Without
D. H. LAWRENCE, MY FRIEND,
AND DONALD CARSWELL, MY HUSBAND,
*this book could not have been. I therefore
inscribe it to them both:*

*That I, for poor auld Scotland's sake,
Some usefu' plan or beuk could make.*

Catherine Roxburghe Macfarlane (1879–1946), was the younger daughter of a Glasgow shipping merchant. She was educated at Park School and Glasgow University, although she never took a degree there. She studied music in Frankfurt for two years before returning to Glasgow to teach art and to write for the *Glasgow Herald* as literary and dramatic reviewer. A short-lived first marriage was annulled in 1908, and she moved to London with her daughter in 1912, to work as reviewer for the *Observer*.

Working in London, she married Donald Carswell, a fellow Glaswegian journalist, and the couple set about earning their living as full-time writers. Catherine became a close friend of D. H. Lawrence and his circle and Lawrence encouraged her with a first novel based on her own upbringing, *Open the Door!* (1920). A sequel, *The Camomile*, appeared in 1922. She wrote little during the rest of the 1920s, but in the three years after Lawrence's death in 1930, she electrified the literary world, first with *The Life of Robert Burns* (1930), and next with *The Savage Pilgrimage* (1932), a memoir of D. H. Lawrence's life and her friendship with him.

Carswell's biography of Burns offended the Burns Clubs of Scotland because of its frankness; and her unguarded remarks about Middleton Murry, another close and influential friend of Lawrence's, led to *The Savage Pilgrimage* being withdrawn and revised under threat of libel. She continued to work as a writer and journalist, collaborating with her husband on an anthology, *The Scots Weekend* (1936), and publishing her biography of Boccaccio, *The Tranquil Heart*, in 1937. Donald Carswell was killed in a car crash in 1939. Catherine died in 1946, and her unfinished autobiography *Lying Awake* was edited and published by her son John in 1950.

Catherine Carswell

THE LIFE OF
ROBERT BURNS

Introduced by Tom Crawford

CANONGATE
CLASSICS
30

First published in 1930 by Wm. Collins & Sons,
first published as a Canongate Classic in 1990
by Canongate Publishing Limited, reprinted in
1996 by Canongate Books Ltd, 14 High Street,
Edinburgh EH1 1TE. Copyright © Catherine
Carswell 1930.   Introduction copyright ©
Thomas Crawford 1990.

The publishers gratefully acknowledge general subsidy from the Scottish Arts Council
towards the Canongate Classics series and a
specific grant towards the publication of this
title.

Set in 10pt Plantin by Hewer Text Composition Services, Edinburgh. Printed and bound in
Denmark by Norhaven Rotation A/S.

British Library Cataloguing in Publication Data
A catalogue record for this book is available
on request from the British Library.

ISBN 0 86241 292 7

Contents

Introduction

Catherine Carswell gives us a Burns seen through the glass of her own temperament and mediated by the example of her mentor, D.H. Lawrence. Lawrence had admired Burns from his youth, and towards the end of 1912 he toyed with the idea of writing a novel around the Scots poet's life and personality. On 17 December he wrote to his friend Arthur Macleod:

> I shall make him live near home, as a Derbyshire man—and shall fictionise the circumstances. But I have always loved him, in a way. He seems a good deal like myself—nicer in most ways. I think I can do him almost like an autobiography.

In the two fragments of Chapter 1 which have survived there is 'a big boned, limber youth of twenty', presumably the Burns figure, with expressive brown eyes and 'a young, eager, peasant face'; whose 'big, raw-boned wrists . . . moved with an intimate intelligence'; and 'who knows more songs than any lad i' th' country'. We see him free a rabbit from a snare: 'it was a living little rabbit-person with dark eyes'—terrified as the mouse was of Burns. Later he has a brief night-meeting with a girl: 'she was breathing against him, live and warm like the rabbit. And it was the darkness he was kissing, discovering. It was the night he had his mouth upon.' Even at twenty, the Carswell Burns is demonstrably more complex and sophisticated than this character of Lawrence's, but the kinship is unmistakable.

A year after he had given up all idea of this novel, Lawrence was making Burns into the symbol of a true, honest attitude to sex and the body, in contrast to the more cerebral authors, and above all the prose writers, of the nineteenth century:

> A big man is big because his power, his horse-power or

vital power, is great—even Shelley and Keats, had terrific vital power. Some men could catch up their sex and everything into their heads—but poets not. Most poets die of sex—Keats, Shelley, Burns. I can't understand it myself, not a bit . . . They've all—not Burns—Baudelaire, Verlaine and Flaubert—got about them, the feeling that their own flesh is unclean—corrupt. And their art is the art of self hate and self-murder.

(To Henry Savage, 15 November 1913)

When Mrs Carswell began serious work on Burns, Lawrence wrote enthusiastically—and warningly—to her husband:

Cath's idea of a Burns book I like very much: I always wanted to do one myself, but am not Scotchy enough. I read just now Lockhart's bit of a life of Burns. Made me spit! Those damned middle-class Lockharts grew lilies of the valley up their arses to hear them talk. If Cath is condescending to Burns, I disown her. He was quite right, a man's a man for a' that, and it's *not* a bad poem. He means what he says. My word, you can't know Burns unless you can hate the Lockharts and all the estimable bourgeois and upper classes as he really did—the narrow-gutted pigeons. Don't, for God's sake, be mealy-mouthed like them. *I'd* like to write a Burns life. Oh, why doesn't Burns come to life again and really salt them!

(To Donald Carswell, 5 December 1927)

In view of Lawrence's diatribe it is of some interest that the *Glasgow Herald* made Lockhart its touchstone; its tepid and ultimately dismissive review claimed that the book 'fails to present as full and true a portrait as Lockhart's excellent Life' (16 October 1930). In the previous month the *Daily Record*, a mass circulation popular newspaper in Scotland, had—and this prior to the publication date—printed extracts in five successive numbers. 'All hashed about of course,' the author wrote to F. Marian McNeill on 17 September, 'but it comes through wonderfully well and I'm so glad of the chance to get at the common reader for whom the book is fundamentally intended. The highbrows can fall into line later if they like.' On three days a week for over a month the *Record* devoted at least a couple of columns to the reaction—letter after letter of what Arnold Bennett termed 'storms, cascades, cyclones of howling and protesting fury', relieved by only a few approving comments. John S. Clarke, Labour MP for Maryhill, saw Carswell as a kind of body-snatcher engaged in 'the resurrection of the ghoulish remains of great men'. To those who had found no truth in the extracts, a woman reader replied that there was indeed truth: 'rotten truth—and the female victims of the poet's lust knew that to their bitter sorrow. Burns was a literary genius, but as a man he was beneath contempt and Catherine Carswell is deserving of commendation for having emphasised this fact.' The issue of 29 September is typical:

BOYCOTT NEW BURNS 'LIFE'

ATTACK BY WOMEN READERS

WOMANHOOD DEGRADED

The first of these headlines points to a very real threat—that the Burns Federation bigwigs of that day (so different from their successors in the 1980s) would actually manage to have the book suppressed. Stewart Seggie, President of the Ninety Burns Club, Edinburgh, is ominously and prophetically quoted: '*If* [my italics] this book is published this year, it will be killed at the Burns Festival in January.' Mr Seggie must have had inside information, for certain figures in the Burns world were trying to get Chatto and Windus to withdraw the book on the pretext that the Federation's copyright had been infringed. They had no sustainable case; the exchange of solicitors' letters was printed in the *Record*; and further details can be found among the thirteen letters from Mrs Carswell to J. de Lancey Ferguson, the great American Burns scholar, in the Mitchell Library, Glasgow. The parallel with the attack on Salman Rushdie's *The Satanic Verses* seems even stronger when one learns that Mrs Carswell received a bullet through the post from a correspondent who signed himself 'Holy Willie' and urged her, by using the enclosed in a quiet corner, to 'leave the world a better and cleaner place'.

After three weeks of unfettered comment, the *Record* printed a lengthy review by William Power on 7 October. 'Never before has the poet been so convincingly or fully presented,' he wrote; 'she sees Burns as an artist in living—passionate, intense, wayward and various.' And ten days later, on 17 October, C.M. Grieve (Hugh MacDiarmid) lent his powerful support in the form of a long letter, though even so he could not resist a little quiet irony at Burns's expense: 'She is guiltless alike of white-washing and muck-raking . . . I have read the book with absorbed interest—not because of its subject, but because of Mrs Carswell's handling.' The majority of the book's opponents, however, saw nothing in it but muck-raking. The most splendidly vacuous of all the anathemas was pronounced by the Reverend Lauchlan McLean Watt in the *Burns Chronicle* for 1932:

> It is essentially a long list, chapter, by chapter, of all that he did wrong; his side-slips from virtue; the women who, carried off their feet by his passionate personality, bore children to him; and the men who drank with him, shouted the choruses of their class with him, got him to write things that outrivalled the candid impurity of old skulduddery fragments the farm-hinds had sung for generations in their wretched bothies; till, at the last miserable page, when you see his poor broken body laid in the grave by a strutting crowd of nobodies, you almost feel as though you ought to be glad that a sordid life is finished . . . It is not far off from being the kind of record Satan might keep near the door of his dark abode, lest a repentant sinner might slip into higher places of peace after struggle, failure, and victory—a book he might bring forward to prove a poor soul's previous convictions, in some final Court of Spiritual Common Pleas . . . It is, in much, an undocumented libel on the dead, compiled on a method of smelling out stories that have grown putrid long ago in the corners where even what had no love or pity in it was content to leave them to oblivion.

What strikes today's reader, sixty years after all the pother, is that the book is a noble 'work of fiction' in the best sense of the word—'that which is made' (as a 'makar' makes poetry), quite apart from the arguable correctness of its presentation of minor details, or even of crucial incidents. Of the major episodes which are open to question today, the most sensational are his affair with Mary Campbell (Highland Mary) in 1786, and the break with Maria Riddel towards the end of his life. All the scanty evidence we have concerning Highland Mary points to a bigamous marriage by declaration followed by her death from typhus. But we can no longer accept that the bones in the child's coffin found in the lair where she was buried are necessarily those of *her* baby. They may well have belonged to Agnes Hendry, who died in 1827 aged six weeks and was buried there. This information did not appear mysteriously in 1932, two years after the book's publication, as has been stated by one biographer, but was communicated to the *Campbeltown Courier* right at the height of the *Daily Record* controversy by Miss J. Hendry of Greenock, and printed in the issue of 25 October 1930. But as Maurice Lindsay has pointed out, other remains were brought to light at the exhumation in 1920, including 'some smaller bones'; since there was no proper forensic examination at the time we have no means of knowing whether these smaller bones were not, after all, those of Highland Mary's child, buried in the same coffin as its mother. The matter is still unsettled.

As for the quarrel with the Riddels in December 1793, most now agree with Mrs Carswell that it took place at Robert Riddel's house, Friars' Carse, and that it was *his* wife whom Burns insulted in a drunken enactment of the Rape of the Sabines. In the Carswell account Maria (Robert's sister-in-law) had not been at the party, and when she cut him dead it was out of solidarity with Mrs Robert and her class. Yet the incident is still obscure; some have felt that Maria must have been there after all and that it was she whom Burns laid hands on, or even that it was a different and otherwise quite unrecorded insult which caused the breach. As usual, Mrs Carswell chooses the interpretation that comes imaginatively closest to her picture of Burns, and presents it without qualification and in bold strokes.

Today, most would feel that her strokes are altogether too bold when she comes to the Scottish background. Calvinism had more going for it than she would have it; country people lived better in the seventeenth century than she claims, except in times of real scarcity; there was more educational progress by 1689 than she admits; we can no longer dismiss so cavalierly the intellectual atmosphere of the Scottish Enlightenment; and it is a peculiar categorisation of literary history which claims that by 1786 the 'romantic movement' had been in full swing in Edinburgh for thirty years. Today's critics and literary scholars, too, would feel that she under-estimates the importance of *English* poetry for Burns before 1786, and that she does not take into account the positive influence of Locke, whom he probably read at Lochlea, or of Adam Smith (*Theory of Moral Sentiments*). No doubt she lumped Locke and Smith in with the other luminaries of the 'spurious culture' which 'misled' his mind—so like the spurious culture of the White Christ, Mrs Grundy, and Middleton Murry, which so irritated Lawrence.

Mrs Carswell was much criticised at the time for regretting that Burns had not been a braver man—why, oh why, did he not lend his voice to those who supported the Convention of the Friends of the People in Edinburgh; why, oh why, did he have to go crawling to the Excise Board? No doubt her other hero would have been more courageous: but then Lawrence had no 'expectant wee-things' to provide for, while his rôle as a 'genius' member of the European intelligentsia made him vastly more confident than Burns, whose spiritual isolation in Dumfries was more crippling than Lawrence's ever was. There is evidence that Burns retained strong democratic and pro-French feelings until at least as late as November 1795.

Carswell's Burns impresses as Tolstoy's Kutuzov and Scott's Balfour of Burley impress. She deliberately forgoes the forbidding reference system of academic biography in order to sweep the reader into and through the emotionally charged narrative that passes before his eyes, and she brings the gifts of a novelist to her task. For the book has a structure over and above any simple 'Burns did this and Burns did that'; it has the shape of a tragedy whose protagonist is pitted against an environment and a philosophy hostile to his inner being, and who is destroyed by his strength as much as by his weakness. As she herself puts it: 'At the best he is confronted by two conflicting evils, between which he must choose; at the worst by two conflicting truths from neither of which he can escape. Such were the warp and woof of Robert's life, like the criss-cross of his plaid.' Arnold Bennett summed up the experience of reading the book in these words:

> Out of it arises gradually the personality of a great man . . . jolly, hard-living, generous, melancholy, unvenal, morbid, dyspeptic and triumphant . . . the very archetype of the supreme creative artist. The spectacle of his career makes English poets seem only half alive. Matthew Arnold was a great poet, but in the master-enterprise of being alive he was a timid grey amateur compared to Burns.

And finally John Buchan, himself both biographer and novelist, in a letter to Donald Carswell:

> It is an extraordinarily able piece of work, beautifully architectured and brilliantly written. It seems to me also essentially a just book . . . The last years are wonderfully done, and the last chapter is a perfect 'falling close'. It is really a wonderful performance.

As the first truly notable Scottish book of the thirties (perhaps greater than *To Circumjack Cencrastus*, which came out in the same year), Carswell's *Life of Burns* greatly deserves revival and revaluation.

Thomas Crawford

PART ONE

Prelude

CHAPTER I

When material improvements are applied with energy to a backward country, many people are bound to suffer; still more will reap a doubtful benefit. It is with a group of such people, and with the good and the evil done to them in the name of progress, that this narrative concerns itself. The principal persons in it are labouring men and women who were characteristic of their time and place, mostly unfortunate, and remembered only because of the accident of genius in one of them. Because of this accident, however, the narrative must include also a certain element of gentility, even of fashion. The reactions between genius and gentility have been at all times worthy of the utmost attention. Perhaps they were never more so than in the period, place and circumstances here assembled. The period is between 1700 and 1800—more particularly within the latter half of the century; the place Scotland.

If ever there was a backward country it was Scotland at the opening of the eighteenth century. Its few resources had been greatly reduced by neglect and misuse, by invasion from without and strife within. Having long since painfully achieved the status of a nation, it had been disappointed again and again through seven centuries of the benefits that should have followed. If ever there was a people that seemed above all things else to need material improvements, it was the people of Scotland just then. Heroisms and treacheries alike, the epic qualities that have made the Scotish struggle famous and, while they lasted, gave a dignity to the national life from the highest to the lowest, were in the end little more than a tapestry concealing the grimmer truth of history, which was the dismal poverty of Scotland's inhabitants. Promise after promise of peace and prosperity had gone down in gloomy confusion. At Flodden the perils of a French alliance had been bloodily brought home. The better reasoned hopes of the Reformation, set in a glow by the communicative and circumstantial genius of John Knox, had faded—less bloodily it is true, but not without shedding of blood and with a disillusioning sadness that was more depressing than bloodshed. The gloom that followed had not been broken but was rather intensified by successive intervals of storm. The accession of a Scotish prince to the English throne, from which so much was expected, had only the effect of involving Scotland in the constitutional troubles of England. The seventeenth century provides the most miserable reading in Scotish annals—a dreary record of fruitless civil war, fanatical folly and brutal persecutions. The old Scotish learning, which in the preceding century had been respectable, dwindled to almost nothing. The Scots tongue ceased to be a literary language as there was no one to write books in it. Ignorance and superstition were in possession. The poverty of the land, once associated with a cheerful if simple well-being, had deepened into destitution. By the time of the Revolution and the Union of Parliaments at least ten per cent of the population—probably much more—were professed beggars; either 'gaberlunzies' who begged by patent, or 'thiggers and sorners' who demanded alms with menaces; and a far greater proportion lived always within sight of famine. The Highlands were worse by a long way than the Lowlands, but even in the Lowlands a laird was accounted well off with a rent roll of £100 a year, two-thirds of which was paid in kind—chiefly poor grain and tough hens. His house, with its dunghill set close in front, had nothing of grace and little of comfort. His garden showed many weeds, some cottage flowers, a few berry bushes and a carefully tended plot of medicinal herbs for use against the prevalent diseases of scurvy, ague and the itch. As for what one pamphleteer has called 'that Honest Part of the Nation call'd the Lower Sort of People,' the English traveller entering by Dumfries or Berwickshire was shocked by their manner of life—by their rags, their filth, their damp and smoky hovels, their almost incessant exposure to bad weather, sickness and want.

A winter's day and a wintry way is the life of man.

. . . In their own proverb there was dire truth as well as poetry.

Yet the Scots never became abject. From that they were saved by a certain quality of heart—a very warm sort of humour—and by their rude but genuine piety. They were able, as the Irish for example never were, to remain sensitive towards the wrongs of others and remarkably stoical towards their own. Sturdy in mind and heart they retained a kindliness that famine itself could not quench. No beggar of all the beggarly crew was sent empty from a door so long as there was anything left in the house to share; no thief of food was to be punished unless he had taken more than he could carry on his own back. Death in a drunken brawl was common enough, but crimes of violence were rare and executions rarer still. Hangings never became the popular institutions that they were in England. The Scots were a humane folk.

They were also a folk much addicted to ribaldry. No doubt the two go together. Probably no other peasantry the world over has been so exuberant in lewdness. The songs of Scotland (in this kind), the stories, the interludes for performance at weddings and other social occasions, have largely been condemned to genteel oblivion. The ancient 'makars,' who were not in touch with the people, mostly held the indigenous lyric unworthy of their Muse. Later the clergy did their best to substitute 'gude and godlie ballates' for those of native growth, retaining only tunes and titles. But scraps enough survive (chiefly owing to the hero of this history) to suggest pre-eminence in a cunning blend of breadth with sweetness, and impudent guffaws with heartfelt sighs and tears. A people poor in the arts, even in the crafts taking a small and imitative place, the Scots had the power of pungent commentary upon life. And they manifested it chiefly by this humanitarian art, so ephemeral-seeming yet conceivably so important, of the common man. In it every mother's son could have a part, and most sons of Scotswomen did. It was indubitably a native product. Being essentially an improvisatory art it was generally circulated by word of mouth, but a fair proportion found its way into rough print that was more perishable than speech. The bawdy chapbooks of Scotland were circulated by the hundred thousand yearly, not only north of the Tweed but well to the south of it, where they exercised the lungs and rejoiced the hearts of less inventive men. This art continued to thrive under all changes of Church and State. The Church took many measures to suppress it: and it luxuriated the more. It derived, if anything, a new, discreditable vitality beneath the shadow cast by evangelical doctrines. Down to the end of the eighteenth century the pedlar's pack continued to hold ribald broadsheets as well as devotional pamphlets. As often as not the same customer would buy both.

If the other saltiness and saving grace of the Scots, their piety, took a militant form, one cannot be surprised. Hope in some shape will survive even where hopefulness has vanished. For generations in the life of the nation temporal expectation had ceased as an active principle. Yet hope persisted. It persisted in the guise of *pietas* towards dubious political 'causes,' and more deeply still in the guise of a piety that occupied itself with an even more dubious blessedness beyond the grave. The last as much as the first involved warfare. You might, despite all you could do, be predestined to Hell, but at least while still on earth you could fight with men who differed from you as to the only possible way of getting to heaven. It is often pointed out that theology is not religion. Neither is it. Yet in the matter of human conduct it has one beneficial effect that religion cannot always claim. A preoccupation with theology will keep a man's head up even when his belly is empty. Stupid he may be, but he will not be slavish, absurd but not obsequious. That the Scot escaped from callousness was in great measure due to his inveterate love of bawdry. That he escaped from abjectness was in equal measure due to his mania for metaphysics. He kept one hand upon the common heart of life: with the other he reached out into the unknown. So it has always been with the Scot, and so will always be as long as there are Scotsmen. When he discards the first characteristic he becomes a prig, where the second, an inferior. Both bawdry and the Bible are needed for the entire Scot.

But man—even the Scotsman—cannot live by the heart, the head and the genitals alone. And how desperate Scottish stomachs and Scotish pockets had become by 1701 was shown to the world by the country's frantic response to the Darien scheme. Six years later, at the date of the Union, there was not to be found in circulation more coin than £600,000 sterling (or 10s per head of the population), including all doubtful currency. Yet upon that frantic glimpse of Darien, no less than £470,000 (£225,000 of it from private and straitened purses) had been poured out.[1]

If the Darien scheme had succeeded, the social and ethical development of Scotland in the eighteenth and nineteenth centuries would have been different—would have been more solidly and ingenuously Scotish. But partly because of its extreme naïvety in plan and execution, partly because its success would not have suited the English, its failure was painful and complete.

When at last in 1707 the orderly conditions needed for progress were established, it was not in the way Scotland would have wished. The Union gave her, it is true, what she most needed, peace and a strong central government. But a grievous blow had been struck at Scotish pride. Some time passed before the exhausted and disheartened country could respond, even to the much-desired chances of material prosperity which had not been gained by her own initiative, but arbitrarily put before her by an enemy of long standing. Wounded dignity apart, there were all the difficulties of adjustment to a new, even a premature situation. Through the Union, which some fifty years later might have come as a crowning blessing, the trade with France was lost, the East Coast fishing ruined by a crushing salt tax, the unorganised but widely spread home industries of spinning and weaving severely checked by English competition. In fact as before—and emotionally as never before—the life of the people was one of squalid misery.

Weighing against these losses, however, and presently far outweighing them in the national balance of prosperity, were certain positive elements introduced by the Union, notably the freedom to trade with the English colonies and the enormous impetus given to agriculture throughout the country. Within twenty years Scotsmen were realising that their land, so long despised as the barren rump of the island, was a place of opportunity. For the first time individual advancement was set within the vision of any man who was at once intelligent, hard-working and independent. He might prosper, it seemed, by farming, by commerce, by manufacture, or by the judicious advancing of monies to fellow-countrymen engaged in these pursuits. Foreign trade, which had never been large and by the time of the Union had grown stagnant (not more than ninety-three small vessels being engaged in it), throve increasingly and along certain lines attained spectacular importance. Once given a tangible chance, men and women alike displayed startling powers of work and of acquisitiveness, and long before the century was out the money spent by the nation on Darien had been made over and over again by single Scotish merchants. Through-out the length and breadth of the land the golden calf was zealously solicited. The gentry were not above participating in trade, and many of them made a speciality of moneylending; the new rich merchants of sugar and tobacco flaunted in gold and scarlet before those less lucky than themselves; women as well as men threw themselves into the dazzling new pursuit. It was through the unconnected but equally unscrupulous efforts of two well-born ladies that Scotland became a world purveyor of linen both in thread and in web. Calico was to follow. Scotish hands learned from the English how to plough, from the Dutch how to plant and weave finely, from the French how to bleach and dye, and in each activity they quickly bettered their teachers in skill and diligence. From the resulting prosperity new industries derived. Coachbuilders, cabinetmakers, upholsterers, glass-blowers and potters were established, stone and slate were quarried, for the first time there was a baker and a butcher in every village. Only the arts lagged behind, and the old Scotish culture, its vigour already gone, found itself sadly outmoded, as did various sections of the community, especially in the remoter country places.

The Kirk was grieved but helpless. Through the darkest years the Scotish ministers, with all their faults, had truly been the leaders of the people, and they had done much to preserve and fortify the soul of the nation. They had also kept a finger on the national purse-strings.[2] They were on the whole worthy, hard-working, unworldly. When the French captured some Scotish trading vessels, with the result that Glasgow one day was £10,999 the poorer, there were pulpit warnings that the Lord was 'remarkably frowning upon our trade in more respects than one since it is put in the room of religion in the late alteration of our constitution.' But unfortunately the ministers' good qualities were more than matched by their illiteracy and superstition. They bewailed the changes they saw around them, but only because such changes gave men other things to think of besides the saving of their souls, and sent congregations strolling in the fields between services to talk of mundane matters. Some instinctive foreknowledge they may have had of the speed with which industrialism would outrun the life of the nation's spirit, but they lacked the clarity and the power to give needful guidance. All they did was to fulminate in the pulpit and persecute out of it, work themselves up over the sins of the flesh which had always been with them, inveigh against uncleanness of speech, expound abstruse points of doctrine. They preached upon the Fourfold State of Man, upon that 'lump of wrath'—a new-born child, or that 'guilty lump of Hell'—a full-grown man. They laid great stress upon the damnableness of heresy and the emptiness of 'works.' And by degrees their flocks withdrew the old allegiance. Other voices with more of pleasantness and peace in them were calling to the people of Scotland. For not all the ministers were stern evangelicals. From the beginning of the century there had been a considerable 'moderate' party, and, as the times changed, these with their urbaner tones, their more comfortable views and their shrewder eye to social and worldly well-being, gained steadily upon the 'high-flyers.' They too were a good class of men—considerably better than their brethren of the cloth of England. They too were reputable in their lives and conscientious in discharging their poorly paid duties. And in addition they were cheerful, rational, well-bred, and in many cases cultured. Strongly disapproving of certain revivalist enthusiasms which broke out here and there towards the middle of the century, they studiously avoided over-stimulation (either emotional or intellectual) for their own hearers. To make up, however, for the dullness of their Sabbath discourses they could give useful advice on weekdays concerning the treatment of a piece of land or the conduct of a bargain. Refusing to strain at points of doctrine—as at so small a matter as a golden calf—they refrained from rendering their congregations uneasy either about this world or the next. Why should they when they were perfectly easy themselves? Out of the pulpit they cherished the virtues of toleration even to heretics, and as their debates with opponents in the Assembly became ever more polite, many men of the stricter clergy began to accommodate their outward behaviour to the new regime. They indulged in supper parties; they wore ruffles and powder, cocked hats and silver shoe-buckles. The old-time minister, with his unclerical homespun clothes and coloured kerchief, his wailing inflections, his orgiastic powers, his passion and his prophecies, became very much a country cousin, and at length an anomaly in the land.

The encouragement given to agriculture was the earliest, as it was the strongest and the most cheerful of the English influences to follow the Union. Though all farming innovations were lengthily opposed by the bulk of the people, they were welcomed with eagerness by the landlords; and the appreciation of the better kind of peasants, if more wistful, was no less eager. The prejudice and sloth of the majority were partly dissipated in an unexpected manner, namely by the rising of the 'Fifteen and its consequences. The work of General Wade and his engineers, who built good roads where before there had barely been foothold for a packhorse (and then only in summer), was a revelation, not only to the Highlanders but to all Scotland. The mere improvement in communications changed the life of the country. Those wonderful 'machines,' that in England were known as carts, began to oust the rough sledges, the ramshackle tumbrils, the creels borne upon the backs of women,[3] who hitherto had been more practicable as beasts of burden than the feeble, thistle-fed ponies. Carriers had begun during the finer months to ply between town and town, and these, to the general admiration, could undertake as much as a quarter of a ton in a single load. That most ingenious of human inventions, the spoked wheel that turns independently of its axle, had scarcely been seen before in Scotland. Accordingly, when a chaise penetrated to the north no Apollo's chariot could have created more amazement, and men bowed low before the driver in the belief that none but the owner would be permitted to drive so magnificent a vehicle. Several new stage routes came into existence. The coach between Glasgow and the capital began to make four miles an hour instead of the former three. Once a month passengers of sufficient wealth and daring could set out from the Grassmarket in Edinburgh with a fair chance of reaching London sixteen days later.

CHAPTER II

Among those who had ridden out in the 'Fifteen in the interest of the 'king over the water' and as a loyal follower of his over-lord, the Earl Marischal, was one Robert Burnes, the son of a farmer in the county of Kincardine. He was a young man still under twenty, and had several other good reasons to think well of himself and his prospects. From the first half of the sixteenth century, perhaps from earlier still, his male ancestors had been workers on the land in that same neighbourhood of the Mearns. They had been poor men, some of them so lamentably poor, even for those days, that they had attracted parish compassion. But in every generation Burnes men had been noted for their good characters, and it so happened that the father of this particular Robert Burnes had contrived, in spite of bad times and Highland robbers, to hand on something besides character to his five sons. Silver spoons (one or two at least) had graced his table, and by hiding his savings in the old box-wheel that lay across the mud puddle of his threshold to form a stepping-stone, he was able at his death to set up his sons as tacksmen and to leave them one hundred merks[1] apiece.

Such things are not to be forgotten. Robert Burnes never forgot them. Nor did he, when he came to marry and found a family, permit his own children to forget them either. It is so that traditions are created in the humblest as in the highest houses, and the pride bestowed is no different from that of the born aristocrat. Robert Burnes assumed the aristocratic pose the more readily in that he was by nature arrogant, sanguine and intelligent. Further, in that he had been not merely one of the Earl Marischal's feudal retainers, but a gardener on the forfeited estates. And while in old Scotland the feudal retainer had always been used to converse on familiar terms with the nobility and gentry, it is still better

12

known how completely the gardener in all countries and times has tended to identify himself with the outlook upon life of those for whom he has worked.

After the failure of the 'Fifteen and the exile of the Earl Marischal with other rebel leaders, Burnes perceived both the futility of the rising and the new openings for agriculture. No doubt too, like his late master, then sulking in Germany, he had come to have a contempt for 'King Jamie.' In any case, though a Tory by temperament and of the 'other persuasion' in church matters by tradition, he conformed to the Presbyterian establishment for peace' sake; and by the time he had settled down as a small tenant farmer in the parish of Dunnottar, taken a wife and begotten ten children, he had put the Stuarts and their cause behind him, as he thought, for good and all. His whole aim now was to follow his father's example and advance the fortunes of his family by any honest means.

Some of the glistening hopes held out to him by the times have been already mentioned. But there were many other items of encouragement. The rebel estates, too often ill-governed by chiefs at war with their neighbours and swarming with ignorant and lazy vassals skilled in nothing but primitive warfare, were forfeit and had passed into more useful hands. Those exiled gentry who were by degrees permitted to return brought with them from Holland and France enlightened ideas of gardening and horticulture generally. The names of new flowers were on the lips of ladies and the lists of landowners. What was more important, new vegetables had at last won their difficult way to the Scotish table. In addition to the eternal kail soup, thickened with hand-bruised oats or barley, there were now for the first time onions, carrots, turnips, potatoes. Though typhus and tuberculosis were still regarded as the will of God and took their toll of most families, the health of the people began noticeably to improve.

In many places the bare and boggy countryside began to show some cultivation other than the savage kind so long unchallenged. Hedgerows—a happy inspiration from Holland—were set protectively here and there. Plantations of tiny larch seedlings, foot-high spruce firs, sapling beeches,

oaks and elms, were being enthusiastically laid out and
tremblingly watched over by the awakened landlords. If not
grubbed up in the night by poor neighbours accustomed to
treelessness and convinced that the roots would rob the soil of
all nourishment, they would one day provide sheltering
woods and more than make good the loss of the ancient
forests, which in the lean years had been cut down, for
charcoal or because they were wolf-infested, or to be sold at
bargain prices to Ireland. The recurrence of famine (in spite
of improved conditions there were three serious famines
within Robert Burnes's lifetime) disposed of the lingering
prejudice against root-crops. Potatoes did far more than
porridge for the well-being of the Scotish people, and it was a
good day for Scotland when bribes were no longer necessary
to prevent molestation of the potato plant as a device of the
Devil. At the mid-century a barley mill—after forty years
under the ban of religion—was permitted to risk the
expected fire from heaven. Fields, as we now know them,
had begun to make their first appearance. That is to say, the
dirty, high-ridged patches of thinly growing grey oats and
bere[2] were being drained, levelled, cleared of moss and
stones, limed, enclosed, manured, subjected to a reasoned
rotation of crops. The custom of using the worst grain for
sowing was no longer universal. Bean or pease flour were no
longer the only alternative cereals to oats and barley. Of
an afternoon at the tables of the gentry small portions of
wheaten bread were served, and of an evening turnips were
ceasing to be regarded as a dessert.

All this, of course, could be done only at the sacrifice of the
old indolence that was dear to most Scotsmen's hearts and in
the past had been dignified by warlike occasions. Scotish
nabobs, returning with fortunes from India, were patrioti-
cally inclined to invest these fortunes in the homeland now
that it was become a land of promise; but neither they nor
other new landlords who had made money in commerce
inside or out of Scotland were weighed down by tradition or
by any kind of sentimental considerations. They saw the
necessity for work if the soil was to be made productive, and
work they would enforce, anyhow upon their underlings. It
was nothing to them that sudden violence was done to the

poor man's pride as well as to his indolence. Payment was offered in good scarce money, though naturally in the smallest possible amounts. The stubborn who would not must suffer with the stupid who could not align themselves with the new order.

Unfortunately to none of its victims does what we call progress bring suffering so acute as to certain of its most intelligent sympathisers—to men, for example, like Robert Burnes, who, neither stupid nor stubborn, certainly not indolent and only quite properly proud, have by the very quickness of their understanding acquired the habit of thinking in terms beyond the limit of their resources.

Of the true East-country type, astute to see his chance and with the daring to seize and the energy to carry it through to fruition, this man at this time should have been conspicuously successful. So, at least, one thinks. A measure of success he himself clearly looked for, and had laid his plans accordingly. Setting, as he did, great store by learning, he was determined that his children should have more than the usual fortuitous education then prevailing in country districts. His farm was somewhat remote from the school of its parish. He therefore stirred up his nearest neighbours to help him build a local schoolhouse—a mere hut of clay but probably no worse than that of the parish—and he found a dominie for it whose poor stipend he paid out of his own none too rich pocket. That such a proceeding set him at odds with the Kirk-session and the parish schoolmaster, whose lawful monopoly of education was thus infringed, Burnes, with all his prudent conforming, was not the man to care. Was he not thereby implanting yet another tradition in his house?

Yet as the middle of the century approached that house had more likeliness than luck about it still. After years of thought and effort Burnes still saw none but horn spoons and wooden platters on his table, and there were no savings either to be used or to be concealed in cart-wheels. His children might be exemplary Burneses as to character and super-Burneses as to education; but the soil of Clochanhill, his farm, had shown itself to be the poorest in a country of poor soils, and his tenancy, which was on the vicious system of two-years' leases then the rule, had coincided with a series of ruinous harvests. A great part of Scotland indeed had been reduced to famine; and though the landlords were giving cash instead of kind for the labour they required, they were also exacting cash in the form of hugely increased rents for their as yet unimproved acres. Thus, while their hopes were still mounting, the hopes of their smaller tenants were apt to be declining, all the more sickeningly for being within sight of legitimate fulfilment.

For Robert Burnes the age of silver seemed farther off than ever. His grown children were willing but underpaid workers, himself an ambitious but ruinously overcharged tenant. There came a day when the rent of his sixty-odd acres of stony ground could not be paid. Not that his eager spirit was to be so easily broken as this. Happily or unhappily, his credit was good. He was able to borrow from a local landowner who had been Provost of Aberdeen. And so the immediate crisis was passed. But no sooner was it passed than he saw the possibility of retrieving his fortune. Two small farms adjoining Clochanhill had become vacant, which, as landowners were beginning at last to realise the thriftlessness of the two-years' tack system, were being offered on leases for seven years. Boldly Burnes doubled his liabilities by taking both. It was the turn of the year. January opened in high hopes of his own enterprise and energy.

In principle he was right. His sole chance lay in an increase of land. But his experience, hard as it had been, had not yet taught him that on the land no amount of enterprise and energy can make up for lack of capital. To transform the monotonous 'in-field' and the exhausted 'out-field,' to drain and lime the ground, to set root-crops, to substitute the new small plough for the huge old one, was not merely a laborious but a costly undertaking. The archaic plough might need the assistance of a dozen oxen and four men to make it scratch over half an acre in a day, but it represented only a shilling of capital outlay, whereas the new plough was not only expensive to buy but demanded a team of stout horses. Seed potatoes were not to be had for the usual barter of skinny fowls and inferior barley. Nothing but money could procure the things that Burnes needed, and money was what he had not got and could not come by. None the less he and his sons set to work with firm belief in the new methods and their capacity to practise them. It was now, however, a question of keeping the home together. Till that date James, the eldest son, was the only one who had left. He was working as a wright at Montrose and was believed to have good prospects.[3] If the new venture failed there would be nothing for it but for Robert and William, the two next in age, to follow their brother's example and take the road to the more prosperous South.

But Robert and William refused to think of failure. They had too much faith in their father and his natural deserts. To the end of their days they held that success had been within their grasp when fate played a last spiteful trick and vanquished them.

Even as their crops were ripening to harvest the 'Forty-five Rebellion[4] blazed up. From that moment the case of the Burnes family was hopeless. The widespread panic and economic dislocation caused by the state of war were alone enough to bring their unstable enterprise to ruin. And there was the additional misfortune of the father's Jacobite antecedents. Burnes himself might have forgotten the 'Fifteen, but there were others whose business it was to remember the incident and every person who had been connected with it. No matter that Burnes was not now, as thirty years earlier, a great noble's retainer, but an ageing farmer who wanted above all things peace. No matter that neither he nor his sons showed the least disposition to 'rise and follow Charlie.'[5] They none the less found themselves for the time being marked men, and to them the time being was crucial. One way and another that summer they suffered for the Cause hardly less than if they had fought for it. Towards the end of the year things were so bad with them that in lieu of rent Burnes had to give his landlord a bill at six months for the sum of £13 sterling. When the bill matured he could not meet it. A few months later he was a landless man.

His sons did all that sons could do. William even made a despairing and most valiant effort to save Clochanhill for his father. One thirteenth day of a winter month he went privily to their landlord and proposed himself in place of the defaulting tenant. But happily for him he was refused. Now there was no resource but by separation. With two unmarried daughters (the mother having died) the old man found refuge in a one-roomed cottage. Come spring, Robert and William would start on their travels.

It was a wise provision of their father's that each had been bred to some trade besides that fatal one of farming—Robert as a mason, William as a gardener. Robert's idea was first to join his brother James at Montrose, and later to work his way into England where wages would be better and winters perhaps less cruel to a constitution already weakened by rheumatism and ague. As for William, he had the notion of Edinburgh—at any rate for a beginning. It was a far journey and he knew not a soul in the capital, but wonderful stories had come all the way to Kincardine of passionate gardening by the Edinburgh gentry, of the laying out of parks and the embellishment of parterres. And he could provide himself with testimonials from three local lairds that would certify him to be 'the son of an honest farmer in that neighbourhood,' 'a very well-inclined lad,' and 'fit to be servant to any nobleman or gentleman.'

Between old Robert Burnes and this third child of his there had always been a special sympathy. William, more than any of the others, had found profit in his father's enterprise of the schoolhouse. And they were both gardeners, born and trained. Black-haired and swarthy, grave, dutiful, with acute sensitiveness well-concealed and irascible nerves under strong restraint, he was a son with whom a father could talk things over as with a brother, may be better. Like his father too he was proud, covetous of knowledge, free from superstition, assured in his innate dignity, capable at times of deliberately rash actions. He was good and he knew it. He was deadly serious. As a child he had listened to the grim stories of the seven years' blight, when the mildewed harvest had to be reaped at mid-winter, and women sold their boys into slavery in the Plantations for food, when men fought for the rags of flesh from a diseased sheep and whole tracts of Scotland were full of the dead and dying. Later, when he was nineteen, with his own eyes he had seen cattle perish by the score and human beings glad to stay their hunger with weeds and rubbish. Now, at the age of twenty-seven, he showed already a deeply lined face. He was possessed by a horror of debt and an abiding fear of destitution. At penny weddings or Hallowe'ens he could not, like so many of his companions, lose life's troubles in orgies of song, dance, Scotch drink and promiscuous embraces. The vivacious, lewdly-worded interludes that accompanied a bridal drew no smiles from him. If ever he married a wife she would be a girl that had bided quiet at home, and he would see to it that any children of his did the same. About religion he had thought much, and had worked out for himself a creed that was considerably more liberal than the Scotish Calvinism of his day, but was not the less binding on himself for that. No doubt the departure from strict orthodoxy was made easier for him by the Episcopalian tradition in his family. Bigotry in any form he disliked. The things he loved best in the world were plants, animals, small children and his own dignity.

One morning before sunrise when spring was well advanced, William and Robert put on the new suits of grey homespun their sisters had made ready for them, drank down their thin porridge, thrust their horn spoons into the folds of their dark blue bonnets, shouldered the bundles that contained their patched working clothes, and said their good-byes. It was in the highest degree unlikely that they would ever see their father again, a fact of which both he and they were fully aware.

When they had walked all forenoon they reached the crest of Garvock Tap, whence they could see backwards to the Clochanhill lands and over the Mearns where all their ancestors had lived. It was the last time either of them would look upon it. So far their way had been the same, so they had each other's company for the ''twal hour' repast, and together they set to upon the mess of boiled beans they had brought with them from home. But after this their roads would divide. Looking forward toward the unknown South, they felt no elation. It was not as if they were in their first youth, and there was so much failure behind them that failure might only too possibly lie before as well for either or both. When at length the brothers parted, William was outwardly the calmer as he seemed the older man. But all his life he remembered the intensity of his feelings at that moment on the hilltop. Many years later, attempting to describe the scene to his children, he made use of what for him was the extreme word, *anguish*.

The capital, to which William directed his solitary course, was still a little city wholly contained within its walls. It was noisy, crowded, homely, uncomfortable, convivial, shabby, unsophisticated, filthy. Edinburgh just then was not so important as it had been nor as it was soon to become. But through all the ups and downs of its history and of its grey and stony perpendiculars, it had remained and would remain a place of inextinguishable character.

When despoiled of Court and Parliament by the Union, the glory of the town and the consciousness of glory in its inhabitants had departed. Vanished for ever was that glitter and rustle of the days when the highest and the gayest in the land had jostled in its alley-ways. And lacking the counter-balance of fashion and of state, Presbyterianism had made its gloomy ruling too complete. The Union had been followed by a long dreariness, a poverty of heart as well as of purse. Hunger for the recapture of grandeur was no doubt respons-ible for much of the passion lavished by the Edinburgh women upon the Young Chevalier during his fleeting residence at Holyrood. But that too had gone unsatisfied. The time was to come when a new flowering, more purely masculine because merely intellectual, would in some degree replace the prouder flowering of the past. At the date of William's sojourn, however, the names that were to make the place a famous literary centre still belonged to babies or schoolboys or, at nearest, to youths who were still vainly seeking recognition of their gifts from their own country-men. Bright lads, like Thomson with the first of his *Seasons* in his pocket, or Smollett with his lancets and his manu-scripts, had taken the road to London, well knowing that they could expect neither honour nor a livelihood from the city on the Forth. Adam Smith, after a long stay at Oxford, was only now about to give a single course of lectures on literature before leaving for Glasgow. Edinburgh was not yet quite ready to be the Athens of the North.

But Edinburgh was getting ready. Both above ground in her lofty (but not airy) flats and below in her many stuffy cellars where men sat to talk, she was preparing herself for what was to be her second period of greatness—and her second-last. The highly intelligent William could not fail to be aware of the stir and rising of the sap. And even if he had been less intelligent than he was, he could not have avoided seeing a great part of the daily life of the town. For to the humblest of its inhabitants this lay open in a remarkable degree. It resembled the life of a continental city in this as in several other respects. As homes were chiefly for shelter and shops for storing, pleasure as well as business was principally carried on out of doors, or anyhow in public places. Entertaining and bargaining were done in the taverns, which were often kept by men of family. Goods were displayed on covered booths in the open stone-cobbled streets. About the hour of noon, when the 'musical bells' were chiming, it was, as somebody said, 'a hundred to one but any gentleman in town may be seen' hanging about the Market Cross on the look out for a drink and a talk. Drink and conversation, indeed, were the chief recreations of the Edinburgh gentry, and there was scarcely an hour of the day unsuitable for simple conviviality—business being arranged accordingly, with regular breaks and many other occasions for adjournment.

The result was a style of social intercourse 'wonderfully easy and captivating,' and everybody knew everybody else's affairs as well as their own, if not better. In the dark, stinking, small-roomed, sky-scraping stone houses (some of them fourteen stories high) the inhabitants dwelt closely packed on top of each other, the richer people on the ground, middle and upper floors, the poorer in the attics and cellars—as many as twenty-eight families sharing a single stair—so that all were well acquainted and passed the time of day as they went in and out of their warrens. Not above two or three families lived in a whole 'up-and-down' house or owned a carriage. Those who needed to drive must hire from the single hackney stand at the top of the High Street, and this they would seldom do unless to be carried out to the country. The streets were quite difficult enough to thread in a sedan chair.

For the quiet young man from Kincardine, entering one May day by the West Bow Port, it was all a great change. His serious thoughts were invaded, and perhaps too some of his heaviness dissipated for the moment by the cursing of Highland chairmen, the ringing of chimes, the cries of fish-wives and vendors of cress, 'crowdie,' larks or cooked beans.[1] The din and press were terrific as the newcomer picked his way in his one pair of treble-soled shoes amid the oyster and mussel shells that bestrewed the causeway. Edinburgh was as yet 'undisturbed by any purification.' Places of public convenience there were none, save the street and the dark entries: disposal of private inconvenience was by way of the pavement and the gutter. In the fetid air of one of these closes on either hand even well-to-do parents could easily lose six infants in succession.

None the less, for those who survived, there was considerable jollity on six days of the week, and many amusements were as free and as easy as the relief of nature. A theatre was still not permitted,[2] but citizens enlivened themselves with liquor quaffed out of tin cans, with cock-fighting, pony races and popular displays. Giants and other physical freaks exhibited themselves on street platforms. A Flying Man slid on his stomach down a hundred and fifty yards of rope from Half-Moon Battery to the Castle Rock. A Fire-Eater broiled a hot collop on cinders on his tongue. A Boneless Man made himself into a hoop and balanced the hoop on a couple of upturned wine-glasses. Only on a Sunday all was still—still, that is, except for the multitudes, soberly modulating their voices and wearing their best of broadcloth, stuff or silk, as they went to and from the church services. The church-goers were like the flow and ebb of a murmurous tide along the grey, shadowed streets. But when they had passed, or while they were at worship, a reverential silence reigned. If, by some mischance, a child had been kept from church and ventured out, it stole over the deserted plainstones on tiptoe and with a fluttering heart.

As for the gentry (to serve whom William was so well fitted) they, of course, added to the grosser pleasures of the town their more refined diversions. They played games of skill, frequented clubs and coffee-houses (wherein no coffee was), organised dances and concerts—to which last had recently been added 'interludes'—performances of an undeniably theatrical nature. The recent improvements in trade and agriculture were helping to do away with the social stagnation; and genial circles, wherein the censures of the old strict Kirk went unheeded, were increasing. Duchess Kitty having resumed occasional habitation of Queensberry House in the Canongate, other fine country folk followed suit. Gaily dressed beaux were beginning to brighten the streets and reoccupy long-deserted lodgings. They wrote verses, studied philosophy and the classics, threw off heavy-footed satires, indulged a passion for music. Since an Edinburgh oboe player had become musician to Queen Charlotte, bringing Scotish melodies into vogue in London, the national lyre had become the vogue in Edinburgh also—but with an added lustre of Scotish pride and English settings. Noble lords played instrumental parts on the platform in the Cowgate, and their young women, wearing chip hats, toupees and sacques, applauded. London must be followed. So the red and green silken plaids had been discarded for dress occasions, and now even the silk-lined hood had ceased to be fashion's latest word. Ladies were still free-spoken and hearty, with a kiss for the stranger of either sex, but they no longer swore or snuffed or entered taverns. Girls addressed their parents as 'papa' and 'mamma,' and preferred the minuet to the reel. Dancing masters arrived and throve, and half-crown Assemblies were held from five in the afternoon till eleven at night in a smoky hired room, with an aged Scots lord selling white gloves at the door. Ministers of the Old Light prophesied the doom of Sodom and Gomorrha. But one minister at least among the New Lights was persuaded (by an article in the *Spectator*) that dancing would make his son[3] a more accomplished preacher if ever the lad should have the honour to mount a pulpit. And now that Edinburgh was beginning to fancy herself once more as a centre, the day was with the Moderates or New Lights. Were

they not all for gentility and innocent pleasures? Were they
not the nurses of intellectual debate, and turning the General
Assemblies in Edinburgh into a school for oratory of the most
courteous, albeit energetic sort?

Accompanying these social activities, happily for William,
were all manner of horticultural changes. It was some time
since the Dutch influence had waned, and the formal mazes,
clipped hedges and prim parterres, so long the ambition of
the Northern gentry, had been supplanted by groves and
rustic arbours, pools, pedestals and 'bustos,' after the pattern
of Mr Pope's garden at Twickenham. But the time of
'admired disorder' was now almost in view. True, people did
not yet rave about Nature's romantic wildness. But Nature,
since her creditable appearance twenty years before in the
scenery of Allan Ramsay's *Gentle Shepherd*, had been given
tactful encouragement, and in the region of Midlothian was
increasingly referred to. There was much competition in the
fresh laying out of grounds, public and private; and with
such success that Edinburgh gardeners were in demand in
the great estates of England and in the palace demesnes of
France.

It was upon a new public pleasure ground that, after many
anxious months, William was fortunate enough to obtain
work that was more than immediately useful to him. He was
employed with others in laying out what till then had been
part of a private estate lying to the south of the town. It was
appropriately named Hope Park. Hitherto, sharing an attic
room with another man as poor as himself, he had lived very
precariously. Yet even so, week by week, he had scraped small
sums from his uncertain earnings, till at length they had
added up to twenty shillings to be despatched to Kincardine
in the perplexing form of a banknote. Now, at work in Hope
Park day after day, he could send more and send it more
easily. He might even spare an occasional penny to carry
home in triumph to his attic for a single night some precious
bound and printed volume from the circulating library. Up
there at the Luckenbooths in old Allan Ramsay's new
premises it was almost worth the money, lingering awhile, to
watch the customers, or overhear scraps of bookish conversation and debate. The shop, with its busts of Ben Jonson and

Drummond of Hawthornden, was the acknowledged resort of men of parts, and of the many 'old originals,' in which, even at her dullest times, Edinburgh was fertile. Here one might see Thomas Ruddiman, the deaf and almost blind grammarian, his stiff old body buttoned tightly into an orange-coloured coat and scarlet waistcoat; or schoolboy-faced Davie Hume; or sedate, clever-featured young Dr Robertson of Gladsmuir, of whom great things were expected, returning in his clerical black and white from the Advocates' Library with the latest batch of notes for his history. Or one might catch a glimpse of more exotic figures—Mr Gay from London, perhaps, on his way to call upon Duchess Kitty; or dashingly-dressed Allan Ramsay, junior, who was now condescending to be the only portrait painter in his native city, and at the same time to lead society there for a short period between his studies in Rome and his appointment as court painter to George III; or the shy, lanky, ill-shapen figure of General Wolfe, who at twenty-two was in unwilling, efficient command of the King's forces in Scotland. Even the perky little ex-wigmaker himself, persuasively selling copies of his own books, and conducting his library in gay defiance of the stricter elements of the town, was a sight worth seeing. Admittedly there was upon his shelves a modicum of 'villainous obscene things printed in London'—the works of Wycherley, for example, and of Mrs Manley. But for readers like the labourer on the Hope Park there were also books like *The Grave* by the Rev Robert Blair, Young's *Night Thoughts* and Hervey's *Meditations Among the Tombs*.

That William was born to be a householder, a husband, a father, was clear to himself as to others. It was at once his duty and his dream. But he was an insecure man and a model son. Perhaps too he was over-fearful of the penny bridal and its accompaniments. Anyhow the dream was to last rather too long and in rather too deep a solitude before the duty in its warm reality was entered upon. Ten years were to pass—ten years almost to a day—between that filial attempt of his to bind himself to an East-country farm, and the binding of himself in wedlock down in the West-country.

It was from the West that many of the gentry came to

winter in Edinburgh. And after two years, weary of city life, William went in spring with one of the westering lairds. The Laird of Fairlie in Dundonald, in the middle part of Ayrshire, was one of the great agricultural innovators, especially in the matter of cattle-breeding. William could hardly have found a more interesting place. He remained in it for two years—a lonely man, but diligent, learning much, and giving satisfaction to his employer. Then, taking with him a new certificate of character signed by the parish minister and the session clerk, he moved to the southern or Carrick district of the county. Near the town of Maybole he worked for two years more with one master, and then— supplied once more with the usual certificate—he returned on his tracks through Stewart Kyle, and, coming to King Kyle in the north, re-engaged himself for two years as daily gardener to a family of the noted local name of Crawford. The Crawford lands were on one bank of the river Doon. William lodged on the opposite bank at the mill and led a frugal, bachelor life.

He was now thirty-six, and it would seem that his lot was cast in this place. Here he would stay. But he had worked long enough for other men and had lived too long solitary under the roofs of others. It was more than time that he should set up for himself. All these years he had been saving to this end, and for some time now his father had needed his help no longer. His savings at last amounted to enough to feu a plot of ground. Presently, near the banks of Doon, he found the place he wanted. Here he would lay his hearthstones and set up the posts of his door.

For it was William's intention to build himself a house and set up as a market gardener, possibly taking up some jobbing outside work for safety to begin with. The seven acres he had chosen were well suited to this purpose. They lay on a slope of low ground near the river where it flowed through the barony of Alloway in Ayr parish. A mile and a half to the north-west was the royal and ancient burgh of Ayr, full of shopkeepers and the lower sort of gentry, and with seats of the greater sort about it on all sides. And to the south—across the Doon in Carrick—the smaller burgh of Maybole had a growing population of cotton weavers and a loom in every cottage clacking from dawn to dark. The hamlet of Alloway was on the straight way—road it could not yet be called—between the two towns. It consisted of a few scattered cottages and a ruined church within ruined walls by a ford.

While still working daily for the Crawfords William began to build his home with his own hands. The neighbours watched him curiously. On the whole he was more respected than liked. He was clearly respectable—his reputation was without a stain; but he was no Ayrshireman, and in the common ways of village chat he was silent and unyielding. When he did speak it was with too marked a propriety, both of matter and diction. And while for a stranger he kept himself too much to himself, it was further against him that he was addicted to the society of his superiors. With them, it was noted, he could brighten and take his place with quiet confidence. He was, for instance, on excellent terms with his master at Doonside, and, given the company of a scholar or travelled person, he showed himself ready enough for conversation. The few friends he made were men of character, such as his near neighbour, John Tennant.

The question was, what girl would this quiet, rather too superior gardener ask to share the four walls he was raising with such careful labour? His was clearly the roof-tree of a man about to marry. A living-room and a kitchen opened off each other, and a door led from the kitchen to the stone-paved barn and byre. Except for two stone jambs and a stone lintel and chimney, the thick walls were made entirely of clay covered with lime. The roof, which contained no attic, was thatched. In the kitchen a bed was built into one wall, and there was a bed-stance made with planks in the other room. Both rooms were a fair size and had small windows, of which one had the upper part glazed. For the rest, light and air were regulated by means of wooden shutters. When completed it was a tidy piece of work, well above the average of its kind both as to style and comfort. William had no cause to feel ashamed of it, and did not. He was exercised, however, even more than the watching neighbours, concerning that business of a wife.

At the mill, where he still lodged, there was a likely enough girl in the miller's daughter. William was on friendly terms with her, a fact which had been duly noted by the gossips of the village as well as by the folk at the mill. The miller, like others of his calling, was a man of substance. Unless he were inhumanly honest it was almost impossible for the miller of any district not to thrive. Quite apart from her gear this particular miller's daughter happened to be the sort of girl that William fancied for his mate. She was home-keeping, modest, and so highly educated that she could even, at a pinch, read handwriting. So William had cogitated long and deeply upon asking her to wife. True, he was not in love with her, but neither was he with any other girl, nor at his age like to be. In any case falling in love was extraneous to the question. A more important consideration was whether her father would regard him as eligible. William shrank from the ordeal of a verbal proposal followed by a possible refusal; but he was at length almost resolved to offer himself—in writing. He had accordingly spent much time in composing a carefully phrased letter, which now lay hidden in his chest along with his few clothes and his many certificates of character. And as he sheered up the clay and placed the stones of his cottage at Alloway, his thoughts dwelt persistently upon this missive and its potentialities.

But one day, after attending the fair at Maybole, he went straight to his lodging, took the letter from his chest, and burnt it. He knew now that it would never be needed. For at the fair he had met a girl in whose presence all hesitation about the choice of a wife vanished. Even before they had speech he had the vision of his cottage tenanted by her and by the children none but she could bear him. Here surely was the reward for all these years of toil and saving and filial piety, that he too should beget filial sons and prudent daughters upon such a wife. Her body was, as they say in Scotland, 'weel set up,' but slender, her eyes brown and well opened beneath dark brows and a square and candid forehead, her hair pale with red in it, her skin the kind that goes with that colouring, transparent but not delicate, and she had bright cheeks. And a man had only to speak with her to discover that her comeliness had no deceit in it. At twenty-four she already had cause to take a serious view of life, yet at the same time she was quick and cheerful, lovingly disposed and of uncompromising virtue. True, she was no miller's daughter, and would bring nothing but herself to a husband. But in herself and by her history it would be difficult to imagine any woman more fitted to captivate the thoughtful gardener. Her name was Agnes Broun.

For more than half her life she had been compelled to earn her own livelihood. Her father, a small farmer on the smuggling coast of Carrick (and without doubt a smuggler in a small way himself) had begotten two families, of which she belonged to the first. His was a Norman stock that had been established in the district since the days of Bruce, and could boast of having provided Ayr with burgesses in the fifteenth century. Yet when he took as his first wife an unlettered servant girl he did not necessarily marry beneath him. She, too, no doubt, had a pedigree that seemed to her as good as that of the Brouns, if not better. Every true Scotswoman brings at least this asset to marriage.

Agnes had been the eldest of six children, and when she was ten, her mother, whom she idolised, had made what was called 'a good end.' That is to say she had summoned Agnes to her deathbed and enjoined upon the little girl that she must thenceforth be responsible for her five brothers and sisters—this with the full connivance of Agnes's father, who saw, no more than the child herself, anything impious in the charge laid upon her. It was not surprising that Agnes never found time to learn to sign her own name. Till then her mother had used to send her daily to a weaver's cottage (along with some other girls not worth sending to the parish school with their brothers) to repeat the Psalms of David to a loom accompaniment: and she had got the length of slowly spelling out a few printed texts from the Bible. But her father, like most Scots of his time and station, held that females were better unlettered. Besides he required what servants he had to devote themselves to his farming and contraband affairs. Agnes must fill the rôle of house-mother. Agnes did her best—for two years.

At the end of that time Broun judged it expedient to marry again, and as the new wife would certainly find the heroic twelve-year-old mother in her way, Agnes was packed off to her maternal grandmother near Maybole. Here she was kept quite as constantly, if less harassingly, at work. Her granny set her to spin within the house, and without to wield the hand-flail and drive the plough-team while the gaudsman held the share to the furrows. When she satisfied the stern old woman she won a small piece of wheaten bread or of oatmeal cake to put as kitchen upon the slice of rye or barley bread that was her usual portion. For recreation she would sing to her granny and to the old blind man, her uncle, that lived with them—songs she had picked up in the fields.

It was a hard life, but Agnes throve upon it. She was strong and willing and neat in her ways—a girl that ran about her work and never sat down unless to her platter, her seam or her wheel. The gaudsman, a young, loverly fellow named Will Nelson, wanted her; and by the time she was nineteen they were tokened. They worked together daily in the field and on the threshing floor. Many of her songs she learned from him, singing them after him line by line, till she got the tune right and knew all the verses. The two of them were very 'chief.' But with a ploughman's wage at £5 a year, both knew that marriage was a thing they must wait for. Unluckily for Nelson, Agnes was not the girl to give herself before marriage; and unluckily for Agnes, Nelson was not the man to tarry a great while in strict celibacy. At the end of seven years, during the whole of which time they had kept company, she discovered him in an infidelity. Fiery-tempered and direct, herself incapable of what she took to be disloyalty, she could neither understand nor forgive. She broke with this William, and broke clean. But the inward uprooting of a seven years' love is a different matter. She was still suffering from it when the other William made her acquaintance at the fair.

It is not difficult to see in what light he must have appeared to her. Few men could have filled more adequately the Scriptural rôle of providing the shadow of a great rock in a weary land. From the first it was clear that he loved her tenderly, and that there was no fickleness in him. From the first his grave, dark sinewy beauty made her all subservient womanhood. And as time went on, and she put him to the test and came to know him, she realised his great worth in the separate world of men. He was the best man she had ever met, and the most intellectual. His undoubted superiority of mind over all she was accustomed to, gave an element of awe to her feeling for him—an emotion almost daughterly, but such as she had never experienced for her own ruthless parent. She was a dozen years younger than William, and he was old for his years. She kept him waiting twelve months. Then she, who had so long been a servant, came to be mistress of the new cottage at Alloway. She asked for nothing better than to serve her husband all the days of her life. As for her husband, this ambition harmonised perfectly with his own long-considered ideas of matrimonial felicity.

PART TWO

Father and Son

'He's a fule wha marries at Yule,' says a Scots proverb—'for
when the bairn's to bear, the corn's to shear.' But as yet, with
his little seven acres, part to be dug for garden stuff and part
left pasture for a dairy of two cows, William Burnes had
happily no need to hearken to sayings made for farmers.
Time enough for that. So he had married Agnes in mid-
December. In any case their first child, a boy, was not born
till thirteen months later.

The night of the birth coincided with a violent storm of
wind and rain, through which the expectant father had to
fight his way and ride the swollen Slaphouse ford for the
midwife. It was one of those births about which legends
are told; but the present narrative is not concerned with
legends. The facts are enough. On 26 January—the morning
after the birth—William, in spite of the weather, brought the
parish minister from Ayr, and assembled for the baptism the
needful witnesses, one of whom was his neighbour Tennant,
a man younger than himself but already twice married and
very fruitful. There was no custom to explain this haste. It
was simply that William could not bear to wait one unneces-
sary hour for what he saw as the consummation of his life.
The ceremony was performed in the kitchen, Agnes handing
the infant to its father from the box bed, and he, after the
Scotish fashion, holding it in his arms to be sprinkled, and
uttering his vows aloud. Never did any man undertake with
more eager solemnity the duties of Christian parenthood.
Never was firstborn more sincerely dedicated to righteousness.

Day after day the gale continued. Along that coast such a
wind could blow from the Atlantic that sometimes it
uncovered the dead in their shallow, sandy graves. In this
case, however, it was the newborn that it exposed. For ere

dawn on the tenth day a gable of the cottage fell and laid the kitchen open to the elements. William had to carry his family through the wet and roaring darkness to the nearest house where hospitality could be sought without loss of dignity—for in a land of large families and two-roomed dwellings it is no small favour to ask for a bed. Then in the inclement morning he went back alone, and set himself to repair the fault the west wind had discovered in his home. Clay and stone are ill to combine. The union between the humble substance of the wall and the ambitious fabric of the chimney had failed. The neighbours spoke their sympathy, but there was some smiling. William was undaunted. So solid was his week's rebuilding that it has stood through a hundred and ninety winters.

The child was thought to resemble his mother because he had her eyes and brows. But his hair was very dark, and his head unusually large. Being the eldest and a son, he was named after his paternal grandfather. So he was Robert Burnes. A second boy would have to be Gilbert, after Agnes's father. This Gilbert arrived a year later. He was followed in due season by two girls, Agnes and Annabella, named after their grandmothers in the correct way, precedence being given to the maternal side.

William Burnes never carried out his market gardening scheme, for before it was well begun a tempting offer prompted him to postpone his dream of complete independence. A new property owner in the neighbourhood, a friend of the Crawfords of Doonside, asked for his help. This was a Dr Ferguson, an Ayrshire man, who, like others of his nation, had practised medicine in London for many years and done pretty well. Now he had come back to his native place to enjoy his money and to be Provost of Ayr. Two years before William's marriage he had bought thirty acres of farm-land, pleasantly situated and very fertile on the banks of the Doon, stretching from below the ruined church at Alloway all the way to Auchindrane. He had built himself a little mansion house, done away with the old farm names of Berriesdam and Warlockholm, and renamed his place Doonholm. All the time he kept adding to his possessions. First, part of the lands of Fauldhead and Whinknowe became his in an exchange deal with neighbour Crawford. Then the lands of South High Corton fell into his hands. Soon he had quite a good little property to leave to his dear eldest daughter Elizabeth, who was the apple of his eye. But throughout all his acquisitions Doonholm remained his home and his family seat, and he wished it to be laid out in the latest style as befitted his dignity. He wanted plantations, shrubberies, a fine garden, walks that would skirt the margin of the river, an avenue of those rare trees—elms. Would the well-spoken-of Burnes undertake the work of overseer and daily gardener at Doonholm?

William could not refuse. He went out to work all day and every day for the Provost while Agnes managed the dairy, and he sold a third of his acres. He still cherished his dream, but husband and wife were peaceful, happy, solvent. And after all he was used to waiting.

For Agnes it was perfection—the brand new house, so trim and convenient, and all her own; her man in a fine job with the gentry who talked with him almost as if he were one of themselves; boy babies and girl babies with bright intelligent eyes following her round; her cows—there were as many as three of them sometimes—that she knew so well; and just enough land to have everything under one's eye. She worked hard, holding to her maiden habit of never sitting still if she could help it. And as she worked she sang. Many of her songs had never been written down, others were from fleetingly printed strips picked from the barrows at Ayr or Maybole, or out of the pedlar's pack by Will Nelson and his like; but since then they had passed so often from mouth to mouth that whole verses had been lost, and new verses added, and lines altered beyond recognition. All the tunes were old, subject to the variations of a hundred scattered singers, alive and dead. Agnes was a good song-carrier, her voice sweet and strong, her memory excellent. The children loved to listen to her, but none so much as Robert, whose appetite for song was never satisfied.

> Kissin' is the key o' love,
> An' clappin' is the lock,
> An' makin' o's the best thing
> That e'er a young thing got.

That was one he often asked for. Another was an old chapbook ballad called 'The Life and Age of Man.' It was one of those dirge-like songs loved by peasants because they voice the sadness of labour, and had been, as Agnes often told the children, greatly favoured by the poor old man, her uncle, who had been 'long blind ere he died.' He had liked nothing better than to sit, shedding tears with his sightless eyes, while she sang it to him. So for Robert it was more even than a song. It comprehended his granny's farm, which he had never seen, the blind man in his chair, the little, hard-driven singing girl now his mother. And at the same time it transcended all these with its sighing refrain:

Ah! man was made to mourn!

But Robert himself could not sing. He tried—how the child tried!—with the violence of despair over his unaccountable, maddening failure. His mother did her best to teach him. But there it was. Though she could set the melody pulsing in him he could not release it. The rhythm was there. It was in his blood. But when he opened his mouth nothing came but unmeaning sounds. It was not that he could not distinguish each separate air. He could, even if they were hummed over without a word. But his baby sisters could sing a tune more correctly than he, and even Gilbert, who did not specially care for music, made a better showing.

When the boys began to go to school (which they did when Robert was still under six) their musical incapacity proved a real source of affliction. Although two of the youngest children in the class—and the school was no more than a class—they won their way quickly to the top in most subjects. In particular they excelled in reading and in all memory-work. But when it came to singing the Psalms of David in metre they were the schoolmaster's despair. He plied the tawse unsparingly, but without results that could be called musical.

In the ordinary course the boys of a cottager would be hired out at eight or nine years old as day-labourers to a neighbouring farmer, or even as resident labourers to farmers at a distance. But William, like his father, had laid plans for his children on a more liberal scale than the district could provide. Moreover he still aimed at an independence that would keep his growing family together. For this, however, he would need control of considerable acres. Soon the cottage would have served its turn. He must sell it and find a small farm. It happened that Provost Ferguson had recently acquired a property of seventy 'unimproved' acres and a steading, up the hill about two miles to the south in Stewart Kyle. William Burnes proposed for it. The rent was high—£40 a year for the first six years, and after that £45. But the Provost, who liked his gardener and knew that he would make the best of tenants, not only made no difficulties, but was willing to lend £100 on the security of the Alloway cottage for the stocking of the farm, and to give an option for the renewal of the lease at the end of the term. William had inspected the place. It was not all he could have wished, but it was his chance. He signed the lease. The family went on living at Alloway—for no immediate purchaser of the cottage appeared. William went on spending his working hours at Doonholm. But in his spare time he began to plant little fruit trees beside the new house, and to clear the stony fields. He brought cart-loads of the best stones down to Alloway churchyard. With Tennant and others he had applied at Ayr for leave to rebuild the ruined walls, and had even raised a small subscription.

Of an evening he laboured over a theological manual he was compiling for the guidance of his children. He had begun this in Robert's infancy—if not before his birth—and had persevered in it with dogged patience ever since. It took the form of a dialogue between father and son, and was designed to convey those ideas of the Godhead and of human life which had exercised his mind as he dug and planted for other men's hire or sat on his obscure stool in the Edinburgh churches. He had the pride of authorship, the gravity of experience, the purity of faith. Unfortunately he was never able to escape from the unreadable jargon that was then the serious mode accepted even by men of respectable understanding. Not that this occurred to him as a drawback. What did trouble him was the poorness of his calligraphy and grammar, which made him more than ever anxious to improve upon his own father's well-meant but defective provisions for learning. He felt qualified to teach his sons the work of a farm and to instruct them in the right conduct of life; but if they were to have more book-learning than himself he must call in the services of another man.

The local school, which the children were now attending, did not satisfy him. It was two miles away at Alloway Mill, and the mill had embarrassing associations for William. Further, Mr Campbell, the schoolmaster, was about to leave, making way for one said to be his inferior. In any case the children could learn little more there than William and his brothers had learned in the Clochanhill schoolhouse. Accordingly, soon after Robert's sixth birthday—about the time the lease of the farm was signed—William decided to have a schoolmaster of his own choosing near home. He had unfolded this scheme to four among the most intelligent of his neighbours and had won their support. John Tennant had a brother, David, who taught at Ayr Academy. Also the English master there, a Mr Paterson, being a native of Kincardine, had condescended to allow 'a certain degree of intimacy' between so worthy a man as Burnes and himself. On Sundays, after the morning service, he would even ask William and Agnes to step into his house for a short time; and William and Agnes (and the children, who waited for them in the street) were sensible of the honour. Through Paterson and Tennant a likely dominie was suggested, and one afternoon in early March William set out by himself for the burgh, having an appointment there with one John Murdoch, a very genteel young man who had but recently qualified as a schoolmaster.

Punctual to the hour, as it tolled from the 'dungeon-clock' at the jail, William crossed the steep, narrow bridge into Ayr. The town had lately been robbed of its gates; but the 'Auld Brig,' though modern citizens were beginning to condemn it as unsafe, remained the only approach from the south side of the river. And at the north end stood Simpson's, a famous place for striking bargains. William rarely entered a tavern either in Ayr or anywhere else, but the meeting with Mr Murdoch was a solemn matter that could not be managed otherwise. Murdoch, coming on his lighter foot from the town side, and passing between the high, gabled tenements with their turnpike stairs, went under cover along the main street because of the wooden balconies that thrust out from either side. He too was punctual to the striking of the dungeon-clock. It was his first encounter with a prospective employer. He was eighteen years of age, full of promise and pedantry.

From the moment of meeting Murdoch felt a warm reverence for this middle-aged, serious father. Later, when most of his life was lived, he was to declare that Burnes was 'by far the best of the human race that ever he knew.' Both men were immediately at one in their worship of learning. Murdoch said that he was musical and had a *flair* for languages. It was his ambition to go some day to France, that he might learn to speak French with a perfect accent. Having been forewarned that he must bring with him a sample of his handwriting he laid it on the inn table to be scrutinised. The time had now come for Burnes to confide the affair of the *Manual of Religious Belief*. Till this was revised, he feared, and copied out in a fair hand, neither young nor old could profit by it. Could Murdoch include such a task with his duties as infant schoolmaster? Murdoch was sure he could. His calligraphy passed muster, and it would appear that he had specialised in the subject of English grammar. To come back to music, he was confident that he would be able to teach even Robert to sing the Psalms of David.

So it was settled. Murdoch was to come to Alloway, where he would be housed in turn with the Burneses and with the four other families whose children would attend daily at a room in the village to be instructed. Besides his keep he would be guaranteed a salary of about sixpence a day. Upon this satisfactory result a drink was ordered at the employer's expense, and drunk to the undertaking. Some six weeks later Murdoch walked over, bringing with him some clean shirts, a spelling-book, *Fisher's English Grammar*, Masson's *Collection of Prose and Verse*, a New Testament, and a new seven-thonged leather tawse.

The arrangement lasted for two years, and was a success. Incidentally it provided Robert and Gilbert with by far the longest spell of schooling they were to have. All later periods of formal education, when added together, were scarcely to equal one-third of their time under Murdoch. On both sides it was made the very most of, and there arose a considerable degree of liking, if not precisely of love, between master and pupils. Murdoch's was a likeable rather than a loveable character. He was above all an energetic teacher. Hustling his pupils through what they still lacked of the 'elements,' he soon had them busy paraphrasing, turning verse into prose, 'substituting synonyms' and 'supplying ellipses.' Masson's enterprising *Collection* (Mr Masson kept a school in Edinburgh on the most modern lines for the children of the gentry at 5s a term) contained elegant extracts from a dozen or so of the greatest writers, from Shakespeare—dead—to Henry Mackenzie—much alive—and selected letters, 'Moral and Entertaining,' from Mrs Elizabeth Rowe. Murdoch made the boys learn many of the passages by heart, which they easily did. He also tried, according to promise, to make them sing the Sternhold and Hopkins version of the Psalms. But here he failed, especially with Robert, even with the aid of the stinging new tawse. At length he was obliged to admit that Robert had 'an ear remarkably dull, and a voice untuneable.' The Dominie had nothing against thrashing as an aid to learning, and he found himself oftener impelled to thrash Robert than the merrier and more docile Gilbert, who was from the first his favourite. It was not that Robert was slow or stupid. On the contrary—save in that one respect of sacred music—he seemed to his master to show almost as marked intelligence as his younger brother. He learned by heart even more readily than jolly little Gilbert, and rapidly became an adept at the favourite synonyms and ellipses. But there was a 'stubborn something' in this thick-set little boy with the dangerous dark eyes that gave an adult pause and called for chastisement.

None the less, the Burnes boys were Murdoch's pet pupils, and he liked to stay in their 'mud edifice,' 'argillaceous fabric,' or 'tabernacle of clay'—as in his rage for synonyms he alternatively called the cottage—better than in any of the neighbours' houses. While there, was he not accorded the full honours due to his learning? And was he not able to engage to the top of his bent in superior conversation? One day, in very different surroundings, he was to sit in princely company and give English lessons to Talleyrand, and other distinguished foreigners. But then he was also to be middle-aged and ill, a dram-drinking, disappointed man. He would never again be so greatly at peace with himself and the world as during these virtuous evenings by the Burnes fireside. Still in his teens he was deferred to by a man far older than himself, and looked up to by clever children as the very fount of knowledge; while that 'very sagacious woman' his hostess, pausing between her endless duties, stood fascinated, uncomprehending, her warm glance travelling in admiration between his face and that of her wonderful husband. Talk at an end, he would slip complacently into the chaff bed, already warmed for him by the sleeping body of little Robert. For Robert was always his bedfellow.

Robert was seven when the family removed from the cottage. It was still unsold, but the time had come to occupy the place in which their work and living now lay. The new farm, Mount Oliphant, stood on bare rising ground to the inland side of the more inland of the two tracks between Ayr and Maybole but nearer to Ayr than to Maybole, and close to the borders of Carrick, the kingdom of castles. To reach it they had to climb with all their belongings two miles to the south east, up the rough hill. It was an austere place, a great change from low-lying, bushy, more human Alloway. From it they had a sight of the sea, and standing up from the sea, fifteen miles out, but seeming much nearer, the sudden stack of Ailsa, with its cloud of birds, and farther still the little craggy mountains of Arran, blue as air.

Not that sea-views gave pleasure to Robert. The inhuman expanse of the sea rather saddened and repelled him. What he loved was to be under trees or beside running water; for then even sadness became a kind of rapture to him, most of all when the branches of the trees were disturbed by a violent wind. He took great delight, too, in the small kinds of birds which shelter by trees and streams. But on the Carrick heights there were no trees, and the birds there were moorfowl that cried and whirred—'vermin' that in spring filled the farmer's heart with despair, and in autumn brought men with guns, and horrid sights of mangled, bloody feathers.

Mount Oliphant itself was a poor rough little place—the house a two-roomed stone cottage, scarcely larger than the clay dwelling they had left, the acres hardly touched by man, and not at all by modern implements. Ayrshire has three kinds of earth—the sandy, the clayey, and the 'mossy and moorish.' It was to be William Burnes's fate to know each kind before he laid his bones in the richest acre of them all. Alloway had been chiefly sandy. Mount Oliphant might have been called 'mossy and moorish,' it might also have been called simply stony. Burnes, setting his fruit-trees the spring before, had already become aware that here was not the best of soil. But his years of happiness had made him hopeful. That April, as it chanced, the weather had been more encouraging than for many years past, so that all growing things were, as the newspapers said, 'in great forwardness.' And the move was made during a radiant Whitsuntide.

The children had to walk to Alloway now each day to be taught by Murdoch, two miles downhill, and two miles up again. And as before, Murdoch came, at regular intervals, to stay with them. Murdoch had become very much one of the family. They counted on him, not only for teaching, but for news of the world, indeed of the universe. At Mount Oliphant there was not even a hamlet, and the father's daily visits to Doonholm were at an end. From Murdoch alone could the Burneses hear how the Forth and Clyde Canal and the Douglas Cause were progressing, what General Paoli was doing in Corsica, what changes were expected any day in the Ministry, how Lord Clive, ill and under a cloud, was on his way home from India, that the Microcosm was drawing crowds in Glasgow and Edinburgh, that the Rev George Whitefield had once more arrived in the latter city from London to preach a Gospel milder than the Old Lights approved, but more evangelical than the New Lights cared for.

From Murdoch's point of view it was perhaps a mistake that he should have chosen a *Life of Hannibal* to lend to Robert at this time. Out of school hours it was the child's only book except the Bible and his father's *Manual*, and for years afterwards he identified himself with the conquering hero, a fantasy hardly calculated to dissolve that 'stubborn sturdy something' in his nature. Such indeed was his military exaltation that even the sea lost something of its terror. If life were to become too difficult at home he could always go off and be a soldier. As life had a way of appearing too difficult for Robert at frequent intervals this soldiering idea was a recurring source of comfort.

The next volumes to enter the house for the children's use were Salmon's *Geographical Grammar*, Dorham's *Physico- and Astro-Theology*, Hervey's *Meditations among the Tombs*, Ray's *Wisdom of God and the Creation*, and Taylor's *On Original Sin*. These were not bought. Each treasure was painstakingly borrowed in turn, either from a book-society in Ayr which Burnes had managed to join, or from one of his superior acquaintances, such as Dominie Paterson, who possessed a 'library'—that is to say, several shelves of books, mainly theological. A single exception was the *History of the Bible* by the Rev Thomas Stackhouse, which a Kilmarnock bookseller was issuing in six volumes. For this monumental work by an English rector Burnes had become a subscriber at three shillings per volume. Vol I in its blue sewed covers (with a Head of Mr Stackhouse taking precedence of a map of the Terrestrial Paradise) had already appeared that March; Vol II (with Egyptian maps) in April; Vol III (with maps of Palestine) in May; and Vol IV would shortly take its honoured place with the others on the Mount Oliphant shelf.

All these printed and bound impossibilities Robert read so far as they were readable. To him the nature of a book had been made so very sacred that to the end of his life he could never surely discriminate between a good book and a bad one. But no book provided by his father could vie with *Hannibal*. That stood for something more even than a book, for something warm, active, personal to himself—for something partaking of the nature of song. To the Scot, then as now, letters were very much one thing and life another.

Quite apart from letters was surely the effect that certain words had upon Robert, when uttered or sung. Why, for instance, when the children repeated in school Addison's paraphrase, 'How are Thy servants blessed, O Lord,' and came to the lines:

> For though in dreadful whirls we hung
> High on the broken wave,

should Robert feel his heart turn over in his breast? It could hardly be due to the literary Mr Addison. The very same thing might happen when old Betty Davidson was singing at the wheel or telling one of her tales, and nobody could connect old Betty with letters. Was their father not always bidding them pay no heed to her ignorant nonsense?

Betty was a kinswoman of Agnes, and sometimes stayed with them for months at a time. It was chiefly out of kindness that Agnes took her in. It meant seven sleeping in the two rooms, but Betty was old and poor, the widow of a cousin, and sometimes ill-used by her son's wife, upon whom she was dependent for food and shelter. And, of course, she could be made useful at Mount Oliphant, spinning, carding, and helping in the house. Agnes, these days, was beginning to find her hands over-full. As for the children, they rejoiced when Betty came, especially Robert. For she was 'remarkable for her ignorance, credulity, and superstition.' Night and day she wore next her skin a string of amber beads against the evil eye; and though life had turned rough for her, and she was old, and unloved, she was full of fun and stories, sayings and songs. Many of these were coarse, all were puerile and unenlightened. William Burnes did not hold with them. But in its own way Betty's mind was better stored than Murdoch's. She had 'the largest collection in the country of tales and songs concerning devils, ghosts, fairies, brownies, witches, warlocks, spunkies, kelpies, elf-candles, dead-lights, wraiths, apparitions, cantraips, giants, enchanted towers, and dragons.' And though the father's contempt and the teacher's rationalism were duly heeded—though all such things were allowed to be trumpery—their charm was not to be so lightly done away with, nor their power. Even as a child Robert knew them for idle terrors. But even as a man, addicted to 'nocturnal rambles' in woods and by streams, he could never shake off the need to 'keep a sharp look-out in suspicious places' for any of old Betty's frightening brood. No such incorrigible hauntings remained from the reading of Taylor's *Original Sin*, although the beliefs there were so highly approved by schoolmaster and father. Again it was the difference between life and letters. Letters were a thing of the intellect; the heart went its separate way.

From the earliest days Burnes had observed his firstborn with pride and also with a certain anxiety. Looking earnestly into the baby's face on the day of its birth, he had formed the opinion, common in middle-aged fathers in a like situation, that he had begotten an extraordinary child. He was the last man to publish a belief of this kind. But, as the years passed, his faith was fortified rather than weakened by the daily pressure of events, an occurrence not quite so common in the lives of hard-driven fathers of increasing families. He noticed with satisfaction the quickness of Robert's mind, and with misgiving the even greater quickness with which one mood succeeded another. Usually contemplative, even gloomy, the dark obstinate little fellow, when roused, was astonishingly vocal, and in states of emotion his eyes, indeed his whole body, spoke for him as well. These things are not the rule in the child of a Scotish cottager, and one day at Mount Oliphant Burnes opened his mind to his wife. 'Whoever may live to see it,' he said, 'something extraordinary will come from that boy.' Robert's mother, however, had not noticed anything extraordinary, unless it was that Robert was by no means a favourite with anybody. As between her two elder sons the more equable Gilbert was her choice.

But Agnes was becoming more and more absorbed in her daily tasks and cares. Three more children were born at Mount Oliphant—William, John, and Isabel. She had to run about more than ever, but she sang less and she saw less, and had begun to take her place without repining upon the working-woman's treadmill. Whatever might be the dreams of that ambitious man, William Burnes, for his children, she herself could hardly fancy any further achievement for a son of hers than to become something like his father.

They had been nearly two years at the farm when the offer came to Murdoch of a more lucrative post. This was opportune, not only for himself, but for his employer. Burnes increasingly needed every penny. It was being borne in upon him that the soil of Mount Oliphant was 'almost the very poorest then in a state of cultivation.' Besides he had come there not to save his children from work, but to keep them under his eye as he laboured, and to combine all the strength of the family in improving the hardly-acquired family property. Dreams, like letters, were not to be confused with reality. Robert, at nine, was old enough to start threshing the grain, and weeding between the furrows for more than childish amusement. Very soon he would be able to help at the plough. The remainder of his bookish education must take its chance. Every night the father would try to give the boys a lesson or two, and the elder children must help to teach the younger.

Murdoch came up to stay the night and to say good-bye. Though he was not immediately leaving Ayrshire—only going to the south of Carrick—it would be too far for any more visits. Besides he hoped to go farther before long. As a farewell present he brought a small compendium of English grammar (this to help Burnes with his continuation classes) and a complete play by William Shakespeare. To celebrate the occasion, the children begged him to read some Shakespeare aloud to them. He agreed.

> She is a woman, therefore may be woo'd;
> She is a woman, therefore may be won;

Thus far the Dominie's reading was a success. The circle round the fireside had been listening intently, but now things went wrong. When the heroine entered 'ravished, her hands cut off, and her tongue cut out,' and was tauntingly asked to fetch water, and to wash her hands, it was too much for young Scotish stomachs. Weeping, the Burnes children protested they could bear no more. Their father was vexed with them for what he considered their ingratitude. 'Very well,' said he, threatening them sternly, 'if that's the way of it I'll ask Mr Murdoch to take the book away with him.' 'If he doesna'—Robert started from his chair, his eyes blazing—'If he doesna,' he cried, 'I'll burn it; I'll burn it!' Such lack of respect called for the tawse; and the tawse would certainly have been brought out, but Murdoch was in an amiable mood, and unwilling to have his leavetaking so disfigured. He pointed out that after all there was no harm in sensibility. So his host let it pass with a reproof; and instead of *Titus Andronicus* Murdoch gave the family a comedy by William Whitehead, Esq, Poet Laureate, which contained an unmutilated heroine, named Araminta, and could be guaranteed to move neither children nor adults to the faintest emotion.

For the next four years the Burneses were a family by
themselves. They could not afford even a woman servant at
£4 a year. At the few times in each twelvemonth when extra
help on the land was a necessity, Burnes would get in some
very old or very youthful person who would be willing to lend
a hand for less than the regular labourer's wage,[1] or a relative
of Agnes's would come for the harvest, and work for his
keep. Otherwise Mount Oliphant was a house unvisited. Up
in this eastern moorish part farms were scarce. The neighbours were chiefly retired tradespeople, who spent much of
their time in Maybole or Ayr, and since the improvement in
trade was rapidly creating new social divisions in Scotland,
such persons felt themselves to be a cut above a small
tenant-farmer. Not that Burnes—who held in contempt all
distinctions except family and intellect—gave them any
chance to air their petty superiority. He had enough to do
without stirring out of his own acres, save on market errands,
or to walk with wife and children, all in their decent best, to
the church at Ayr on Sundays to hear the lengthy but mild
discourses of the Rev William Dalrymple—the same that
had been summoned to baptise the one-day-old Robert—then
home again to the one afternoon of the week upon which,
except for the feeding of the beasts, they could cease from
work.

Each weekday, soon after dawn, or in winter perhaps
before it, the first task was to thresh with heavy hand-flail
enough grain for the day's needs. That done, the horses must
be rubbed down—especially the two precious little Gallo-
ways, upon which Burnes had spent more of his capital than
he could spare, but on these uplands the cheaper horses
from Ireland were little use. Next the cows must be milked
and seen to—the short-legged, taper-horned, rough-coated

breed, brown streaked with white, which the Laird of Fairlie had helped to introduce into Kyle. These gave the right sort of milk for the sweet-milk cheeses that Agnes made. After the byres there was the outdoor work, and the sun was not high by the time William Burnes was about in his fields with Robert and Gilbert attending him. Robert was good with the beasts, and bade fair to have a fine sowing-hand and to be clever at the plough. He was developing, too, into a strongly built muscular lad, though round-shouldered and something lacking in physical stamina. Perhaps it was because he was constantly over-worked and under-nourished that he suffered from gloom and exhaustion. None but skim milk could be kept for the children, and meat they never had. Whatever the cause, Robert slouched, and he ached, and sometimes he shrieked out during the night. But there was nothing for it. Principle and the day's routine were sacred.

Principle and the day's routine; that was it—to exclude from existence all but duty, self-improvement, and the fear of God; to exclude particularly any indulgence of nature, any ebullitions of mirth or passion except in the matters of family affection. Here was the ideal figure of the thoughtful, well-doing Scotish father upon which thousands have since tried to model themselves with varying success. William Burnes compelled the admiration of his sons, and was so far from being knowingly unkind or unjust that any rebellion against him seemed to the rebel as wickedness indeed. Of this he took no base advantage. In theory he would have used the tawse for obstinacy, untruthfulness, carelessness, disobedience or bawdy speaking. In practice his tawse was hardly ever needed. Within his seventy acres his word was law, and a mere look was enough to quell any incipient difference of opinion. But what a look that could be! He was himself so passionately devoted to duty that he expected a similar devotion from those about him as a matter of course. He failed no more in tenderness than in duty. His sympathy with the younger children was perfect. He spared time to teach them the names and ways of wild flowers and the different kinds of grasses. With the animals he was invariably gentle.

He was not gentle, however, with human foibles, and any sort of human excess found him not merely unyielding but subject to explosions of rage. One day an old man who was working for him uttered what Murdoch's elegance described as 'smutty innuendoes or *double-entendres*.' William's rebuke was of crushing severity. Because he was of noble nature his home was not unhappy; but it was restrained in all but effort, suppressed in all but anxiety.

It is the eldest son—especially if he is also the eldest child—that bears the brunt of a father's personality. Robert was the chief victim of William Burnes's intensity of righteousness. From the first he felt all that was noble in himself (and from the first he was conscious of nobility), submitting to his father's views, and only what was ignoble urging to unreasoned rebellion. Gilbert, with his less impassioned nature, came off more lightly. There were fewer contacts between him and his father, and he needed neither to submit nor to rebel. As for the younger ones they were set somewhat apart and screened by the elder, as younger ones are. But for Robert there was no escape. He was hemmed in by righteousness. With a particular eagerness he embraced his father's ideal of intellectual superiority by means of unremitting self-improvement. Every day throughout those four years Burnes made it a point to converse with his two elder sons familiarly, but seriously, on enlightened Christian principles and in the most correct language. As far as possible he avoided Scoticisms. It was what the learned were doing now in Edinburgh. (So far had it got that one Aberdeen divine and versifier,[2] who was universally admired, had laid it down that 'to write in vulgar broad Scotch, and yet to write seriously was now impossible.') Burnes, who had always found the Ayrshire dialect, like the Ayrshire nature, somewhat rough and coarse, had a preference for 'gentle' speech. So between meals he talked 'English' to his boys, and during meals he allowed, indeed encouraged them to read English books. At table each male member of the family who was old enough sat silent over his bowl of porridge or broth, a spoon in one hand, a book in the other. At night, family prayers and supper over, Burnes took from the shelf a book of geography, theology or natural history for the instruction of his children.

Not till these educational duties had been discharged, all

by the light of a single candle, did the head of the house allow himself to open his little memorandum book of farm-entries. But long after the children were in bed he would sit pondering over this discouraging volume or painfully adding to its contents. The produce of a successful farm, as Burnes well knew, ought to bear equal division by three as follows: one portion should cover the rent, a second should provide for running expenses, while the third remained for living and profit. As this worked out, the man with a farm of 500 to 1000 acres might well make a fortune, while on a 40-acre farm of similar land there was no more than a bare subsistence. It was the same dilemma in Ayrshire as in Kincardine. Burnes with his seventy acres had been in hopes of making at least a living. But he had not taken into account the peculiar poverty of these acres. Even with good seasons the soil up there needed far more capital spent on it than he could come by. And the seasons after that first too hopeful spring had been uniformly bad. The debt to Provost Ferguson remained unpaid, the cottage unsold. Disease and accident had thinned the byre.

Life was drab now that Murdoch was gone—especially in the winter. There were long months of the West Coast rain and sea-mist—of all-pervading dampness and mud. Frosts came rarely, though there would sometimes be a heavy fall of snow, to be followed by more mud than ever. In their efforts to save on the living-and-profitmaking third of the farm, food was poor and none too plentiful. Robert for days on end was plunged in gloom. As the eldest son he was infected by his father's horror of debt and by the morn-to-night heartbreak of a farm that is not doing well. He had even more than the normal child's capacity for dramatising the fears it reads in a parent's face. At times he was overcome by sympathetic despair. At other times he rebelled against a world where things were so hard for a good man like his father, while men not half so good or so gifted lived pleasantly. He questioned life but received no satisfactory answer. Again his rebellion would take a subtler form, and he would be filled with envy of the beggars that went from cottage to cottage. They never did a hand's turn, yet they never went empty away. All were free from care, some were wonderfully jolly. Why not lead the beggar's life? It is not poverty so much as respectability that racks the nerves of such as the Burneses. Powerless because poor, they were joyless because they were respectably poor. Robert must go on in the way of his father, and his father's father. Proper pride, Scotish stoicism, the consciousness of respectability—these were their only consolations. But something in Robert leaped in response to the mood of the beggar who could be careless no matter how great a rascal he was.

As the end of the first lease approached William Burnes became desperately anxious to leave Mount Oliphant. He knew now in every drastic detail that the place was a 'ruinous bargain.' Unless he could get away he would be tied down to it for another six years and at an increased rent. But how and where was he to go? He was still in debt. Even if a suitable new farm offered how was he to stock it? To be successful the new farm must be either larger or richer, in any case more expensive. He made an effort to find a profitable sub-tenant for Mount Oliphant. None appeared. There was nothing for it but to stay on. At least they had a considerate landlord. Provost Ferguson had driven a good bargain for himself, but he was friendly and would not press the date of a difficult payment.

And things happened now and then to brighten life. A beggar with his meal-bag would have a tale to tell or a song to sing—possibly a song that bore witness to a more rollicking existence than Mount Oliphant could know. Some 'excellent new ballad' would be hawked at the door by a voluble pedlar, and if Robert had a penny it went upon this. On a Sunday the Patersons would allow an improving book to be taken home from their 'library.' Above all, not long after the weary beginning of the second lease, Murdoch came back to Ayr, where he had been appointed a master at the Academy. His four years of wandering had taken him beyond Carrick, away to Dumfries, and even farther.[3]

What seemed yet more wonderful to the Burneses was that Murdoch kept faith with them in spite of his new importance and his travels. Naturally they could not see so much of him as before, but he was as friendly as ever, and reasonably often he devoted a half holiday to providing them with what all (including himself) agreed to call a 'mental feast.' Once more there were improving evenings at the farm—more improving than before because more exciting. Occasionally he brought with him from the town one or two friends whom he was pleased to describe as even 'more intelligent than himself.' This was an event for which the memorandum book must be laid aside, perhaps forgotten. Burnes, when his distinguished guests were furnished with suitable refreshment (of which Murdoch seemed to need a larger supply since his travels) would propound some question of moral or natural philosophy. The 'more intelligent ones' would reply at length, and Murdoch would permit himself a few well-chosen 'observes.' For relaxation there was the news of the day—how narrowly war with France had been averted, how dangerous to peace with Spain was the dispute over the Falkland Islands, or—nearer home—how the great Dr Johnson was even now in Ayrshire, visiting the learned Laird of Auchinleck in the company of his Lordship's much travelled young son, young Mr James Boswell.

Robert sat by, for the most part silent, even morose, but listening intently. He was too proud to be merely grateful and content, as Gilbert and his father were, with this meagre trickle of news from the great world. He would have had it otherwise—more in keeping with the Burnes capacity and deserts. Besides, did it not bring home more sharply than ever their humble isolation? Yet, with all this, his eyes would betray how gratefully the occasion moved him; and when at length—as it had a way of doing—the talk turned on France, he could no longer refrain from an impetuosity of question that made the interest of the others seem pale. Robert could not hear enough of France, its ways, its language, its new blaze of ideas kindled by a watchmaker's son from Geneva, which was now throwing its heat far enough to warm the heart of an Ayrshire ploughboy. *La Nouvelle Héloïse* had appeared in 1759—the very year of Robert's birth—and *Émile* six years later. Robert, of course, had read none of Rousseau's books, but their content of emotion reached him none the less. Murdoch was a Whig of the Left. He was all for equality and nature and France. Certainly after *Émile*, France had become too hot for the Genevan philosopher, and he was glad to accept a pension from a reactionary English monarch, and a home from a Scotch Tory historian. Nevertheless (so Murdoch assured his Ayrshire hearers) in France alone did the world of fashion pay due homage to learning. Edinburgh had something of Paris in this respect, London nothing. Even in Edinburgh the fine ladies did not treat Davie Hume as he had been treated in the French capital.

From such topics Robert would not let Murdoch rest till he had wrung from him the very maximum of information. Murdoch was good-natured about it. He had never been averse from giving information. Moreover he promised, if the time should come that Robert could be spared from the farm for a week or so, to teach him to read the French language, and even to speak it with the authentic accent.

Meanwhile Robert's education had been proceeding on its earnest but erratic course. William Burnes, with the best will in the world, was not a good teacher of boys. Arithmetic was one of his weak points. Accordingly he had seized the chance, when a brother of his wife's was staying with them—a man better at figures than himself—to have the *Ready Reckoner, or Tradesman's Sure Guide* brought home one day from Ayr market. At the same time somebody had the happy thought that they should have the *Complete Letter Writer*. This popular manual was known to give examples of how one should write to a creditor or debtor, a bereaved friend or one newly wed, of how to draft a proposal of marriage, or to refuse one without unduly wounding the feelings of the rejected. When, however, after a full day in the burgh, the uncle returned, it was found that by some accident he had brought, not the *Complete Letter Writer* but a collection of letters 'by the Most Eminent Writers' of the reign of Queen Anne, together with a few 'sensible directions for attaining an easy epistolary style.'

For Robert it was a splendid mistake. He seized the book, and for weeks life was illumined by this ray from the polite world of letters. He had no actual correspondents upon whom to practise. Imagination supplied the defect. Of an evening he would compose epistles to fictitious persons of culture. He was facetious and philosophical, allusive and alliterative, pointed and parenthetical, flowery and brief.

He conveyed his compliments and condolences, modestly accepted congratulations, worked up to a peroration, and at its height broke off with a humorous aside—all in the approved manner of the wits of Queen Anne. Such were his diligence and aptitude that he mastered the art of polite letter-writing—so far as mastery may be attained by a boy of fourteen without experience, with nobody to write to and nothing to write about.

But his handwriting was bad. So was Gilbert's. Murdoch's incomplete teaching had lapsed and the plough-handles had finished the mischief. Their father took notice and decided that both boys must go for a term to Dalrymple school, three miles away. With the harvest coming on both could not be spared at once. They went week about, and even so it was a sacrifice on their father's part. Well aware of this Robert and Gilbert made the most of the opportunity. Both acquired a small and neat but characterless hand. During his week at home each felt the need to make up for his brother's absence by working doubly hard. Robert now was the principal labourer at Mount Oliphant, and was doing the daily work of a full-grown man.

The following summer, that he might profit by Murdoch's offer of some teaching free of charge, he was again released, first for a week, and later, just before the harvest, for two weeks more. He shared the master's bed at Ayr, and learned from him during his spare hours. Some of the lessons were actually given in bed at Murdoch's lodging, some in the street on the way to school and back. The first week was devoted to English grammar, and Murdoch could not speak highly enough of his pupil. He introduced Robert as a likely lad to Mr Robinson, the writing master; and Mr Robinson, a self-taught classical scholar, gave the boy a Latin grammar, admonishing him that without the Latin tongue no man could attain real culture. Robert was also introduced in person to the Patersons' library. For the first time he saw copies of the *Spectator*, Pope's Homer, Goldsmith, Spenser and Gray—copies, moreover, which might kindly be lent to a well-doing respectful, promising young ploughman.

Among these books which stood to Robert excitingly enough for culture, there was one volume that was different, alive, a peculiar discovery. This was Ramsay's *Tea-Table Miscellany*. Most of the verses it contained had been falsified by the genteel editor, and the other 'ingenious gentlemen,' his assistants. But many of them were still recognisably country songs, while some were substantially the same songs that Robert had learned long ago from old Betty, or his mother. And here they were printed in a real book that was valued (in spite of the passion for English) by serious men and fine ladies in the city. At the end of the week Robert was allowed to take it home. Later, when his second stay with Murdoch was over, he returned bearing a French dictionary, a French grammar, and Fénélon's *Aventures de Télémaque*. During these two weeks he had learned to read and understand simple French prose very creditably, though perhaps not quite so well as Murdoch liked to make out.

More important than either French or English were the 'superior people' with whom Robert mingled at Ayr. Immediately on his arrival he had been made welcome at the house of a relation of his mother's, who kept a shop for selling smuggled tea, and did very well out of it without his reputation being the worse. But very soon the boy had gone higher than this in the social scale. French, as it happened, was having a vogue with the more ambitious youth of the place, and the fact that Murdoch had spoken here and there of his pupil's facility created a certain interest. In one or two quarters Robert became friendly with boys of his own age, but of a station above his own, among them, the sons of a doctor. These were new experiences. Though at Dalrymple school he had, in Scottish fashion, sat alongside of all sorts and conditions of boys—the minister's, the doctor's and the laird's—he well knew that outside the school gate not one of these gentry would call him friend. The good Provost might like a chat with his intelligent tenant—almost, you might say, as man to man—or he might stop Robert on the road to ask kindly how things were going up at the farm. But the sons or grandsons of these excellent people would no more have dreamed of taking Robert home for play or talk, or of accompanying him to Mount Oliphant, than they would dream of being themselves invited by the children of the Earl of Stair.

Yet in the town, because he had been quick at French, the boys of a doctor could seem hardly to notice the 'immense distance' between them and their barefoot fellow-student. Robert was grateful, passionately so. But Robert was also proud, and prone to self-despair. For him that 'immense distance' remained an instant reality. He never ceased to be conscious of his clouterly clothes and rustic manners; and while he watched his new friends rehearsing their parts for what he conceived as an 'enviable appearance upon the stage of life,' he saw himself as more than ever 'destined to drudge behind the scenes.' These boys, when they were a little older, would be leaving their homes, perhaps their country, with a reasonable chance of making names for themselves. Quickly they would acquire for the poor who had once been their neighbours and schoolmates, that 'proper, decent, unnoticing disregard' which already Robert had found occasion to observe. It was not their fault, of course, that things were so. He could no more blame them than he could invite them to Mount Oliphant. He hid his feelings from them lest the short pleasure of their society should be spoilt. But the feelings remained and rankled.[4]

Nevertheless life was opening out. Upon Robert's return from Ayr a fairly constant circulation of volumes had set in between the Patersons' shelves and the farm; and the boy of fourteen—the voracious age for a reader—filled himself full. Even when he found the reading dull he persevered in his blind pursuit of culture. At intervals he addressed himself to his *Rudiments of the Latin Tongue*, which bored him; but he reminded himself of what Mr Robinson had said as to the superimportance of Latin, and when he found the language defiant he was inclined to give up hope of himself. At other times he would ask himself why. Of what use to him were Latin or French or even the almost equally foreign culture of English? Suppose he acquired them all, would they make his life—the life of a farm lout—any more tolerable? He knew they would not. Yet his father's ideals, and something in himself as well, drove him on. Ramsay's *Miscellany* apart, there was little real enjoyment in his reading, still less discrimination. He had neither guide nor chart, nor even choice. It was merely that through two generations the fetish of book-learning had been handed down to him, and that he happened to be in most things a quick learner. He now knew that he was clever. But he was confused and unhappy and without an aim.

But through the confusion and novelty the old clear call of harvest sounded—and with it for Robert a call still older and clearer.

Immediately upon his return from Ayr he was forced to lay aside self-culture for the fields. The fields claimed every hour of the day, and every hand in the family—some extra hands as well. One pair of the latter—rather too soft and small for the thistle-rich garnering of the Burnes acres—belonged to Nelly Kilpatrick, the blacksmith's daughter from Dalrymple way. Fair-haired, neat, charming, in her fourteenth year already a complete little woman, Nelly was coupled with Robert for the gathering and binding. All day long the two worked together, and often they would stop at the end of their row of sheaves for Robert to pick out the nettlestings and thistle-prickles from the girl's aching palms. As he did so, his own large hands trembled, and it seemed to him that a drum was beaten furiously in his breast.

This would have been enough, but there was more. Nelly could sing. Her favourite air was called 'I am a man unmarried,' a dance measure, of which all the words except the title had been lost; but she had many others with and without words, and she could not sing too many or repeat them too often for her partner. Nelly silent could make his heart behave like a drum, but Nelly singing transformed it into that more mysterious wind-and-string instrument, an Æolian harp. He said nothing to her of this drumming or thrumming, and supposed, therefore, that she was unaware of it. Perhaps she was. But at the close of each day, when the sun had set and it was too dark to work longer, she would hang behind the others till Robert fell back too and joined her. Far ahead, across the dim stubble, William Burnes's forward-leaning figure led the bandsters and shearers home to supper. He had walked like an old man these ten years and more.

Everybody saw that Robert was in love. His eyes alone would have betrayed him, but there was in addition an agitation of his whole body which made his brothers laugh but gave his father serious concern. Robert was far past caring what any of them saw or thought. What they did not know, and he did, was that Nelly had revealed something besides love to him—that wrapt up in love there was a further revelation. These drums and harps, set throbbing by her knowing little hand, were not for her alone.

One of her songs had new words, so she had told him. A young man she knew had fallen in love with one of the servant girls in his father's house, and to please his sweetheart had made fresh verses to an old tune. Here was a discovery eclipsing the discovery of Ramsay's *Tea-Table Miscellany*. A lad in his own neighbourhood, not much older than himself, nor much above him socially, the son of a small laird, who assuredly knew more of shearing sheep and cutting peats than of Latin or French, had caused his beloved to be envied and himself to be admired by making a song for her. Robert was nothing if not emulative. He was fresh from intellectual triumphs in Ayr. He knew himself to be a brighter lad than most. He had been reading the *Tea-Table Miscellany*. And he was in love. Again and again he made Nelly hum the wordless air that was her favourite, until he felt he had mastered its rhythm. A tune he must have. Who could make words without a tune? Then, leaving her, crooning it over and over in his tuneless voice till it pounded in his heart-beats, he walked about the fields. In response to the music and his love, lines seemed to come of themselves. Transported he welcomed each line, furiously fashioned and re-fashioned it—till in a very short time he had seven four-line verses with a chorus of *Fal-lal-de-ral*, the whole to be called 'Handsome Nell.'

It did not occur to him to write the song down. It was for singing, not for reading; besides he could trust his memory. He repeated it to Nelly till she could sing it to him, which she did, delighted with it and him and herself. One verse in particular pleased her as it would have pleased any woman. It ran:

> She dresses aye sae clean and neat,
>> Baith decent and genteel;
> And then there's something in her gait
>> Gars ony dress look weel.

But harvest was quickly over. Nelly departed. The dreary isolation of winter descended upon Mount Oliphant and its inhabitants. Now there were other things than love to think of—sheep in fold and cattle in byre to be fed with bog hay. There were also other things than Latin to despair of. About the middle of the second lease Provost Ferguson died. His place was taken by a factor whose duty to the deceased's estate did not permit of generosity. Letters from him were frequent. William Burnes found them insolent and threatening. More perhaps than their contents it was the very painful effect these letters had upon his pride that made Agnes and the children burst into tears when one arrived. Burnes had no means of withstanding legal pressure except that which he had before tried in vain—namely, to make use of his option of renewal by sub-letting the farm. It was a measure which savoured of cunning, loathsome to his proud stomach; for renewal had never been intended as a means of escape. It also meant that for the next two years they must all live 'very sparing'—more so than before in the effort to save for the move.

To Robert, following his bright glimpse of another world in Ayr, this turn of the screw came doubly hard. In spite of his unpresentable appearance he had discovered in himself an aptitude for social life. He had found himself hilarious in congenial company, and well able to hold his own in talk. From his own feelings and the faces of others he had known himself to shine. In Nelly the whole female sex had smiled on him. Now he was condemned more rigorously than ever to what he saw as 'the cheerless gloom of the hermit.' Solitude, unless it were to string rhymes, plunged him into terrifying melancholy. The society of his family had become austere, harassing, inadequate. Almost every night he had a dull headache.

Soon after his sixteenth birthday a further blow was struck

by the removal of Murdoch from Ayr in circumstances painful to all his friends and particularly so to the Burnes family. Their much respected minister, Dr Dalrymple, had taken occasion to reprove the schoolmaster, who, to his liberal principles and general Frenchification, had lately added a weakness for the pothouse. It was reported that in consequence of this reproof Murdoch had spoken against the reverend gentleman, both in a weaver's house and in an inn-parlour, calling him a hypocrite and a damned liar. That might have been allowed to pass as vulgar abuse, but Murdoch had gone on to say that the Doctor was revengeful as Hell and false as the Devil: which being clearly an exaggeration, gave the young man's enemies the chance to present a petition against him for the utterance of 'unworthy, base, reproachful and wicked expressions.' The magistrates accordingly deprived him of his post. After a hurried leavetaking, he set out for London, not to return.

Robert had never had less time for reading. The unconquered *Latin Rudiments* menaced him from the shelf, along with the last volume of Stackhouse containing heads of the Roman Emperors. But perhaps, too, he had less inclination for study. Darkly he questioned 'bookworm philosophy.' With Nelly he had discovered 'the highest, and indeed the only enjoyment of life'—that is to say, love and poetry, which for him sprang from a single root, and must be for ever indivisible. Was not all else by comparison with these either sordid or worthless? He saw the disappointment in his father's face, noted the silenced voice of his mother, questioned the infertile mud of Mount Oliphant. Even if things went well, what better was there in the lives of the most prosperous working-people than love and poetry? At the best such prosperity as they could attain had to be got and held, not merely by never-ceasing vigilance but by the detestable methods of 'little chicaning bargain-making.' For workers on the land there was neither freedom nor fame. Of supremely good things there was only the single 'delicious passion,' and springing with this there was song. *Amor vincit omnia!* That was all the Latin needed by a farm-labourer.

But love, no less than Latin, made its demands and called

for self-improvement. Robert had managed to impress Nelly by his versifying, but he had felt loutish in her eyes, and he had compared himself bitterly—'a rude and clownish solitaire'—with his town friends. He had no doubt of his intrinsic superiority. There was a force within him that made him take the lead with boys of his own age irrespective of class or chances. Yet he was self-conscious, envious and easily humiliated. If only he had the necessary polish how much more surely could he gratify his passion to shine! But what within the reach of a plough-hand could confer the necessary polish? The answer was a course of dancing-lessons. A dancing-class was held in a barn near Dalrymple. Other lads of his own age, and girls—Nelly perhaps among them—would be going. Now that he was a full-time labourer his father was paying him a small wage. He would spend some of it on joining the class. This announcement met with his father's firm disapproval. The lad was too old to be in terms forbidden, but William Burnes made it clear that if Robert persisted it would be regarded as an act of defiance. He would become a disobedient son.

Robert's heart was sore, but he did not hesitate. He performed the act of defiance, and was numbered for the first time among the disobedient. Each dancing evening, as he set out from Mount Oliphant, he was made to feel an ingrate and a rebel. But he enjoyed the lessons none the less. They provided an escape from the increasing horror of solitude. He became 'distractedly fond' of dancing. Though he could not sing, he responded quickly and unerringly to rhythm, and in spite of his rather clumsy build and cruelly rounded shoulders, learned to dance well. The music intoxicated him. There, in a dusty barn that was lighted by a few tallow candles in the rafters, he felt as if nothing could humiliate him again. At home nothing further was said on the subject. William Burnes was no nagger. He even relented so far as to allow the elder girls to join Robert later at the class. But, rightly or wrongly, Robert felt that his father's feelings towards him had undergone a subtle change—that where before he could count upon encouragement, admiration, and love, there was now what he could only describe as 'a kind of dislike.'

Poor William Burnes! Mount Oliphant was not his only disappointment. Without being in any way discreditable, Robert was developing in an uncomfortable manner. He had taken to studying but one book, a collection of English songs, made by schoolmaster Masson and lent by the Patersons. He carried it about with him constantly, even while he drove the cart or minded the beasts. He considered it line by line, murmured the verses aloud, noted rhythms, felicities, falsities of feeling. It was a foreign currency, but at least he could ring its coins over for the sounds of true and counterfeit. His work in the fields of Mount Oliphant often marked time while he was marking rhymes, and his leisure went in making imitative verses. Altogether, William Burnes reflected, it would be well to send Robert away from home again, and this time for a substantial period.

At Kirkoswald village, where relatives of Agnes still lived, there was a schoolmaster named Roger, who had a great reputation for the teaching of practical mathematics. Lads in their teens from different parts of the countryside were sent to him for a summer course of surveying and mensuration. Robert, his father felt sure, would soon pick up anything that could be taught, and the necessary study would divert his mind from dancing and poetry. Poetry might be a good thing in its own place, but to what could all this versifying lead? To what dancing led every wise man knew. A knowledge of surveying, on the contrary, could not fail to be a solid advantage. William, as a landscape gardener, had often felt the want of it. More immediately it would be useful to the whole family in a new and ambitious venture that he was planning. Somehow they had pulled through the last difficult years, and there was only one more to run. By mortgaging the Alloway holding in favour of Ferguson's eldest daughter they had placated their creditor. A new farm had been found with entry at the following Whitsunday. At the same time the chance had at last arisen to dispose profitably of the renewed lease of Mount Oliphant. That Burnes should launch from failure into a much larger enterprise was characteristic. The new farm, which was called Lochlie, and lay ten merciful miles to the north, consisted of 130 acres. The rent was exorbitant, 20s an acre—and William could remember farm land at 2s an acre!—but its greater extent would provide scope for enlightened farming. Robert and Gilbert were now almost men and could take part in a man's venture. Robert would be surveyor as well as chief labourer. The ground could be skilfully laid out and cunningly improved. They could grow flax and sell it at the weaving village of Tarbolton, not three miles away. Later, the whole place might be turned into a lint farm. Flax, as a crop, was much spoken of those days, and had much to recommend it, especially to those who had never tried to grow it. Spinners and weavers were on the increase. Tarbolton was a growing place even as Dalrymple was a dwindling one. Another winter, another concerted effort and endurance, and they could leave the ungrateful land of Mount Oliphant for ever.

On the green but bleak and poorly cultivated slopes of Carrick, a mile to the south of Kirkoswald village, lay the little farm of Ballochneil, where Agnes Burnes's brother worked. Here, as in many Scotish farms, the servant had married his master's daughter. The couple lived in a single room outside by the mill. As they had no extra place for a visitor, the farmer, Mr Niven, allowed the boy from Mount Oliphant to share his own son's attic bed in the farmhouse. Young John Niven, like his brother-in-law, worked for his father, and had no time, nor indeed inclination for book-learning. His cousin, William Niven, however, who led the grand life of a shopkeeper's son at Maybole, was to join Robert at Kirkoswald school each day and to share his studies there. He was slightly younger than Robert, but he had the advantages of town life and had already taken a classical course at Maybole Academy. He was intelligent, personable, lively—quite ready to be both friendly and patronising to his clod-hopping companion.

To begin with, he informed Robert, they would have to take Dominie Roger to an inn and stand him treat. This was the proper procedure. So to 'The Ladies' House' they went, all three—the famous mathematical teacher, middle-aged, arid and supercilious, but fond of his dram, the bright new town pupil and the unbroken scholar from nowhere, heavy but observant. It was the first time Robert had entered a tavern. He took note of the way in which William called for the drink—'tipenny' ale for themselves and something stronger for Roger—and felt that he was seeing life. He felt rightly. Kirkoswald, especially when reviewed from a tavern bench, was a very different place from dead-alive Dalrymple or sleepy Alloway. With six miles of conveniently indented and caverned coast the parish had long been a hot centre for contraband, and most of the widely-scattered farmers throve by the trade. When a lugger put in from Ostend or Gothenburg or one of the French ports, it was the custom for whole families—men, women and children—to keep up a drunken orgy for three days and nights on end. Every cup and crock and can was needed to hold the neat spirit. On one farm, where not so much as a water-jug remained unfilled, the sodden servants would boil the breakfast porridge in proof brandy. Even apart from such extremes the district abounded in simple-souled smugglers, who lived for the next cargo, and outside of the church walls took no account of original sin. At first Robert was shocked and a little nervous. Never before had he seen a tavern brawl, and here they were of everyday occurrence. But horror soon gave way to tolerance, and tolerance to enjoyment of the spectacle. There was refreshment in the careless comedy of Scotish life, in seeing the weakness as well as the strength, the earthiness and eccentricity as well as the noble self-control of the Scotish character. At Mount Oliphant all excrescences were carefully shorn. At Kirkoswald excrescence was the rule. Yet Kirkoswald was as truly Scotland as Mount Oliphant. Robert's perception of this brought with it a sense of release. In the poorest man's existence there might be more than he had imagined.

He worked honestly, if without enthusiasm, at his daily lessons. The subject held no interest for him, and Roger was harsh and sarcastic. But he had come for the course at great cost to his father, and the fact that there were competitors put him on his mettle. It was not in school hours, however, that he most truly exercised his faculties. Between morning and afternoon classes William Niven and he talked, he doing most of the talking. William was good-natured. He was also clever enough to see that he must revise his first attitude towards this countrified cousin who, though outclassed by himself at dancing and by John Niven at wrestling, leaping and putting the stone, had so much more to say than any classical scholar from Maybole school and said it better. In a very short time the Carrick boy's patronage evaporated and his friendship warmed into something like hero-worship.

It was not merely that Robert talked so rapidly, so succinctly and upon so many subjects. It was the lighting up of his face and eyes as he talked and the unusual quality of his voice that subjugated William. In a debate or a question of general knowledge William was prepared to back him any day against old Roger himself. And William was not the only one to note the voice and eyes and the eloquent face that went so oddly with the clumsy frame. The Kirkoswald minister's two playful daughters were clearly interested. Mr Burnes's clothes were poor, but there was that about him that made one willing to see more of him, besides a most engaging dimple in his chin. One day the girls caught sight of him alone on the other side of the street. He was muttering to himself and staring at the ground. They crossed over giggling. 'Fancy looking at the ground,' said the bolder, 'and talking to yourself when we are here to be looked at and talked to!' He was quicker than any minister's daughter and not easily flustered. 'Madam,' said he, confounding her with his gaze, 'it is a natural and right thing for man to contemplate the ground from whence he was taken, and for woman to look upon and observe man, from whom she was taken.'

At the end of each week he usually went with his 'cousin' to Maybole to stay over Sunday in the little house above the shop. On their way they had to pass near the ruins of Crossraguel, loveliest of Scotish abbeys, the cloisters of which at that time were still intact. No better place could be for serious youth to discuss the universe on a summer afternoon. Why, Robert wanted to know, were not Presbyterian places of worship beautiful? Pacing together among its thyme-scented stones the two lads discussed theology, sought for a practical philosophy, dived into metaphysics, examined all they knew of life. What was there to be said for the Old Lights as compared with the New? Could one by right thinking or religion be consoled for the defeat of all one's natural ambitions? Might a man look for happiness with a woman above him in station or even gifts? Robert thought not.

At Maybole they could take part only in the humbler diversions of the place, but it was a lively little burgh where more than one side of life was to be seen. As the capital of

Carrick it had what even a generation later was described as
'a certain degree of massive and metropolitan magnificence,'
and if its narrow streets could no longer boast 'twenty-eight
winter residences of noble and baronial families,' at least that
mansion still stood from which a legendary Countess of
Cassilis had come tripping down to be 'off with the raggle-
taggle gipsies.' But Maybole's age of dignity was past. Its
aristocracy now consisted mainly of the worthy tradespeople; its common folk were weavers; and a considerable
floating population of beggars and riff-raff, attracted to a
rising centre of industrialism, kept the taverns busy on
Saturday nights. Robert Burnes and William Niven visited
taverns and were amused. But they also met other knowledgeable youths and found books to read. Robert read the
works of Thomson and Shenstone, and managed to carry
away as his own property a volume of songs called *The Lark*,
which was a treasure to keep for the lean days ahead at Mount
Oliphant. Besides English ballads and ditties, Restoration
songs, old political squibs, and indecencies from d'Urfey's
Pills to Purge Melancholy, it contained songs by known
Scotish poets—such as Allan Ramsay's 'Song of a Begging
Soldier' ('. . . with my rags upon my bum,' etc.) and Mrs
Cockburn's sophisticated version of 'The Flowers of the
Forest'—and better still some anonymous Scotish folk-
songs—lyrical like 'Waly waly,' full of tolerant humour like
'Toddlin' Hame,' or racy and bustling like 'The Blithesome
Bridal.'

So far there seemed neither time nor inducement for
versifying. Robert had mastered the first six books of Euclid.
Now he was at trigonometry, struggling with sines and
cosines, dialling and surveying and taking altitudes. At the
same time he had been trying to prove his quality in other
ways upon his schoolmates. He had offered from time to time
to dispute with any of them upon any subject, human or
divine. But the boys were too dull to offer flint to his steel,
and some were hostile. When, with William's support, he
went on to urge them to form a debating society, they
reported the project to Mr Roger.

'So you think you are great debaters and can put the world
right and improve our minds here in Kirkos'le, eh?' the

master inquired of the innovators before the assembled class.

Robert's eyes were threatening, a flush rose to his forehead and his lower lip quivered. But his friend, who sat *vis-à-vis* at the same desk, whispered him something; and nothing if not swift, he understood and nodded his agreement. Next moment the class heard William making his civil apologia. He and Robert, he said, had no other idea than to improve their own minds by the daily formal discussion of interesting topics, and here surely should be nothing objectionable to a schoolmaster.

'Fancy that now! And may I ask what are some of your interesting topics?' queried Roger with his unpleasant smile.

William named their latest—'Whether is a great general or a respectable merchant the more valuable member of society?'

'Indeed! And am I to understand that there's more than one reply to sic a silly-like question?'

The sneer won a cheap laugh, but it was Robert's turn now.

'If you like, sir,' he said, 'to take your choice of either side, I will debate on the other and the class can judge of the relative value of our arguments.'

It was a challenge not to be refused without loss of prestige. Besides surely the foolish youth had delivered himself into the hands of his castigator? Mr Roger complacently took the side of the conquering general. The contest did not last long. After a few interchanges the schoolmaster glanced at the clock and announced that enough precious time had been wasted. His hand was observed to shake as lessons were hurriedly resumed.

Of all times in the year autumn was to Robert the most disturbing. Why he could not tell, but unfailingly as July passed and August came he was subject for whole days on end to extreme physical and mental excitement. As a child he had felt most violently alive at this season. Now there was the further association of his first love with the yellowing of the grain—Nelly Kilpatrick and the happy autumn fields— Nelly's little head that matched the rigs of barley—Nelly's voice. The stacked corn would always stand for love to

Robert. It would always be the blonde girls that would seem to him not only the loveliest but the most loving.

And now it was mid-August at Kirkoswald. In another week he would be finished with his mathematics and would take the soft hilly road back to Mount Oliphant to help his father and Gilbert with their last harvest there. The work for Mr Roger was mapped out to the last day. Robert, the model pupil, had every intention of carrying it through. But just outside the schoolhouse autumn was lying in wait for him.

Mr Roger's classes were being temporarily held in a ground-floor room in the main street of the village, which had strips of kitchen garden behind each house. More than once of late, from the school window, Robert had noticed a girl moving about domestically in the garden next door, and had found it increasingly hard to concentrate upon his lesson. The struggle was at its height when he heard himself being ordered to go out. Mr Roger had desired him to take the sun's altitude. He obeyed without loss of time. Next moment he was in the garden. The wall was not high. Soon he had spoken to the girl and found her friendly. She was called Peggy Thomson and her hair was as fair as Nelly's. Sun, moon and stars forgot, he set about persuading her to meet him that same evening after school. She said she would.

For the rest of his time at Kirkoswald Robert did not work. William Niven was startled by the transformation in his clever friend, who seemed clever no longer except in the matter of devising meetings with his girl. William had seen love-lorn swains before now. His cousin John, for instance, as everybody knew, was sweet upon Dominie Roger's daughter, and hoped some day to marry her. But Burnes seemed to go clean crazed. All day he thought only of that moment in the evening when he would be able to steal out to join young Peggy. And at night, even during the short time that his head lay on the pillow (as John Niven could testify), he did not sleep a wink.

The lovers' meetings were as innocent as they were sweet. That he was with Peggy, alone and by appointment, was enough to fill Robert's cup of happiness. The two exchanged a few shy words and shyer caresses. Timidly, as it grew dusk, he put his arm round her waist. When he left her the spring

of words and music bubbled anew in his mind. He walked
about for hours in an ecstasy of composition. Single lines and
then verses formed themselves into a song to autumn and to
Peggy. The rhymes were not all they might have been, and
the poem remained unfinished, but he hoped to finish it later.
It was in the politest, if not the best English style:

> But, Peggy dear, the evening's clear,
> Thick flies the skimming swallow;
> The sky is blue, the fields in view,
> All fading green and yellow:
> Come, let us stray our gladsome way,
> And view the charms of nature;
> The rustling corn, the fruited thorn,
> And every happy creature.
>
> We'll gently walk and sweetly talk,
> Till the silent moon shines clearly;
> I'll grasp thy waist, and fondly prest,
> Swear how I love thee dearly:
> Not vernal showers to budding flowers,
> Not autumn to the farmer,
> So dear can be as thou to me,
> My fair, my lovely charmer!

Parting from Peggy was sad; but when he reached home at
the end of the week Robert was in a cheerful frame of mind.
He felt that his stay at Kirkoswald had done him good—
polished him up. He had seen life from a different angle and
had measured himself against different people without
finding himself unduly wanting. His manners were improved, he was sure; the circle of his friends was widened; he
had walked under the moon with a girl of his own choosing
untroubled by paternal vigilance. These were helpful times
against the winter months on an isolated farm. At last, too, he
would be able to practise upon real correspondents what he
had learned from his book of elegant exemplars. William and
John Niven were only two of several who had promised to
write to him, and his wages began to go on writing materials
and payments to the letter carrier. Hardly a post arrived from
Maybole without something for him. He became delightedly
sophisticated on paper, pluming himself on being able to

adapt both style and matter to the character of his correspondent. With one he was plain and manly, with another playful, with another learned, with another rude. And of every letter he carefully preserved a copy, both because he thought it worth preserving, and that he might compare it—always favourably—with its reply.

So the winter passed, and the spring. When Whitsuntide came the Burneses took their leave of Mount Oliphant.

To mark the new departure William Burnes now fee'd his two eldest sons as ploughmen at the market rate which had lately risen to £7 a year. This was policy. Ploughmen and servants, they were preferred creditors. It was also an economical arrangement. Out of their £7 both lads would pay for their clothes (made at home) and meet their little personal expenses. It was even expected that they could save.

The house at Lochlie was in a hollow, close by the loch (really marsh) that gave it its name. At the bottom of the loch lay a prehistoric dwelling still guarding its cold hearth and its fruitless store of grain; but the Burnes family discovered only the pervading dampness of the place. The lands rose higher than the house and lay mostly along a ridge between the valleys of the Ayr and the Irvine. From this ridge the Arran peaks and Ailsa and the sea could still be seen away to the south-west, but near at hand there was the more pleasing sight to Robert of wood and water. There were the Coyle, the Faile, the Cessnock, the Lugar—lovely tributaries of the two greater streams, and all had trees. For the past nine or ten months, going to and fro on austerer slopes, he had pondered over the elegies of Shenstone and had memorised most of the songs in *The Lark*. As the humour took him he had revised in memory pieces of his own, adding a stanza here, altering one there, comparing them with printed verse. Surrounded by the new joy of water, he devised a new song about a crystal stream, a sunny beam, wild birds singing, flowers springing, a storm that shook the branches of the trees, and a manly heart, which, he trusted, would support him still. It was closely modelled upon a song in *The Lark*—so closely that some phrases were borrowed. But the Lochlie household were none the less impressed when Robert recited it. William

Burnes was particularly pleased with the sentiment about manly hearts. Here was poetry in its proper place.

Trees and streams were not the only cheerful novelties at Lochlie. The parish of Tarbolton was even more stimulating than Kirkoswald. There were no active smugglers, but the farms were numerous, closely set and populous, the village animated. Linen, cotton and even silk were woven there. The one long straggling street was full of rowdy life. Groups of webster lads (known as 'the mechanics') stood about of an evening. There were shops and inns. There was a tailor who was a local bard. Once there had been a schoolmaster, Peden by name, who still after a hundred years was reverenced as prophet and martyr. Now there was one, Wilson by name, who was a cheapjack doctor. On Beltane's Eve in May there were great ongoings when the 'fires' were lighted on the curious little round hill just outside the village. None but the young men might stand by the rising flames. The women and the older men must stay below, walking round and round the base of the hill while the lads fed the fire and leapt with shouts over it in their dance of fertility. About this same hill in June a great cattle fair spread itself, with shows and booths. In July there were the Tarbolton races.

Robert welcomed the end of his solitude, but Tarbolton found him an awkward 'incomer.' Though he was anxious to make friends with the more intelligent among the farmers' sons, with the 'prentices and the sons of the blacksmith, his itch to shine, at their expense if necessary, was too evident to be pleasing. The elder people were astonished by his ready knowledge of the Bible, but they found the uses to which he put it neither judicious nor decent. Some of the younger ones were fascinated, but they found his silences too brooding and arrogant, and his speech too pointed and swift. He argued to refute, overwhelmed his listeners with unfamiliar quotations, and emitted a torrent of appropriate words that inspired the villagers with some admiration but more suspicion.

Certain works of fiction, the first he had ever opened, had recently come into his hands. He had read the *Sentimental Journey*, *The Man of Feeling* and two odd volumes of the three-volume *Pamela*. The effect was not quite happy. He was only eighteen. His critical faculties were unawakened. The little guidance he had been given about books had been pedantic and ignorant. He had known moments of insight; but his very gifts, which conflicted so painfully with his station, drove him again and again to accept standards that were alien, if not actually false to his nature. If Richardson or Sterne had been less brilliant their sophistication might have charmed him less. If Mackenzie's banality had not been backed by the whole trend of polite Scotish sentiment, he might have taken the so-called 'Scotish' novelist's measure. As things were, the novelists proved to be yet another in the series of subtly confusing and disingenuous influences to which this ploughboy had been subjected since the first dawn of his intelligence. Not that Sterne in himself should have been misleading. The discovery that a fine mind could be partial to bawdry should have encouraged a country fellow to be himself. But it was Sterne's whim to smile behind the mask of gentility, and his Scotish admirers—all trying their hardest to be themselves genteel—looked at the mask rather than at the face. This same gentility was largely responsible for the vogue of Henry Mackenzie. People believed that in him they had a Sterne purged and a Fielding void of offence, when all they really had was a monument to shoddy sentiment. For a whole winter and more Robert went about his field work with one of the world's worst novels in his pocket (he had been unlucky enough to secure a pocket edition), ardently believing it to be the world's best. He thumbed it over devoutly till the binding was worn through, and then bought a new copy. Upon *The Man of Feeling* he would model himself. He took to leaning his head upon his hand and his elbow on his knee in the correct attitude. He cultivated a dripping heart and was subject to pregnant silences, appropriate tears and bursts of rapture. Such endeavours do not add to a young man's popularity among the males of his own village. But there were, of course, the females. Here there was no complication which was not of service to him. Tarbolton was full of lively amorous girls, and though when left alone with one of them Robert was still shy and tongue-tied, he soon found a way through them of gaining importance among certain of his own sex. Already at seventeen twice deeply moved by love, he made an ideal confidant for youths who were themselves in the way of wooing. However fond he might be of hearing his own voice declaim upon abstruser subjects, in the matter of love he was the king of listeners. Intensely interested, wholly sympathetic, he combined a natural insight and delicacy where women were concerned with a zeal to assist the male. So far in his own experience he had known love only as the most powerful and clarifying of emotions. Now he became an apprentice to the niceties of lovemaking, and he set himself to serve his time with a good will.

Country boys find solitary wooing impracticable. For half a dozen excellent reasons an accomplice is needed. In all the parish of Tarbolton none proved a readier accomplice than Robert Burnes. Night after night, should the weather favour love, he might have been seen (but took good care not to be) slipping out, barefoot and silent, after the household was asleep, to join Johnnie Lees, the shoemaker's apprentice, or one of the Candlish boys from the forge, or maybe a ploughboy from the Bennals. At the signal of a low whistle the conspirators would meet—perhaps after a whispered colloquy to separate again for a time, perhaps to go far afield together. They might go uphill to Coilsfield, where pretty self-respecting Peggy was housekeeper, or downhill to the inn at the ford of Faile, where sulky Maisie and 'smiling Jennie' were the landlord's daughters. Robert's part would be to tap at the girl's firmly closed window pane, and with well-chosen words to coax her out, while his friends lay low behind the byre or among the corn-rigs waiting. Very soon he knew every move and trick of the game on both sides, and could quickly take the measure of the girl's reluctance, scorn, or inclination. When further it became known that he could write impressive letters suitable to any given circumstances, his help and companionship were more sought than ever.

Though Robert, given the chance, would talk about most things, there was one matter often in his mind which he confided to nobody. The more he came to know his own countryside the more conscious and passionate his feeling for it became. He had grown to love particularly the slopes and valleys round Lochlie. These streams by which he walked with his love-stricken friends, these hills he climbed on their behests, these trees he lingered under alone with his thoughts, filled him with discontented rapture. He wished them to be praised and celebrated. But the Anglified praises of Scotish hills and streams that he had read and imitated did not seem to ring true. One might sing till one was tired about crystal streams and sunny beams, but all the while the dark waters of Cessnock and the rust-red current of Faile flowed on, lonely and unsung.

This discontent and rapture were increased by a chance reading of Blind Harry's rhymed *Life of William Wallace*. The little chapbook—small enough to go into a waistcoat pocket—was an abridgement made from the ancient work fifty-five years before by a West-country laird. It was to be found in most cottages, though, strangely enough, not in William Burnes's. Candlish, the Tarbolton blacksmith, had lent it to Robert. One Sunday afternoon—the only daylight hours of the week on which he could count for himself—he walked alone to Leglen woods six miles away. It was the shelter to which Scotland's other 'most famous and valiant champion' had more than once been driven, and Robert, dipping into his chapbook and wandering there till the daylight faded, worked himself up into a state of fine frenzy. Had even Blind Harry done justice to his theme? Were not the glory and the misfortune of this hero, like the charm of the Ayrshire streams, still to be sung? Emulating his politer hero, Mr Harley, Robert wept.

He fell upon his knees. It was Harley's habit alternately to be 'bathed in tears' and to 'drop one tear, no more.' Robert, accordingly, had set himself to master the art of weeping, and when moved had usually a tear or two at command. He really was moved by Leglen woods and thoughts of Wallace and Bruce, so the tears came readily. If only, he declared to the Ayrshire skies, he might one day make a song of Wallace that should be worthy of Wallace; he would ask no more of life!

Life was hard enough at Lochlie, but not yet too hard. Instead of the stones and moss of Mount Oliphant, there was sour clay, undrained bog, rushy pasture to contend with. But the pressure had been lifted. The family had made yet another hopeful start, and hopefully they continued their 'uphill gallop from the cradle to the grave.'[1]

William Burnes had the happiness of seeing his children growing up about him in virtue and vigour. For some time he even ceased to be anxious about his eldest. Allowance being made for youth and a ready tongue, it seemed as if Robert were shaping into a man after his father's pattern. He was dutiful. He took a serious view of life. He was taciturn with strangers. He could plough six roods day after day, throwing a furrow sixteen inches wide. The younger ones loved him for his fun and patience and story-telling. Round the fire in the evenings he gave them lessons in the King's English. There was a space between his return from Kirkoswald and the departure from Mount Oliphant when he had fallen into one of the old gloomy fits and had seen himself as a tragic rebel:

All devil as I am, a damned wretch,
A hardened, stubborn, unrepentant villain—

and he had made a rough broadsheet doggerel—full of rebellious feeling, though clumsy and poor as ever pedlar carried—about a ruined farmer and the fickleness of fortune. But in the social atmosphere of Tarbolton he had turned to more cheerful themes such as the Tarbolton girls and other natural joys of the countryside. It was as if he had set himself to accept the life of a labouring man and to make the best of it. That we are set in our walk of life by Providence was a sacred belief handed down to him through many generations. After all his was a lot of which none need be ashamed. It had its advantages and its alleviations, even its exquisite moments.

He liked, for instance, ploughing and sowing, not merely because they left his mind free while his body was engaged, but for their own sake. He loved Maggie, the willing old mare, and Luath, the old mongrel sheep-dog. It amused him to make pets of particular sheep. Then there were those times when, even in the dreariest tasks of the farms, a rapture would rise in him and take possession.

In these circumstances he could grind out a cheery song upon the ploughman's life, or in good-humoured verses resign himself to being one of the proper young men of Tarbolton parish.[2] Henceforth he would expect the daily round to be lightened only by its moments of ecstasy, by the leisure it gave to the mind, by the stringing now and then of a set of verses, and by the common possibilities, friendship and love. Thus he saw the humble stage set for his existence, with no further events to look for until the curtain was rung down.

In the dark November days, when loneliness most threatened, he persuaded Gilbert and five other country boys to form a club. They called themselves the Tarbolton Bachelors and began by meeting once a month for discussion and a social evening at the cottage of one of the village members. Soon, in spite of the jeers of the village mechanics (who were not admitted), other lads from the outlying farms were clamouring to join, and the Bachelors met weekly in the upper room of a tavern. Each member paid threepence towards ale, which was kept till last thing in the evening, when toasts were drunk to sweethearts. It was laid down that

> every man proper for a member of this society must have a frank, open, honest heart; above anything dirty or mean; and must be a professed lover of one or more of the female sex. No haughty, self-conceited person, who looks upon himself as superior to the rest of the club, and especially no mean-spirited, worldly mortal, whose only will is to heap up money, shall upon any pretence whatever be admitted. In short the proper person for this society is a cheerful, honest-hearted lad, who if he has a friend that is true, and a mistress that is kind, and as much wealthy as genteelly to make both ends meet, is just as happy as this world can make him.

The rule about sweethearts was certainly the founder's,

but it was probably Gilbert and the others who insisted later that religious subjects should be barred. Robin, as they called him, was too much given to disputation upon matters of theology and church government. On a Sunday morning in the churchyard between services he would hold forth on original sin to anyone that would listen, and on the way home from a funeral would exercise his wit at the expense of Calvin's doctrines. So far so good, but for the amenities of a social evening Scotish feelings might easily run too high on such questions. Robert was agreeable so long as all other topics were open. 'Should there be reserve in friendship?' 'Is a good education an aid to happiness in a labouring man?' 'Is a savage or a civilised peasant the happier?' 'Is love or friendship more satisfying?' He was fertile in subjects, and every one he suggested showed in what channel his mind was running. He formulated the first question for debate as follows:

'Suppose a young man, bred a farmer but without any fortune, has it in his power to marry either of two women, the one a girl of large fortune, but neither handsome in person nor agreeable in conversation, but who can manage the household affairs of a farm well enough; the other of them a girl every way agreeable in person, conversation, and behaviour, but without any fortune—which of them shall he choose?'

The Tarbolton Bachelors grinned. The 'girl of large fortune' might be imaginary, but it was not difficult to identify the girl who was 'every way agreeable in person, conversation, and behaviour, but without any fortune.' They might rate her natural gifts less highly—Gilbert found her commonplace enough—but her 'tocherless' condition was beyond question. She was Alison Begbie, a Galston farmer's daughter, who was servant at a small farm down on the Cessnock. Robert had been seen hanging around there of an evening lately, which Gilbert had noted with amusement. All Robert's geese were swans, he said. He himself was inclined to look somewhat higher for a wife. Perhaps his brother, with his picture of the plain, rich, prudent marriage, was having a return dig at him now. Robert, having made careful notes, delivered a powerfully reasoned speech in favour of the less prudent view. There may have been some malice in it.

Gilbert, he knew, had already suffered a rebuff at the hands of Jean Ronald of the Bennals, who could boast that her father was a laird of sorts with £200 a year. Robert liked Jean's sister, Annie,—could have liked her more than a little—but sooner than risk a similar humiliation he would never go near the place again. That was his way.

There had been Peggy too, the self-confident young housekeeper to the gentry up at Coilsfield. Sunday after Sunday in church Robert had watched her. She sat further along in the same pew as the Burnes family. She was dainty, demure, but alas! disdainful in the knowledge that with her dowry she could take her time and make her choice among the best that offered. Indeed it was rumoured that she had already made it. But how he could have loved a portionless Peggy! How angrily he did love her, in spite of her portion, for more than half a year, murmuring between his teeth, instead of the Psalms of David, words of his own:

I'll kiss thee, yet, yet,

—and fancying himself a 'baron proud and high,' with overwhelming horses and servants at his command that he might make the Cophetuan gesture!

But being, like Shakespeare, 'no such matter,' he must assuage his high intolerance of rivalry and find the best not good enough for him. His study of parochial loves, as well as his instincts, forbade the position of a doubtful *prétendant*. For him it must be the magnanimous, the careless or the defiant gesture. The bride must take all at his hands, compare him with no other and bring him nothing but herself.

So it came about that in all Tarbolton parish there was not to be found a more suitable wife for Robert Burnes, ploughman, aged twenty-one, than the servant girl, Alison Begbie. Besides being dowerless she had three attributes most admired by this wooer—namely, fair hair, a good figure, and the ability to read and write. She could actually read handwriting, which argued a very superior education. Further she could talk sense, her cheeks were red, her eyes were bright, her character good. Such girls give every promise of wifely qualities. Gilbert might laugh when he listened to Robert descanting upon her extraordinary beauties, but Robert was the better judge of women. Perhaps he was not more in love with Alison than he had been with Annie Ronalds or with Peggy of Coilsfield—not nearly so much as with Nell of the harvest-fields, or with Peggy at Kirkoswald, of whom he still thought often and tenderly—but when he was with Alison he felt soothed out of his restlessness. If not madly enamoured, he was assuredly in love with the prospect of marriage with her.

To the girl herself he had as yet said nothing. Though an adept lover in theory and as proxy, he had never had to make a formal declaration, and he felt extremely shy. Their meetings were chiefly in company and by chance—at village parties or on Sundays, when the youths and girls stood about talking after church. Even when he had managed a more private meeting they had talked only generalities and gossip. More than once he had come to her determined to speak and had left her without so much as skirting the subject of love. Yet he was sure that she was only waiting for him to say the word. Why else should she receive him so amiably when she must know from his eyes and his manner what his intentions were? Besides in the Cophetuan attitude there is no room for doubt.

He had found various means by which to 'fan the sweet connubial flame' in himself. First he had composed a long panegyric upon the beauties of his mistress, called 'A Song of Similes' (how pleased Murdoch would have been!) modelled upon the Song of Solomon. Then, warming to his work, as he lingered at night outside her window, he had made two more songs. Finding a technical difficulty in the name Alison, he had turned her into a Nannie, and again into a Mary, but what's in a name? The Nannie song was full of virtuous intention and obedience to Providence. Robert found it suitable to repeat to his father. The Mary song was different:

> Yestreen, when to the trembling string,
>   The dance ga'ed through the lighted ha',
> To thee my fancy took its wing—
>   I sat, but neither heard nor saw;[3]

There is no record that he submitted this one to his father's judgment. To Alison neither song was disclosed.[4] Emerging from the rapture of production he even told himself that in the serious, life-long business of marriage among working people, passion was out of place. Besides, Alison's behaviour to him had been so calm and friendly that he felt she would be offended by too warm an expression of desire. To win her he must show himself a grave and prosy wooer. This being so he decided that he would put everything in train for his marriage, and leave the proposal till later. On however small a scale he must set up for himself. But how?

So far the plan of a lint farm had not matured. Gilbert and Robert had cultivated flax on a part of Lochlie made over to them for the purpose. But like most other farmers they had as yet grown little more than would supply their mother's wheel. The yarn of her spinning went to the village to be woven for home needs, or it was exchanged after long bargaining for some of the ready-made sheetings that the travelling webster with his pony carried from door to door. Within these household limits flax was known to be a 'robbing crop.' To make it a paying one the new spinners for profit and the six-loom weavers must be supplied. Hence the growers must have a practical knowledge of flax-dressing. For Lochlie to strike out in this new line Robert must become a flax-dresser. A new line had never been so badly needed. The American war had affected ordinary farming. Root and cereal seed prices were soaring. The Burneses had long had the flax idea in mind; and now Robert saw in it as well the only way in which he might keep a wife without severing himself from his father's only too precarious interests.

This meant going to Irvine ten miles away, and remaining there for some months. He would have to learn ripping and retting, grassing and scutching, heckling, spreading, drawing and roving. Could his father spare him? As it turned out his father could. At last there were negotiations for the Alloway cottage. The Ayr Guild of Shoemakers wanted it for an ale-house.[5] After discharging outstanding debts William Burnes would still have something over. He would be able to engage a woman servant and a herd boy. Robert should have this further chance of knowledge. It was near the end of the year; Robert should go at midsummer.

Seeing that Alison had proved elusive of personal wooing, Robert had begun to send her long letters. He took trouble

with these letters and was pleased with them, so much so that
he was confident of the impression they must be creating,
though he never got any reply to them. By the turn of the year
he had sent her three. Among the verses he had *not* sent were
these:

> O Mary, canst thou wreck his peace
>   Wha for thy sake would gladly dee,
> Or canst thou break that heart of his
>   Wha's only faut is loving thee?
>
> If love for love thou wiltna' gie,
>   At least be pity on me shown;
> A thocht ungentle canna be
>   The thocht of Mary Morison!

What Dominie Murdoch's good pupil did send was the
following paraphrase:

> Once you are convinced I am sincere I am perfectly
> certain you have too much goodness and humanity to
> allow an honest man to languish in suspense only
> because he loves you too well. And I am certain that in
> such a state of anxiety as I myself at present feel, an
> absolute denial would be a much preferable state.

While Alison was deciphering this (for she did not read
handwriting so very easily after all) and wondering over it,
and comparing the picture it gave of the writer with the more
temperamental impression made by him in person, she
received another letter, about three times as long and even
more in the style of the polite letter-writers of Queen Anne's
reign, in which he categorically disclaimed such things as
irrational passion, flames, raptures, warm fancy and youthful
spirits, giving it as his opinion that the married state was
'only friendship in a more exalted degree.' After which she
was still friendly and met him and talked with him on
indifferent topics, but still delayed her answer.

Robert was afraid only that he had alarmed her on
occasions by the ardour of his manner. So he continued to
steal down after nightfall to the Cessnock farm, and, without
being seen, to leave further sententious assurances in writing. His love, he would have Alison believe, was no 'giddy
rapture,' but rather a kind of Christian affection.

Whatever Alison may have thought of this description, William Burnes had begun to doubt its accuracy. He had noted his son's deep excitement, his comings and goings, and his increasingly late hours, and he feared for the young man's virtue. One night, instead of going to bed at the usual hour, he sat up grimly waiting. It was late winter, with a high wind, scudding clouds, and moving shapes on the moor. The truant was long of returning. When at last he slipped in softly the reprimand was ready, but he was readier still. His face was glowing and friendly, and he had verses for his father—light-hearted disarming ones about the darkness and the wind and the devilish shapes the thorn-trees had assumed on his way home. As he recited them in his persuasive voice the older man was convinced of his innocence, and the two sat together for another hour talking over the fire. That spring, having heard from his eldest brother's son[6] at Montrose, William set forth the family news in óne of his rare letters. 'Two of my sons,' he wrote, 'and two of my doughters are men and women, and all with me in the farming way. I have the happiness to hope they are virtuously inclined . . .'

It was true. All these months Robert had been dead serious in his preparations for marriage. It was partly with the same end in view that he presently became a Freemason. Free-masonry would provide a further bulwark against poverty and debt, that double nightmare bequeathed to him by his father. But of course there was more in it than that. The brotherly idea of the Order made a strong appeal to him. In summer he was admitted an apprentice at Tarbolton Lodge, which held its meetings in a cottage—meetings not unlike those of the Tarbolton Bachelors, but more festive, and with more than threepence a head spent on drink—and it was understood that when he went to Irvine he would be welcomed by the Masons there, more especially after he had been duly passed and raised.

Now it was time for him to go, and still Alison had said nothing. Robert wrote one more letter begging her to reply soon and in writing. It is as stilted and as sincere as his other letters, but lower in tone and with a note of uncertainty. When he is in her company, he tells her, 'foreboding fears' and 'mistrustful anxieties' crowd into his mind; and when he sits down to write to her he is 'altogether at a loss' what to say. He can merely repeat his grave, modest proposal of marriage. Only then, when all was ready for his departure as a man betrothed, did Alison's reply come. It was a refusal in classic feminine form. She was very sorry, but his feelings were not reciprocated. She wished him 'all kinds of happiness.'

Robert was shocked; no Laird of Cockpen could have been more so. His agitation was so painful that his father felt afraid for him, and his brother, for once unable to smile, looked on in amazement. At first, reading and re-reading the letter, he had hardly been able to believe what had happened; but there was no getting away from its message, and fury and despair possessed him in turn. Alison had led him on and jilted him. Alison had acted like the wise virgin she was, in rejecting one so clearly destined for failure. In either case he had lost the one thing likely to make his life endurable. More immediately, he had been robbed of his private motive in consenting to go to Irvine. Nevertheless go he would—if only because Tarbolton was now intolerable to him.

He took Alison's refusal as final. No woman should get the chance to refuse him twice, to change her mind about him or drive him to an appeal for pity. He did not visit her again, and did not even reply to her letter till within a day or two of his leaving, when he wrote praising her delightful qualities and hoping for her continued friendship and correspondence. He refrained from reproach. To have shared life with her, he said, would have given life a relish that wanting her he can never taste. So model a composition—firm, manly, and in measured prose—did something to restore his self-confidence, and he took care to make and keep a copy. He knew, and he knew Alison would know, that from no other young man in the parish could she have received such a letter. He wrote also to Will Niven. He was done, he said, with women, and would never again involve himself in courtship.

One day in midsummer Robert Burnes walked up the main
street of Irvine. It was the biggest town he had yet seen. Once
it had ranked as the third seaport of Scotland, and it was still
the largest town of Ayrshire. But for many years its trade had
been declining, and now, in spite of its superior size, it was
generally regarded as a poor place compared with Ayr. It was
noted chiefly for flax-dressing establishments or 'heckling-
shops.'

In the ten miles' journey from Tarbolton Robert had had
to pass Dundonald, of which his father had often spoken as a
place to be remembered in his obscure Odyssey. But to this
traveller the place was dominated by the old brown castle of
the Bruce, set like a child's toy on the top of its round hill.
Eight years earlier an eminent English tourist had burst out
laughing at the idea of a king with any claim to kingliness
living in this three-roomed tower. It was like so much else in
Scotland and Scotish history—brave against the landscape
when viewed from a distance, but at close quarters astonishingly poor. Robert, however, never felt less like laughing.
Had he been in Boswell's place he would have turned
black-browed on his companion, for all his eminence. The
mere recollection of Bruce recalled his boyish ambition and
showed it put aside. Fate seemed against him in the matter of
heroic poetry as in matrimony. Here he was at twenty-two
about to become a flax-comber—one of the despised mechanics—and his past like his future was difficult to contemplate
without despair. As at Kirkoswald, he was to live with a
relative of his mother, though a more distant one than the
Nivens—a young man named Peacock, who professed
flax-dressing and for a small payment would take him into his
shop and teach him the trade. The better end of the town,
where the well-to-do citizens had their houses and shops, was

to the south-west, the way by which Robert entered. Peacock lived in the north-east. Turning off near the top of the High Street into a crooked dirty lane called the Glasgow Vennel, Robert stopped before the second door on the right to announce his arrival and to ask if the Tarbolton carrier had arrived yet with his meal-sack and his box. Carefully packed between his shirts was a fiddle which he had not yet learned to play. Peacock's was a two-roomed cottage of the usual kind, and, tucked in behind it, reached by a narrow passage, was the heckling-house, littered with gear and filled alternately with steam and fibrous dust. Here Robert would work during the day. At night he would sleep in an adjoining closet.

Peacock was a skilful heckler, and Robert set himself with such a good will to learn from him, that in a few weeks he had mastered the essentials of the business. But Peacock was also disagreeable and mean, and one day in the autumn there were high words between him and his pupil over a question of money. Robert in wrath packed up his belongings. Round the corner in the High Street, a few doors from the King's Arms, he found another heckling establishment, where a man and wife were willing to give him a bed and take him into partnership for a small payment.

He had arrived in Irvine in low spirits. The experience with Peacock had depressed him, and heckling was not really to his taste. The confined, finicking, dirty, and noisy process of raking the tow from the line gave little satisfaction as work, and it was unfavourable to all his habits. He missed the harvest fields, and was cut off from the familiar sources of happiness. He was also underfed and uncared-for. The time of year that usually brought him exaltation passed unnoticed. He grew more and more melancholy, and in October definitely ill. Though he could see nothing much in life to make life desirable, yet his symptoms frightened him, and the thought that he would soon die took fearful possession. One night, waking suddenly in terror, he fainted. This experience was repeated on other nights. When not followed by loss of consciousness the terror seemed only the worse. The mere thought of it kept him awake. Somebody recommended a remedy then popular for all manner of obscure human ailments. He was to keep a tub full of water by the side of his bed, and when threatened by an attack to plunge into it. This he did. The shock relieved his nerves for the moment. Then damp and shivering the rheumatic young man crept back into his cupboard bed. As the heat of his body revived he found he could fall thankfully asleep.

Persevering in this treatment he contracted a pleurisy. His father came from Lochlie to see him, bringing what dainties the farm could produce. Though concerned about his physical state William was glad to see that his son's mind had taken a religious turn. Robert had been pondering over those gloomier portions of the Scriptures, that with their profundity of pessimism have helped to unnerve many a sensitive youth on the threshold of life. He had paraphrased some passages from the Old Testament:

Ah woe is me, my Mother dear!

and composed two Prayers on the Prospect of Death:

Why am I loath to leave this earthly scene?
Have I so found it full of pleasing charms?
Some drops of joy with draughts of ill between:
Some gleams of sunshine 'mid renewing storms.

He was oppressed by a sense of guilt in the face of a just but angry God.

On his side Robert was struck by the change in his father's appearance. William was noticeably thinner. He coughed and there was more than the usual anxiety in his deeply sunken eyes. He could give no good news of the farm. The belated terms of peace with America were creating even more trouble than the long suspense which they had ended. In addition a new worry had developed. He had entered Lochlie without a detailed agreement in writing, and now the landlord, a Mr McLure, was objecting to the proportion of ground laid under flax. Burnes in his turn had alleged McLure's liability for the draining of the loch. With the obstinacy of a failing man he was contemplating litigation. It was as black a cloud as any they had known.

Robert mended slowly. Till Christmas he remained shaky, but he was able to go on working, and he had begun—no doubt through the Freemasons, who were strong in that neighbourhood—to pick up acquaintances in Irvine. He was still depressed. He made a 'Dirge to Winter' that ended with resignation, and a 'Prayer under the Pressure of Violent Anguish' that breathed submission. He searched the Bible for comfort and found some, especially in the verses from Revelation descriptive of Heaven. He searched his other 'Bible' too—the one by Henry Mackenzie—and in a letter to his father assumed not only his hero's sentiments but his actual words (used on the occasion of Mr Harley's last illness). 'I am not formed,' he wrote (without quotation marks), 'for the bustle of the busy, nor the flutter of the gay.' He lamented, too, the effects on his 'whole frame' of 'the least anxiety or perturbation.'

In the usual course he would have gone home for Hogmanay. No other festival in the Scotish calendar was so much regarded in the family circle. But it happened to be a busy time in the flax trade, besides which Robert had a special reason for not wishing to leave Irvine just then. The couple in the High Street had turned out to be dishonest, and their shop little more than a disguise for thieving. They were pleasanter people than Peacock, and as new types Robert had found them interesting, but they wanted watching. So two days after Christmas (an unregarded date) he wrote to tell his father of his decision, and to ask for more meal. After a fairly hopeful description of his bodily health he gave an account of his spiritual condition.

> . . . my principal, and indeed my only pleasurable employment is looking backwards and forwards in a moral & religious way. I am quite transported at the thought that ere long, perhaps very soon, I shall bid an eternal adieu to all the pains, & uneasiness, & disquietudes of this weary life; for I assure you I am heartily tired of it, and, if I do not very much deceive myself I could contentedly and gladly resign it. . . . As for this world, I despair of ever making a figure in it. Indeed I am altogether unconcern'd at the thoughts of this life. I foresee that Poverty and Obscurity probably await me, & I am in some measure prepared and daily preparing to meet and welcome them. I have but just time and paper [to] return you my grateful thanks for the Lessons of Virtue & Piety you have given me, which were but too much neglected when they were given, but

which, I hope have been remembered ere it is yet too late. Present my dutiful respects to my Mother. . . .

To William, it is to be feared, this too Christian picture was more gratifying than shocking. He did not seriously believe his son's health to be in danger, and after all it *was* a truly Christian picture and admirably executed. Not another father of his acquaintance was likely to receive so well-expressed a letter from his son. If it was a little too well-expressed, that might be put down to superior education. Therein lay its only difference from a letter William himself might have written when a young man.

But the common country gossips had come nearer to the truth when they averred with a headshake that young Burnes had 'a great deal to say for himself.' With him an emotion must be expressed in words, and an emotion expressed was an emotion discharged. His letter was none the less genuine for being already a dead letter by the time it reached Lochlie. At most it was only the record of a mood, and the mood immediately succeeding it would not have tallied with any picture of his father at any age. Before the ink was dry upon the fair copy that he kept for his collection his inveterate sociability had re-asserted itself. It had become imperative for him to seek his fellows; and this not more to escape from the ghastliness of solitude than that he might take his shining place among them.

On New Year's Eve he joined in a carousal at the heckling shop. Like everybody else he had his share of ale and toddy. Of recent years whisky, an innovation from the Highlands, had become popular in the South, and illicit stills were everywhere. It was fire-strong stuff, proof spirit, pre-eminently the drink for this occasion. In Irvine too 'duty-free' brandy of the best French variety was obtainable, and that free of charge. It was a merry evening. Blackguards the company might be, but at Kirkoswald Robert had discovered that perfectly respectable people do not necessarily make the best company, and that a blackguard with a tankard before him may provide companionship of a highly amusing and instructive sort. In Irvine this discovery was confirmed. He himself could not drink deeply of any stimulant. His stomach would not stand it. A very little lighted him up to become the

life of a party, and without any translation to a better world
he summarily bade adieu to the pains, uneasiness, and
disquietudes of this. His eyes, instead of smouldering,
glowed; his voice resounded in the attractive cadences that
were so lamentably absent from his singing; his feet performed the complicated steps of the reel with zest. Nobody
from the description of himself, penned in all good faith three
nights before, would have recognised him that Hogmanay.

Unfortunately, amid the uproarious welcome given to
1782 by the flax-traders and their friends, some one knocked
over a lighted candle, which lay blazing unnoticed on the
floor. Tow burns briskly. Before the company knew what
had happened the whole rickety place was on fire. They had
barely time to get out before it was burned to the ground. The
woman of the house blamed Robert. Robert blamed the
woman, who certainly was drunk. But whoever was to
blame, all Robert's possessions and any money he had saved
were gone with the shop. He had nothing left but the clothes
he stood up in.

Yet he did not go home. It would have been his easiest
course; but he did not go. For in spite of his misfortune he
was no longer melancholy. He had begun to make friends in
Irvine. He was fascinated by the spectacle of life in a seaport
town—and there were other things. He was not going home
yet. With remarkable speed he found work enough to keep
him (with the food supplies from Lochlie he could do with
very little money), and back in the Glasgow Vennel, a few
doors from Peacock's cottage, he took a single room in a
tenement house at a shilling a week. Here he swept his own
floor, lighted his fire, cooked his own porridge and potatoes.
For the first time in his life there was nobody to overlook his
doings. He carved his initials on the stone mantelpiece, and
set himself with ardour to study poetical rhythms.[1]

He had lately found a very practical means of enlarging his
knowledge in this respect. In the same street as the burned
premises was Templeton's bookshop. Even when Robert
first arrived in Irvine he could not afford to buy books, and he
could still less afford it now. But at least he could go where
books were, and it had been his recreation to turn over with
envious fingers the pages of volumes he could never hope to

possess. Now he went to the bookseller's daily. Soon he had increased his knowledge of fiction by two-thirds of a three-volume *Peregrine Pickle*, and the same of *Ferdinand, Count Fathom*. A far greater attraction than fiction was provided by the ever-changing ballad sheets.

Seeing this, the good-natured Templeton had got into conversation with his unprofitable customer, speedily discovered his real interest, which was not fiction, and introduced him to the shop's stock of Scotish verse. Robert read *The Evergreen* collection—sham antiques in a delightful, complicated Jacobean stanza by Allan Ramsay; rhymed 'epistles' that had passed between old Allan and an impecunious young Renfrewshire laird, Hamilton of Gilbertfield; Hamilton's elegy on his dead greyhound bitch; 'The Piper of Kilbarchan,' the work of another laird, Sempill of Beltrees, having a measure that accompanied Robert (as it had accompanied the troubadours of the twelfth century) in sleeping and in waking. Back numbers of *Ruddiman's Weekly Magazine* contained some nimble astonishing pieces in that same troubadour measure—bearing the signature Robert Fergusson. They were on low themes—'The Farmer's Ingle,' 'Caller Oysters,' 'Hallowfair,' even 'To My Auld Breeks'—and in the homeliest vernacular; but they were poetry. The author, said Templeton, a mere copying clerk in Edinburgh, had created some interest in the metropolis and had made as much as £50 sterling out of a book called *Scots Poems*; but it was now seven years and more since he had died, young, obscure and in distressful circumstances. The price of Fergusson's book was half-a-crown. Perhaps Robert bought it. Perhaps Templeton gave it in return for the amusement of hearing his young friend—seated at ease upon the counter—declaiming aloud from the latest batch of ballad strips. Those that were bawdy received a rendering especially felicitous.

With his good memory Robert was able to carry away the words of any ballad, tragic or comic, more surely than if he had merely paid his penny for it. From every visit to Templeton's he came murmuring verses, stepping in time to a new rhythm, alive to fresh subject matter. He was finding Irvine a wonderfully educative place.

The education was not wholly of a kind that would have

met with his father's approval. Indeed Irvine, with its mixed population of dissolute industrials and free-and-easy seafarers, was hardly calculated to confirm that 'inclination to virtue' of which the elder Burnes had so lately boasted. The younger Burnes held no great opinion of industrials. But sailor-men were congenial, and with one of these he now struck up a rapid and enthusiastic friendship. Richard Brown had all the glowing virtues and the easily forgiveable weaknesses of his calling. He was open-handed and brave, unlucky and lecherous. Robert had only to learn his history—outlined by Brown in colours ultramarine—to feel warm toward him. A poor weaver's son, who had been for some reason adopted by a gentleman and educated beyond his station, he had, he alleged, been thrown on the world by his patron's death. In the classic manner he had gone to sea. He had been marooned by American privateers on a wild and barren coast. He was an inveterate lover. He bore a remarkable resemblance to Tobias Smollett's heroes.

After more than three months of painful and solemn thoughts this man's companionship acted upon Robert like a well-prescribed tonic: it soothed and it stimulated. As at Kirkoswald with William Niven, so now at Irvine with Richard Brown, he discussed life at length. On Sundays they walked to Lord Eglintoun's woods two miles away, strolled among the high trees—the oldest in Ayrshire—where once had walked the author of that ancient Scotish poem 'The Cherry and the Slae,' and never ceased to talk. Viewed from the criss-cross shadows of Eglintoun, many things in life looked other than they had looked from the simpler shadows of the Crossraguel cloisters. Matrimony, for example, hardly came into the picture except as a condition to be avoided. Brown, a true sailor, was marriage-shy. He had likewise the poorest opinion of platonic relationships between the sexes. He believed equally in winning a woman and in riding away. Robert, always willing to learn, once more proved himself the aptest of pupils. In the matter of female acquaintance the two formed an effective alliance—Brown with his bluff sea-dog air (Robert described it as a 'cheerful vacancy of thought') and the dark, witty young landsman, still shy, but with his dark stare and winning voice, his dimpled chin and somewhat tip-tilted nose, equipped for more than sailorly audacity.

There happened that year to be unusual opportunities in Irvine for young bachelors who wanted to advance their knowledge of womankind without committing themselves. A Sabbath or two before Robert's Hogmanay calamity the town had been scandalised by the appearance in the pulpit of a female who proclaimed herself the Third Person of the Trinity. In this divine capacity Elizabeth Buchan, an inn-keeper's daughter from the North-country, declared that persons upon whom she breathed would never die, but would be lifted bodily through the air into Heaven, all in a rejoicing company. Since her effective breathing upon Mr White, minister of the local Relief Kirk, her following had begun to alarm the magistrates, not so much on account of their heavenly as their earthly tenets. She preached free love with fervour and dispensed absolution for all moral lapses. Robert was not the man to fall under the spell of the 'Friend-Mother'—thus she styled herself. But he was interested in any creed, still more in its effects upon people. In this case his investigations were assisted by the peculiar elation prevailing among the Buchanites. The cult appealed especially to women. Some of the devotees were young and pretty. Robert became acquainted with one named Jean Gardner. She could not persuade him to enter the flock of 'Old Buchan'—as he irreverently called the prophetess though she was only a few years senior to himself. But willing youthful embraces—none the less that they are spiced with erotic religiosity—are sweet to one fresh from the hands of a prudent maiden and worn by long communing with death and despair.

One Sunday in the woods Robert paused, and excluding all expression from his voice, recited some of his own verses to Brown. Brown was struck with them, especially with the 'Dirge to Winter.' He suggested that they might be accepted for print by some magazine. Why not send them in somewhere and try? While Robert knew better than to believe that any verses made by himself could be 'like printed ones,' he was restored yet further by the sailor's praise.

Robert stayed in Irvine seven months, but his future as a flax farmer had faded long before that time. From Lochlie came word that litigation had begun. McLure had not proved more yielding than his tenant, and however the case might go the Ayr lawyers would soon pocket William Burnes's small savings. Robert must go home at once. Even if things had not been so bad, the life he had led since the New Year could not have continued.

Just how bad things were he learned from the others on arriving. Their father's health was not improving, nor his temper. It was true that he was gentler than ever with the younger children. When little Bell was herding cattle in a storm, he had gone out to sit with her that she should not be frightened by the thunder. But older people—even their mother—went in fear of his nervous explosions. There was the afternoon when he had come back from an interview with the lawyers to find a lad wasting a trifle of hay—his sharpness had been something to remember. There was the scene over a poor old wretch caught fibbing, when their mother had been fiercely turned upon for saying a good word for the sinner. They all dreaded the visits to the town from which the master of the house returned looking like death and unfit for any more work that day. Under the shadow of exhaustion he was a man to be feared and spared. Even the lighter tasks were sometimes too much for him. Once that spring he had left the morning threshing undone, and at noon, dragging himself in from sowing, had sunk upon his chair, saying that there was nothing in the bin for the horses' feed. It was Bell who told Robert this and how her mother and Lizzie Paton, after exchanging a look, had gone out to the barn and set to upon the grain themselves. She, the eleven-year-old child, had gone with them to help. But Robert could see without much

99

telling how things were. His father was failing; his mother
and Lizzie Paton, the strapping servant girl of twenty, had
formed a close alliance—a new and separate factor in the
farm.

William was not the only one with whom his children had
to go warily. Agnes had always had a red-headed temper of
her own, and as the russet faded from her hair, and at the
same time she saw hope fading from her husband's life, that
temper grew no easier. She was still vigorous, but of late her
always slender figure had become spare. She had shrunk and
grown a little crooked. The two elder girls, aged twenty and
eighteen, had gone out to service in neighbouring farms.
They were faithful in bringing their wages home every
Saturday, but they preferred to work away from Lochlie. It
was with Lizzie that their mother was now at her best,
magnanimous and laughing.

Age apart, mistress and servant were not unlike. Both were
by nature willing, kindly, cheerful, untaught—perhaps
unteachable except by experience. But whereas the clear
colours and pleasant features of Agnes had rejoiced the eye,
Lizzie's face was notably plain. She had a fine figure,
however,—strong-hipped, straight-backed, full-bosomed.
With all her youth upon her she had a careless cordiality and
softness such as the older woman had never been able to
indulge in herself. It may have been this that endeared the
girl to Agnes, and from the first gave a warmth to their
relation. Upon reaching middle life the upright wives of
grave and upright men often find themselves acutely in need
of a younger friend of their own sex. On that day of William's
collapse, as they wielded the hand-flails together in the
dim barn, the woman of fifty had felt her own youth return
to her. She was a girl again in her teens, working in her
granny's barn, with young Will Nelson to help and to make
love and to teach her the latest song—poor Will, who was
unregenerate, but just because of that for ever young in her
eyes. And she wondered about life. Experience does not
always make us glad that we have resisted temptation.
Glancing across the husk-filled space at the uplifted arms
of her servant lass, she smiled with a more than maternal
tenderness. Would Lizzie find it in herself to withstand a

Will Nelson? If she did not, who could blame her? Certainly
not Agnes.

> Kissin' is the key o' love,
>> An' clappin' is the lock,
> An' makin o't 's the best thing
>> That e'er a young thing's got.

In spite of all difficulties Robert retained his cheerfulness.
At Irvine he had lost his wardrobe and his virginity, but he
had gained something more precious than both put together.
The mood of Christian resignation which was imposed had
given way to the mood of reckless acceptance which was vital
to him. Let him once feel reckless, and something bubbled
up from a deeper source than he could command for any flow
of pious ejaculations.

> O why the deuce should I repine
>> And be an ill-forboder?
> I'm twenty-three and five feet nine,
>> I'll go and be a sodger.
>
> I gat some gear with mickle care,
>> I held it well thegither,
> But, now it's gane—an' something mair,
>> I'll go and be a sodger.

In subject these verses might be attributed to the foiled
Militia Bill of that year, to the fears of a French invasion
and the consequent Scotish volunteering fever; but in spirit
they derived from the New Year blaze at Irvine. They were
nearer to the pagan Hannibal of childhood than to the
tear-bathed Harley of adolescence, and they declared for
Richard Brown and his like, the coarse, sweet, unconver-
ted old Scotland, as against the care-burdened, rigid-
thinking, suppressed-emotional Scotland of the goodman of
Lochlie.

If he could have escaped from that second Scotland! But
its God—the God of the Burneses—was too powerful.
Inscrutable, yet just, punishing guilt, yet pledged to wipe
away all tears from penitent eyes, He lay in wait for him,
compassed him about and dwelt within him. Rebellion was
unthinkable. All a man could do was to play truant, and this
Robert did. But in truancy there is no freedom.

It was the truant mood that prevailed at Lochlie that summer. Things were no less desperate than they had been. Robert still saw himself as destined for obscurity in all save temperament, still cursed the misfortune that condemned him to write 'we who are of the lower orders of mankind' when, as Depute Master of the Tarbolton Lodge, he had to address an appeal for funds to Sir John Whitefoord, the Provincial Grand Master. He was still threatened at intervals with the nervous symptoms of his illness at Irvine. But he had thrown a load off his heart. To a lively North of Ireland tune he had picked up among the hecklers— 'The Weaver and his Shuttle, O!'—he made a nine-verse song:

> My father was a farmer upon the Carrick border,
> And carefully he bred me in decency and order.

It was rhymically crude, but had vigour and a swing to it, which was more than could be said for any of his religious outpourings. Other improvisations followed, in which he addressed fortune in sailor fashion, fingers to nose, or calmly contemplated existence as a wandering beggar. What mattered worldly success when life was so entertaining a spectacle, and love so sweet and easily got? Let him henceforth be nothing more than an observer and a lover, life was still worth living.

It is a more attractive pose than that of the bowed head, even than that of the head that is bloody but unbowed. Robert's presence drew the eye as never before. He was bold and he was glowing. Since the founding of the Tarbolton Bachelors he had shown some inclination to dress to the part of a village beau. Davie Sillar, a neighbour who wrote verses, played the fiddle and fancied himself as a parish Don Juan, had joined the club chiefly because Robert's appearance had aroused his curiosity. The two had become friends and it was with the aim of becoming a 'brother-fiddler' that Robert had taken up the instrument. Practise as he might, he would never be able to rival Sillar as a musician, but as a figure he was easily first. Even at a distance he was unmistakable because of the dashing manner (unlike anyone else's) in which he folded his plaid. The plaid itself was of an unusual colour—reddish yellow like an autumn leaf. He was the only

young man in the place to tie his hair, and from beneath
his scone bonnet two black locks escaped in careless kiss-
curl whiskers. Sillar was fascinated and jealous. Saunders
Tait, the village laureate, found it necessary to miscall his
budding rival. Gilbert, though sometimes scandalised, fell
under his brother's spell. He could well believe the tale
that one day down at the smithy, old Candlish, hammer in
air, had let his iron cool sooner than lose a word of Robin's
rant.

Among the Tarbolton girls it became understood that
when Rab from Lochlie started to talk they should gather
round to listen and laugh and watch his face. Often
unpromising and heavy, it could, as they had learned,
transform itself upon occasion, and their presence was
usually occasion enough. Emboldened by his Irvine experiences he made love with great success at home and abroad.
He knew—as the girls knew, but as Sillar with all his
amorousness would never know—that love was the single
flower of life for poor country people. It began to be
whispered that an hour with him in the dark was worth a
lifetime of daylight with any other lad. Once this is whispered
a young man's way is clear.

> Notwithstanding all that has been said against love,
> respecting the folly and weakness it leads a young
> inexperienced mind into; still I think it, in a great
> measure, deserves the highest encomiums that have
> been passed upon it.

Such was the first entry in an album, neatly bound in
leather and fitted with clasps, on which he had lately spent
some of his wages. It was to contain 'observations, hints,
songs, scraps of poetry, etc.' The observations and hints,
such as the foregoing, were to be his own, the songs and
scraps of poetry chiefly other people's. For his own verses he
could trust his memory. Now and again he might include a
stanza or two of his own but only for purposes of comment
and criticism. Paper was an expensive, dignified material
sacred to prose and the pursuit of culture. He was proud and
sure of his prose. Was it not based on the most elegant
English models? Had it not been perfected by close
study of 'The Man of Feeling'? On the title-page of his

'Commonplace Book' he outlined himself as a Harley in homespun . . . 'of a rustic way of life. . . . Robt. Burness; a man who had little art in making money, and still less in keeping it; but was, however, a man of some sense, a great deal of honesty, and unbounded good will to every creature, rational and irrational. . . .' While making the most of the ploughman pose, he immediately appended some quotations from Shenstone to show what an unusual ploughman he was. Some day these entries might be examined by other eyes than his own.

Of his poems he was neither proud nor sure. Brown's suggestion of printing had pleased and stimulated him, but he shrank from taking it seriously. Consumed by poetic ambition, he yet found the idea of public comment terrifying and the idea of remuneration deeply distasteful. It was bardship he coveted—above cavil, ridicule or gain. As this seemed impossible, he took refuge in an excessive humility. After all he was not the only rhyme-stringer in this or any other parish. Davie Sillar—now gone from the country life he hated to be a grocer in Irvine—had made the same suggestion as Brown that Robert should consider print; but Davie thought every bit as well of his own poems as of Robert's—perhaps better. Saunders Tait could throw off a stanza quicker than he could cut a pair of breeches, and be proud of them too, even when Rob and Davie jeered. So could the lousy little tailor, Rankin of Ochiltree. As for the gentry of Ayrshire—the readers of verses published in magazines—these were used to improvise themselves and to listen to the practised performers of the Edinburgh clubs during the winter. All over Scotland people were making bad verses, and calling them good. There was keen competition and criticism. It was easy enough to make a fool of oneself, still easier to be made a fool of. So Robert compromised. His own poems were 'for fun,' for relief, for escape and secret indulgence: they sprang from emulation, discontent, imitation—anything except inspiration: at most they would serve to amuse a trusted friend or an ignorant girl. He had seldom got so far as to 'say' one of them to several of his family together at the farm. Nor had he ever composed a line with paper before him and a pen in his hand. If, when he was

out and about, a stanza rose in his mind and floated there
without attaching more to itself, he would scrawl it, when he
came home, upon a little slate, so as to fix it the more firmly in
his memory. Later it might come to him to add more and to
improve. But that too would be while he was in the fields or at
market or warming himself by the peat-smothered fire before
going, last of all the family, to bed.

Yet what would he be without the deep and agitating
reverie into which he was thrown by this fugitive activity,
without this torture of music that he could not sing, without
the heady charm of finding words that would sing the music
for him? He might pretend to himself that it was all part of
the superior education got for him by his father; all of a piece
with the culture he strove after so blindly, the books he read
every meal-time so assiduously: but he knew better. These
had their bearing on it, but they were none of them its source.
Its source lay hidden. There were times when it seemed the
best thing in himself or in life: again times when he regarded
it as a secret vice, as the vomit to which the dog returns.
It was damaging to his farm work. His reason belittled it.
His will and his pride refused to take it seriously. But
reason, pride and will combined could not make him give
it up.

That spring he made a new sort of poem. It was about a
sheep. The four brothers had been ploughing the lea together
all morning—the two elder ones driving the furrows while
the younger ones managed the teams, cleared the stones and
ran off the water, which at Lochlie was a continual curse. The
shapes of Robert and Gilbert in their coarse working clothes
were manful against the steep field, and fifteen-year-old
William stood up stockily enough, but young John was
cruelly revealed as a reed of a creature all unfit for farm work.
They were returning from the house to their work from the
tawl'-hour brose, plodding across the in-field with the horses
and ponies, when a little scarecrow figure—Hughoc Wilson,
the half-wit herd from the next farm—came shambling
across, mouthing and gesturing some bad news. In the ditch
that divided the farms, he told them, Robert's pet ewe Mailie
was dying with her two lambs crying beside her. Robert's
concern was great. He had recently bought the creature and

her twins with his own money, more as a fancy than as a farming investment. But Mailie was not dying. She had merely taken a twist of her tether, rolled over, and with her four trotters in the air was patiently awaiting human assistance. Having untethered and set her on her feet, he went back to the plough laughing. Then he remembered Gilbertfield's 'Bonny Heck.' When all the light was gone and the horses had been unyoked and headed for home, he repeated to Gilbert 'The Death and Dying Words of Poor Mailie,' thirty-three couplets, in which he had pictured the respectable mother sheep as laying her solemn dying injunctions upon her offspring. Gilbert was amused and surprised—as well he might be; for though in the same metre that Hamilton had used, and though the idea of a dying animal making its last will and testament is one of the oldest in folk song, 'Poor Mailie' was a far better poem than 'Bonny Heck.' It was, in fact, the best poem of the sort yet made by a Scotsman, and could have been placed without impertinence beside Skelton's 'Philip Sparrow,' which Robert certainly never saw.

The first entries in the 'Commonplace Book' were made in April, but after that it lay closed all summer. Before April was out William Burnes's illness had taken a sharp turn for the worse. They had all seen the change and had accepted it with fatalistic quiet as something that brought added work as well as abiding grief to each member of the household. The sons must toil harder and take more responsibility: the wife must look out the grave clothes, hang them in the sun and fold them away ready: the younger womenfolk must wait upon the stricken man. By the early summer he had barely the strength to write a few short notes to those of his wife's brothers who had helped him from time to time. His own brothers were far off, and soon he would be gone leaving his affairs in disorder. He wrote painfully with his own hand, discharging as ever his duty as he saw it, setting down in strictly unemotional language his gratitude, his confidence in their future kindness, his farewell. For the longer more formal letters to his own relations he would have to depend upon Robert and Gilbert.

Robert's letter to the prosperous Montrose cousins was a

comprehensive news-sheet. Having informed them sadly but firmly of his father's approaching dissolution, he proceeded to a lengthy and exact disquisition on the state of trade and the causes of agricultural depression in Ayrshire, which proved him to be a diligent reader of the newspapers, a close student of current politics and a careful observer of local conditions. The lairds, he said, many of them ruined by the failure of the Ayr Bank eleven years ago, were asking far too much for their land. They were enthusiastic over farming experiments which had been carried out successfully in England and in parts of Scotland where there was natural rich loam, as in the Lothians; and they expected the same results without loss of time or extra expenditure upon their own obdurate acres. It was the same problem as had been presented to their grandfather in Kincardineshire thirty years before, but with the aggravation of a higher standard of living. In Ayrshire there was only one way for poor men to make a bit of money, and that was smuggling, and unfortunately, money made by smuggling was lost as easily as won. In conclusion he sent his cousins a small cheese left over from last year's stock, and his father's warmest wishes for their welfare—'probably for the last time on earth.' It was a letter that proved to William Burnes that at least none of his educational efforts had been wasted.

But education seen under the shadow of death has a dwindled importance. Of late, watching with a sick man's insight and from a sick cottager's post of vantage, the kitchen bed, Robert's father had marked much that might otherwise have escaped him. Now, seated solidly before the table, neatly addressing that admirable letter with his stumpy pen, Robert appeared all that an eldest-born Burnes should be. But suppose Lizzie Paton were to come in, would he not look up, and would not the two go out together, leaving the letter forgotten and unsealed? With the tenderness of the dying toward life, William caressed the old collie Luath, which liked to lie within his reach. With the accusing eyes of the dying toward the living, he searched Robert's face. He was sure of Luath. If only he could be as sure of Robert he could die content.

Having said good-bye he should have departed. But he had

always been a slow man, and his ailment was of a cruel, lingering nature.[1] Autumn came and went, and another Hogmanay, and Robert's twenty-fifth birthday, and William Burnes was still above ground. He was little more than a skeleton in his cupboard—the pain-racked shadow of a man, but still the head of the house. So in all their plans—and plans were urgently called for—Robert and Gilbert were hampered by his presence. Stung as they were by sorrow, they must in everything take both his living and his death into account; and they must hope that he would not survive till the following Whitsun when their seven years' tenancy of Lochlie would be at an end. If he did they would be sold up without any prospect of finding another farm. They might even be faced with that ultimate Scotish disgrace, a pauper funeral. They knew he would die insolvent. For the head of a Burnes family to lack a decent coffin, a bought grave, a stone, and fitting refreshment for mourners would be a shame never to be lived down.

Here was a situation such as the high-souled Harley had never been confronted with—a situation pressing hard upon young men 'of a rustic way of life,' even if these could credit themselves with 'a good deal of honesty, and unbounded goodwill to every creature, rational and irrational.' As usual in the face of reality sentimental idealism functioned only in the shape of righteous indignation unaccompanied by scruples. Landlords who inconveniently and with menaces demanded their rights came under the heading of neither rational nor irrational creatures but of 'reptiles.' McLure, the landlord of Lochlie, answered particularly to this description. Reptiles must be tricked, and thanks to an astute friend and brother Mason in the neighbouring parish of Mauchline, Robert thought he saw a way of tricking McLure.

The astute friend was astute by profession, being, like his father before him, the man of law in a village of a thousand inhabitants. He was well-to-do, well-connected, and something of a local character. Gavin Hamilton was his name, and his house and office, which occupied two sides of a corner of the big Mauchline churchyard and part of the site of an ancient monastery, was imposing enough to be nicknamed 'the Castle.' In the ordinary way, even with his Freemasonry,

Robert could hardly have looked for anything like equal friendship with such a man. But a 'Bachelor' crony of Robert's, one John Richmond, a skittish, intelligent youth of seventeen, worked in Hamilton's office. And Hamilton had a genial reputation. He liked to be called 'the friend of the poor.' His clerk's account of affairs at Lochlie afforded a cue he could not miss. Besides the youth's description of Robert had piqued his curiosity.

The two had only to meet to take heartily to one another. 'The Clerk'—as he was called in Mauchline—was of the breezy type admired by the moodier Robert. He was tall, stout, handsome, free-spoken, fond of the good things of life and sure of himself. He used many damns in his speech (even before the minister), hated the spectacle of suffering, and had every aptitude and inducement to live up to his reputation of having a heart of gold. He rejoiced in liberal views. His father and mother had been obliged before their marriage to accept the Kirk-session's rebuke for unseasonable fruitfulness. Robert bore himself admirably upon the introduction, and came away brimming with enthusiasm. Being himself aristocratic by temperament, he had felt at home in Hamilton's company, as he had never done in the genteeler company of ministers, doctors and schoolmasters. The first interview at 'the Castle' was followed by others of a more confidential nature.

Hamilton, among other things, was factor to the great local landlord, the Earl of Loudoun. Some little time before his acquaintance with Robert, he had become his employer's tenant for Near Mossgiel, a farm of 118 acres on the high ground about a mile north of the village. He had intended it to be a dairy supply and summer holiday place for himself and his growing family. To this end he had rebuilt the original hovel of a cottage, furnished the outhouses with dairy gear and put some cows on the rough pasture, leaving the land otherwise unimproved. He had, however, either grown tired of the notion or found it unprofitable. When he heard how the Burneses were placed with McLure, whom he disliked, he had a bright idea. Robert and Gilbert should take Mossgiel from him at £90 a year, and they could begin to work the place quietly at once. He would deal very reasonably in the matter of dairy stock, and all would be in readiness for their occupation upon their father's death. So long as they got the spring planting done at Lochlie they could sell the growing corn to Tarbolton buyers after they themselves had cleared out. McLure, of course, would make the devil of a fuss, but he could take no legal steps against them for what was no more than a piece of sharp practice, and the Tarbolton worthies could be trusted to claim anything they had paid for. As to the insolvency, what was to prevent all six children, as well as any other workers on the farm, from ranking as the old man's first creditors? His sons were already his servants. Let his daughters become so too. And that there should not be a penny for McLure to seize when the time came, let them all put any savings they now had into Mossgiel. It was a cunning and practical scheme, over which a legal champion of the poor might well rub his hands. Incidentally it predisposed Hamilton more than ever to his *protégé* Robert. The preliminary arrangements were soon made. By November Robert and Gilbert, unknown to McLure, were lease-holders of Hamilton's farm.[2]

Now it only remained for William to die. Mackenzie, the Mauchline surgeon, said it could not be long, but February came and they were still waiting. On the morning of the 13th Robert and Bell were alone together in the room with the stricken man, who was almost too far gone to speak. The little girl was crying, but not for her father, though she adored him. That morning a terrible thing had happened. Luath, which the night before had been missing from his usual place by the bedside, had been found by Robert lying dead outside the door. Some hostile neighbour had done it. The incident was kept from their father, but it threw its shadow over the household. Robert, though it was a week-day and he should properly have been at work, stood at the little window looking out at the winter bushes and rough frozen grass. He did not try to comfort his sister, but let her cry her fill. It was their father, tender to the last, who roused himself and tried to speak consoling words. Ethical too to the last, he marshalled what remained of his breath to drive home with all the force of the occasion those maxims which had so consistently governed his own life. 'Shun every vice,' he murmured to the sobbing Bell—and with a supreme effort of that will which had never yet failed him—'. . . walk in the paths of virtue.'

While he fought to collect the last scattered shreds of his strength, his son still stayed by the window, blotting out the thin February light with his massive head and shoulders, leaning his cheek on his hand in the favourite attitude of the Man of Feeling which had now become his own. Conscious of Robert's presence as of the ache in his own breast, the father spoke again. 'There is only one of you all I am afraid for,' he said. As Robert still did not stir William repeated his fear for one and one only of his children.

At last the young man came to the bed. 'I suppose it is me you mean?' he said. His father's eyes left no doubt as to the answer. Returning quickly to his post at the window Robert burst into tears such as Mr Harley had certainly never shed. Later in the day William Burnes died.

It was some comfort that they could give him a good burial. Years ago he had laid aside the needful three or four pounds, and his children would sooner have starved than have drawn upon this for any other purpose. They could have a 'first quality' coffin and mort-cloth, and provide the several courses of bread, cakes and scones, the correct amount of ale, tea, snuff and tobacco. If some of these were smuggled articles, acquired through the Broun connexion, they would taste none the worse for that. And there would be cheese and oatcakes of Agnes's own making for the assembled poor. The presence of a minister was not strictly necessary, but it would be fitting as well as decent to ask old Dr Dalrymple from Ayr to bless God's good gifts. Late that Friday night the Tarbolton bellman, toddling slowly from end to end of the long village street, uttered on behalf of Lochlie his ancient call. 'All brothers and sisters, I let you to wot that there is a brother departed out of this present world, according to the will of Almighty God.' And as the people ran to their doors, he gave them the dead man's name and a general invitation to the house for the death ceremonies. Thus it was proved to all that William Burnes in Lochlie was no pauper.

For anyone to refuse such an invitation would have been neither friendly nor Christian. On the Sabbath evening the middle-aged and elderly women crowded into Lochlie's kitchen to witness the coffining, finger William's winding sheet—made from wool which according to custom his wife had spun in the first year of their married life—and enjoy tea and bannocks. Tea, though now drunk daily by the gentry, was still a luxury to villagers, and was especially appropriated to funerals. On the Monday the men came up in a body. Many were merely poor or curious folk who had no connexion with Tarbolton but never missed a funeral if they could help it. When all had been into the house by relays to eat and drink and take stock of the deceased's possessions, the coffin, preceded by the beadle with his bell, was brought out, the stragglers fell off, and the procession, consisting entirely of men, formed up. The presence of the minister had preserved decorum among the mourners, and kept the proceedings from becoming, as they were apt to do, over-festive. Further, as William had wished to be buried at Alloway kirkyard within the walls that he had repaired, the bearers and true followers—distinguished by their muslin 'weepers'—had the sobering distance of twenty miles to cover. The coffin was tied to long poles slipped through the stirrups of two saddled farm ponies which walked tandem. One of the ponies had been sent by John Tennant who, now the Countess of Glencairn's factor, lived at Glenconner, seven or eight miles away.[3] 'They'll be wae and dowie at Lochlie the day,' he had said to his son James. 'Tak the pownie and gang ower and help at the funeral.' Robert led the Glenconner pony, which was put in front. Gilbert followed leading the other beast.

It was a busy day for Agnes. She had now to prepare a substantial meal for the faithful hungry ones who should later return from the graveside. But withered and bent as she was, none could do this sort of thing better than she, and today she had her two grown daughters to help her as well as Bell. This was something to be thankful for, as Lizzie Paton was sick and looking blue beneath the eyes. Her mistress knew well enough what ailed the girl. She hoped her husband had died without noticing anything. He would have taken it to heart. She herself was not unduly put about. Such things came to pass and they were vexing. But Robin was a good-hearted lad. He would marry the girl when her time came, if not before. Agnes had nothing against Lizzie as a daughter-in-law. She had been too soft, but she would make a good wife. What with his versifications and Masonics and stravaiging ways, the sooner Robin was wed the better.

PART THREE

Mossgiel

Robert was head of the house. He wore the badge of authority, his father's silver watch. When called upon he assumed even more than his father's dignity. On weekdays he gave the orders. On Sundays he led the way to Tarbolton kirk and with becoming gravity took his place at the end of the pew. On such evenings as he found it convenient to be at home he conducted family worship. It was his pleasure as well as his duty. Coming from his father's lips the phrase 'Let us worship God' had often moved him. Now that he had passed from the spectator's to the performer's place, he recognised it as poetic material. This, with his ability to identify himself for the moment with his father, gave style and feeling to his own utterance. His reading of the Scriptures had a fine solemnity; his extempore prayer had passion and power.

On such evenings as Robert did not find it convenient to be at home—which often happened—Gilbert did his best as deputy, but was felt to lack unction.

Now that he was Robert Burns[1] in Lochlie people took new note of him—and it suited his notions to be noted,—but when they spoke of him they were apt to smile, which they had never done when speaking of his father. Sometimes they even winked. Neither gesture is compatible with the use of a surname. After the removal to Mossgiel, a few weeks after his father's death, Robert became Rob Mossgiel, or Robin, or even Rab to both his villages.

To the Burns family the circumstances of the removal were inevitably painful, but to the detached onlookers at Tarbolton they were highly amusing. They were indeed slightly scandalous. When McLure heard that a notice had been put up on Tarbolton church door advertising the sale of the Lochlie corn, he was very angry. He informed the parish by tuck of drum that buyers would buy at their own risk. To make assurance doubly sure he posted himself outside the church on the Sabbath day and cried the same warning as the worshippers were leaving the morning diet, from which the worshippers had the satisfaction of inferring that the corn would be going cheap. It was a clear occasion for a doggerel bard. Mr Saunders Tait, who had already some old scores to settle with Robert, improved it to the tune of seven verses. Tarbolton laughed at them, but in his anxiety to expose Robert as a knave the tailor exposed McLure yet more conspicuously as a fool. In the circumstances the intended victim could afford to join in the laughter. He had gained some cash and a reputation for astuteness.

But in addition to the immediate scandal of McLure there was the prospective scandal of Lizzie Paton. Her condition might not as yet be visible to the casual eye, but in villages there is the casual nose to be reckoned with. Lizzie's devotion to the new master was every bit as evident as her dejection. Mrs Burns was on her side. She thought Robert ought to marry the girl. What would his father have said? But Robert's father had gone to where there was neither marrying nor giving in marriage, and Robert's mother's spoken words, unlike her words that were sung, carried little weight. He was no mother's boy. He had a great respect for Lizzie, as all his life he had for any woman who yielded sweetly to him, and he felt a tender championship that was also self-regarding. When one of the local girls passed him with haughty averted face on the moor above the farm, he revenged himself by declaring:

There lives a lass in yonder park,
I wadna gie her in her sark
For thee, an' all thy thousan' mark!
	Ye need na look sae high.

It was the truth. He could neither admit unworthiness in any woman upon whom he had bestowed the most fleeting attention, nor withdraw his affection from one who had, however briefly, roused his desire. At the same time it had to be allowed that Lizzie was rough and uneducated to a disgusting degree, and that the issue between them had been as simple and indeterminate as her face, and that at no time had he led her to expect marriage. He was not in a position to marry, even were he inclined, and he was not inclined. The abstract idea of marriage, which had charmed him during his wooing of Alison Begbie, had at Irvine suffered a sea change. If it had been Peggy Thomson now. . . . He still thought with warmth of Peggy, and looked eagerly for news of her from his Kirkoswald friends.

But Lizzie Paton he could not see as his wife. Neither could Gilbert nor his sisters. If they had been of their mother's opinion the united family might have been too much for Robert. But Gilbert was emphatic. The like of Lizzie Paton was no match for a Burnes.[2] As for the sisters, one at least was to be of the Mossgiel household, and she wanted a particular girl friend of her own to live with them and help. There would be more than enough young women on the farm; besides a bachelor brother makes an easier master than one with a wife. Agnes Burns having been reduced to a disapproving silence, Lizzie was packed off to her widowed mother.

She made no complaint. She had, it appeared, a clear—some called it a masculine—outlook on life. She admitted that she had not been taken advantage of or misled by promises. She had merely been heartily, perhaps hopefully in love. If her face had been a little less plain, or if her hair had been a little fairer, or if her schooling had been more extensive, or if she had been able to sing, her story would have been different. Such is fate in Ayrshire and elsewhere.

The young people at Lochlie had won, and probably they were right; but they could not count their honours. Robert entered in his Commonplace Book a score or so of commonplace lines on Remorse revised from the blank-verse tragedy he had begun at eighteen and had never been able to finish. At eighteen he would have made more practical reparation. At twenty-five relief at his escape was stronger than remorse, and stronger even than relief was satisfaction at having vindicated his manhood. He was sorry about Lizzie, but his sorrow, though sincere, was superficial. The nature of his feelings appears most truly in the jovial and graceless 'Welcome to his Bastart Wean' composed a few months later.

Meanwhile he was busy settling at Mossgiel. The getting out of Lochlie had been vexatious but successful. The irate McLure had taken steps to sell up the home, only to find himself once more baffled. Acting on Hamilton's advice, William Burnes's children had claimed as servants of the deceased for arrears of wages. They were thus preferred creditors as against McLure. In this way they managed to save the bulk of their household goods and farm stock for Mossgiel. Robert had his troubles and his occasional twinges of conscience. He sorrowed truly for his father, wrote an epitaph for his headstone (thereby discovering a new poetic vein and vehicle for irony), and made good resolutions such as his father would strongly have approved. He undertook to put away verse-making, bought a new memorandum book for the farm and seed for the spring sowing, determined volubly that he would attend markets, study nothing but farming books, think of nothing but crops. But really his life had leapt up and away.[3] He was in new surroundings, and, as it were, re-delivered from his father's influence, which had lasted too long and had irked him more than he knew. His first entry in the farming memorandum book was a poem, his spring seed was a bad lot, he handed over to Gilbert those tasks which called for steady application and reserved for himself those which would leave his mind free or take him into company. Gilbert would keep the accounts and attend to the business of the farm, while Robert would plough and sow and make journeys into Mauchline.

Especially make journeys into Mauchline. Not farming pretexts nor the pursuit of self-improvement, nor even the comparative nearness of Mauchline could explain the frequency with which Robert was to be seen traversing that mile of steep road with his dog—the faithful successor to Luath—trotting at heel. The truth was that Mauchline, more than any other place he had seen, served both as a bright microcosm of the world for his observation and as a stage upon which he could display his whole repertory of parts. When he set out there was always a readiness in his air. He was a young man bent upon adventure and at the disposal of fortune. Nothing escaped his lively vagrant eye. But on the return journey he was always wrapt in thought. He seemed oblivious of the outer world and even of his own proper self. When he reached the farm, if nobody was about outside, he would pull the string of the outdoor latch and enter softly;

and if nobody was about inside, he would climb the ladder at the back of the little entrance hall and disappear through the trap-door in the ceiling.

The upper floor of the cottage was an attic divided into three small compartments. That on the west side had a tiny deep-set gable window, and was the sleeping room of his young brother William and a Broun cousin, Robert Allan from Irvine way. That on the east was a windowless lumber cupboard. The middle compartment contained the bed which Robert shared with Gilbert. There was a sky-light in the thatch, under which stood a small deal table, Robert's special property. It had a drawer in which he kept his slate, his Commonplace Book, his letters and notepaper—and a growing heap of poems. Shortly before leaving Lochlie he had begun to write his poems down, and from being written down they began more and more to occupy his time and thoughts. He even carried pen, ink and paper about with him, and his pockets as well as the drawer in his table were stuffed with scraps of verse. His untidiness, already a byword in the family, became worse than ever—Robert could never find anything. If a plough-wedge or a horse-shoe nail were missing Gilbert would make him turn out his pockets. It was certain to be found there, with perhaps something else which had been long sought. His thoughts were much in his attic. At meal times he got into a habit of gulping down his food and slipping off before the others were well begun. He could see no other way of squaring his conscience but by spoiling his stomach. This was a pity, for with him the latter was by far the less recuperative organ.

Both gave him considerable trouble, however. He alone knew how Protean were the guises in which he made his descents upon Mauchline. With Gavin Hamilton he was manly and deferential and full of reasonable, enlightened discourse. But with Hamilton's clerk Richmond and with James Smith (another youth of seventeen, who kept the haberdasher's shop at the entrance to Mauchline in the Backcauseway) he led the way in bawdy talk and in bitter invective against the rich and the censorious. He particularly loved Smith, who was witty, dark, delicate and amorous. With the casual young men of the village—'the unthinking rabble of mankind'—he was sometimes contradictory and arrogant. Observant people noticed his variousness and did not think the better of him for it.

Mauchline gave him the variety he needed of scene and behaviour. Here was no stagnant pool, but rather a river pool, which has the qualities of peace and permanence, and yet is full of change. At Mauchline Cross six of the busiest roads in Ayrshire converged. There was no more notable rendezvous for wayfarers in all Scotland. April brought race week,[4] when the stretch of road between the Cross and Mossgiel bore the imprint of every kind of Scotish foot, naked and shod: Tarbolton in race week was nothing to Mauchline. July brought the cattle-market, famous throughout the shire and far beyond it. In August the stage was set for the greatest function of all—the open-air Communion services, when the population swelled in a day to fourteen times its normal thousand, and the surplus thirteen thousand camped promiscuously out of doors (largely in the churchyard) there to indulge in orgies of piety, love and drink. Even everyday occasions were showy. The place was full of pretty, well-dressed girls. A Mauchline wedding was something to write about with its silk gowns and stockings and a powdered head for the bride's father—there had been nothing of the kind at Tarbolton.[5]

Even about the way Mauchline was built there was something encouraging to a various sociability. From a central green, part common, part churchyard with a great tree full of rooks' nests to mark the middle, the short streets ran out to the country in every direction; and all round the green stood houses and taverns, which, though they mostly presented their backs to it, presented also their back entrances. Visible from all sides, the square, bare sentry-box of the church was set like a reminder or at times a menace. Near it, pleasantly ruined and snuggling in its ivy, the old priory, built by the monks of Melrose, afforded a sanctuary for lovers. Often what was done secretly in the Priory had to be publicly expiated in the church.

As for taverns, there was a far finer variety than at Tarbolton. Any week-day, by merely sitting in Johny Dove's in Main Street, Robert could hear all that the most respectable

village gossips and the most ponderous village wiseacres had
to say of life. On Sundays he could slip through from the
churchyard by the back way into Nance Tinnock's discreeter
tap-room, to listen to the complacent godly who were used to
take refreshment there between sermons. As yet their
discourse concerning their own righteousness and the sins
and duties of others was unchecked by the presence of the
silent, dark young man lately come from the next parish.
When these palled he could drop more warily into Poosie
Nancie's at the corner facing the market. Because of her
peculiar contumacy in sin Nancie had been 'excluded from
the privileges of the church.' She was a drunken slut and a
receiver of stolen goods. With her villainous, black-bearded
husband she kept a lodging-house and tavern for thieves and
beggars. Her servant was a doxy off the roads, her daughter
Jess a half-wit, nicknamed 'Racer' because she could run like
a hare and would any day for a wager or a fee. At the Elbow,
too, kept by a sailor, things were to be seen and heard. At all
four taverns there was good Scotish material, and plenty of it
for the farmer from Mossgiel to ponder over as he walked his
homeward mile. A world was contained within a hundred
square yards.

The farm house stood on the breast of a fallow ridge—
all the Mossgiel land was too fallow by half—and had a
south-westerly aspect. Its outlook over the wooded valley of
the Ayr made it a pleasant place in summer, but in winter it
was comfortless enough. Hawthorns made a high ragged
hedge round the back that gave some protection from the
wind that came rushing down from the moors of Galston
and Muirkirk. A few old trees overhung the roof. They
looked well but shut out the light. The outhouses formed
a big detached quadrangle about the duck-dub. Inside, the
ground-floor of the house consisted of two rooms—by far the
best the family had yet occupied—separated by the little
entrance with its ladder and trap. On one side was the
kitchen, which had concealed beds all along the back wall;
here all the womenfolk slept. On the other side was the
'spence' or parlour—an apartment with which Robert was so
pleased that sometimes he invited the Tarbolton Freemasons
to hold their meetings in it.[6]

Besides the nine people sleeping in the cottage, there were three who lay in the stable loft above the four horses. The stable sleepers were the gaudsman John Blane and two eight-year-old herd boys. It was to save his own sons from this sort of childhood that William Burnes had made such persistent efforts and in the end helped to bring ruin on himself. Robert did not forget. He made much of the herd boys, Davie and Willie, gave them rides on his shoulders on the way from the fields, told them stories, spared them family worship—though on Sundays he examined them in their Shorter Catechism—and sometimes by the fire at night instructed them with young Bell in the King's English. The cleverer of the two boys, Willie Patrick, could not make Robert out. The field work would be held up for minutes at a time while he crouched to stare at some little thing on the ground, some wood or weed or small beast, that no farmer in his senses would have thought worth looking at. And while he stared he heard not a word that was said. Yet when Willie was sent running, as he often was, to deliver a letter at Mauchline and fetch the answer back, it was clear enough to him what his master was after. It was clear, anyhow, that these urgent affairs in Mauchline had nothing to do with farming.

As a letter carrier who would be unobserved Willie was useful. But the most useful of all the children in the farm to Robert was Bell; because Bell could sing, and to have a voice at his disposal, even a child's voice, was become a necessity to him. His fiddle, though he had practised it long and ardently, had failed him. He would not admit this. Against all evidence he would style himself a 'brother fiddler' when he wrote to Sillar at the Irvine grocer's shop. But failed him it had. The mortification of being defeated by Latin was as nothing compared with this inability to learn what was for him the very 'language of nature.' It was very strange and maddening. He could compose an air consisting of four successive parts, which was so clear that he could and did write words to it. Yet because he could neither sing nor play it nor write it down (unless it was first played or sung to him) it was doomed to remain for ever a melody unheard—words without music though to music they had been composed. He dreamed tantalisingly of harpsichords, and of spinets such as he knew were to be found in the houses of rich people. He had never seen either instrument, but he felt that given a keyboard he could utter forth those infuriating themes to which his secret life was lived. By devoted application he had learned to 'prick down' on paper the notation of a simple melody if he heard it often enough repeated;[7] and once it was in his head he could hum it aloud after a fashion. He had become a passionate cadger of music. Not a tinker, tailor, soldier or sailor strolling along the road beneath the farm was safe from his solicitations; not a gentleman, ploughboy or thief in the Mauchline taverns but might be asked to sit and deliver, if he had such a thing as an ancient tune about him. But he needed a familiar, and if possible a household voice, and Bell had one. She would sooner sing than spell any day. Often when she should have been at her lessons or her household tasks, her brother made her hum over and over again some tune he had taken down from the lips of a strolling beggar or an incorrigible tippler at Poosie Nancie's.

In return for her singing he let her into the secret of his table drawer, and sometimes, when he was out of the way, she climbed the ladder to his room and pried. She did not think Robert so clever as her father had been. Nobody on earth could be that. But it was wonderful how like singing some of the lines on these bits of paper sounded when you managed to read them aloud—still more when you got Robert to 'say' them to you. Here, for instance, was one that almost seemed to sing by itself:

> It was upon a Lammas night
>   When corn rigs were bonie,
> Beneath the moon's unclouded light,
>   I held awa' to Annie;
> The time flew by wi' tentless heed
>   Till, 'tween the late and early,
> Wi' sma' persuasion she agreed
>   To see me through the barley
> Corn rigs, and barley rigs,
>   And corn rigs are bonie:
> I'll ne'er forget that happy night
>   Amang the rigs wi' Annie.

That circumstances have so often warped and destroyed men of genius is a sad fact of human history; that the man of genius does not merely defy circumstances, but draws from them all the nourishment his genius demands for its flowering, is of all facts the most magical and consoling. Robert's spine had been bent by excessive labour and insufficient food at a tender age; his instincts had been thwarted by a crippling moral code, and his mind had been misled by a spurious culture. Yet, as much by the futility as by the violence of his struggle, as much by his defeat as his mastery of untoward surroundings, as much by his lapses as by his aspiration, he extracted the vital elements from a forbidding soil. Beneath the dreariness and the false ideals, between the submissions and the rebellions, the acceptances and the evasions, between belief in his father's God and truancies from Him—truancies more human than rebellion and more poignant than escape— the slow distillation of emotion had proceeded in secret. Now the cisterns of his being were full. It only wanted such little matters as the death of an old man, the move from one village to another, the birth of an unwanted baby, to remove the long pressure; the jet would shoot all the higher because of it.

He had entered Mossgiel telling himself that rhyming was a reprehensible habit and that as the master of a new farm he must lay it aside. Yet all that summer he rhymed harder than ever, and he rhymed now, not to escape from the poverty of life, but to give expression to the new richness of life as he found it in Mauchline. What he had long fitfully and faint-heartedly pursued was now itself in pursuit. The table-drawer filled; it overflowed. He knew the exultation of flowering genius. Nevertheless his problem remained. What could poetry do for him? Could it bring him fame? Commonsense told him that it was most unlikely. The utmost he could hope for was a local reputation as a clever versifier. To become famous one had to get one's poems printed in books or magazines, and that was out of the question for anyone who was not of the gentry or at least college bred like Fergusson. And after all what had poor Fergusson made of it? He had died young, destitute, mad. No, Scotland could and would do nothing for him as a poet, but he as a poet could and would do something for Scotland. This revelation came to him quietly but it inspired an emotion as profound as ever determined the direction of a man's life. Once conceived, the idea possessed him. He would identify himself with the nameless, unrewarded bards who had made the songs of the Scotish people.

But with Robert the sublime and the sordid and the ridiculous always came treading on each other's heels. The autumn advertised Lizzie Paton's condition to all and called for action on the part of those whose sacred duty it was to rebuke sinners in the Lord's House and before the face of the congregation. Elders of the Kirk made due inquiry. Admissions were obtained. One Sabbath Day Robert Burns in Mossgiel was formally cited from the pulpit to appear as a penitent in due course.

Mauchline church, like other Scotish churches, had no choir. Immediately below the pulpit there was a box that housed the precentor, whose function it was to chant each line of each psalm in solo ahead of the people, so to provide them with the words. Between the precentor and the first row of worshippers, somewhat to one side, was a small platform like the throne for an artist's model, so placed as to be in the view of all. Here any member of the lower orders who had been detected in Sabbath-breaking, blasphemy or lechery was required to sit throughout the service, sometimes throughout many services week after week, upon a small uncomfortable three-legged stool. At the close of the sermon, on the summons of the beadle, the culprit stood up to receive pastoral rebuke, the length of which was determined by the speed with which convincing evidence of contrition was obtained. Sometimes this was a slow business. There were sinners who turned a deaf ear, even sinners who argued. Once an Ayrshireman had called the minister to order. 'It isna' adultery I'm here for,' he objected, 'it's but simple forni'.' For the most part, however, the power thus placed was hard to withstand and easy to abuse. In the early days, when 'affectionate' eloquence was demanded of the ministry and when the victim had to wear a garment of sackcloth, many young women committed suicide rather than endure the cutty stool. For this and other reasons its use had lately been discountenanced by the New Light clergy. But the minister of Mauchline, the Rev William Auld, was faithful to the Old Light. The most he would yield to modernity was occasionally to permit evildoers to stand up for rebuke in their own pews. Where it happened that a man and a girl of the same class and parish had transgressed together, it rested with him to decide whether they should stand in their respective pews or side by side in the high place of humiliation. If, however, the man happened to belong to the land-owning class he was absolved from appearing, and got off with a private censure before the Kirk-session and a substantial fine for the poor-box.[1] The Scotish sense of fitness could not abide that a broadcloth bottom should come in contact with the sinner's seat.

In this case there was no exemption from the cutty stool for either sinner. Impassive but arrogant Robert stood up in Mauchline church to listen to the homily of the old man (a brother Mason) in the pulpit. Mr Auld—he was not an unkindly man, though rather stupid—pushed the rebuke no further than was strictly necessary. Still the strict necessity alone inflicted severe humiliation on a proud man.[2] From his obstinately wide-open eyes the penitent could see the embarrassment of Gilbert, the amused sympathy of Smith and Richmond (who never knew when they themselves might be in his place), the intense satisfaction of all the 'unco guid,' who felt certain that nothing of the kind could ever happen to them or theirs. Among the latter were the Armours. Mr Armour was the builder in the Cowgate, a man of substance and high respectability and, of course, a Freemason. Mrs Armour was a woman of unspotted virtue. Their son Adam was also virtuously inclined. He enjoyed nothing better than to assist in ducking a whore in the village pond. There were also daughters. The Armours knew little

of the Mossgiel incomer, and what they did know they did
not like. It did not surprise them that he should now be
exposed for what he was—a loose and dangerous fellow, so
reprobate that he would not even atone for his transgression
by marriage. They had a special reason for regarding the
day's ceremony with approval. It would be a lesson to their
daughter Jean. For the deplorable fact was that Jean had
somehow come to be on speaking terms with Mossgiel.

The Armours might have felt less secure had they known
that it was not Mossgiel who had scraped acquaintance with
Jean, but Jean who had perseveringly made up to Mossgiel.
Being on the dark side in her colours she had not immediately
drawn his eye, which looked out ever for corn-coloured
heads, but she had not failed to mark him more and more. On
the Monday after race week, while crossing that part of the
village green where the women bleached their linen, and
whistling his dog off from fouling the clothes, he heard
himself boldly hailed. 'Weel, Mossgiel, hae ye gotten ony lass
yet to lo'e ye as weel's your dog?' Robert looked round
sharply. He seemed to recognise the voice. On the Saturday
evening he had been at Morton's tavern. Morton's on
holidays was the great resort of young men and girls, for
upstairs there was a clear floor and a fiddler who would play
at the rate of a penny a reel. The girls stood along the street
on the other side of the churchyard, like so many cattle or
servants at a feeing-market, each waiting for some young
man to choose her as his partner and lead her over the
gravestones into the tavern. That Fair night Robert's dog,
which had been left outside, had found its way upstairs and in
seeking its master had ruined a reel. He had kicked it out
with the characteristic remark, 'I wish I could find a lass that
would lo'e me as weel's my dog!' There was a roar of
laughter. Mossgiel was never to be seen without the dog well
to heel. Now he knew that this girl had been one of the
laughers, who had escaped his notice in the candle-light. In
the April sunshine he took a good look at her. She was a girl of
nineteen or twenty, in 'short-gown'[3] and kilted petticoat. She
had a pleasant square face, small square hands and frank,
widely-opened, desirous eyes. Not his type, perhaps—the
eyes were too dark, but there were lights in the straight

brown hair which a poet might easily describe as golden. Her bare legs were strong and shapely, her feet remarkably small. She was as shy and as bold as a blackbird. He guessed that she would hold love, as he did, to be 'the first of human joys, our chiefest pleasure here below.' Before he continued on his way they had arranged an early meeting. He had found out that she could sing; she should sing for him. Piqued by the news of Peggy Thomson's approaching wedding, he looked out the old Kirkoswald love-song for suitable revision. This was easy. 'Jeanie' could be substituted for 'Peggy' and (O happy chance!) 'Armour' for 'charmer.' It even passed through his mind that he might marry her. 'To have a woman to live with when one pleases,' he wrote to one of his Kirkoswald friends, 'without running any risks of the cursed expense of bastards and all the other concomitants of that species of smuggling— these are solid views of matrimony.' But when he stood up in Mauchline church the cursed expense and other concom-itants weighed so heavily upon him that thoughts of matri-mony were put aside. Much better to clear out. Why not sail away overseas to Virginia or Jamaica? This, like his old notion of soldiering, was less a decision than a dramatisation. As he had seen himself in distant lands wearing the King's uniform, so now he saw himself in distant lands herding gangs of negro slaves. He needed just that extra fillip. Something very timid in him, something deprecatory and even despairing, that had been imposed by his upbringing, always impeded his natural boldness until he could receive or manufacture some stimulus from without.

A stimulus more powerful than any change of sky was supplied in a very simple manner. He became a father. Much has been said of the effect of motherhood upon the normal woman. Not so much has been said of the effect of fatherhood upon the normal man. Possibly an element of ridicule has interfered. Yet the effect is real enough. Robert in the simpler human emotions was eminently normal. The proof of his virility wrought upon him with releasing force. His public shame was great; his private exultation in paternity was greater. The birth of little black-eyed bastard Lizzie was the turning-point of his life as a man and the beginning of his conscious career as a poet. Only the slightest additional impetus was needed to make him take his decision, and it was given. As often happens at a crisis it came from an unexpected quarter.

Between Lochlie and Largieside (where Lizzie Paton lived) Robert had a farming friend, who, though of his father's generation, was so different in character from William Burnes that during the Lochlie days the acquaintance had not been much cultivated. John Rankine in Adamhill was prosperous—he had a carpet in his parlour, upon which Robert was afraid to step as it was the first he had ever seen. He was of the best Ayrshire type—downright to roughness, but quick-witted, fun-loving, and avowedly human. His bent was Rabelaisian. He had further the habit of rhyming. Now that Robert was his own master he liked to go over to Adamhill of an evening for talk and toddy, and he was courtier enough to pretend that it was in honour of Rankine's daughter Annie—an uncommonly plain, grenadier-like girl—that he had written 'Corn Rigs are Bonie.' When Rankine heard the gossip about Robert and Lizzie he was moved to write to Mossgiel. Was Robert indeed the begetter of this new Tarbolton parishioner? If so, he was a sad, bad young fellow—but Lord, how much less sad and bad than the worthies who gloried in his fall, with eyes turned up and mouths turned down! The writer would be glad to have Mossgiel's account of the affair. It was a quizzing but sympathetic letter—a comradely slap on the back. A reply came promptly—and in verse. Prose could not voice the gratitude and sudden joy. It was an hilarious acknowledgment of the Paton affair—surely the least contrite confession ever penned—with the impudent opening

I am a keeper of the law
In some sma' points, although not a'.

For the first time Rob the Rhymer stretched himself and was at his ease among familiar friends; and by that outward ease what had hitherto been only a tremulous defiance was changed into a smiling confidence. He knew how shallow his shame in Mauchline church had been, and how deep was his contempt for poor old 'Daddy' Auld, for the gaping gossips, for the tight-lipped Armours and their kind, even for his own humiliation. In this knowledge contempt gave way to

laughter, and laughter to serene acceptance. Of course if his
father had been there, to suffer and make him suffer, it would
have been different; but as it was—well, one could put one's
fingers to one's nose and pass on.

In this new assurance he presently wrote again to Rankine—an epistle—enclosing a few poems. The epistle was
in verse. It was long, brilliant and quite shameless.

> As soon's the clocking-time is by,
> And the wee pouts begun to cry,
> Lord, I'se hae sportin' by and by,
>   For my gowd guinea:
> Though I should herd the buckskin kye
>   For 't in Virginia.

To his delight he found that to write an epistle in verse was
easier than the elegant Augustan letter-writing that he had
practised with such pains, as well as being far more
satisfactory. The lines came at call. They stepped after the
fashion of Ramsay's epistles, but—and he recognised it with
a leaping pulse—they were charged with a fun and feeling
that was all his own. The 'Epistle to John Rankine' marks the
end of Rob the Rhymer and the beginning of Robert Burns
the poet. When 'the clocking-time' was by—that is when the
baby Lizzie was born—he wrote 'The Poet's Welcome to his
Bastart Wean,' the rollicking and tender verses that set the
seal on his defiance. He had achieved paternity and poetry
and what did anything else matter? He could even think of
himself from the death-bed point of view; and with a heart
warmed to the man who had held out a hand to him at the
right moment, he wrote his own first epitaph:

> He who of Rankine sang lies stiff and dead
> And a green grassy hillock haps his head.
> Alas, alas, a devilish change indeed!

In November young John died, and they buried him in
Mauchline churchyard. For this funeral they could afford
only a 'second quality' mort-cloth. Things were not looking
very bright on the farm. The first Mossgiel harvest failed
through Robert's having bought bad seed. The later crop was
ruined by the heavy cold rains that beat the hay to the ground
and left the corn blackening in the ear long after the reaping
time. Barely the half was saved. At the oncoming of winter

Near Mossgiel was a mire of what the agricultural writers of the day called 'obstinate shiftus,'—a dense, slippery clay as heart-breaking as the stones of Mount Oliphant or the moss of Lochlie. 'Friends of the poor' have not infrequently an eye to their own benefit. Hamilton was exacting a high rent. But the more fate worked against Robert as a farmer, the more he gave himself to poetry. Day after day, as he ploughed for the winter wheat, he composed all the while, and every night he wrote down what he had made during the day. There was no effort, only abandonment and a sense of mastery in production. Through the years of foggy, aimless and often unhappy pursuit of a learning from which he could foresee no good results, he had been shaping the instrument that now lay ready to his hand. English and Scotish poets—good and bad, but mostly indifferent—he had studied, mimicked and stolen from: all had been haphazard and he had been given little choice. His poetical lineage was far from pure. Even on the Scotish side he was very much on the wrong side of the blanket. Of Dunbar, Henryson, Douglas and the old 'makars' he knew nothing. From Ramsay he had absorbed a poetic speech—an artful, though natural-seeming blend of English with Scotish words, that easily passed as the mother tongue, but was far more flexible. From Fergusson he had learned that the humblest and homeliest themes were the best for treatment by this composite vocabulary. As long as he could remember, the rhythms of Scotish folk-song and the refrains of nameless bards had rung in his ears like the pulsing of his blood. His borrowings were extensive and unashamed; his subjects were seldom new, his metres never. Yet the poems which now flowed from Mossgiel had every one the freshness of a mountain spring.

The figure of water persists. From childhood a running— or as he liked to call it, a 'trotting'—stream had been the very image of beauty to Robert, and until his dying day it was his symbol of life and song. Now that he was giving himself up to life and to singing, it was his fancy—pleased with his own name—to call himself Robin Ruisseaux. He would look to his native streams for the inspiration he had sought in vain from bookshelves. The Ayr, with its high red cliffs, should be his library, the leafy Faile his lexicon, the chattering Coyle his college. As a conscious poet he would capture something of the 'wild irregularity,' the 'warbling cadence,' the 'heart-moving melody' that belonged to these waters as to the people's song. His blood threw off, if only for a time, the weakening virus of Scotish education.[4] He could treat learning lightly and so disregard the long inferiority and strain it had imposed upon him. Men went into college 'stirks and came out asses.' He could even laugh at his own weakness for clerkliness. And with this impassioned substitution of brooks for books went a further hearty resignation and acceptance. He was able to write now without bitterness—as one who, having despised his heritage, rediscovers it as something doubly precious—'my compeers, the common people.'

There are country vintages, heady, full-bodied and pure, that will not travel. Apart even from the difficulties of language, it is hard for casual readers of print to appraise the unique flavour and potency of the poems written by Robert Burns between his twenty-sixth and twenty-eighth year. They have survived in spite of the printed page rather than because of it. There is a very real sense in which they are not 'printable.' Though he took to writing them down, even the longest narrative poems were composed and vocally communicated to others before pen was put to paper. The epistles, crammed with local and personal allusions, were despatched direct to the friends for whom they were particularly designed, in Robert's clear, characteristic handwriting—next most intimate thing to speech—with the ink hardly dry upon them. The songs, written directly to music, were intended to be sung. The epigrams, epitaphs, satires and character-sketches were for tavern laughter, secret handing about, or, when all else failed, for furtive display on the prickles of a roadside bush.

Notwithstanding his unceasing activity as a poet Robert reached his twenty-seventh year without the idea of making a printed book. His contemplation of print went no further than that some day, perhaps through the kindness of Hamilton, he might get a stray piece or two published in an Edinburgh magazine. Yet this was enough to make him write everything down and continually work over and improve what he had written—always taking special pains with pieces that had met with applause on their first hearing. The calling, which he had with his whole heart accepted, was not that of world poet, but of rustic bard. A bard cannot be independent of listeners. His first business is to enlarge his circle; he dare not diminish it. Robert Burns was a greatly gifted artist and he knew it. He was quite capable of the 'take it or leave it' attitude, but he had to consider his circumstances. If ever poet produced to please and amuse a known audience it was he. It was not for him to shoot arrows into the air, but to aim darts in the presence of witnesses (including rivals) at a visible mark—and a village mark at that. Village critics are nothing if not critical. The humility thus enforced had its reward in a supple and perfect craftsmanship.

With a new piece he was wariness itself. First he tried it on Gilbert or on Smith or on the womenfolk, watching their reception carefully, enjoying their praise with heartfelt joy, acquiescing in their indifference, inferring the nature of their disapproval and calculating its worth. He endured and made use of his listeners' comments. Never would he be able to endure or make use of criticism that professed to be literary.

His first attempt at satire was as safe to himself as it was damaging to its helpless object. At a Lodge meeting early that spring he had been annoyed by the prosiness of the Tarbolton schoolmaster, a harmless but self-important creature who supplemented his wretched stipend by selling groceries and quack medicines, adding to the latter 'advice in common disorders given gratis.' On his way home Robert imagined a dialogue between himself and Death, in which Death grumbled at this village competitor in a fashion that exposed his absurdity to perfection. Gilbert's malicious rapture, when he heard it repeated next day at the plough, was so evident that Robert had no doubt of a successful circulation. To all save its victim it gave the same immediate, intense delight. The author had to spend far more time in making copies for handing about than had gone to the making of the original.[1]

Being now assured of laughter he grew bolder. Having ranged himself with the New Lights—a position that was no departure from his father's teaching, but only a passionate intensification of it made easier by the trend of the times, the Old Lights became his natural butt. His first opportunity came when two Old Light ministers fell out publicly over a childish practical joke that one had played on the other while out on their ponies. Robert celebrated the occasion in 'The Twa Herds.' For so jubilant a performance the family circle was too small. Making a copy in a disguised hand he passed it nonchalantly to Hamilton, alleging that it was by a fellow unknown to him, that he himself thought it 'pretty clever,' but that he would be glad of another opinion. Hamilton, who was not deceived, laughed himself nearly into an apoplexy and took good care that it went the round. It met with a particularly discerning and unchristian welcome in New Light manses. Robert acknowledged it. He made many copies in an undisguised hand and knew that next time he could go twice as far. From ministers to lawyers, from bellowing farmers to smirking schoolmasters, through parishes as much as five miles away, the satire circulated. One appreciative reader sent a laboriously rhymed epistle of his own to Mossgiel. Robert responded eagerly and easily—his wit alight, his sensitiveness basking in the warmth of approval. More and more such 'letters' went flying out from Mossgiel to known and unknown friends. Before he had even thought seriously of printing a line he had won an eager public within his five-mile radius.

Any notion of Robert as a dreamy-eyed young man weaving rhymes while loitering behind the plough, is as prettified as his portraits. An unwelcome energy informed his speech and his movements. Into his Freemasonry, his friendships and loves, he poured the full violence of living. Increasingly sure of a hearing from the best minds about him he was wildly stimulated by the head-wagging of the others. He walked godlike on his slopes, breathing poetry as he breathed the air, without effort or forethought. The germ of a poem came into being for him—a line, a verse or a string of verses—without his volition. But once there, he grasped and worked at it with artful ardour. His power of improvisation became stupendous. In race week, after a more than usually entertaining session at Poosie Nancie's, he threw off for his tavern companions a 'cantata' called *Love and Liberty*, which consisted of eight pieces of rhymed narrative and as many songs with choruses.[2] Even his less memorable improvisations reveal the sureness of a finished artist. So great an excitement cannot be continent. It overflows in all directions. Even on the farm Robert worked, for a time at least, not less but far harder than in his father's lifetime. He lifted heavier loads than anyone else, ploughed a straighter, quicker furrow, threw a truer cast of seed and showed his practical ingenuity in many ways, including the invention of a new, painless method of unhorning steers. Everything in his fields was fuel to his flame—the failing crops, the rain or hoar, the field mouse scuttling from the ploughshare or the daisy bowing before it, the gaunt old mare waiting patiently for him—all were the stuff of poetry. His glance became more arrogant than ever, and more dangerous. If any woman could have resisted him at this time her name was not Jean Armour.

'The Twa Herds' angered but did not alarm the Old Lights. They never guessed that it was merely a sighting shot and that the real bombardment was still to come. If they had, they might not have exposed themselves as rashly as they presently did. In a fatal moment Mauchline Kirk-session resolved upon a moral purgation of the parish. The moving spirit in this was not the minister, but one of the elders, William Fisher by name, who enjoyed great influence in Old Light circles owing to his doctrinal austerity, though it was whispered that his private and practical austerity was—at least in certain respects—not so marked. With a courage unusual at that time the Kirk-session directed their attack against upper-class persons on the reasonable ground that the lower orders could not be expected to behave unless their betters showed them a good example. Gavin Hamilton, who was notoriously lax in his church attendance, was in the first batch of victims. He was cited before the Session and formally reprimanded. Well able to look after himself, he appealed to the Presbytery of Ayr which, while piously enjoining Sabbath observance, sustained the appeal, absolved the appellant from censure, and pronounced the Mauchline Session over-zealous. The discomfited Session took the case from the Presbytery to the Synod of Ayr, only to have their defeat confirmed.

Robert, who had delightedly attended his patron throughout the proceedings, celebrated the triumph with 'Holy Willie's Prayer.' As usual he read it first to the family circle. They laughed—it was impossible not to laugh—but they were appalled even in their laughter. The poem was scurrilous, brutal, indecent, and horribly profane. They implored him not to circulate it. But their entreaties fell on deaf ears. By this time Robert's eyes were fixed on a horizon beyond the Ayrshire border and he was reckless. Besides he had known that his family would be shocked. The point was that they had laughed in spite of themselves. Laughter was the true test of 'Holy Willie's' quality.

So it proved. Not Hamilton and his circle alone, but the whole opposing faction of the Moderates[3] hailed it with unholy glee, and various quite unshocked reverends became anxious to see and shake by the hand this rustic with the deadly command of ridicule. Hamilton was willing to introduce his tenant who, on such occasions, did great credit alike to his landlord and his father. The curious among the black-coats were presented to a tallish, round-shouldered, fine-eyed but coarse-featured young man of great assurance. The assurance, backed by admirable English and ready quotations from the most elegant authors, impressed them perhaps more than the verses themselves. But when the young farmer took his leave a certain thoughtfulness, not wholly pleasant, descended upon his would-be patrons. One at least of the New Light ministers, surprised on a Sunday by the unlooked-for sight of Mossgiel's black eye-brows amid his congregation, was so much overcome by nervousness that he could hardly continue with his discourse. As bard and satirist this fellow had to be reckoned with. He now numbered readers in Ayr, in Maybole, in Kilmarnock, in Irvine, as well as in the villages and farms and country mansions—below and above stairs. In one house at least which might be reckoned county[4] copies of his songs, bestowed by him amorously in the kitchen, had found their way to the drawing-room. The lady had bidden him come up for her inspection. In the act of making pretty, patronising speeches, she had found herself unmistakably excited.

But most of the Mauchline neighbours were nervous of themselves and jealous of him. Petty and uneasy in their living they disapproved of Mossgiel and his works. He was too provocative and perilous a member of their society. His chosen associates—publicans and sinners—would alone have marked him out for suspicion in a Christian society. In addition he was an acknowledged leader in impudent immorality. Instead of conducting fellow-bachelors, as at Tarbolton, along the path of mutual improvement—although he had talked of a 'Conversation Club' at Mauchline—he had formed a gang which called itself the 'Rebel Four' and of which fornication was the principal and avowed interest. At Tarbolton it had been necessary for each member of Robert's club to be 'in love,' but for membership of the Mauchline 'Club of Fornicators' a man must have given proof of his fruitfulness. Richmond, Smith and another lad named Hunter, all still under twenty, had so qualified under Robert's stimulating guidance. Each awaited his summons to the cutty stool in consequence, and they made it a habit to meet at Johny Dove's, there to review, condemn and sentence in mock tribunal those of their neighbours— especially the old and reputable like Mr Fisher, whom they believed to be no better than themselves but merely more careful in escaping consequences. The idea of this 'Court of Equity'—to give it the more decent of its titles—was Robert's, inspired no doubt by his attendance at Gavin

Hamilton's case. A grotesque blend of Scots civil and ecclesiastical procedure was invented. Robert, of course, presided as judge, Smith was fiscal, Richmond clerk, and Hunter messenger-at-arms. The preses himself drew up the decrees of the Court in rhyme. These met with much applause.[5]

From its nature the institution had no permanency, and it broke up that spring. Richmond, having stood in church over an affair with a girl called Jenny Surgeoner, fled to an office in Edinburgh. Smith—clever and careless, the one of all the young men Robert loved best—was in particular disgrace. His 'fault'—a servant of his mother's—was more than twice his age, so that he was become a laughing stock as well as an 'example' in the village; and though he made it a point that none should laugh more than he, he would presently depart to Linlithgow. In prospect of his going (though it would not be for some time) Robert made for him this tender epitaph:

> Lament him, Mauchline husbands a',
>   He aften did assist ye;
> For had ye staid whole years awa,
>   Your wives they ne'er had missed ye.
> Ye Mauchline bairns, as on ye pass
>   To school in bands thegither,
> Oh, tread ye lightly on his grass—
>   Perhaps he was your father.

As for the preses himself, early in the year Jean Armour had discovered to him that once more he 'wore the promised father's tender name.' It was embarrassing—the more so that her father was a brother Mason. But he was very fond of her. He would do the right thing by her. He would make her his wife at once, though privately, by the simple exchange of consent which satisfies Scots Law and can later be converted into a public and regular marriage by registration in legal form. His clear conscience, together with the knowledge of her condition—which pleased him in spite of his embarrassment—rendered their meetings and partings all the sweeter during the few weeks before the 'holy beagles'—as he named the Kirk authorities—had nosed out their secret. He gave Jean a written declaration of marriage to which both put their signatures (Jean's scholarship was confined to signing her own name with difficulty) in the presence of Smith and another witness. Besides these marriage lines he gave her others—a woman's love song such as many a woman would fain have written but no woman ever could:

O wha my babie-clouts will buy?
Wha will tent me when I cry?
Wha will kiss me where I lie?
   The rantin dog, the daddie o't.

Wha will own he did the faut?
Wha will buy my groanin-maut?
Wha will tell me how to ca't?
   The rantin dog, the daddie o't.

When I mount the creepie-chair,
Wha will sit beside me there?
Gie me Rob, I'll seek nae mair,
   The rantin dog, the daddie o't.

Wha will crack to me my lane?
Wha will mak me fidgin fain?
Wha will kiss me o'er again?
   The rantin dog, the daddie o't.

She had become the nucleus about which his recurrent dreams of marriage and a fireside and children of his own reassembled. At Shrovetide the Burneses had given a party, and, sitting round the fire in the room Robert loved as he had never loved any other room, they and their guests had given story and song about. One song was of married happiness. It was new to Robert and moved him deeply. 'When I upon thy bosom lean . . .' it began. And when he learned that it was by an old Ayrshire man named Lapraik,[6] living some twelve miles eastward, he had begun to send fervent epistles to the author. Once more he was almost as much in love with marriage as with poetry. Jean went to Paisley—her parents having judged it wise to absent her from Mauchline for a time—but he thought of her none the less securely and passionately and honourably.

Sitting one midnight in the same parlour where the singing had been, listening to the rats in the rafters, pondering over his difficult situation, he vowed himself formally and all afresh to a Scotish Muse that was clothed in flesh much resembling the flesh of Miss Armour, especially about the legs. Crowned with holly, the rural goddess appeared to him in the firelight. The sublimity of the occasion demanded a tribute—a long, sustained poem in an elevated direction almost English. This he achieved before going to bed. Master now of his craft, and fortified further by a vision, his productiveness doubled. Henceforward not one of his correspondents—not even the Surveyor of Taxes—was too prosaic for a poetic reply.

It is not given to all to be creative, even for a brief space during their lifetime; to few is it given to be creative for long. Perhaps the supreme test of human conduct—of simple goodness and worth—may lie in our reception of this condition in ourselves and in others, when it exists. Its recognition and welcome—perhaps nothing else in life is so important, seeing that life continues only by new creation. Certainly the suppression, impediment, persecution of individuals possessed by the inconvenient fury by which we all live has been our wickedest activity down the ages, as to deny or ignore the fury itself has been our stupidest. Robert had accepted his holly wreath, prickles and all. He was a man inspired. The more innocent of the beings near him rejoiced therefore. It was his coming that the penned-up cattle welcomed most loudly, and on his knees that the children clamoured to sit. His mother, Gilbert and his sisters, though he caused them misgivings and could give them no help, bowed happily and simply before him and were meekly proud of his fame. When Lizzie's baby was weaned and he wished to have the child, she was brought to Mossgiel and his mother cared for her. They did not, could not approve of his doings nor of many of his poems; yet they let him be, and their kindness never wavered.

He considered them too. The farm was going from bad to worse after the failure of their second crop. He had not been, could not be, very helpful. Soon—as he saw no chance of an early registration of his marriage with its weight of responsibility—he would bring another scandal on the house. He must go away across the detested sea. As early as February, with this idea firmly fixed in his mind, he went into Ayr and obtained the promise of a certain Dr Douglas that he would write to his brother in Jamaica asking if there were any posts for book-keepers on his estate. It would be many weeks before the reply could come, but from the moment of that interview Robert took his departure for granted and looked on Mauchline with the eyes of an emigrant.

With the sound of the sea in his ears and his gaze upon the mountains of Jamaica, his life took on a new intensity. Like one condemned to death and standing full of health and youth before the grave he has dug with his own hands, he was beside himself. He had always dramatised himself. Now he saw himself from the outside as never before, dead and gone, and the place where all his life had been spent knowing him no more. In sober prose, a penniless man who went from Scotland to Jamaica was as good as dead and gone; and Robert was a poet. Loving Scotland, particularly loving Ayrshire, he endured immediately the nostalgia that lay before him, and immediately savoured the emptiness of his fields, his riverside walks, his tavern seats, when he should be gone. Like his father thirty-eight years earlier he looked backward and forward at once and was gathered up in anguished perception. But he was not like his father, dumb. Under the pressure and in the agitation he determined to create a memorial of himself. He would make a printed book.

Well-placed friends—Ballantine, an Ayr banker, and Muir, a Kilmarnock wine-merchant, encouraged the idea: but it was really the mountains of Jamaica and the equally unconscious Jean that between them had urged him to a frenzy stronger than his timidity. He had long known that his poems were good. His only doubts had been as to their reception, and these were removed with his own imminent removal. To be praised after he was gone, to be spoken of as a 'clever fellow,' even if it never reached his ears, would sweeten exile: to be blamed or called foolish could not trouble him with the seas between: it would indeed be better than not to be spoken of at all. And there the book would be for his friends at least to remember him by. He had sowed bad seed in the Mossgiel earth; but with a wife and two children and a book, the soil of Scotland would have something of him for ever,—no matter whether he returned to claim his harvest or died of fever far away.

He knew the book would have to be published by subscription. He did not expect or wish to make a penny by it. What had poetry and pence to do with one another? His holly-decked muse would never consent to print on any mercenary excuse, nor would his bardly pride endure it. For fame and fame alone he would publish. If, between them, he and his now considerable circle of manuscript readers could muster enough subscribers to cover the printing and binding of a modestly priced volume, he would be more than content.[7]

He sounded several printers—one as far away as Glasgow—unsuccessfully. Seeing that his scheme was impracticable without influence he consulted Hamilton. Hamilton thought well of it—was indeed enthusiastic. (Rent was owing for Mossgiel.) Robert had already confided his emigration plans to the Clerk, from whom it was that he had the introduction to Dr Douglas of Ayr.

Still more enthusiastic than Hamilton was one of his friends, Mr Aiken, lawyer and Surveyor of Taxes at Ayr. This fat little man, known locally as 'Orator Bob' from his love of spouting,[8] was the most vocal of all the admirers of young Mossgiel's verses, and had done more than any other single individual to make them known. He wore tight clothes, and his test of a poem was the number of buttons that his emotion burst from him when he declaimed it. Soon after the mooting of the publication project, he received one that made the buttons pop off like whinpods in August. It was a long, highly polished idyll in a measure and manner such as no Scotish poet had ever before attempted. There and then 'Orator Bob' made up his mind. Rob Mossgiel was far more than a village virtuoso. If he chose he might command the applause of the most refined and elevated circles. 'The Cotter's Saturday Night' proved it.[9]

In the first days of April Robert drew up the following:

PROPOSALS for publishing, by subscription,
SCOTTISH POEMS, by Robert Burns.

The work to be elegantly printed, in one volume octavo.
Price stitched, three shillings. As the author has not the
most distant mercenary view in publishing, as soon as so
many subscribers appear as will defray the necessary
expense the work will be sent to the press.

> Set out the brunt side of your shin,
> For pride in poets is nae sin:
> Glory's the prize for which they rin,
>   And Fame's their joe;
> And wha blaws best his horn shall win,
>   And wharefore no?

It was run off by a Kilmarnock printer named Wilson,
whom Aiken and Hamilton had found for him.

But April brought other business besides publication proposals. On the first Thursday of the month the Kirk-session of
Mauchline met. The Rev William Auld, moderator, having
information that Jean Armour had left the parish in such
circumstances as to leave behind her a *fama clamosa*, moved
the court accordingly, and Messrs William Fisher and James
Lamie, elders, were appointed to speak to the parents. A
week later the two 'holy beagles' walked up the Cowgate and
knocked at the Armours' door. Mrs Armour opened. Her
husband had taken care to be out.

After the usual village preliminaries the mission was
disclosed. Was it true, what all Mauchline was saying,
that Jean was with child, and to Robert Mossgiel? Or could
Mrs Armour contradict and utterly abolish the deplorable
report?

Mrs Armour was powerful in ignorance, stout in surprise.
There was certainly nothing, she assured her visitors, so bad
to be said of Mossgiel that she and Mr Armour would not
gladly say worse. But did they not know that poor Jean was at
Paisley with her uncle Purdie the carpenter merely by way of
a change? And that she was as good as tokened to young
Robert Wilson the weaver, who was doing well himself there
now, and was devoted to the girl, visiting her constantly at
her uncle's house—ay, and giving her valuable presents?
The Session had surely been misled. But Jean would shortly
be home again and could then reply to the baseless charges
herself. Meanwhile would not Mr Fisher and Mr Lamie take
a little drop of something? If Mr Armour had not so
unfortunately been out he would have offered them snuff as
well. Refreshed but unconvinced, the hounds of heaven went
on their way.

A few days later Robert entered the Armours' kitchen to

find both husband and wife awaiting him. He knew, as did all the parish, of the deputation. He knew also that Jean's departure to Paisley had been arranged by her parents in the full consciousness of her condition. And he was aware that Jean's mention of the marriage paper, which he had given her to be her shield and buckler, had only angered them the more. But Jean in her hurried last meeting with him had not been her usual frank self. She had been hiding something from him. What this was he must now find out. At the same time he would dispose of the *fama clamosa* by showing his own honest, husbandly hand.

He had strengthened himself for the interview by turning in upon his way at Johny Dove's in Main Street.[1] Not only was Dove's connected very practically with his love for Jean, but the occasion called for extra sustenance. Of late, under the stress of life and the excitement of impending publication, Robert had discovered anew what magical virtue lay for him at the bottom of a well-timed glass. He was not given to drink—neither his purse nor his stomach would stand it. But was he oppressed by one of those moods of gloom, self-distrust, impotent rebellion, which dulled his every faculty? Was his Muse sluggish or timid? Was he unable to face the world with the kingly gesture that best suited his soul? Let him only take a fair swallow of Scotch drink and all was well again.

So, though the Armours' greeting was frankly hostile, he felt himself perfectly in command of the situation. Prepared for reproaches he bore them equably. The author of 'The Cotter's Saturday Night' heard himself accused of 'studied, sly, ensnaring art' and of 'perjured, dissembling, smoothness.' He had sat at the board of a fellow-cottager, had knelt at evening worship with him; and how had he repaid his host? By seducing the daughter of the house—a girl trusting, inexperienced, respectable, and so much younger than himself!

It had to be admitted. Robert was able to go further and glory in it—beneath the meekness of admission. For his was the complete reply of marriage. Secure in his husbandly status and in the modicum of drink taken, he pointed out that Jean was his wife. He had given her his signed declaration. The child would be legitimate. Did the Armours doubt the existence of the paper? He could assure them solemnly that Jean had it, and it merely awaited public confirmation, which could be given at any time. So long as neither party repudiated it, the marriage was and would remain valid. For his part he would stand to it, privately and publicly. Could they ask more?

They could and did. Mr Armour could ask, for instance, about the Mossgiel crops and the arrears of rent owed to Mr Hamilton. And Mrs Armour could frame a still more pointed questionnaire anent Lizzie Paton's baby. Suppose, for the sake of argument, that Jean did possess the paper he described, what sort of provision could such a husband as Robert make for a master builder's daughter?

Taken aback but still on his mettle, Robert outlined his plans as attractively as possible. He was bound to admit that he had not at the moment much to show in a worldly sense. But if they would have a little patience and kindness . . . If Jean could remain with them yet awhile, he would sail to the West Indies, work there hard as any slave, and return as soon as he had money enough to set up house for her and his child. And of course he would send home to her all he could spare. Mauchline would know she was his wife. With persuasive art he conjured up the picture of himself returning prosperous across the Atlantic. Though as yet no reply had come from Dr Douglas's brother, he felt as certain of a Jamaica post as if it had already been offered and accepted. Nor was this easy optimism—a thing of which Robert in his most heightened moments was incapable. It was simply that Jamaica was easy as hell to get to once the mind was set—if not *via* Dr Douglas then by some other channel.

But the Armours were not impressed. Ramming a huge pinch of snuff up his wide-winged nostrils[2] Mr Armour pronounced the name of McLure. Robert might hoodwink a poor creature of a Tarbolton landlord, the Tarbolton people being notoriously 'uncontaminated by reading, reflection or conversation'[3] but the men of Mauchline were not so easily beguiled. Irregular marriages even with witnesses had been repudiated before now, and would be again. In any case everybody knew what happened to penniless young men of loose character who indentured themselves for the plantations. Many things happened; but a speedy and eligible return to their native village was not one of them.

What Robert had not counted upon was the strong, personal detestation of the Armours toward himself—the hatred of him and of all he stood for, which overbore even their care for Jean and their considerations of family honour. It was notorious in Mauchline that Mr Armour could not 'bear the sight of' Mossgiel. If Robert was the last to realise their loathing he saw it now clearly enough in Mrs Armour's eyes, heard it in her malicious words, repaid it with a sudden and violent hatred of his own. But how far reduced he was, how deeply stung by the truths thus painfully brought home, how determined to establish at all costs his good faith, emerged in his response to their jibes. He offered to give up Jamaica. He would become a common labourer. He had failed as a farmer, but even the Armours must allow that he was a first-rate ploughman. As such he could offer Jean a poor but immediate and honest roof. It was a hard thing, but it was practicable, and he would do it.

Now when the suppliant was stripped and humbled, as much by his own hand as by theirs, was the moment for the Armours to let fly their poisoned shaft. On no account, they informed him, would they have him for a son-in-law, now or later, marriage paper or no marriage paper. And they had happily brought Jean to their way of thinking. Not only had they heard of his precious declaration of marriage from her lips, but they had it in their keeping and from her own hands. As a sign of her repentance and submission she had given it up to them before going away to do with as they should think fit. If it were legal they could not annul it, but they chose to be doubtful of its legality, and on the first opportunity they were going to consult Mr Aiken at Ayr. With Jean things were arranging themselves at Paisley without help from Robert. The faithful and eligible Wilson had been told of her imprudence and was willing to overlook it. Already she had accepted from him the financial aid which her betrayer, with all his papers and protestations, had not yet offered. Her marriage with the admirable weaver was merely a question of time. There, where her lapse would not be known, she would settle down when the date was convenient. The child, of course, if it lived, would be conferred upon the Mossgiel household as soon as it was weaned.

Robert took his leave so quietly that the Armours could only hope their hatefullest that he was covering his hurt by a mighty effort of will. In reality he was for the moment stupefied by the force and unexpectedness of his defeat. As he crossed the green with his long heavy steps and passed the church, he was deaf even to the clamour of the building rooks in the great ash tree. But turning into Backcauseway he came mercilessly to himself, and when he plunged into his friend the haberdasher's little dark shop he was in the grip of a lunatic frenzy. His rejection by Alison Begbie had been nothing to this concerted rejection. He was seared so deep in the quick of his pride and his manhood that he felt his sanity trembling. Smith, who, unlike Richmond, was genuinely fond of Jean, perceived that any word for her must wait. Robert could see only that she had lied, broken faith, sided with her horrible parents—especially with her thrice horrible mother—against him in his rôle of husband. And from this to believing that she had betrayed him also in love was but a step. Did he not know how ready a lover she was, and in this readiness how irresistible to men? Was she not as realistic and immediate in her habit as he was himself idealistic and remote? Since finding herself with child by him she had demanded his embraces more insistently than ever, enjoyed them more frankly. And here she was willingly exiled, taking money from this base mechanic, seeing him every day, appealing womanlike to his lust or chivalry or both! If Wilson had indeed offered her marriage, it was surely as a forsaken woman or because the Armours had bribed him—in any case as part of the Armour plot in which Jean was implicated. But perhaps the story of the offer was merely a part of the plot in being a lie? Perhaps the weaver was only out for his own fun, so that Jean was as greatly to be pitied in the future as blamed in the present? Let her suffer then! The one clear thing was that she had conspired to be rid of him—all because he was poor, unlucky, outspoken, a poet, instead of being a prosperous hypocrite! Rid of

him she should be. As she had chosen to repudiate the
marriage, so would he. He could easily control his witnesses.
There were other girls in Mauchline. Yet how he had loved
her!

Thus Robert returned to Mossgiel to the polishing and
preparation of his poems for the press. Taking from his table
drawer *The Vision*, he removed Jean's name from the passage
wherein her legs were described, and put in Lizzie Paton's
instead. If indeed it were to see print, the honour of those legs
would belong not to the 'perjured' and he feared 'eternally to
be damned' Armour, but to poor devoted Bess. Glad enough
would Bess have been had he given her a paper of marriage
with all the seas between. Not that he had the least intention
of so gladdening her.

Within the next day or two he called at Mr Aiken's office in
Ayr. The busy little tax surveyor and man of feeling bade his
visitor be seated, but though friendly as ever he was not in
oratorical vein. Watchful rather. Indeed restless as a hen on a
hot girdle. That same morning he had received Mr Armour,
and had given advice, with the result that Robert's and Jean's
names had been cut out from the marriage paper, which, thus
mutilated, remained in Armour's hands.

In spite of what he already knew—in spite too of his belief
that Jean was no longer anything to him—Robert, when he
heard this, felt as if the disfiguring knife were scoring his
heart. The blood drummed in his temples; his face darkened
and was contorted; he uttered words of accusation, repudiation, self-defence. Never had Mr Aiken less need of strong
attachment to his waistcoat buttons. He was deflated. Yet he
still felt that he could take the Armour point of view without
forfeiting his patronage of Robert; and as that young man
stalked away estranged beneath the piazzas, he consoled
himself by determining to do everything in his power for the
poor fellow's book. His office was one of the best centres in
Ayrshire for circulation and advertisement. Approving as he
did the sound of his own voice in declamation, secure as he
usually was from slighting behaviour—for it was the interest
of most callers to keep on terms with him—he should be able
to dispose of more subscription bills than anybody else, and
to do so more fruitfully. So his benevolent chest swelled once
more.

Before leaving the town by the Old Bridge, to which
a modern rival was soon to be built a little way down
stream, Robert turned in at Simpson's. If all else in Scotland
failed him there was still Scotch drink. Let him sip it while
he might, and feel his tumults turn under its benison to
ordered verses. There was drink and there was poetry.
The Old Bridge outside—so old that its origins were
mythical—would, as night fell, be grumbling sadly against
the grand new Adam structure. Robert had seen the plans
for this. Now he began to imagine a dialogue between the
bridges, which might well be modelled after one of Fergusson's poems—a piece in which causeways and pavements
were the protagonists. In moonlight and to the sound of
running water there would go forward the eternal debate
between Old and New. So on the worn seat where his father
and Murdoch had pledged their bargain twenty years before,
he for whom they had planned, drank a fierier potion laced
with his own genius; and all the way home to Mossgiel their
honest efforts came to blossom in his brain. At the same time
in the stuffy little burgh office he had left, the busy,
well-meaning insect powers of Aiken were planning successfully how to combine the furthering of poetry with self-
conceit.

At the farm Robert found awaiting him printed sheets of
his proposals—a whole eight dozen of them assigned to
himself for distribution. They were far more than he knew
what to do with, but late into the night he sat addressing
copies (often accompanied by a long and bawdy letter) to all
the people he could think of as in any degree interested.[4] To
save expense he would have to deliver many himself. His
farm work would suffer. It was already seriously suffering.
Sitting up night after night with pen and paper after the
others were abed, he found himself unable to rise when they
were stirring in the morning—for he was not one who could
go without his sleep. His family understood these things.
They had been generous. But he knew it was time he made
over Mossgiel to Gilbert. Every letter of this period contains
fears of the disgrace that might follow his publication. He
must go away.

To the last, of course, neither he nor his family would

consider that he should be excused his modicum of daily duties on the farm. But now he and his fields were seen always against the alien background of Jamaica. The noise of the dread Atlantic was in his ears, the thunder-cloud of ruin and death hovered overhead. The colours were intense, the forms significant in every detail as just before a storm. Each object, each smallest creature and flower, was bathed in the rainbow light of farewell. It was the same indoors. He dandled his baby Lizzie and returned her cheeky black stare with one of paternal passion. Anyhow *she* was his; and he would leave all he had to her when the world had done its worst. Trying to record one-thousandth part of what he saw and felt, he covered paper in a fury (and that too cost money!). Of his many long letters some would have done credit to Mr Micawber, others to Joseph Surface; others again—and these his best—might have come from the hand of Joseph's brother. And as fast as he wrote letters he wrote poems.[5] He wrote a rhymed dedication of his book to Gavin Hamilton, bade farewell in verse to Scotland, to Jean (and several other girls), to the Freemasons, to various men friends and to himself. One of these last was a gay and flattering ode 'On a Scotch Bard gone to the West Indies,' another a pleading and remorseful epitaph. He wrote Laments and Odes to Ruin and Despondency. He penned twelve lines of heartfelt denunciation on the back of a pound-note. It was in this vehement agitation and deep passion of leave-taking, not in any mood of pastoral reverie, that he made the verses to the mountain daisy:

> Ev'n thou who mourn'st the Daisy's fate,
> That fate is thine—no distant date;
> Stern Ruin's ploughshare drives, elate,
>   Full on thy bloom,
> Till, crush'd beneath the furrow's weight,
>   Shall be thy doom!

Never was a young man more dangerous to women, never women more necessary to a young man. Robert believed he had overcome any lingering fondness for Jean. But as the weeks of her absence were prolonged the urgency of his deprivation became extreme. For the first time he occasionally went to a tavern to get drunk. La Rochefoucauld has

pointed out that 'the heart, while still agitated by the remains
of one passion, is more susceptible of another than when
entirely at rest,' and besides that Robert had the desperate
desire to leave a wife behind him in Scotland. He began to
hover hawklike over Mauchline. He saw himself as a hawk or
a stalking fox that had the mountains of Jamaica as its cover.
But though the girls of Mauchline liked him and were ready
enough for a flirtatious word, they knew too much and were
too worldly-wise to let themselves be taken by so fugitive a
wooer. It was not until he had sighted amid the prudent herd
a little blonde and foreign doe that he was able to strike with
effect.

In the matter of church-going at all times he was regular.
That is to say, he rarely missed going twice each Sunday to
public worship. But his two diets of worship were by no
means always in the same church; for he had the habit of
sermon-tasting, which habit among the intelligent youth
of Scotland continued to a time within living memory as
the sole alleviation of the rigours of Sabbath observance. In
the morning, therefore, he punctually attended his parish
church; but knowing too well the flavour of Daddy Auld's
discourses and wearying of them—though to be sure they
offered to a practised listener fine opportunities for later
reproduction by way of mimicry among cronies—he habitually 'wandered' in the afternoon. Sometimes he went to the
little church at Tarbolton, which was so full of memories
that, sitting there, he grew sentimental: at other times he
went farther afield and might be seen intently drinking in
the Word under strange ministers. He had thus become a
leading authority, not only upon Old and New doctrines, but
upon matters of delivery, phrasing and pulpit demeanour
generally, which with his admirable memory and turn for
caricature was an inexhaustible source of delight to his tavern
friends.

In Tarbolton church the previous summer he had often
observed with interest one of the most modest and devout of
the female worshippers—so much so that for many weeks he
had neglected other afternoon houses of God to concentrate
there. She was young—not so young as Jean but a good five
years less in age than himself; her face was gentle and

steadfast; her hair, long and fine as silk, coiled up under her woollen head-plaid, was perfectly golden. When the minister gave out chapter and verse she was slow to find the place in her small Bible, but once found it was followed with attentive forefinger—all of which to Robert's way of thinking was very 'love-inspiring.' So he had spoken with her and discovered the reason of her extra care and slowness. She was no Ayrshire girl, but was from the Cowal coast of the Firth of Clyde, where they spoke the Gaelic. With pleasure he had heard her soft, singing, delicately broken speech, with delight had looked into her shy, sincere and amiable eyes. He had learned her name—Mary Campbell—that her father, once a preventive man, owned a small coaling vessel, and that she was a dairymaid. It may have been on his recommendation that in November she left her Tarbolton place and became nurse-maid at 'the Castle' to Gavin Hamilton's new baby—his second boy, born that summer.[6] But all through the winter and early spring Jean had been in sturdy possession, and April brought the *fama clamosa*. Even if Mary did not know before, she knew then all that was said of Robert.

She was of the retiring sort. When he asked her one day in April to meet him that evening in the ruined tower of the Abbey she refused. But on hearing from his own lips that he was deserted, that he was free, that he was crazy with a young man's longing and that he wanted a wife, she was not able to go on refusing. For she was in love. La Rochefoucauld might have added as a rider to his other observation that 'the heart, while still agitated by the remains of one passion, is also more likely to inspire passion in another than when it is entirely at rest.' Very soon Robert and Mary were meeting as often as meetings for such work-ridden creatures as themselves were possible—that is to say, every Sunday in daylight and every weekday that could be managed after dark. And because of her outlandishness and his desperation these meetings brimmed with a peculiar sweetness. Jean had been willing with the homely and hearty willingness of a young heifer. But Mary was wilder, gentler in her yielding. She was quiet, superstitious, with a delicacy of spirit and a capacity for sacrifice to which Jean would always be a stranger. She fulfilled his boyish dreams. And he had sought her out and won her, not she him. Would she marry him he asked? Seeing him tender and sincere, she said she would. Would she also trust him? For good reasons they could not immediately celebrate their marriage. Though morally free, Robert had still to receive ecclesiastical discharge from his promise to Jean, which discharge Dr Auld would give him, he was assured, when he had stood in church for his three rebukes.[7] Would Mary trust him? Mary would and did. During the last fortnight of April and the first fortnight of May they loved without reserve. Not even Smith shared their secret. Before May was well advanced Mary knew that in due time she would bear Robert a child.

Meeting at night beneath the still tightly closed buds of the hawthorns the lovers measured themselves against fate. They kissed and made their difficult arrangements. Mary must still trust Robert and do as he said. She could not remain in Mauchline—not till the faintest suspicion might be aroused. Term day—May the fifteenth—was near. She must give the Hamiltons immediate notice on the usual plea that her mother needed her at home to help with the younger children. She would tell her parents that she was tokened and had come home to prepare for her speedy marriage. Robert would send them a letter setting forth his honourable intentions. As soon as things were cleared for him he would come for her; or if this were prevented, she would meet him at Greenock, where she had an uncle in the carpentering line, or at Glasgow—if it was from Glasgow port he would sail. At either place they would be publicly married. They cherished the idea that they might then even sail to the Indies together. In the interval she would not be able to write to him, but he would write to her and send her the songs that welled from his heart at every thought of her.

So they made their plans, as daring and well-meaning a pair of lovers as ever kissed. But Mary was Highland. Before she went she would have Robert swear on the Holy Book itself and would herself so swear. And she would have their vows repeated across running water, so to placate the grudging powers of nature. Only thus could she travel away alone and face her parents.

Robert was the last man to deny these requests. So the jeering prophecy of Mrs Armour was fulfilled. He purported to contract another irregular union. This time he would put such awe upon the woman that she would dread faithlessness as a danger to her very soul. For himself, the more firmly he was committed the better he was pleased. Therefore on Sunday evening, the fourteenth, when Mary's little box was corded in her attic, they met under Stairaird crag at that quiet ferny place where Mauchline burn runs over a shelf of rock into Ayr river. Leaping across the narrower water Robert knelt by Mary's direction (he being less knowing than she in such procedures); and he on the further bank, she on the nearer, they joined hands under the current, thus solemnly to pledge their troth. Then they exchanged the Bibles each had brought. Robert's was a smart, two-volume one, gilt-edged, and with his name, his Mason mark and the Mossgiel address on its fly-leaves. Producing his ink-horn and 'old stumpie,' his quill—which he was used to carry with him for the taking down of stray song-music—he first added Mary's name to his own in each volume, and then he wrote on the blank pages opposite these awful words:

On vol 1—'And ye shall not swear by My Name falsely—I am the Lord.—Levit. 19th chap.: 12th verse.'

And on vol 11—'Thou shalt not forswear thyself, but shalt perform unto the Lord thine Oath.—Matth. 5 Ch.: 33rd Verse.'

What he wrote in Mary's Bible for his own reminder will never be known,[8] but surely it was every bit as solemn and binding. Mary was satisfied that she was truly married according to Scots Law and the Evangel, as well as by the rites of jealous nature. And so indeed she was, unless Robert should choose to perjure himself, which was unthinkable. Next day, sad but confident, she set off on her tedious journey by cart and sail to Campbeltown in Kintyre, where her parents were now living. And Robert, sitting that night in the rat-haunted Mossgiel parlour, his heart melting at the thought of her, his chair balanced on its back legs, composed the following lines—for a son of Mr Aiken's who was leaving home for the first time:[9]

> The sacred lowe o' weel-plac'd love,
>   Luxuriantly indulge it,
> But never tempt th' illicit rove,
>   Tho' naething should divulge it.
> I wave the quantum of the sin,
>   The hazard of concealing;
> But och! it hardens a' within,
>   And petrifies the feeling!

There was nothing of the 'illicit' in his feeling for Mary. He was 'luxuriantly' possessive and had bound himself 'by secret troth and honour's band.' By his own code he was as truly married to her as if all the powers of Church and State had tied the knot. After swinging a while longer on the back legs of his chair and chewing 'old stumpie' he smiled and sat foursquare and wrote further:

> If ye have made a step aside—
>   Some hap mistake o'erta'en you,[10]
> Yet still keep up a decent pride,
>   And ne'er o'er far demean you.
> Time comes wi' kind oblivion's shade,
>   And daily darker sets it;
> And if nae mair mistakes are made,
>   The warld soon forgets it.

Jean came home from Paisley on the 9th of June to find awaiting her a summons to appear before the Kirk-session for interrogation. She had had Robert's letters, but they were too intimate for answering by means of dictation. For many weeks past there had not been a letter to answer. He made no move to communicate with her even now. Her condition would soon be apparent to all—was so already. Her parents were in no comfortable mood. They gave her their version of Robert's visit.

She went round to Smith. Could he not help her with Rab? Though she had given up the marriage paper, it had been under violent pressure. And supposing her parents, with her interests at heart, *had* repudiated it, what was to prevent Rab from still making public acknowledgment of a marriage which had certainly taken place? As friend and as witness to the marriage surely Smith was the person to help her and bring them together. She could assure him that there was nothing in the story of Wilson, except that he was in love with her and willing to marry her if she would take him. But it was Rab she belonged to, and her parents would surely come round in time if they saw him serious and firm. Could not Smith persuade him to make her openly his wife, and to give up the mad Jamaica notion? With so many genteel friends such a man as Rab could find work in Ayrshire other than that of a common labourer. It was natural that the Armours could not approve such a calling in a son-in-law. With Smith's promise that he would do his very best for her with Rab, she returned across the kirkyard.

Robert might be moved by Smith's appeal (made by letter), but he was no longer free to act. He replied:

. . . Against two things, however, I am fix'd as Fate: staying at home, and owning her conjugally. The first,

> by Heaven I will not do! the last, by Hell, I will never
> do! A good God bless you, and make you happy up to the
> warmest weeping wish of parted Friendship. . . .[1]

Yet he could not deny himself the sweets of magnanimity;
neither could he stifle his longing to see Jean, to speak with
her, to know from her own lips why and under what pressure
she had betrayed him. So he added:

> . . . If you see Jean tell her, I will meet her, So help me
> Heaven in my hour of need!

Though a 'poor heart-crushed devil' he enclosed the latest
edition of his 'Court of Equity' for Smith's benefit. To another
friend, gone from Mauchline, he wrote of the 'ill-advised
ungrateful' girl.

> Never man loved, or rather adored, a woman more than
> I did her; and, to confess truth between you and me, I
> do still love her to distraction after all, though I won't
> tell her so if I see her, which I don't want to do. My poor
> dear unfortunate Jean! how happy have I been in her
> arms! . . . those who made so much noise at the thought
> of her being *my wife* may some day see her connected in
> such a manner as may give them more real cause for
> vexation. I am sure I do not wish it. May Almighty God
> forgive her ingratitude and perjury to me, as I from my
> very soul forgive her. . . . I can have no nearer idea of the
> place of eternal punishment than what I have felt in
> my own breast on her account. . . . I have run into all
> kinds of dissipation and riot, mason-meetings, drinking-
> matches, and other mischief, to drive her out of my
> head, but all in vain. And now for a grand cure; the ship
> is on her way home that is to take me out to Jamaica; and
> then farewell dear old Scotland! and farewell dear
> ungrateful Jean! For never, never will I see you more.

Next day, having ignored the summons to appear in
person, Jean signed this form for the Session:

> I am heartily sorry that I have given and must give your
> Session trouble on my account. I acknowledge that I am
> with child, and that Robert Burns in Mossgiel is the
> father. I am, with great respect, your most humble
> servant, JEAN ARMOUR.

It meant, as she well knew, that in another three weeks or

so, when her pregnancy should be still more evident, she must stand along with her alienated lover for admonition on three successive Sabbaths. Jean was very sad.

Not so Robert. He was 'humbled, afflicted, tormented'; he had moods of gloom and of desperation; but his excitement was far too great, and things were happening far too fast to allow of sadness. He had received the offer of the post in Jamaica, and counted on embarking early in October. His publication proposals had met with between three and four hundred subscribers—enough to ensure the printer against loss. He had been busy planning and prefacing his book.[2] It went to press the same day that Jean signed her admission for the Session. Then there was Mary to be written to, and there was a redoubling of farewells all round. He had only one foot left on shore; the other was well in the Atlantic. He almost welcomed his church rebukes, for these ensured his freedom to honour Mary. His interrogation by the Session—now that it was nothing new—he made the subject of the wittiest and by far the most impudent of all his epistles.[3] Having braved the bogies over Lizzie Paton, he had lost his respect for them. He would leave Mauchline without admitting blame or asking for pity.

But he was beset with nightmares. He had accepted the Jamaica offer, but the post—bookkeeper on a plantation at £30 a year for three years—was neither well-paid nor congenial. It was indeed a terrifying prospect, alleviated only by the fact that his master would be an Ayrshire man. There was the question too of passage money. To travel to Port Antonio at his master's charges on terms of indenture meant working for a year and more after his arrival without pay and in conditions far worse for the unacclimatised white overseer than for the negro slaves he must drive. Yet he could see nothing else for it. And even if he indentured himself he would need cash for outfit and incidental expenses. Day after day what little he had was melting into the paper and letter-carriages upon which his darling hope depended. As for the idea of borrowing, it was congenitally hateful to him. Besides to a man already in debt borrowing might not be practicable.

Musing on these things, gazing with exiled eyes upon the

new unfolded hawthorns, red and white, and on the stream
by which he had pledged himself to Mary, he was trespassing
one evening in neighbouring policies. An experienced trespasser, he had long had the habit of annexing the incom-
municable treasures of trees that were the property of others.
He often walked in the private plantations of Barskimming,
Catrine, Montgomerie, or those of Ballochmyle. Till a short
time before, this last well-wooded and watered property,
with its larches that had been grown in greenhouses, had
belonged to Sir John Whitefoord, a kindly old country
gentleman, a Mason of high degree and Provincial Grand
Master, and Robert saw no harm in borrowing its precious
foliage and bird-song as from a brother Mason. But Sir John,
impoverished like many another local landowner by the
failure of the Ayr Bank, had been obliged to sell to a wealthy
retired paymaster from Bengal; and now at sunset this
contributed a further undertone to the melancholy of
Robert's thoughts. Not he alone was passing away, but also
the old Scotland he adored and fain would celebrate in song at
once homely and lyrical. The warm, rude careless ways were
everywhere perishing unchronicled, being done away by
trade and the new emulation. A showy, ill-founded bridge
was to be thrown across the Ayr; a great ugly cotton mill was
to be built on the Ballochmyle acres, employing hundreds of
hands and defiling the little river with cotton waste; so the
rumour went. Leaning against a tree he had become one with
its shadow, still as its bark[4] that he might not at all disturb the
birds, when the flutter of a gown betrayed the presence of
another human being and recalled to him the fact that he was
not only a trespasser but possibly an unwelcome one. What
should he do? Not far from him, though still apparently
unconscious that she was not alone, wandered the young lady
of the house—Miss Wilhelmina Alexander, sister to the new
laird. Charmingly she completed the rural prospect, a fact
which Robert was not too embarrassed to note. She was
youthful, female—surely she would excuse, imaginably she
would rejoice in such an encounter? Moving from beneath
his tree he turned upon her his fully-charged dramatic eyes,
and was ready to salute her respectfully as befitted his sex,
silently as befitted his station. But in her affrighted gentility

she gave no sign that she had seen him and made off in a
flutter. At home, after description and question, she identified the bold stranger with that rhyming fellow Mossgiel
whose reputation was not of the best sort. Robert returning
to the farm made a song to her which pleased him greatly.[5]

O had she been a country maid,
    And I the happy country swain,
Tho' sheltered in the lowest shed
    That ever rose on Scotia's plain!
Thro' weary winter's wind and rain,
    With joy, with rapture, I would toil;
And nightly to my bosom strain
    The bonie lass o' Ballochmyle.

True to his promise he saw Jean. He even went to the
Cowgate to see her under the eyes of her parents. The
interview was not a success. Jean did not seem to compre-
hend how basely she had acted. All she could see was that it
was not yet too late for a securer marriage ceremony.
Robert's inability to see this baffled her and put more power
into her parents' hands. Little did she or they guess that
through their action he had now given himself irrevocably
elsewhere. Had they so guessed, his leave-taking might
have been unpleasanter than it was. As it was, Mr and Mrs
Armour told him they never wished to see him again.

Yet he returned across the kirkyard with feelings for the
faithless one that surprised him by their tenderness and
passion. He had seen easily enough (Jean was not one to hide
such things) that she still loved and quite simply wanted him.
She wanted him even more than she wanted marriage, which
was very loveable of her. Besides she was imbued with the
most endearing common-sense. As she must pay, why should
she not have her fill of love? Somehow she had managed at
parting to convey this view to him, and it was a view in which
it was impossible for him not to rejoice. Mary had been gone a
month, and a month is in certain respects a long time. He was
certainly going to marry Mary. But there was still the attic
window in the Cowgate that communicated with the back
window of Johny Dove's. He loved, he revered, he wor-
shipped Mary. But an honest loving lass is an honest loving
lass, for a' that and a' that. . . .[6]

He was too busy to see Jean often, even if it had been easier for them to meet. He spent much time now at Kilmarnock seeing his poems through the press; he looked up subscribers there, at Irvine, at Maybole and all over the country, renewing his boyish friendships as he went. Willie Niven, now prosperous, wanted to help; so did Sillar and Rankine. Muir had ordered forty copies. He began once more to attend his Lodge meetings, which he had been neglecting of late, and sat much in taverns to talk and to be well-wished.

The appearance of the book was fixed for the last day of July. On the 9th Robert stood for the first of his three times in church, and he was allowed by Mr Auld to stand in his own pew. He was to stand again on Sunday the 30th and on the first Sunday in August.[7] Then he would be a free man.

But on 20 July or thereabouts he suddenly changed his plans. He had learned somehow what the Armours thought to keep secret from him—that Mr Armour had obtained a warrant *in meditatione fugae* to lodge him in jail until he should find security for the maintenance of the child. Now the reason for Armour's retention of the mutilated marriage paper was made clear to him. Without the names it would have no matrimonial value, but being in their hands, it might be an instrument for the extortion of money. The idea, characteristic of a half-educated villager, might not be feasible, but to Robert in his present situation it was alarming. He felt himself a hunted man. The reported sum sought by Armour was 'enormous,' the prospect of being arrested for failure to pay it before his ship sailed, too bad to risk. Robert heard of another ship—the *Nancy*—advertised to leave the Clyde for Savanna on August 10. No matter that he must now give up all hope of paying for his passage: no matter that upon reaching Savanna, which is on the south coast of Jamaica, he would have to make a fresh journey by land before reaching Port Antonio, which is on the north— the desire to be off without more delay was overmastering. In the *Nancy* he would embark, and until she sailed he would hide himself from all but the very few people he could trust.

On 22 July he executed a settlement of all his property, including any profits from his poems, in favour of his daughter by Lizzie Paton, and appointed Gilbert trustee. Two days later the document was duly read aloud from Ayr Cross. Leaving his little hide-covered chest packed at Mossgiel, where the family was united with him in wrath at the Armours' action, he fled to his cousins, the Allans, at Fairlie.[8] Here he was safe from his pursuers to sleep through his numbered nights. From Old Rome Foord—as the farm was called—he slipped in and out on his last errands, sacred and profane. He went to his printer's, to his Lodge meetings, to Kirkoswald to say good-bye to Peggy, who was now married; and Peggy's farmer husband walked with him five miles on his road home, both men shedding tears at the parting handshake.[9] When it came to his second standing in Mauchline church, though he had just heard that the *Nancy* had somewhat postponed her sailing, he was now a man departed and it was all one to him. But before setting out on his seven-mile walk back to his lair, he met his church partner to condole with her forgivingly if non-committally. That night, 'in a moment of rage,' 'exiled, abandoned, forlorn,' he wrote to Richmond:

> I know you will pour execration on her head, but spare the poor, ill-advised girl, for my sake; tho' may all the Furies that rend the injured, enraged Lover's bosom, await the old Harridan, her Mother, untill her latest hour![10]

The next day—Monday, 31 July—the poems appeared. At a Tarbolton Lodge meeting on Wednesday night the reception he had from the brethren was of the sort which heralds a local triumph. By the Sunday following, standing his third and last time in church, he knew that his book was succeeding beyond all expectations. So did his friends and his enemies. Every eye in church dwelt hungrily upon the face of the fornicator whose printed words had caused so great a stir, brought such wild delight, aroused such a fury of anger for miles around. Subscribers had been showing their copies about and reading passages aloud amid laughter and tears and shouts of glee; those who had not subscribed were hastening to secure copies before they were sold out; servant girls and plough-lads were doing what they had never done before—spending their savings on a bound volume of verse, going without what they had saved for in order to read what one of themselves had written for them.

It was good—a very great satisfaction. No poet has ever had a greater. But there was nothing in it to alter his plans save that he could escape indenture by paying his passage. With the full intention of embarking on the *Nancy*, now due to sail from Greenock any day within the month, he called the next Sunday on Dr Douglas in Ayr to say good-bye and settle any further formalities there might be with regard to the undertaking. Here, however, he met a couple of knowledgeable travellers—man and wife—who had not long come from Jamaica themselves and were scandalised by the idea of the Savanna route. A 200-mile journey across country lay, as they pointed out, between that port and Port Antonio. Mr Burns, without experience and making it at the worst season, would certainly catch the 'pleuritic' fever, in which case he would be nothing but a burden on his master. Not only so, but this land journey alone would run his master into something like £50—which, with the sea passage, would take the employee some two years' wages to repay. It was stark madness. Mr Burns should rather sail in Captain Cathcart's boat, the *Bell*, which was going from Greenock direct to Kingston in September. Dr Douglas joined in condemning the *Nancy*. Cathcart was a good fellow and a friend of Gavin Hamilton's; he would no doubt be reasonable in the matter of passage money; and as the guineas for the poems were now coming in surprisingly and waiting here and there for collection, Mr Burns might be able to put down the necessary sum and arrive in Jamaica unembarrassed.

From this unsettling interview Robert set out for Mossgiel.[11] On the way there he managed to see Jean—and they could not help being very happy together. He knew for certain now that, however weak she had been with her parents, she had not loved Wilson or any other but himself: and though he continued in his firm refusal of marriage she was content to have him on any terms—which contentment warmed the very cockles of his heart toward her and all women. He reached Mossgiel in high spirits, slept well, and the next morning wrote gaily to Smith, making light of his troubles and extolling the sex. That week he would be busy gathering the scattered payments of the book, delivering copies—sometimes as many as twenty at one house where a friend was acting as distributing agent; receiving congratulations in person at this tavern and that cottage and this other superior mansion of the county, where the lady desired to speak with him—all the while keeping as clear of Mauchline and the old Armours as he could. On Thursday morning early he would be setting forth on his pony upon a cheerful round, making inns his centres for two nights at a time. If, for a marvel, Smith could be out of bed by 7 o'clock, they could have a word together as Robert rode south unnoticed through the village on his way south. Whether or no, Smith was assured that his friend was going to 'laugh and sing and shake his leg' to the last, and to the last celebrate the most excellent goodness of woman!

Of the edition of 612 copies, 350[12] had been subscribed for beforehand. Almost as soon as the subscribed copies had been distributed the others were sold. The single copy that might have been to spare for Robert or his family was given to a friend. Gavin Hamilton rubbed his jolly hands, saw his debt paid and began to talk of a second edition of 1000 copies. Already Robert had hastily paid (lest Armour should hear of it) the nine guineas which was his fare into exile.[13]

He was shaken about the *Nancy*, but in spite of this did not at once give up his intention of sailing by her. His chest was on its way to Greenock. As he took it by pack-horse part of the way himself across the Galston moor for the carrier to pick up, he composed what he fully believed to be his last song on Scotish soil and his positively last dirge to his native land. His mood was matched by the weather. The wind blew; rain streamed from the dark sky. His farewells were said—almost.

One that remained to be said involved a new acquaintance. Among his subscribers and declared admirers was George Lawrie, parish minister of Loudoun, at Newmilns on the Irvine. Newmilns was on the road to Greenock. If it was not actually to break his journey that Robert was invited to spend the night there, it was certainly when he was under the immediate shadow of the journey; and upon arriving at the manse—which had the words 'Jehovah Jireh' carved over its front door—he was poignantly affected by the warmth of his welcome.

There were four young people—a son and three daughters—and the eldest daughter, Christina, played the spinet, which he now saw for the first time. His book lay honoured on the table. Guests came in and, as Mr Lawrie was a New Light, the room was cleared for dancing. Outside, the night had gone still after the storm and the moon was risen. From the manse windows it could be seen shining on a flowing river, a ruined castle, bare hills:

> Sae merrily they danced the ring
> Frae e'ening till the cock did craw;
> And aye the ower-word o' the spring
> Was 'Irvine bairns are bonie a'.'

In the embrasure of one window the enraptured guest swiftly wrote this and another verse on a scrap of paper and handed it to Miss Christina with a look in his eyes that was an embrace. At last bedtime came, but Robert was sleepless and wrote verses to his host and hostess far into the morning, when he dozed over and breakfast had to be begun without him.

But instead of going on to Greenock then or a few days later, he went back to Mossgiel and let the *Nancy* sail without him.[14] Now he would go by the *Bell*, which, on account of the recent storms or other causes of delay, would not sail till 20 September. On 1 September, in his letter to Richmond, his excuse for the postponement is that the *Nancy* had only given him two days' warning and that this was not enough for all he had to do. But in the same letter he admits that he is 'anxious, very anxious' about Jean's approaching confinement. This anxiety is underlined by his friendly remonstrances about Jenny Surgeoner and her baby. The poor girl, he says, is even trying to learn to write so that she may be more worthy of Richmond. (Such remonstrances, he allows, are on delicate ground!)

Lawrie as well as Jean, however, had delayed his embarkation. The minister had felt and had strongly said that something could be done to keep an Ayrshire poet at home. If Robert would only wait a few weeks he would at once write to Edinburgh—to no less a poetical pundit than Dr Thomas

Blacklock, who was a ministerial friend—enclosing a copy
of the poems and suggesting that they might be shown to
the still mightier pundit—the Great Panjandrum of the
Northern Athens, Dr Blair himself! If the interest of these
men could be aroused in Robert's favour, Lawrie felt sure
that a living at home was assured. Robert was more than
doubtful; but the eagerness of a man like Lawrie, joined to
other more secret pleadings, was not to be resisted.

On the evening of the 3rd—which was a Sunday—young
Adam Armour made his way through a hurricane, pulled the
bobbin of the kitchen door and was blown in with his news—
Jean had borne twins—a boy and a girl.

Robert was tickled to the soul by this wealth of paternity.
He promised Adam that the boy should be brought up at
Mossgiel, told him that the Armours must be responsible for
the girl, and sat down to write to Richmond again.

> Wish me luck, dear Richmond! Armour has just
> brought me a fine boy and girl at one throw. God bless
> the little dears!
>
> > Green grow the rashes, O,
> > Green grow the rashes, O,
> > A feather bed is no sae saft
> > As the bosoms o' the lasses, O.

And to Hamilton he sent 'Nature's Law,' on the line of
Pope—'Great Nature spoke; observant man obeyed,' with
wit harnessed to a Psalm tune:

> Let other heroes boast their scars,
>   The marks of sturt and strife;
> And other poets sing of wars,
>   The plagues of human life;
> Shame fa' the fun, wi' sword and gun,
>   To slap mankind like lumber;
> I sing his name, and nobler fame,
>   Wha multiplies our number.
>
> The Hero of these artless strains,
>   A lowly bard was he,
> Who sung his rhymes in Coila's plains,
>   Wi' mickle mirth an' glee;

> Kind Nature's care had given his share,
>   Large, of the flaming current;
> And, all devout, he never sought;
>   To stem the sacred torrent.
>
> He felt the powerful, high behest
>   Thrill, vital, thro' and thro';
> And sought a corresponding breast,
>   To give obedience due:
> Propitious Powers screen'd the young flow'rs
>   From mildews of abortion;
> And lo! the bard—a great reward—
>   Has got a double portion!

On 5 September Daddy Auld baptised the babies, which being bastard were not named for their innocent grand-parents, but their parents—the boy Robert, the girl Jean. When he was weaned the boy would come to Mossgiel to be another charge upon Agnes. Jean Armour, unlike Lizzie Paton, was no great favourite of hers, but it seemed she welcomed all babies.

And what, all this while, of Mary? Ever unassuming, she had retired into the background of Robert's life. But there she was established in modest supremacy, blooming sweetly and many-rooted as a daisy plant. He was faithful to her in his, and in nature's fashion; his tender loyalty was not dimin-ished but rather increased by the turmoil of his life and by the unexpected turn things had taken. But his life *was* in turmoil, and things *had* taken most unexpected turns, and Mary's was a waiting part.

Small comfort all this was to her as her body grew heavier with the weight of Robert's child, and her heart with the secret she was trying to keep from her parents. For she was their eldest and their much loved and trusted daughter, always frank and good, kind and trustworthy, helpful with the four younger ones. The only cause of uneasiness she had ever given them was her tokening to an Ayrshire man she hardly knew and of whom doubtful stories were told. As summer passed and autumn drew on and still Robert's letters told of postponement, she saw the race with nature grow ever more desperate. But she had still every reason to believe in Robert, and his letters continued to come, and his loving songs. He would be meeting her at Greenock in August . . . in September . . . in October. . . .

For again her secret husband had put off his coming. The *Bell* sailed without him on 20 September. The harvest was nearly got in. And still Robert waited for a word from Lawrie, and Mary for a clear word from Robert. His future, which had been dark but distinct, might now be brighter to a casual eye, but it was painfully vague and threatening to his own. To stay on after one's leavetaking is bad enough, but here there was worse; and lingering among the scenes to which he had bidden farewell, Robert was tragically at a loss. Closing around him he could feel the meshes of a net invisible to others, which was the work of his own 'folly-devoted' hands. His very success was tightening the knots, for he had laid his plans for failure and departure. Would he be able to avail himself of the best-meant plans of his friends, based as these were on his staying at home, when the truth of his circumstances was discovered? His known position with regard to Jean would make it hard enough for those who tried to obtain an Excise or other post for him. (And there was no getting away from it that when he looked at Jean suckling his twins he realised how deeply his affections were engaged and how gladly he would make provision for the three of them.[15] But what when they learned of his solemn pledge to Mary? Yet with Mary he could never break faith, and he must indeed act quickly if he was to avoid what he would deeply have agreed with De Quincey was 'an abiding pang, such as time could not abolish, of bitter self-reproach.' For the most part he still saw nothing for it but Mary and Jamaica, and that as soon after harvest as might be. But he had consented to wait until Lawrie had heard from Blacklock, if only for the chance of a speedy second edition, which might help to solve the still pressing problem of money. Armour had withdrawn his threat, so that Mossgiel farm was safe to live in, but the situation of its tenants was not as yet materially affected by the success of the poems, which remained strictly local. Here was yet another paralysing factor—the hope of fame. Robert could not forgo the verdict of Edinburgh. Mary, after all, might benefit and could not suffer by that verdict. She was but five months gone. She could still wait a week or two.

Enthusiastic ladies and gentlemen of Ayrshire the while were bidding the poet to their houses, as much to see how he comported himself as to tell him how much they had enjoyed his poems. He always went—for triumph, curiosity, distraction; and his hosts and hostesses always expressed their surprise at his self-possession and simple dignity. It would seem that some were not a little piqued to observe that he appeared free from embarrassment in their presence. He for his part—though fully sensible of their kind condescension and apt in epistolary expression of the same—found a different piquancy in these drawing-room visits to mansions where he had been long conversant with the byres, the stables, and the situation of the servants' bedroom windows.

Dr Blacklock, who was stone blind and old for his age at sixty-five, did not dictate a reply to Lawrie's letter till the day after the twins were born. This delay was due to the writer's intention of 'expressing his approbation' of Mr Burns's poems in verses of his own. But 'whether from declining life or a temporary depression of spirits' it had proved impossible 'to accomplish that agreeable intention.' He therefore contented himself—after the said lapse of time—with praising Mr Burns's poems very warmly and at length, promising that one of these days they should be laid under the august eye of Dr Blair,[16] and concurring in the desirability of an immediate second edition. He also mentioned—and this was peculiarly interesting—that, even before receiving the book, he had already had some acquaintance with Mr Burns's work through Professor Dugald Stewart, who had received several pieces in manuscript from a Mauchline friend, Dr Mackenzie. Whether from the same causes that had delayed the writing of this letter, or because of some unexplained withholding on the part of Lawrie or Hamilton—through whose hands it passed on its way—it did not reach Robert till the third week in September. The sweeter for coming when he had almost ceased to expect it, here was the first word from the great world. The singer's experienced ear could not mistake in it the ring of genuine applause. To his family and

friends it gave substance to the hope that a post
found to keep him in Scotland. To him its m
importance lay in its reference to a second edition. He w
to Richmond:

> I am going perhaps to try a second edition of my book. If
> I do it, it will detain me a little longer in the country; if
> not, I shall be gone as soon as harvest is over.[17]

At the beginning of October he went to Kilmarnock. With
Blacklock's encouragement and the fact that the first edition
had been sold out within a month of publication, he had no
doubt that his printer would proceed. But the cautious
Wilson saw the matter in a different light. He argued that, so
far from justifying a second edition, the remarkable success
of the first rendered it a ´tempting of Providence, for
obviously everybody who could be imagined as wanting to
read the poems had now had the opportunity. The utmost he
would offer was to print 1000 copies for £15 or £16, the
author to pay for the paper in advance, which would be
'about £27' more. Robert was bitterly chagrined. His net
profit on the previous transaction was barely £20,[18] and he
had not another penny in the world. Ballantine offered to
lend him the money, but he would not take it. Ballantine saw
wisdom in this. He thought with Aiken that they should let
local printers alone and take a strong line. Aiken would write
to Edinburgh for information as to how they should approach
a city firm. As soon as the winter session of the University
opened, many of the Ayrshire gentry would be in the capital,
and surely some of those who had been so loud in their local
praise would use their influence for him there. Moreover
there was Professor Stewart, who, when he was not teaching
Moral Philosophy at Edinburgh, was an Ayrshire laird and a
near neighbour, and had been interested enough to subscribe
for the book. Presently indeed Professor Stewart went even
further. He invited Dr Mackenzie to bring the much-discussed
poet with him to dinner at his house near Ballochmyle. The
date fixed was 23 October, shortly before the host would
leave his pleasant white-washed country house for his dingy
winter quarters in the Canongate.

Mr Dugald Stewart of Catrine was a very ethical,
academic, facetious young gentleman, thirty-five years of

age, of whom all the world had a very high opinion in which he himself very cordially, though modestly, concurred. Abhorring subtleties and prone to expatiate at large, he was 'without genius or even originality of talent'[19]: but he could both clear his throat and spit (which, being of an asthmatic tendency, he had to do at frequent intervals) in a perfectly gentlemanly manner. His gestures were formal, his forehead domed, his eyebrows bushy, his voice rich and burring and his heart fairly kind. He was a Freemason, and had great pleasure in greeting Robert ceremonially as a Craft brother. Having excellent family connexions, he used them to augment his income—for his stipend as professor and his revenues as laird were alike meagre—by receiving young noblemen and gentlemen into his house as boarders and pupils. One of these was with him at Catrine. This was Lord Daer, son of the Earl of Selkirk.[20] His lordship, who had recently returned from France, where he had made the acquaintance of Condorcet and adopted liberal principles, was exactly the same age as Robert. The two young men got on famously. Robert was surprised and delighted by his lordship's unaffected simplicity; his lordship was equally surprised and delighted by Robert's dignity and ease. Dr Mackenzie, who regarded Rab Mossgiel as a sort of Jekyll and Hyde, was relieved to see him play the better part; Professor Stewart's intelligent grey eyes beamed on them all. Possibly the ploughman poet evinced a tendency to lay down the law in a manner that was not strictly becoming to one in his station and situation. But his fluency and 'avoidance of the peculiarities of Scotish phraseology' were certainly amazing.

It was a delightful evening. For the time being Robert forgot his gnawing anxiety and on the way home composed good-humoured verses on the occasion:

> This wot ye all whom it concerns,
> I, Rhymer Robin, alias Burns,
>   October twenty-third.
> A ne'er-to-be-forgotten day,
> Sae far I sprachled up the brae,
>   I dinner'd wi' a Lord.

I've been at drucken writers' feasts,
Nay, been bitch-fou 'mang godly priests
   (Wi' rev'rence be it spoken!).
I've even join'd the honor'd jorum,
When mighty squireships o' the quorum,
   Their hydra drouth did sloken.

But wi' a Lord!—stand out, my shin,
A Lord!—a Peer—an Earl's son,
   Up higher yet, my bonnet;
An' sic a Lord!—lang Scotch ells twa,
Our Peerage he o'erlooks them a'
   As I look o'er my sonnet.

That same afternoon, while the poet was taking wine with Lord Daer at Catrine, earth was being shovelled over the body of Mary Campbell in Greenock churchyard. The same grave contained her dead baby. Round the grave the men of the Campbells and the Macphersons were cursing the name of Robert Burns as the Armours had never cursed it.

It happened in this manner. When it had begun to seem urgent to Mary that she should get away from home if she was to keep her secret longer, she arranged to take a situation in Glasgow[21] from the November term. Even if she were to get as far as Glasgow her lover could easily come for her there; but she prayed she might not get beyond Greenock, where she could stay with a cousin of her mother's—a shipwright named Macpherson—till Martinmas and hope for the best. As her younger brother Robert was on the point of being apprenticed to Macpherson, their father took the family in his boat from Campbeltown to Greenock and went with them himself to stay in their cousins' tenement house so that he might see his son through the 'brothering-feast.' There would be a party to admit young Robert to the craft: Mary would help with everything: it would be a family occasion.

So it was; but next morning the new-made apprentice fell ill—too ill to go out to work. Everybody made a joke of it. Mary said he had drunk too much. Macpherson observed that it was a mercy he had lately bought a grave, as it was no easy matter getting one in Greenock just then, unless a man were a stranger or a pauper, when he went to the common corner of the churchyard. Still the boy Robert ached and drooped; and instead of throwing off what seemed like nothing more than an attack of low spirits he began to shiver and burn by turns, to breathe quickly and to vomit. His head pained him; there were noises in his ears and throbbings in his temples; his eyes lost their brightness and seemed sunk in their sockets; his skin darkened and his teeth and lips looked blackish. When he began to wander in his speech and purple spots appeared here and there on his body, all knew it was the 'putrid' or 'malignant' fever.[22]

Mary, of course, minded him. Mary was always good. She was a devoted nurse, but Scotish methods—especially Highland methods—were the reverse of hygienic. With small, low-ceilinged, crowded bedrooms (and even beds), closed windows, absence of drainage, the presence of many bewailing friends, 'the fivver' had a way of spreading itself throughout whole households and parishes. As Robert grew better his sister began to hang her head. She developed the characteristic symptoms. But to the consternation of her cousins and her father she also displayed symptoms which were unusual in the disorder. The strange frenzy of her manner was not to be accounted for by common delirium. It must surely be that she was 'smit,' bewitched, under the evil eye. So the one-eyed man, her father—he had lost an eye in the Revenue service—went to where two streams meet, and from the joining of the waters he chose out seven well-matched smooth pebbles. These were put to boil in new milk for the correct time and the milk given to Mary to drink. But Mary only grew worse, and soon the reason for her peculiar frenzy was revealed. She gave birth to a premature infant. Within a day or two both were dead. Before the burial her little sister went privily and cut off a lock of the corn-coloured hair.[23]

A week or so later the Mossgiel household were all sitting in the kitchen. The harvest being now in, the men were idle—but one at least of them restless. The women were making ready for the winter spinning, and young Bell was being shown how to use the 'big' wheel, which had just been got out, when the carrier arrived with a letter for Robert. Looking up from her thread, Bell marked how her brother scanned the direction on the cover, as people do when they see an unfamiliar hand, and how he went to the window for light and privacy. She watched him slyly with her black eyes, saw his face darken and convulse, and then hastily resumed her work as he turned, crushed the letter in his hand and left the house.

Robert wrote to the Campbells, but there was no reply. He wrote again pleading his honourable love, beseeching for some word of how Mary had come to die, begging for at least a handkerchief or ribbon that she had worn—with the same result. At Greenock and at Campbeltown Mary's father gave orders that neither her name nor Robert's should be mentioned in his hearing. All the letters and poems she had received were destroyed. Only the mutilated Bibles were kept as a shameful memorial; and the little sister, who had hair as yellow as that she had cut from Mary's head, knew some of Robert's verses by heart from having heard them often repeated in confidential hours.

Shock and grief apart, Mary Campbell's death affected Robert's life crucially. On her account he had freed himself from Jean; now he was freed from her. Before this freedom there is no sign that he had thought of going to Edinburgh; after it, almost at once, he decided that he would go. No definite news had been received about a second edition, but the last few weeks had brought new influential admirers, and old admirers like Aiken thought it might be well for the poet to visit the capital in person. Richmond was written to for a bed. If the visit were a failure Robert could still sail for Jamaica—from Leith instead of from Greenock. He had heard of a ship that was leaving Leith before Christmas.

PART FOUR

Edinburgh

Richmond, now aged one-and-twenty, had been above a year
in an Edinburgh writer's office, and had endured various ups
and downs, unfortunate illnesses and changes of situation.
He lodged in the Lawnmarket, hard under the Castle on the
east side—Baxter's Close, first stair on your left and first
floor, looking out into Lady Stair's Close, at the head of
which was the humble shop of Mr James Johnson, maker,
mender, tuner and hirer of musical instruments, and not far
from the flourishing establishment of Mr William Brodie,
cabinetmaker and Town Councillor, who had lately (though
he did not advertise the fact) started a profitable side-line in
wholesale burglary. It was an ancient stone house, with little
mullioned windows, and large panelled rooms, beautifully
proportioned and fairly verminous. For his room there, with
its single window, sanded floor, deal table and chaff bed,
Richmond paid 2s 6d a week. When one day early in
November he told his landlady that a country friend—older
than himself and warranted sober and respectable, though
possibly under the necessity of departing for Jamaica—desired
to share his room until such time as the ship should sail from
Leith, she consented in consideration of 6d a week extra.
Mrs Carfrae was a well-doing widow of forty-five, who had
a sore trial in the 'gandy-goings' of certain 'base jades'
occupying the second floor—they being neither more nor
less than common whores who, unfortunately, pursued their
avocation in an independent manner.[1] Gladly, she said, she
would have lived in a house with none but douce country
folk such as Mr Richmond and his expected friend. But in
these bad days even respectable householders could not
afford to pick and choose their quarters. Not so long ago such
a house as this would have had none but genteel inhabitants
on its middle floors and honest poor above and below; but

now the gentry was all for the New-town—with their houses that looked like New Light Greek temples; and their places were taken by riff-raff with that easy money which was an overflow of the new trade.

On Monday evening, 28 November, a jaded pony stumbled down the rough causeway stones of the Grassmarket; and its rider, a heavy, round-shouldered, short-necked, swarthy young fellow, in buckskin breeches that were obviously new, dismounted and stared about him, much as another round-shouldered and swarthy man of the same age had stared about him on first entering the capital thirty years before. Like his father, Robert Burns at twenty-seven looked quite ten years more than his age. When in repose his deeply marked, coarse-featured face was thoughtful to melancholy; and it was with the hard glance of one already assaulted by life that he examined the sloping square, the overhanging bulk of the Castle rock and the advertisements of Balloon Ascents and Learned Pigs, so far as these famous things were visible in the November gloom. But the eyes of the later arrival were wider, bolder and more intent than those of the earlier had ever been, and when they lighted upon something to anger or amuse them, they could still blaze boyishly.

The square was crowded, for Edinburgh was all agog for the first arrival of that miracle of speed, Palmer's mail coach from London, which was already some hours overdue.[2] Our traveller, however, was safely met by Richmond and another Ayrshire friend, John Samson, brother to a Kilmarnock seedsman who had recently been celebrated by Robert in a tavern impromptu. Samson had not come in pure welcome. He wanted to borrow the pony to ride home upon next day—a matter upon which there was some debate, for Robert, who had himself borrowed the beast, had promised its owner to return it by carrier.[3] But when Samson declared that Mr James Dalrymple of Orangefield had countenanced his immediate use of the pony, he carried his point. Dalrymple—Mason and man of influence alike at Mauchline and Edinburgh—was among the few upon whose town interest Robert might reasonably count.

Since mounting that same pony on the Sunday morning he had been hard put to it, having been lavishly entertained *en route* by admirers of his poems who longed to meet him and had twice his physical endurance and thrice his capacity for strong liquor. His theories upon Scotch drink and his reputation as an entertainer had both been put to the severest tests. On the Sunday evening, at Covington Mains in Lanarkshire, a well-attended and vehement supper party had lasted till well into Monday morning. At the next farm the whole neighbourhood had been summoned to a breakfast party. At the next again there had been a similar broadcast invitation to a dinner. The journey had been a bardic progress, rejoicing and reassuring to the heart, and at each place the bard had kept the company alternately entranced and roaring with laughter. Now he was paying for his triumph in head and stomach. But before he and Richmond could settle down to sleep—both in the same bed beneath the low ceiling from which the faulty plaster was shaken in flakes by the noisy, wine-bibbing wenches upstairs[4]—there was much to be said. There was all the Mauchline gossip—how Jenny Surgeoner was going on,[5] how Smith's mature 'fault' had conducted herself 'upon the seat of shame,' full particulars of the suicide of the Earl of Loudoun, whose affairs had been going from bad to worse since the failure of the Ayr Bank, and whose estates were about to be sold by public roup in Edinburgh, a matter upon which Robert had undertaken to report to his Lordship's factor, Gavin Hamilton. Also Robert had in his pocket Daddy Auld's certificate of bachelorhood, which had to be submitted for his friend's expert opinion, with full and confidential explanations of how it had been got out of the deluded old man. *Item*, there were questions to be asked about a vessel, the *Roselle*, now lying at Leith and 'positively sailing' for Savanna on 17 December.[6] *Item*, there must be a full and true account of the farewell meeting of the Tarbolton Lodge, when the celebration had lasted till five in the morning and Robert had been the hero of the brethren not in poetry only but in purse. *Item*, Richmond must be consulted as to the wisdom of his guest joining in the Grand Lodge celebration on St Andrew's Day.[7] *Item*, confidential descriptions had to be given of local persons of quality, known to Richmond by name and sight only, who had lately become on interesting terms with his friend. There was that mature lady, Mrs Dunlop of Dunlop, who on reading 'The Cotter' had been miraculously raised from a bed of mourning to send a servant with an order to the poet for six copies of his book and a command for his company at dinner. On the other hand there was the undoubted snub of the parvenus at Ballochmyle. There was only one name Robert did not mention—that of Mary Campbell.

Next morning all the novelty of Edinburgh could not tempt him out of bed, much less out of doors. He lay the whole day ill and despondent, and though he rose the day after, he still felt the effects of his too glorious journey. He had the vaguest notions of how to proceed with his business, which was, in the first place, to find a publisher for an emended and enlarged edition of his poems, and, secondly, to secure if possible the interest that would save him from Jamaica by getting him a commission in the Excise. In spite of the encouraging generalities of his Ayrshire patrons he had not brought one letter of introduction and his pride forbade that he should present himself uninvited to Dr Blacklock or even to Dugald Stewart. He had wit enough to know that Edinburgh and Ayrshire were very different places, and that consistency of behaviour was not necessarily to be found in the gentry who were equally at home in both. In his rough country coat, with his black hair unpowdered and rather long, the details of his dress careless, and his riding whip in a restless hand that sometimes slashed it at his thigh, sometimes cracked it loudly in the air, he neither felt nor wished to feel at home among the smug strollers on the city 'plainstanes.' Yet he did not escape what has well been called the 'double anger of the upstart and the artist,' and he had to summon his conscious pride in self-defence. What to him were these broadcloth gentry who passed him unnoticing to greet one another so importantly? What to them were he or his verses any more than the Learned Pig that performed daily in the Lawnmarket? He thought with passion of his 'elder brother in the Muses,' Robert Fergusson, who had trodden these same stones in witty obscurity and died piteously before the wild rose of boyhood was gone from his hollow cheeks. Knowing that Fergusson was buried in the Canongate churchyard, Robert went there that he might kiss the earth where the adorable poet lay, but it was a sleeveless errand. He could not find the grave. It was unmarked and unknown. So much for Edinburgh's love to man if the man was poor and a genius!

A less tragic pilgrimage was made to the house in the Luckenbooths up against St Giles's where Allan Ramsay had once had his shop and library. Here, as he bared his head in reverence, he was observed by the beady grey eye of the present proprietor of the shop. Who that proprietor was and how easily an introduction might be effected by means of certain Ayrshire connexions Robert knew, but again his pride restrained him. He passed on to a less showy establishment further down the High Street, which did nothing but printing, and inquired there if the master would consider a volume of poems as a business proposition. The master would not consider it, and, looking his visitor up and down, expressed his opinion in so injurious a manner that Robert desisted from further explanation. But he would make this bumptious nonentity regret his churlishness. Before turning away he drew from his pocket a lavish handful of silver, carelessly displayed it and thrust it back again.[8]

Edinburgh had greatly changed since William Burnes's day. For the last ten years the old scenes had been going down, and the New-town going up, with its different architecture and thoughts and ways. The gentlefolk were more and more forsaking the Canongate and the High Street, losing touch as they did so with their simple neighbours and becoming thereby a little vulgar themselves; and, though the Old-town still held its own as the heart of the place, with Parliament House and the High Street taverns and closes, a spiritual change-over was evident. There was a real theatre in the New-town, to which it was correct to go and see the most modish English plays, and the little amateurish old concert-room (modelled on the opera-house at Parma), with its Scotish music and its amateur style, was about to be abandoned for something brighter and more professional and Anglified under the auspices of Signori Stabilini, Urbani, Corrigiani, Corri and Schetki. Fergusson had sung the dirge of the Scotish Orpheus. For a quarter of a century the romantic movement had been in full swing, and at the same time trade had prospered exceedingly. In the church Moderatism had almost ousted the old austerity. Gentility had gone on from strength to strength. The fashion of sentimentality had undermined the old taboos. Moderatism itself was yielding to a new Evangelicalism.

What preserved the shape and in a measure the charm of Edinburgh was her undiminished capacity for producing and maintaining 'characters.' At the moment, it is true, she lacked a really Great Man. David Hume had been dead these ten years—a misfortune for Robert, who would have loved his boyish nature and admired his manly intellect. Adam Smith, though still technically alive, was debarred from playing a part by chronic stoppage of the bowels; and though the widow Dunlop had written to him about the new poet, the author of *The Wealth of Nations* was too busy thinking about a prospective trip to London (where he was going to try a cure at the hands of his sapient countryman Dr John Hunter) to take any notice. Principal Robertson was handicapped by his immense importance and his ear-trumpet. Still High Street and Parliament Square were rich in figures conscious and striking—'old originals' who, if not great men, were well accustomed to playing the great man's part to their own satisfaction and the enjoyment of everybody else. In High Street there were still dwarfs and giants and men who went up in fire balloons. As for Parliament House, that circle has been called 'the dullest in Christendom,' but this is surely a misnomer for persons who possessed so enviable an appetite for life, such unshakable conviction of their own importance and so extended a leisure in which to play out their every eccentricity. Their own *clique* and their own *claque*, they were in love with themselves, with one another, with Edinburgh. Most of them were oldish men, but counted upon being very much older. Adam Ferguson, Professor of Natural Philosophy—who, having had a stroke twelve years before, now lived on milk and vegetables, dressed entirely in fur, and gave weekly parties at his suburban house which the wits named Kamtschatka—was to attain his century. Others at the age of fifty had acquired all the advantages of senility while retaining a vigour of enjoyment which was perfectly youthful. Nobody worked hard. Everybody talked prodigiously. Whatever the Shorter Catechism might declare, the 'chief end' of the Edinburgh worthies was 'to glorify and enjoy themselves for ever'—all in the most correct manner, if you allow for a little over-drinking.[9] They led indeed the existence of hardy and long-lived butterflies that rejoiced in their freakish markings and were blissfully unconscious of their futility. Everything in their town—lighting, water, education, trade—was under the control of a Town Council which was 'omnipotent, corrupt, impenetrable, silent, powerful, submissive, mysterious and irresponsible' as the Venetian Senate.[10] But this affected them not at all; and, in spite of their heartiness and broad speech, for them the 'Lower Orders' had no existence.[11]

Their political Jove was Henry Dundas (afterwards Viscount Melville), already Pitt's 'Grand Vizier' and 'uncrowned king of Scotland.' The election of the Scotish representative peers was in his hand, and he controlled thirty-nine out of the forty members of Parliament and all the offices worth mention. At this time he was forty-two years of age—cool, capable and enormously forceful, but 'a sad fellow in his private capacity' as Boswell said,[12] and in public matters completely unscrupulous. 'Damned sagacious,' Robert called him, and from first to last every report of the one man to the other was antipathetic. The shadow of Dundas, all-powerful and, in our particular connexion, certainly malevolent, may be said to darken the background of the poet's life from now to the end.

Their ecclesiastical head was Hugh Blair, minister of the High Church (St Giles), who combined holiness, rhetoric and *belles-lettres* in a manner that commanded universal applause. He was sixty-eight and enjoyed a pension from the King, who had been known to wish that 'the Bible and Blair's Sermons might be in the hands of every youth in the United Kingdom.'[13] Edinburgh found those sermons full of 'sublime grandeur and awful dignity,' and the man himself worthy of 'respect with humble veneration.' On the same day that Robert rode into Edinburgh Dr Blacklock, dictating a second letter to Lawrie, nervously opined that 'most, if not all' of the Kilmarnock poems would fail to gain the approbation of Dr Blair, whose 'taste is too highly polished and genius too regular in its emotions to make allowances for the sallies of a more impetuous ardour.'

Of what Robert called the 'noblesse' the two most prominent for him were James fourteenth Earl of Glencairn and Jane Duchess of Gordon. Both were still in their thirties. Glencairn was a conventional, pleasant, intelligent, weak man with poor health. But for his rank and notable good looks he would scarcely have been remarked. Jane was of another type. Hers was the only female voice of the moment in an essentially masculine society, but it was a voice that would have made itself heard anywhere and in any social circumstances. Her father, a dissipated country laird, had abandoned his wife and three handsome daughters, giving them £100 to live upon, which they had done, 'keeping up a good countenance and the best society,' though without troubling about the three r's. One night at Comely Gardens—the Edinburgh equivalent to Vauxhall—she captivated the Duke of Gordon who married her forthwith; and her sisters did hardly less well in their alliances. She had been for many years a model wife; but now, having educated herself along with her young children, she had grown weary of faithfulness, notwithstanding which, being truly gay as well as beautiful, warm-hearted and dauntless, she remained the absolute leader of fun and fashion in Edinburgh, as none had been since the great Countess of Stair with her negro manservant. Her Scots tongue was notoriously frank, and she had wit—broad as her speech—a great gift of mimicry, and complete disrespect of persons. As 4 A.M. was her regular bedtime and five hours all she needed of sleep, no party was too late for her, and she was never too tired to dance, talk, play cards and provide material for the gossips. Her London manners were the same as those she displayed in Edinburgh. The King doted on her. Mr Pitt and Mr Dundas did some of their best drinking at her house. That her husband, the Duke, quietly solaced himself at his Castle gates was an open secret.

Messrs Henry Mackenzie and William Creech, leaders of the *Literati*, were both men of forty. The former, who fifteen years before had written 'the most popular novel of the decade in Britain,' was the Addison of the North, Scotland's pride, show-piece and arbiter of taste. He it was who had put the seal of approval (posthumously it is true) on the poems of the young shepherd, Michael Bruce; and he was later to welcome Campbell, to give Scott his first impetus towards fame and to encourage Byron. Fergusson he had ignored; but then Fergusson, an impudent guttersnipe without reverence or taste, had put forth a work named *The Sow of Feeling*, so naturally the rest was silence. He was of good family, and for some years had been the acknowledged head of a very gentlemanly literary and legal group calling itself the Mirror Club. There had also been *The Mirror* magazine, which he had edited during its two years' existence. He now edited *The Lounger*, which was entering its second year. Having enjoyed five years of London literary society and being endowed with 'very soft and engaging' manners and a nice taste in wines, he was always delegated by the united consent of Whig and Tory to greet distinguished visitors to the Northern Athens. None except Samuel Johnson had ever been known to ruffle his urbanity. He was always sitting for his portrait, which was no wonder, as he was elegantly tall, spare, and beautifully dressed, with a touch of old-fashioned affectation and an expression of the liveliest good-nature. To look at him nobody would have guessed that 'the Man of Feeling' loved nothing better than a cockfight or that he was by profession a successful conveyancer.[14]

William Creech, bachelor, bookseller and publisher, who now owned Allan Ramsay's shop, though not his library, was also a dandy, but with a difference. He too had a self-created character part to sustain and he dressed to it with care, favouring a somewhat out-moded sort of clothes—breeches of black velvet or silk according to the season, and notable shoe-buckles. English on his mother's side he had lived in London for a year, and for shorter periods in Holland, France, Switzerland and Germany. Of all the Edinburgh wits he 'wrote the most like a gentleman'; but in soul and breeding, as in stature, he was as little and mean as Mackenzie was long and marginal. While at college with Mackenzie and Lord Meadowbank, he had founded the famous Speculative Society. Early in life he had given up the study of medicine for the book trade; and after a useful interval of travelling in the youthful company of Glencairn—his mother having been a country parish minister's widow who took in aristocratic student boarders—he had become a man high in the Edinburgh Town Council and sole proprietor of the chief establishment in Scotland that combined publishing and bookselling. 'The Lord's anointed Bailie of Edinburgh'[15] was a man to be reckoned with. In the March of that year he organised the first public masquerade in the capital. Possessed of a practised tongue and a vast talent for the back-stairs, he rivalled Mackenzie in the manufacture of reputations, and his life was exceeding pleasant. To attend 'Creech's Levee' the most respectable as well as the most amusing worthies of the town passed each morning through the narrow alley and up the long winding stair which led, in defiance of the new fashion, to the eyrie where he lived. Here was drink and talk till noon, after which Bailie Creech descended to prosecute his business, of which the guiding principle was to take no risks and to postpone the settlement of accounts till they could be postponed no longer. By one o'clock he was again at leisure, but this time among his wares, to receive the flocks of visitors, who treated the shop as 'a very delightful lounge,' and to repeat by request one or other of his few but perfectly rehearsed anecdotes till it was time to dine with some of the chosen at an inn convenient. At the stroke of four he left his clerks in charge and returned to his own or a friend's house with the consciousness of a day's work well done. Among other things he was a paragraphist of power, and so to be courted and feared.

The lawyers, of course, were many, all more or less literary and some of noble blood. Among the latter the Hon Henry Erskine, Dean of the Faculty of Advocates, was a person of peculiar privileges. He too was a man of forty, younger brother to the Earl of Buchan and elder brother to the brilliant Thomas Erskine.[16] It was less his family, however, and his position as head of the Scots Bar than his unusual beauty, wit and gentleness that set him apart. He had an 'aerial' quality that made him adored, particularly by men. (In Edinburgh it was not uncommon for two men so to identify themselves as to be called by all their friends 'husband and wife.' At a later date Harry Erskine became 'married'—as might be Beauty to the Beast—to one who was in no other respect 'at all entangled with the graces,'[17] namely the clever, cantankerous, misshapen John Clerk, afterwards Lord Eldin.) The darling orator of Parliament House was not only a Whig, but also one of the few who was to remain a stout and consistent Whig when French affairs meant danger and exclusion from preferment. The Bench was filled with oddities. There was Lord Eskgrove, whose special privilege was absurdity, he being a man greatly gifted in the solemn, unconscious cutting of capers. Another eccentric was old Lord Monboddo, who was certain that babies were born with tails. He may well have remembered Robert's father, for it was in his own father's garden at Monboddo near Clochanhill that William Burnes learned his trade—anyhow, he could speak to the good repute of the Burnes family in the Mearns. To enumerate names, however, would be tedious. It is enough to say that Edinburgh contained a great array of not very learned men, who were lawyers, doctors and professors, and who took themselves and were taken by others with immense seriousness. Among them Dugald Stewart held a high place.

Naturally it was through Stewart, Dalrymple, Mrs Dunlop and other well-connected Ayrshire readers, some of whom were even then in town, that Robert must draw attention to himself and his needs. Without patronage from the circles in which they moved he might as well be in Jamaica. Any hope of independent publication had been quenched by his rencontre with the High Street printer; and to look for an independent livelihood that should be obtained without patronage would have been still more absurd. Often during his first strollings in the Edinburgh streets—baffled, unsure and uninformed—he thought that Jamaica would be preferable to a place where there was no accommodation to be had for such as himself save by the sort of humble appeals and flattery that he loathed. But after all he could still go aboard the *Roselle*.

Unable to present himself at once in any of the obvious quarters, he brought himself on his fourth day to make the only sort of appeal which seemed tolerable to him, namely a written one in the form of an expression of gratitude for some favour which could be assumed as having been rendered unasked. He wrote to old Sir John Whitefoord, who was in town. Sir John was connected by marriage with Dugald Stewart, but there was no mention of this in Robert's letter. What there was mention of was the noble way in which Sir John was reported to have spoken in defence of the writer's moral character, which some Edinburgh ill-wisher had lately traduced in the course of private conversation. The incident had somehow been reported to Dr Mackenzie of Mauchline and by Mackenzie passed on to Robert before his departure. No doubt it had increased his sensitiveness in the matter of paying calls. Even if we may regard the letter as a clever ruse on Robert's part, it makes painfully apparent the discord there was in his spirit.

> ... I have, Sir, in one or two instances, been patronized by those of your character in life, when I was introduced to their notice by [social] friends to them, and honoured acquaintances to me; but you are the first gentleman in the country whose benevolence and goodness of heart has interested him for me, unsolicited and unknown. I am not master enough of the etiquette of these matters to know ... whether formal duty bade, or cold propriety disallowed, my thanking you in this manner, as I am convinced, from the light in which you kindly view me, that you will do me the justice to believe this letter is not the manoeuvre of the needy, sharping author, fastening on those in upper life, who honour him with a little notice of him or his works. Indeed the situation of poets is generally such, to a proverb, as may in some measure, palliate that prostitution of heart and talents they have at times been guilty of. I do not think prodigality is, by any means, a necessary concomitant of a poetic turn, but I believe a careless, indolent attention to economy is almost inseparable from it; then there must be in the heart of every bard of Nature's making a certain modest sensibility, mixed with a kind of pride, that will ever keep him out of the way of those windfalls of fortune which frequently light on hardy impudence

and foot-licking servility. It is not easy to imagine a more helpless state than his whose poetic fancy unfits him for the world, and whose character as a scholar gives him some pretensions to the politesse of life—yet is as poor as I am.

For my part, I thank Heaven my star has been kinder; learning never elevated my ideas above the peasant's shed, and I have an independent fortune at the plough-tail. . . . With a tear of gratitude, I thank you, Sir, for the warmth with which you interposed in behalf of my conduct. I am, I acknowledge, too frequently the sport of whim, caprice, and passion—but reverence to God, and integrity to my fellow-creatures, I hope I shall ever preserve. . . .

Of this—and there is more of it, though nothing more explicit—Robert made a careful copy. It was to serve as the model for only too many other letters, full of protest and uncalled-for gratitude, uttered with ever deepening nausea.[18]

In a couple of days Sir John replied. Perfectly comprehending the purport of Robert's thanks, he wrote:

I do not pretend to much interest, but what I have I shall be ready to exert in procuring the attainment of any object you have in view. I have been told you wished to be made a gauger; I submit it to your consideration, whether it would not be more desirable, if a sum could be raised by subscription for a second edition of your poems, to lay it out in the stocking of a small farm. . . .

'The stocking of a small farm!' Robert's heart sank at this fateful phrase. Yet Sir John's letter was warming in its clear, if distant, friendliness. 'Any object you have in view' was a reassuring admission that a poet might be allowed to choose, even to know, what best suited him. And the desirability of a second edition was not questioned.

Actually—and the letter implied without stating the fact—there had been considerable talk in Edinburgh literary circles of a certain ploughman poet, and several persons had been bestirring themselves to help him. This was especially the case since 3 November, when (apparently unknown to Robert and his Ayrshire friends up to the time he left Mauchline) a review of his poems had appeared in Sibbald's *Edinburgh Magazine*. Sibbald, himself a farmer's son and once a farm servant, was now a leading light among Edinburgh bookseller-editors. He had bought Allan Ramsay's library and set up for himself in Parliament Square. He was known to be conservative in his tastes. He admired Dunbar and Drummond of Hawthornden and the old 'makars,' and was accustomed to sneer at later writers in the vernacular—such as Gilbertfield, whose 'depraved taste' had led him to 'pen elegies on pipers, and dying speeches of hounds and horses, in the familiar dialects of the meanest vulgar.' Yet here he was in his October number quoting lavishly from an obvious imitator of 'Bonny Heck' and 'The Piper of Kilbarchan,' declaring this imitator to be 'a striking example of native genius bursting through the obscurity and poverty and the obstructions of a laborious life,' pronouncing his 'observations on human character acute and sagacious,' 'his descriptions lively and just,' 'his rustic pleasantry rich,' his 'softer scenes touched with inimitable delicacy.' This, though safeguarded by the assurance that the Ayrshire poet had an 'untutored fancy' and 'many faults,' was enough to make the coffee-house connoisseurs take serious notice : and when, in the first week of December, Sibbald came out with more selections from the Kilmarnock volume, the *Literati* were well agog. Sibbald's second number was closely followed by a long and even more authoritative article by Henry Mackenzie in *The Lounger*[19] (which, being in a bad way, was glad of anything in the nature of a novelty). At almost the same time the London *Monthly Review* published a reserved but arresting appreciation, which ended thus :

> The objects that have obtained the attention of the author are humble; for he himself, born in a low station, and following a laborious employment, has had no opportunity of observing scenes in the higher walks of life; yet his verses are sometimes struck off with a delicacy and artless simplicity that charms like the bewitching though irregular touches of a Shakespeare.

Without this there would have been enough, but the *cachet* of London gave a final flourish to the affair. Mackenzie had been careful to hint at particular misfortunes, to mention a compulsory departure to Jamaica, and to claim in set terms the shelter and support of Scotland for so gifted a son of her soil. People went about begging for a sight of the book, turning on their tongues the delightful titbits from *Sibbald's* and *The Lounger*, and asking for information. Ayrshire landowners—of whom there were many, including the Lord Provost—were questioned and were pleased to reply with the sort of stories that build a legend.

It happened just then that the association between Edinburgh and Mr Burns's home county was very strong and romantic. Early in the century an Ayr wright (and fiddler at weddings) had given houseroom to people poorer than himself—his wife's widowed aunt, a washerwoman, and her son. Going abroad, the boy had become Governor of Madras and, returning rich and childless to his native town, had adopted the destitute family of the then dead violer. With his name and fortune and push (for the orphan was a gallant pusher) these had done well for themselves in Scotish society. One daughter had married the Sheriff-clerk of the county, so becoming the mother of Dalrymple of Orangefield and sister-in-law to the mild old minister who had baptized Robert. Another was the dowager Countess of Glencairn, mother of the fourteenth earl, and aunt to Captain Macrae, a very agreeable rake and man about town. One of her younger sons had lately married an Erskine, which had further fortified the Edinburgh-Ayrshire connexion. Between them the Glencairns, Dalrymples and Erskines could set what fashions they pleased in the capital.

So Robert's pride was saved. There need be no appeals from him. Quickly it became known that he was presentable, that he was fascinating, that he could talk, that he was a Freemason, that he was in town. Those who wished to meet him had only to approach Stewart, Dalrymple or Whitefoord. Invitations and callers of the most genteel kind arrived at Mrs Carfrae's first floor. Her lodger packed away his country coat, and bought a new one of blue English cloth with buff facings and brass buttons, a double-breasted waistcoat of blue and canary stripes,[20] top boots and a cambric neckcloth. Before his stomach had well recovered from the rural hospitality of his journey thither, he was being pressed to eat and drink in the highest social and literary company of the land.

Nothing like it had ever happened before, and Edinburgh went crazy with curiosity and self-important benevolence. The Ayrshire ploughman was the most talked-of man in town. You might not have been so lucky as to have seen his book—it is doubtful if there were half-a-dozen copies to be had—but if you had not had a word with the author of the charming 'Daisy' and the tear-compelling 'Cotter' (extracts of which you had perused in Sibbald's or Mackenzie's magazines or even in the *Evening Courant*) you were sadly without the pale. Soon there would be no excuse for not having read all the poems in the Kilmarnock book and more. For already in the middle of December the subscription bills were out for a 6s octavo volume (5s to subscribers) and the list of subscribers was dashingly headed by the signatures of one hundred members of Scotland's smartest club—the Caledonian Hunt.

The Caledonians were anyhow in a good humour. Come January they were to open the New-town Assembly Rooms with a brilliant ball led off by Lord Elibank and Lady Haddo, and attended by 'all the people of fashion in town,' to the number of three hundred and fifty, the ladies wearing coloured satins covered with crepe and decorated with flowers, turban caps trimmed with feathers and precious stones, or 'pink-coloured Spanish hats,' which had a 'very pretty appearance' and might cost anything up to twelve guineas. Except for the Great Room at Bath (which it exceeded in 'elegance and just proportion') the Edinburgh Assembly Room was the largest in Britain and it had cost £8000 to build.

So gladly the Club lifted the ploughman on the crest of its wave and decreed that he should be the catch of the season. Though his book would not appear till April and nobody quite knew what would be in it—apart from the 'Daisy,' the 'Cotter' and some other *morceaux*—the author was invited to a Grand Visitation at St Andrew's Lodge[21] and there treated to 'multiplied honours and repeated acclamations as "Caledonia's Bard, Brother Burns."' At this he was 'down-right thunderstruck,' as well he might be. But once started, the

Edinburgh people were set on doing the thing handsomely, and without pause this unread Laureate of Scotland was bidden to assemblies, concerts, theatres and clubs. Erskine befriended him. Glencairn became his protector. Duchess Jane announced that he had swept her off her feet. Dr Blair invited him to breakfast and was pleased to 'make allowances' for him. Each person was more anxious than the last to 'make allowances.' Soon Robert had dined with so many lords that he lost count of them. He still carried his whip in his hand and kept his hair unpowdered, and the very things which had marked his obscurity now made him one of the Edinburgh figures to be pointed out. He sat for his portrait in oils and had his silhouette cut. His subscription papers were despatched to every point of circulation in Scotland. The most distinguished covering letters, Presbyterian and Papist, carried them to the Court of St James's, the Scots Colleges at Paris, Douay and Valladolid, the Scots monasteries at Ratisbon and Maryborough. Nearly three thousand copies were at once subscribed for; Mr Creech would publish 'for the sole benefit of the author,'[22] Glencairn would appear as patron, and there would be an entirely new dedication 'to the noblemen and gentlemen of the Caledonian Hunt.' Certain of the more hilarious of these gentlemen—including my Lord Glencairn and his jolly cousins Dalrymple and Macrae—permitted themselves to celebrate the occasion by bidding the Bard to a supper at which their partners for the evening were raffish ladies of the town.

The *Roselle* 'positively sailed' on 17 December without a poet on board.

Some public acknowledgment on the part of Mr Burns was expected by Edinburgh. Which expectation Mr Burns understood only too perfectly. The pride that might not stoop to appeal must rise all the more quickly in gratitude. On the very first opportunity *The Caledonian Mercury* published the 'very beautiful' poem which began

Edina! Scotia's darling seat!

and went on to say:

Thy sons, Edina, social, kind,
    With open arms the Stranger hail;
Their views enlarged, their lib'ral mind,
    Above the narrow rural vale;

This was shortly followed by an eight-verse 'Address to a Haggis,' in more festive, but still somewhat reciprocal vein. Thus all tastes were served. Though it was uncertain if the second production had been wholly composed in or for Edinburgh, there could be no doubt about the first; and the word went round that the ploughman could improvise verses for any occasion. It was vaguely known that he had to his credit a whole body of as yet unprinted poems, vaguely believed that he had many more 'Cotters,' 'Mice' and 'Daisies' up his homespun sleeve. But few of those who now extended their patronage had any idea that he was a powerful satirist or a practised song-writer. Even of the 'Kilmarnock Burns' Edinburgh drawing-rooms knew comparatively little: of the Mauchline Burns they knew nothing.

As to his social behaviour, we who know him as the son of William Burnes, the pupil of Murdoch and the master of Mossgiel, will take something for granted. His less informed Edinburgh hosts, however, must be partly excused for their amazement that he managed, not only to behave, but to hold his own in polite circles. What bearing they expected of a tenant farmer who was also the author of 'The Cotter's Saturday Night' has never been stated. It is clear that they (and many others since) found less to wonder at in his poetic gifts than in his conversational powers, his general culture[1] and the 'manly simplicity' of his demeanour.

It caused surprise, too, that he showed no signs of having his head turned by the flattering notice of so many of his important superiors. This was the plain fact. His letters home were at first calm and amused, and later critical. If, later still, they betrayed agitation, it was not of the sort that can be associated with vanity. That he was gratified, that he was enchanted, is certain. There was great satisfaction in thus quickly having found recognition in the great world. But his practised country eyes almost as quickly showed him that the august Edinburgh figures, so long reverenced from a distance, were no more worshipful than the corresponding Mauchline figures which he was used to ridicule. Most were but 'ill-digested lumps of chaos,' and some were in addition 'strongly tinged with bituminous particles and sulphureous effluvia.' No poetical youth, but a grown man of fearless judgment and incomparably greater experience in living than his patrons, he observed that the kindly Glencairn was not above toadying to fools, that the much-travelled Creech was an ignorant, impotent monkey, and that the immense Blair himself was 'meerly an astonishing proof of what industry and application can do' with a 'heart not of the finest water' and 'natural parts such as are frequently to be met with . . . in short . . . a truly worthy and most respectable character.' That he might relieve himself by writing such things down (which he might not speak aloud in Edinburgh without the most frigid and painful results), he bought a new common-place book; and in letters to intimates or to women he 'took to pieces' with savage gaiety 'Right Honourables, Honourables and Reverends not a few.' Some of these letters were stolen unposted from his lodging; others, like so much more of his less guarded writings, have been piously destroyed.

Decently deferential as he tried to be in company, he was not used to the attitude, and presently the first glowing verdict of his 'wonderfully good' behaviour was opposed by other verdicts less favourable. The Man of Feeling laid it down that the gifted ploughman was 'a little too independent of mind for his station.' Others then found him 'somewhat authoritative,' or his wit at times 'unpleasing and unhappy,' if only too ready; or his partisanships—notably in the case of Fergusson—too violent for one of his breeding. It was unseemly that he should express such fierce anger and contempt over the matter of Fergusson's grave. And though it was easy to excuse his not always knowing 'when to play off and when to play on' in good society, it was not so easy to condone flat contradiction. Having taken to heart Mackenzie's dictum that 'to call forth genius from the obscurity in which it had pined indignant . . .' was 'to give wealth an enviable superiority, to greatness and to patronage a laudable pride,' the good people of Edinburgh naturally found it a little improper that the indignation of genius should be turned upon themselves. True, as somebody said, Mr Burns was 'never rude nor boorish when unprovoked by insult.' But 'yon impudent staring fellow,' as one gentleman called him, was surely above himself in his readiness to perceive insult—as when, to the invitation of a lady of title who had neglected to obtain an introduction before asking him to her party, he replied that he would 'do himself the honour of waiting upon' her, 'provided her ladyship' would 'invite also the learned pig' from the Grassmarket. Edinburgh was used to a malice more 'playful' and an indignation more 'virtuous.' Naturally also a good deal was expected of the author of 'The Cotter' in the way of appropriate sensibility and well-timed raptures. And naturally Robert was not always above conventional ecstasies. But very often he was. At one literary breakfast-party, wearied by the pompous ignorance of a ministerial talker he shouted down the aged gentleman, nay called him a 'damned blockhead.' Asked at Blair's own table whose preaching he had most enjoyed in town, he unhesitatingly said Dr Greenfield's.[2] Even when it was subtle, as it could be, his wit was calculated to cause discomfort. Sounded on the merits of Elphinstone (whose work had been published by Edinburgh subscription five years before) he remarked that 'the poetry of Elphinstone can only equal his prose notes'; and when of some worthy it was observed that he had grown fat of late, 'When you have told that,' said Robert, 'you have exhausted the subject; fatness is the only quality you can ascribe to the gentleman.' He was appalled by the tedium of genteel talk. It must have been an Edinburgh drawing-room that inspired him later to write:

Dulness, thou portion of the truly blest!

It was as certainly an Edinburgh drawing-room that evoked his address 'To the Unco Guid.'

On both sides it was a strain. At night he had to get Richmond to read him to sleep, or his frayed nerves would have kept him tossing. What with his own tradition of behaviour, both as to courtesy and independence, his need to assert himself, his very real sense of gratitude, and his resentment of a situation where all the gratitude was supposed to be on his side, between the glamour and the disgust, he suffered the more that he put a good front on the situation. Often he wondered if he would not have been better in Jamaica. Beneath his triumph, which was naturally intense, he felt so distrustful, that, within a week or two of his fame, he wrote to Greenfield enclosing some poems by village boys 'such as I lately was, and such as I believe I had better still have been.' He doubted with village caution the eventual good of so sudden a change of fortune; and meanwhile he was compelled to compromise, to perform, to betray at suitable moments a tearful sensibility modelled on the Man of Feeling. His nature was far too dramatic to let him refuse clearly and consistently the rôle thrust upon him. He could and did pump up tears and load his voice with feeling as well as any of the Edinburgh *Literati*. But in certain things he was incorruptible. In the recitation, for example, of his own poems, his delivery was 'slow, articulate and forcible, but without any eloquence or art,' the while he looked steadily out of the window instead of using his eyes upon his audience.

With the women he was in an especial dilemma. Though perceiving that after all the men in town and country were much alike, he had to admit that 'a refined and accomplished woman was a being almost new to him.'[3] He was charmed, and in return easily made himself charming. After all here were women, and he was at ease with them though here were, at the same time, ladies. He could keep them listening in rapture as long as he would, while he poured out for them the treasures of his wide experience of rural courtship and answered their questions concerning country loves. In return they were delighted to admit his conquest. But what did it amount to? He soon found out. The friendly, elegant creatures competed to invite him, to dance with him, to display their bosoms and shoulders, even in their genteel way to flirt with him; and though he had the peasant's inveterate disapproval of low-necked ladies, he could not escape provocation. But when it came to honest love-making, crash!—he was up once more against the merciless wall of class distinction. Mr Burns was too familiar! Mr Burns must recollect where he was, and what!

Against this barrier all his skill, knowledge and boldness were unavailing. He raged. He was in the height of his powers, his passions and his fame. Mary was dead. Jean was lost to him. The Edinburgh girls, whom he met socially— handsome, playful and intelligent—were inaccessible. He greatly admired Lord Monboddo's girl, Eliza, with her squeezed-up breasts, ringlets, exquisite features (in spite of the misfortune of bad teeth) and talent for versifying, had some tender passages with the daughter of a suburban farmer to whose house he went as a guest, and formed a friendship with Miss Margaret Chalmers, a pleasant young connexion of Gavin Hamilton's who had the further link that her father had once had a farm near Mauchline. But while he showed both taste and wisdom in his selection he knew himself disregarded as a wooer.

The inevitable happened. Not caring for the regular prostitute—though his feeling was not of the same sturdy description as young Adam Armour's—he did not consort with the women of Baxter's Close; but he easily found, among the more or less honest poor of the town, girls of his own class who were willing enough to take up with him. One Highland servant called May Cameron he attached in this way to himself. He was safe with her, knowing her already frail—for merely frail or amorous women he had a sympathy—and her associations by name and race with Mary Campbell were an attraction.

It was nobody's fault, or rather everybody's, that Edinburgh had no defined place for a genius of humble birth, and that with all their kindness and admiration the Edinburgh drawing-rooms compelled Robert to lead a double life. He gravitated more and more to the rougher side of Edinburgh society. At Johnnie Dowie's, in Liberton's Wynd, or at Daniel Douglas's, in Anchor Close, his uproariousness, scorn and 'wicked wit' could find a ready audience any day of the week. These taverns were frequented chiefly by more jovial and less eminent citizens than he met elsewhere, but they were also attended in moderation by unimpeachable gentlemen from the drawing-room world, who were unbent under the influence of pies, porter and punch.

The respective and highly respectable landlords of these 'howffs' were as different as any two of the trade could be. Johnnie was one of the characters of Edinburgh, a perfect Boniface, paunchy and weak-legged, with so many chins sunk so deep into his chest that he seemed to have neither chin nor neck. Fergusson had been one of the many to descend into his little cavernous rooms (one of them so dark and narrow that it was called 'the coffin') to the familiar greeting of 'Come in, gentlemen, come in. There's plenty o' corn in Egypt yet!' He purveyed the two specialities of the house and served its two excellent grades of ale with a Hyperborean grace, drank the company's health gravely and retired till next his services were called for. But on the stroke of twelve he became a despot, benevolent but inexorable. Not another drop of drink would he sell. It was time for gentlemen to go home. There was no arguing with Johnnie.

'Dawney' Douglas, on the other hand, was the meagrest, meekest man that ever bore the name of Daniel, enjoyed an ample and dominant spouse, and made a snug fortune out of sixpenny dishes of tripe, hash and haddock, with their proper liquid accompaniments. His tavern, with its sustaining texts above each lintel, was practically next door to the shop of William Smellie, Creech's printer, who had founded there a convivial club known—from Dawney's single song which he plaintively warbled—as the Crochallan Fencibles. Smellie was a man in whom Robert was bound to take delight—untidy, careless, vital, a 'veteran in genius, wit and bawdry.' Even sedate lawyers like Lord Craig and William Dunbar lost some of their starchiness in his company. Most of the Crochallans, however, were not sedate. Among them were love-lorn Alexander Cunningham who, though connected with the Glencairns and a nephew of Principal Robertson, seems not to have had the *entrée* to the highest circles; Cleghorn, the farmer from Saughton, a man of the Rankine type, jolly and of rude wit; the two dominies, Cruikshank and Nicol, who taught at the High School; Robert Ainslie, the harum-scarum law apprentice; Peter Hill, Creech's chief clerk, between whom and his employer no love was lost; Johnson, the music engraver of Lady Stair's Close, ignorant, almost illiterate, who yet was an obstinate enthusiast for folk music and the inventor of a cheap process which substituted pewter for copper plates. Smellie had known 'poor Bob Fergusson' and had printed his poems.[4] He and his club-mates had their faults. Some of them were merely coarse, others perhaps definitely ill-conditioned fellows; but at least they were free from solemn nonsense, and a man could say what was uppermost in his mind without fear of discomposing the company. They filled up Robert's glass and acclaimed his sallies, as indeed well they might, having found a prince of entertainers. He put at their disposal not merely his wit, but the whole store of his unprinted, memorised poetry. The Crochallans soon knew more about their guest's genius than all the drawing-room folk. Besides his best talk he gave them 'Holy Willie,' 'The Epistle to a Tailor,' 'The Contraband Marauder,' and 'The Court of Equity,' and cheerfully admitting of bawdry that if it were the sin against the 'Haly Ghaist' he could not hope to be saved, he produced for their further entertainment a 'curious' compilation of rude and rural rhymes, collected at first hand and, where defective, restored by himself in a manner at least equal to the original. It was contained in a little manuscript book which passed nimbly from one Crochallan hand to another but was most appreciated when the compiler gave readings from it. He called it *The Merry Muses of Caledonia*, described it as 'not for Maids, Ministers or Striplings' and wrote by way of preface:

Say, Puritan, can it be wrong
To dress plain Truth in witty song:
What honest Nature says we should do,
What every Lady does, or would do?

Among the Edinburgh actors, too—the first stage folk he
had ever met—he was at ease. He especially liked William
Woods, a man eight years older than himself, who had been
Fergusson's friend and had often given the poor lad free
passes for the play. It was with real pleasure that he wrote
a rhymed speech for Woods to recite at his benefit night.
He was ready to love any man who had been fond of
Fergusson—Smellie, Woods, and later Peter Stuart, the
newspaper man, who once delighted him by insisting that the
living poet as a companion was barely equal to what the dead
one had been, 'whose richness of conversation,' 'plenitude of
fancy and attraction,' and 'felicitous manner' had 'enraptured every person around him and infused into the hearts of
young and old the spirit and animation which operated in his
own mind.'

His association with the Crochallans, though gay, was far
from idle. It was through it that he was later to meet the
music-engraver, Johnson, with his project for a collection of
Scotish songs with music. No project could have been more
fascinating to Robert, or more useful. In Johnson and one
Clarke, organist of the Episcopal church, who was his
musical editor, he found the only men in Edinburgh who
agreed with him in preferring the Scotish country tunes as
country people sang them, to the embellished versions of
Signori Stabilini, Urbani, Schetki and the rest. Johnson was
so impressed by his knowledge of the subject, which was as
extensive as it was peculiar, that he practically handed over
the general editorship of the collection, now in accordance
with Robert's suggestion renamed *The Scots Musical Museum.*
The editor undertook to provide words (including original
contributions), music and footnotes. He asked for neither fee
nor reward and got none.

At Sibbald's Library in Parliament Square he found a
different source of enjoyment. Having duly thanked the
learned librarian (in writing) for his review, he now went
often there, handled old Allan's books, and in the Maitland

MSS became acquainted with the old, classic Scotish poets, whose very names till then he had hardly known. How he grudged them their freedom, and their lovely traditional diction that was as easy (or as difficult) for English as for Scotish readers! It was at Sibbald's he read that most tenderly bawdy and most Scotish of all love duets, having for the male speaker the refrain:

Ye'll break my heart, my bonie ane!

Nobody in Scotland (except perhaps Sibbald) read Dunbar then. The *Scots Magazine* found him 'much tinctured with immodesty,' and his Muse likewise. But Robert would set that line afresh to music, so that it should sound for the first time in the mouths of simple singers who had heard neither of Dunbar nor of the *Scots Magazine*. First he must find a tune for it. The Highland air, 'Cambdelmore,' or 'Ballindalloch's Reel,' if taken slow, would do.[5] Then the rest of the words came by themselves:

Thou'll break my heart, thou bonie bird
    That sings beside thy mate;
For sae I sat, and sae I sang,
    And wist na o' my fate,

with variant versions constantly recurring to be written later.

One day at Sibbald's he was handed a packet containing ten guineas, this being ten pounds in excess of the anonymous well-wisher's subscription for two copies of the new edition. Who could this be that in generosity was not to be outdone by Glencairn himself? Sibbald had no information, so Robert pocketed the money, all the more grateful that the delicacy of its conveyance called for no set gratitude—with gratitude's painful accompaniment of ploughmanly protest of independence. In spite of the cheap lodging and the lavish hospitality of Edinburgh the old question of a livelihood was not silenced. Creech had a mind above advance payments. The first of the subscription money that came to hand had been sent to Mossgiel where the situation remained critical. Even with all that could be expected from the second edition the future was uncertain as ever. Nobody in town seemed inclined to help in the matter of an Excise post, which seemed to patrons less poetical than a farm. But Robert knew how a farm ate up inadequate capital. Besides, for all he might say of independence at the ploughtail, he was sick of the soil and distrustful of himself in relation to it.

He was sick of the soil, yet it held him. It was deeply involved with his poetry, it showed up the empty, rootless existence of the city, and he missed it. For the first time in his life he was not lending his strength to the fruits of the earth. Neither was he producing any more poems of the kind that came with a leap of the heart. Were the two things perhaps bound up together? Anyhow he could not contemplate any permanent life for himself in Edinburgh. It was no more than 'a hare-brained adventure,' in which, even while it lasted, there was much for him to resent. But how its excitements would mock him when he 'returned to his shades.' They were at the same time of questionable worth and deeply upsetting. Edinburgh would soon be done with him and he with Edinburgh, yet Mossgiel, because of Edinburgh, was become less than nothing to him. He was like the fabled bird of Paradise which, having no legs, cannot anywhere alight, so must live in mid air. Should he not still go to Jamaica? His thoughts circled sorrowing and self-accusing over Mary's grave. They circled also over a certain cottage in the Cowgate, Mauchline. There was Jean to be considered and at times longed for. With all his 'simple dignity' and virile independence, the man of the moment in Edinburgh looked down into his future as into 'the bottomless pit.' When not in company he was subject to weariness. At night he was threatened by his old nerve trouble and dominated by terror. Richmond was kind. He would light the candle and get out the bed book; and by day he often helped to transcribe the poems that Smellie was demanding to set up. But the friendship felt the strain of inequality.

One solid satisfaction there was. A monument—fifty-four square feet of polished Craigleith stone—would stand where none had stood before, or would have stood for many a year had he not come to Edinburgh, namely upon Fergusson's grave, and it would stand there not for Fergusson merely, but as a symbol of reproach against a society that had no easy, honourable place for poets. Its erection had been no light undertaking. He had first written to the Magistrates of the

Canongate asking their permission. Their reply—disclaiming all power in the matter and advising him to apply to the Managers of the Kirkyard—was worded so offensively that he blasphemed. He kept the letter and a copy of his reply. One day perhaps his fame would allow of the newspaper publication of both documents to court a public verdict. Meanwhile, having duly approached the Kirkyard Managers, he obtained their kind permission that the finest poet produced by their town should be thus honoured at the initiation and expense of a poor, low-class stranger from the West-country. Robert ordered the stone with triumph. He caused to be engraved on it, with Fergusson's name and dates, four lines from a poem he had lately written on the subject:

> No sculptur'd marble here nor pompous lay,
>> 'No storied urn nor animated bust!'
> This simple stone directs pale SCOTIA's way
>> To pour her sorrows o'er her Poet's dust.[6]

Soon afterwards, presenting (one suspects not very suitably) a copy of the dead boy's book to the wife of the Greek professor, he wrote on the fly-leaf his Irvine paraphrase, beginning:

> Ah, woe is me, my Mother dear!
> A man of strife ye bore me.

And in another copy, given (one suspects still less suitably) to a young lady versifier, he wrote:

> Curse on ungrateful man, that can be pleas'd
> And yet can starve the author of the pleasure.
> O thou, my elder brother in misfortune,
> By far my elder brother in the muse,
> With tears I pity thy unhappy fate!
> Why is the bard unfitted for the world,
> Yet has so keen a relish of its pleasures?

Again and again in verse, prose and talk he was to repeat the thought contained in the last two lines. 'There is not,' he wrote, 'among all the martyrologies that ever were penned, so rueful a narrative as Johnson's Lives of the Poets.' And he noted the 'irresistible impulse to some idle vagary,' which 'shall eternally mislead the poet from the paths of Lucre,' while at the same time the unfortunate has 'a keener relish than any man living for the pleasures that only lucre can bestow.'

His enthusiasm for Fergusson, in season and out of season, did him no service among the *élite*. As weeks wore on and novelty wore off, it was felt to betray a 'propensity to coarse dissipation' which was further borne out by sundry whispers. Crochallans like Lord Craig and busybodies like Creech, with lightminded gossips who had become Masons and club-members for no other reason than that they might share in the spectacle of Mr Burns in his unguarded moments, carried reports from tavern to drawing-room. It became known that the author of 'The Cotter'—that sweet poem which had 'much of the same kind of merit as "The Schoolmistress"'[7]—was also the acknowledged author of pieces calculated to 'offend the serious.' After all, even of the Kilmarnock selection Mackenzie had been careful to say that certain poems breathed 'a spirit of libertinism' and that parts of others were 'offensive to delicacy.' And while taking into account the 'ignorance and fanaticism of the lower class of people,' 'the habits to which the poet must have been subject,' 'the society in which he must have mixed' and the fact that in his own walk of life 'our poet had, alas! no friends . . . from whom correction could be obtained,' it was also to be recollected that there was now at his disposal all the taste of the Caledonian Hunt and the culture of Parliament House.

The effusiveness with which that taste and culture were pressed upon him bade fair to rival the initial curiosity and hospitality of his Edinburgh hosts. These had begun by being 'blind to many faults for the sake of numberless beauties.' Now they felt impelled to indicate the faults, using the beauties merely to give point to their criticisms and counsels. Doubtless carried away by their own generosity, they had gone further in their praises than was suitable. In February the *English Review* had eschewed comparisons with Shakespeare, and in subtle withdrawal had feared that the ploughman poet was 'by no means such a poetical prodigy as some of his *malicious* friends have represented,' that he did not 'excel in the plaintive or pathetic,' that he possessed 'too great a facility of composition,' that he was 'too easily satisfied with his own productions,' that 'The Cotter' was 'without exception the best poem in the collection' and that Scotland was rejoicing in 'a natural though not a legitimate son of the Muses.' As London set the fashions, these were sayings to make Edinburgh pause and perpend.

The Caledonian Hunt at all events having sponsored the forthcoming book, must see that the right things—like 'Edina! Scotia's darling seat!'—were put in, and the wrong things—too numerous to name—left out. Parts of 'The Dream,' for example, were, to say the least of it, ill-advised. 'Young Peggy Blooms our Boniest Lass' and 'The Bonie Lass o' Ballochmyle' were not for the fastidious. They contained too much of the 'vehement familiarity' which Mr Burns had yet to learn was replaced among the refined by that sort of 'chivalrous gallantry' which dreams not of 'locked embraces and midnight rencontres' but instead 'sues for a smile' or 'melts in a tear.'[8] Dr Blair had utterly contemned 'Love and Liberty' (*The Jolly Beggars*) and 'The Prophet and God's Complaint.'[9] Mackenzie, who gave even 'The Daisy' a low place, advised the omission from the Edinburgh book of all dialect poems. Dr Moore,[10] writing from London, thought the same—unless, of course, Mr Burns could write another poem like 'The Cotter,' which began to seem unlikely. Dr Moore, who had been introduced by Mrs Dunlop, had produced in his sixtieth year the admired philosophical novel called *Zeluco*. So he knew. Mr Burns, wrote Moore, should study Greek and Roman history, and French and English history (especially from the beginning of Henry the Seventh's reign), and heathen mythology ('on account of its charming fancifulness'), and the best English poets; he should plan a large work 'upon some proper subject,' write many more short pieces like 'Edina! Scotia's darling seat!' and 'deal more sparingly in the future in the provincial dialect.' Equally full of written suggestions for omissions, emendations and new undertakings was Mrs Dunlop of Dunlop. 'The Twa Dogs' must not seat themselves so inelegantly: in 'The Cotter' itself 'unhappy' was the wrong epithet for her ancestor Wallace. The Earl of Buchan,[11] too, was anxious to be helpful. While admiring 'these little doric pieces,' his Lordship (with a few lapses in spelling and grammar) hoped that the Scotish laureate would not 'suffer the wings of his Pegasus to be sullied or curtailed by the grosser or more polished invaders of his genuine Invention,' and that he would 'Keep his Eye upon Parnassus and drink deep of the fountains of Helicon, but beware of the Joys that is dedicated to the Jolly God of wine.' Officious goodwill of this kind, however absurd, rarely offended Robert. He thanked his friends and evaded their advice. As he confessed to one of them he was 'not very amenable to counsel.' But two things appalled him—first, that two-score pages of his precious new edition must be devoted to setting out the names of his fifteen hundred noble and gentle subscribers; secondly, that he must omit those poems to which his noble and gentle subscribers objected on the score of indelicacy. His refusal would make them doubt his sensibility and gratitude. His mere idea that a piece like 'Holy Willie' would do outside the Crochallan circle (within which, of course, it was extremely amusing) argued a lack of right feeling.

On every point he had to yield. The subscribers' names and dignities went in: 'Holy Willie,' 'The Lass o' Ballochmyle' and 'Young Peggy' were left out. He might and he did 'damn the pedant frigid soul of criticism for ever and ever,' but there was nothing for it but to submit with expressions of that gratitude, which, from being the refuge of his pride, was fast becoming his secret shame and plague. He wore a ring on his finger and carried a snuff box in his waistcoat pocket that were the gifts of my Lord Glencairn, and it was my Lord Glencairn and his friends who were paying for his book. These people must have what they wanted. His fame was of their making, and if they regarded him as their creature it was not for him to blame them.

On 21 April the book appeared. The list of names was impressive. The dedication to the Caledonian Hunt, which took the place of the homely Kilmarnock preface, was skilful and in its fashion dignified. The contents included 'Edina,' the edifying religious pieces written at Irvine, 'The Ordination' and 'The Address to the Unco Guid.' The *Scots Magazine* gave a long review consisting of the dedication quoted *in extenso* and a one-line reference to 'this extraordinary young man.' This did not mean that the contents of the book did not give general satisfaction. They did. Amid friendly congratulations which drowned a few vague murmurs of dissatisfaction the poet set about his departure.

He felt bound to write letters of thanks to his patrons and friends. To many he enclosed as a memento a little engraving of his portrait, the same which had appeared as frontispiece to the Edinburgh edition. To others he sent a book or some personal trifle. He loved to give presents. In the more formal letters reiterated thanks were combined with assurances that he did not overrate the attentions paid him. The carefully effusive, and at the same time carefully manly, phrases could not conceal an encroaching weariness. 'I am afraid,' he confided to Dunbar, 'my numerous Edinburgh friendships are of so tender a construction that they will not bear carriage with me.' To Dr Blair (and others) he wrote: 'I have made up my mind that abuse, or almost even neglect will not surprize me in my quarters.'[12] In the same vein he wrote to Mrs Dunlop, but because his correspondent was a woman he felt valiant enough to add that he 'set as little by lords, clergy, critics, etc., as all these respective gentry do by my bardship.'

Before going home he would make a month's tour of the Border counties. It was a chance to see something more of Scotland, and he would collect all the old songs he could from these parts for the Museum and his own pleasure. Already he had given Johnson four songs, two being of his own composition. (One of these was 'Young Peggy Blooms'—the rejected of Edinburgh.) His light-hearted young friend Ainslie, who had managed to get a fortnight's holiday, agreed to accompany him on the tour. They would go on horseback. Robert had bought a mare and christened her Jenny Geddes on account of her obviously protestant principles. Ainslie's company was congenial because he was amorous and talked chiefly nonsense. His youth and feather-brained gaiety provided a blessed relief from the genteel solemnities of Edinburgh; and it was to be feared that similar solemnities might have to be encountered at frequent intervals during the tour, for Robert was armed with introductions and invitations to the most respectable houses and country seats in every district through which their route lay. He needed all the distraction he could get. Nothing had come of the Excise idea. He had been offered a farm near Dumfries on terms that his Edinburgh friends assured him were attractive, and though the attractiveness was less apparent to him, he must in decency see the place and come to a decision. After twenty-two-and-a-half weeks in the capital and an unprecedented triumph there, this was as far as he had got towards solving the problem of how to live.

Thus, roundabout and trailing sundry provincial clouds of glory from East Lothian, Berwick, Roxburgh, Selkirk and Dumfries, the poet came home. He had been away six months. The first night he put up at Johny Dove's, but before sleeping he went to the Cowgate to see Jean and his baby girl. He had not warned the Mossgiel folk of his arrival.

During the five weeks of his tour he had been almost continuously on show and had been made much of, chiefly among the bigger farmers and smaller gentry, for the provinces were not to be outdone by the capital in welcoming a national bard. The prosperous farmers of the South were not much to his liking; it did not escape his notice that the richer the farmer the poorer and worse educated were his labourers. Some family parties, however, he had enjoyed (being always at home in the domestic circle), and he had flirted blamelessly with several pretty girls. He had been lavish with his money, which had come in tempting sums from subscription centres here and there and reached him *en route*. His keenest pleasure had been in stravaiging many miles off the itinerary his Edinburgh friends had planned for him. He must needs see any glade or hill which he connected with a familiar song or thought likely to yield an unfamiliar one. The barest line of a song heard in childhood, a stray refrain or the name of an air was motive enough for a day's journey. He would have been happy to tour all Scotland with an old song-book as his guide, restoring and repairing, discovering where air and words had been wrongly mated, noting down bawdy verses for his *Merry Muses*, feeding his own lyrical fount at what for him remained the true source of inspiration. Unfortunately the weather was bad, and he was often soaked through.

Once he was so ill that he had to get a manservant to sit with him all night. Colic and a high temperature were accompanied by what he now described as his 'nervous ailment,' and for twelve hours or more he would be a prey to fear of death, disgust of life, self-contempt, remorse for the past and acute anxiety for the future. Almost invariably these attacks ensued upon a mood of extreme agitation and elevation. While in the Border country, for example, on finding himself about to pass from Scotish to English soil, he had thrown himself on the last of the Scotish earth in an ecstasy of dedication, which borrowed nothing but its outward form from Henry Mackenzie, and which in due course was followed by the night terrors. When these passed, though weak, he enjoyed some hours of exquisite serenity. His nerve storms were thus succeeded by a condition which was a corridor to the wildest frolic or to the deepest religious emotion.

At the end of a fortnight Ainslie returned to Edinburgh. After that Robert had to be content with a staid middle-aged companion, who afforded 'not one hearty mouthful of laughter.' At Dumfries, as at Jedburgh, he was made an honorary freeman. But he received bad news. May Cameron from being with child had lost her place. The information came from a Mrs Hog, an Edinburgh inn-keeper, who had taken pity on May and now respectfully appealed to Mr Burns. Going by what he called 'the Devil's Day-book' for his dates, Robert suspected foul play. But he must help the girl. So he wrote to her, and from Thornhill he sent directions to Ainslie*—fellow-sufferer in a like case. Having viewed the suggested farm with discouragement, he turned his face homeward and arrived at Mauchline, tired, out of love with humanity and none too pleased with himself.

He found nothing in Mauchline to counteract these feelings. No poet ever experienced more completely or in more rapid succession the miseries of obscurity and the malignant emptiness of fame. He had wished for it so much—to be talked of and called a clever fellow,—and here

* See note at end of chapter (p.224).

he was, acclaimed in the capital and far beyond it in the very character of his desire. But all it had done for him was to put some dubious money in his purse and show him mankind as it was. Edinburgh had somewhat sickened him of human nature in high places. It had made him an admirer of Satan, so much that he had bought a pocket Milton to carry about in place of the *Man of Feeling*. He now studied 'the sentiments, the dauntless magnanimity, the intrepid unyielding independence, the desperate daring and noble defiance of hardship, in that great personage Satan.' Yet none of his city experiences depressed his opinion of the entire human species so alarmingly as the reception he now met with from the 'plebeian brethren' his 'Compeers, the rustic inmates of the hamlet.'

Those who had most disapproved of him were the readiest to fawn, and the same men and women who had alleged moral grounds for their active spite now overlooked everything in the hope of his favour. The Armours were not only ready but greedy to eat out of his hand. They made it abundantly clear that there was never a more desirable son-in-law, and pushed the ever-willing Jean into his arms. As for the rest, to put it at the highest, he had exchanged the old privileges and freedoms of obscurity for an all-encompassing responsibility. Beneath Hamilton's congratulations it was easy to feel his financial assertion; beneath the pride of mother, brothers and sisters, their reliance upon the famous one to set them right with the world. Gavin Hamilton must be paid; Gilbert must be disembarrassed; William must be found a good place; the womenfolk must be enabled to make a suitable show in church with silk dresses and cloaks. Such is fame. It was all very natural, and some of it, no doubt, right. Another man might even have relished it. But Robert, like all true satirists, was an impassioned idealist. He had dreamed of something different, and he found his whole being jarred by the impact of human opportunism. At the same time he was alarmed by the unforeseen demands enjoined by his success. He was not one to refuse them, yet how was he to accept? His idealism told him that he must not live by his poetry, his realism told him that he could not. So far as the fashionable were concerned he strongly suspected that his vogue would not last. He had lived long enough in Edinburgh to know that Edinburgh was bound to reject the three-quarters of himself that constituted his value as man and poet. Yet, in returning to his shades, he could not hope to make the sort of living that was expected of him save by exploiting his vogue and soliciting the influence of fashionable friends. This process would be almost if not quite as distasteful as turning out verses for money, and what at best would be the results? He looked round at the Mauchline faces, recalled the talk of the Border farmers. It had been bad enough to find that Edinburgh was no better than Mauchline: it was far worse to come back and find Mauchline no better than Edinburgh—indeed not so good. Culture, after all, was something. If hearts were nowhere what they might be, the usages of good society did provide a substitute for charity in the covering of a multitude of shortcomings. He missed, too, in village talk the agility and skill of urban wit. If Edinburgh rejected him, he rejected Mauchline. Again the limbo of Jamaica seemed to offer the only solution.

First, however, he would see the North of Scotland as he had seen the South, make a pious pilgrimage to Kincardine, the land of his fathers, and collect more songs. So much at least he would get out of his fame, and some of the money from his book would be justly expended. Before leaving Edinburgh, indeed, he had discussed the project of a Highland tour with his Crochallan friend, Nicol of the High School. Henry Mackenzie had furnished many distinguished introductions. An itinerary, punctuated with visits, beauty-spots and song localities had been planned. Robert greatly admired Nicol as one who had nothing slavish in his composition and could be at once a Jacobite and a hearty disrespecter of persons. Such a man, he premised, would make the best of travelling-companions. However, they were not to leave till late in August, when the school vacations began and all the Highland mansions would house their noble lords; and there was much to be done before then which involved the further spending of money and the postponement of earning it.

Naturally Robert had taken up again with Jean. It was no

fault of hers, poor girl, that her parents were despicable. He had long since ceased to doubt her fidelity or to reproach her with what he now knew to be a yielding under menaces over the marriage paper. It was enough that since then she had asked him for nothing but his embraces, and had taken them as gladly when he had nothing else to give, as now when he had something which he would not give. For he still made it clear that there was nothing matrimonial in his love. Unlike many men in a similar position, he found girls the least calculating of friends; and the frank greetings given him by various young women in Mauchline had been among the happiest incidents of his homecoming. Girls, of course, liked presents, and they had a predilection for marriage; but there was a purity of emotion in the amorous relation that was not to be found elsewhere. In Mauchline, as in Edinburgh, the young women—and for that matter the young men—would have been very well if only they had been left to themselves by their elders.

Restless at home, in less than ten days he went off, ostensibly to attend to the sales of his book in Glasgow,[1] and to order silk there for the Mossgiel womenfolk—black lute-string of the best quality. He was gone a week, but did the business in much less; and, while the Ayr dressmaker was busy making up the silk (sent home by carrier) into 'Sabbath bests' for Agnes and the girls, he was in Greenock seeking out Mary's grave and calling on her parents. Mrs Campbell, being in Greenock at the time, was prevailed upon to see him. She was even melted by his account of himself, so that he went away comforted in that degree. But nothing she could do or say had any effect on Mr Campbell. Robert, however self-reproachful he might be, could not abide to be so hardily withstood. Having departed hastily to visit the Clyde lochs, he wrote on the window of an inn at Inveraray these lines with Glencairn's diamond ring:

> There's naething here but Highland pride,
>   And Highland scab and hunger;
> If Providence has sent me here,
>   'Twas surely in an anger.

The ostensible occasion of his spleen was the indifference to his comfort shown by the landlord, who, like everybody else in the Campbell capital, was just then engrossed in providing for a great house-party which his Grace of Argyll was entertaining at the Castle. Humble wayfarers must shift for themselves when the MacCallum More (a subscriber, by the way, to the Edinburgh edition) was being served. But the epigram may well have owed its acrimony to a far humbler member of Clan Diarmid—Mr Campbell, skipper of a coal boat.

On his way home, visiting Loch Lomond, he met with a riding accident, the result of a prank following upon two successive nights of revelry, in which all the parties had become what Robert called 'bitchified.' He took it light-heartedly, but the injury to his leg was serious enough to trouble him for several weeks, and helped, with other things, to depress him throughout July, the whole of which month he spent at Mossgiel.² It was the busy time on the farm, and he had ample opportunities both of seeing how bad things were there and for gauging his own distaste for all but the poetical aspects of the soil. The season had again been bad. Everything was puny and unripe. He was plagued by a severe and extended series of nervous nights. Against his instinct he was persuaded to write an elegy on Sir James Hunter-Blair, the Ayrshire Lord Provost of Edinburgh, who died on 1 July. It was a bad elegy and he knew it. It was duly published in the Edinburgh and Ayrshire newspapers, all, of course, for love. He wrote, too, an autobiographical sketch in the form of a letter addressed to Dr Moore. It was not the first time he had thought of doing this for a friend's reading.

In the first days of August he set out for Edinburgh again, *via* Glasgow, where—either by accident or because he wished to have the comments of some friend there before it should be despatched—he left his autobiographical letter. He also left Jean once more 'as women wish to be who love their lords'—to use a favourite quotation of his own. As Jean, however, was probably still suckling the baby girl it may well be that neither she nor Robert suspected the fact. Arrived in Edinburgh on 7 August, he was straightway served with a writ in respect of May Cameron and, admitting his liability, duly received a week later the document of 'liberation,' the back of which, without delay, he utilised by scribbling down on it the latest addition to *The Merry Muses*. After spending the first night with Richmond in the old Lawnmarket quarters, he moved to Nicol's house in Buccleuch Square—a more fashionable part of the Old-town—where he had the exclusive use of an attic room. Richmond, though he knew of his friend's coming, had arranged for the place in his bed to be filled by a less famous companion as from 8 August.

Robert's main object in coming to town nearly three weeks before Nicol could be free for the Highland tour was that he should settle his accounts with Creech. Thanks to Mackenzie—for the Man of Feeling was above all a man of business—Creech had been bound by hand and seal to pay a hundred guineas for the copyright of the Edinburgh edition, but so far he had not paid a penny, and Robert needed money. In addition to the first emergency sums sent home from the earliest subscription monies he was now lending Gilbert £180, free of interest, to be repaid when convenient. His Border tour, his comparatively idle month at home and the journeys he had taken, though they cost no extravagant amount, had made inroads on his capital. And now there was May Cameron, three weeks in Edinburgh—with Lord knew what financial calls and complications—and the coming Highland tour. His voluminous correspondence meant a steady drain of money. Hardly a post now but brought him bad poems from young ladies or old gentlemen or ambitious village mechanics, for the perusal of which he had to pay in money as well as in time and integrity. If there was any merit, or even any real emotion in the effusions he had to read and advise upon, he felt impelled to be kind. Himself sensitive to criticism, he could not be harsh but in the face of effrontery or pretentiousness, when he lashed out with a violence which betrayed his pent-up feelings. So it was his fate to be accessible to every horny-handed male or lily-handed female in Scotland who could string a few rhymes—the understanding being 'If you, a Mauchline ploughman, can have such a success, why not I, and I and I?' When, in addition, his hobby of collecting new as well as old songs became known, he was kept busier than ever.

In spite of these things, in spite of the fact that Creech was far too busy with his levees and other important matters to descend to a question of a hundred guineas, Robert's spirits rose in town. On August 23 he wrote to Ainslie, who was away on holiday, promising that if Ainslie would christen his new-born bastard Achitophel or Zimri Burns, he would return the compliment by naming his own 'get,' when it should arrive, after Ainslie. And on the 25th he stepped in cheerful mood with Nicol into the two-horse chaise which Nicol had insisted upon for the comfort of his corpulence in preference to the less costly mode of travelling upon horseback.

At Linlithgow, their first stop, he hoped to see Smith and to assure himself that at least his dear former 'fiscal' was free from that slavishness which now smeared all the world. But Smith was gone from home, and his friend had to content himself with a call at the shop—where he noticed some attractive Paisley shawls—and a gossip with the house-keeper.

Robert's new companion was stimulating and, being sixteen years his elder and a married man, had more influence over him than the callow Ainslie. Indeed the poet saw in him the best that Edinburgh had to offer. Nicol was against the powers that be, yet was learned in the classics and a man of considerable culture. He was swift to pounce on the falsities and faults of others, especially of those above him, and he had an acrid wit. If he showed also a certain roughness, even violence of temper, his country friend was always ready to account this for righteousness in a character otherwise sympathetic. At Stirling Castle he fanned the ever latent flame of Robert's romantic Jacobitism, with the result that Glencairn's diamond left some dangerous lines on a pane of glass where all comers might see them. They ended thus:

> The injured Stewart line is gone,
> A race outlandish fills their throne;
> An idiot race, to honour lost;
> Who know them best despise them most.

But alas for the vanity of democrats! It had been slily noticed by an Edinburgh observer that, with all Robert's contempt of

the great, he was often 'rather more than enough flattered' by
their notice: and he was now to find that Nicol was rather
more than enough displeased when another was selected for
distinguished attentions. By the time the tour was well
started, travelling with Nicol was like sitting beside 'a loaded
blunderbuss at full cock.' At Blair Castle, when the ploughman was ensconced *en famille* with the Duke and Duchess of
Atholl and their children and the Duchess's two young
sisters—one of whom, a charmer of seventeen, had been
born in Russia where her father was ambassador—the
enraged Latinist, having had a good look at the ducal library,
began to fume with impatience to be off. Graham of
Fintry—a man of great influence in the Excise—was a
fellow-guest; Henry Dundas himself was expected any
moment. Robert, finding everybody delightful and being
found delightful by everybody, would never have a better
chance of establishing himself in life without humiliating
himself in the process. But at the summons of a comrade who
resented having to play second fiddle he turned good-
naturedly away. The pretty diplomat from Petersburg,
realising the situation as keenly as she relished the poet's
company, tried to bribe the chaise driver to damage a wheel
and so delay the departure. But she quickly discovered the
difference between Slav and Scotish coachmen. Hospitable
pleadings were equally vain. Neither Mr Burns's pride nor
Mr Burns's principles would permit him to give even the
semblance of preferring greatness and gain before plain
friendship. 'King Harry,' when he arrived, was not likely to
take a favourable view of such conduct, however it might
recommend itself to young ladies. This was hardly the sort of
action he would absolve from foolishness, or regard as a
recommendation for public employment. It does not appear
that Mr Dundas evinced any regret at having missed the
poet, or ever afterwards showed any desire to make his
acquaintance.

The same thing, though in very different circumstances,
happened in Kincardine, when Robert visited his father's
sisters and their husbands—and Nicol had not even a library
to keep him from irritable boredom. And again at Kilravock.
And again at Gordon Castle. Here in her 'world of a house' on

the Spey, with its vast frontage, its high towers and great domed vestibule, Duchess Jane displayed her 'great gift of homeliness,' and her guest had never felt more at home in any cottage. He too was in his sunniest temper and radiant of his charm, to which she was peculiarly sensitive. But he wanted to include Nicol in the general warmth, and Nicol, because he judged his inclusion to be no more than courtesy on the part of his titled hosts, refused peremptorily to be included. He had the horses harnessed: he stamped up and down: it was in vain that the Gordons sent a gentleman—accompanied by Robert—to beg him to dine with them. With or without Robert he would leave Fochabers according to time-table— which was that very moment. Robert went with him. Of the whole matter Robert made no more than a rueful face and a polite apology. As the chaise containing him and his surly companion swayed and bumped along the road, he found occupation in writing complimentary verses to the Gordon family. That same night, at the next stopping-place, he joked over the incident and poked fun shrewdly, but quite gaily, at the crusty classic. He was never to see the Gordons again.

Before deciding about the farm that he had half-heartedly inspected while at Dumfries, Robert wished to make a serious attempt for the Excise. Also he wanted that hundred guineas of Creech's. After visiting the Burness relations at Montrose, where he promised he would do what he could for Uncle Robert, who was now living in a very poor way in the South-country, he reached Edinburgh on 16 September. The tour had lasted only twenty-two days instead of the intended calendar month, which had proved too much for Nicol's uneasy temper. Nevertheless Robert enjoyed it far more than he had enjoyed the Border tour. After all, the North, not the South, was his ancestral country, and his spirit responded to its wilder beauty and richer music.[3] He was happier with the Gordons and the Atholls than with the complacent farmers of the South, who 'talked nothing but high things.' All the same he was pleased to think that in one of the northern castles, being left alone in the library for a few minutes, and remarking a Shakespeare splendidly bound in tooled calf, which upon inspection proved to be both worm-eaten and unread, he had been able privily to leave his autograph on the fly-leaf:

> Through and through th' inspired leaves,
>   Ye maggots, make your windings;
> But O respect his lordship's taste,
>   And spare the golden bindings!

NOTE. *See* p.215: 'I am very sorry for it, but what is done is done. . . . Please call at the Jas. Hog mentioned & send for the wench & give her 10 or 12 shillings, but don't for Heaven's sake meddle with her as a *Piece*. I insist on this on your honor; & advise her out to some country friends. . . . Call immediately, or at least as soon as it is dark, for God's sake, lest the poor soul be starving. Ask her for a letter I wrote her just now, by way of token. It is unsigned. Write me after the meeting.'

Barskimming woodland, on Ayr river, was one of the many private properties which Robert had used as happy hunting-grounds for love and poetry before fame—more relentless than any Dominie Murdoch—had paraphrased his life into prose. Now the owners of these high waving trees and running waters—the lairds and their ladies of Montgomerie, Catrine, Ballochmyle and Stair—had turned into his hosts, his patrons, his advisers and his critics. Where once he had been glad to sit on the edge of the kitchen table, or may be on the chaff mattress in one of the servant girls' bedrooms, making love in the vernacular or intoning a song for which the laughter had to be painfully smothered, he now sat on an upholstered chair with his boots without apology on the drawing-room carpet, conversed gravely in irreproachable English, and occasionally 'recited' some new complimentary piece, which would be received with condescending applause. All these estates had established some rights of obligation with him; but there was one, that by a curious coincidence of character and circumstance exercised a decisive influence on his life. This was Barskimming. The laird of Barskimming was a very exalted personage, Thomas Miller, Lord Justice-clerk of Scotland.[1] It was as Lord Barskimming that he had taken his seat on the Bench; and though, on succeeding to an older family estate in Kirkcudbright, he had seen fit to change his judicial title to Lord Glenlee, Barskimming remained his usual country seat and the permanent seat of his affections. Naturally he had become a subscriber to the Edinburgh edition, but his interest does not seem to have gone much farther. Not so the interest of his Lordship's younger brother Patrick. He it was that had left the timely ten guineas 'for the Ayrshire bard' at Sibbald's Library in the days when the *Roselle* still hung at anchor in Leith harbour; and he was prepared to do much more.

Mr Patrick Miller was the best-meaning man in the world, perhaps even in Scotland. While in this and many other respects typical of his time, country and class, he was distinguished by certain other characteristics more interesting and less comfortable. With his severe nose, his long upper-lip and jutting under-lip, his somewhat pendulous cheeks, his kindly but absorbed eyes, his brown wig that came low on the forehead giving the whole face a slightly old-womanish look, and his plain dark clothes, he appeared to the casual observer very much what he purported to be—namely, a successful business man of good county standing and with no nonsense about him. A friend of Mr Coutts the banker, he was himself a director of the Bank of Scotland, and also, among other things, chairman of the celebrated Carron Company. It was through men of his kind that the nation, almost without money, had survived the upheaval of the seventeenth century and prospered. Following the example of the Kirk, which in country places had long been a moneylender, shopkeepers and merchants (who were often the younger sons of the landed gentry) had established the practice of financing their customers at five per cent. This had been especially the case in Edinburgh, where such men, without in any degree infringing their public or private honour, met their customers in the taverns or at the head of the High Street to negotiate bills, accept deposits, give loans and, as time went on, to issue small notes that passed into circulation before banks had been so much as thought of. The elder Mr Coutts had combined such useful dealings with his wine business, and many a substantial loan had been arranged in his dark little wine vault among the claret bottles. Though the younger Coutts and Patrick Miller now carried on business through the medium of banking companies, they were close enough to the older and simpler ways to partake of their manner of thought.

So much for the façade presented to the world by the Lord Justice-clerk's banker brother. It was sincere and solid, but it was only a façade. For Patrick Miller was a prey to two of the most calamitous passions known to mankind—mechanical invention and agricultural experiment. Under the wavy brown wig his head was in a perpetual whirl of cranks and pistons, new sorts of naval guns, long-haired Spanish sheep, special breeds of swans, seeds of marvellous grasses, roots from Sweden that would prove the salvation of man and beast—a thousand and one 'bright' ideas, each with its own particular weak point, which in the first instance was invariably overlooked by the sanguine projector. In harmony with these material dreams were political convictions of a highly radical description. Miller had led an adventurous life—he boasted of having been to sea before the mast—and had made every penny of his large fortune by his own efforts. It was natural that he should be in sympathy with the new spirit in France, and heartily disapproving of the Dundas *régime* in Scotland. Nevertheless he contrived to remain on friendly, even intimate terms with the Dictator, who was his fellow-director on the Bank of Scotland and whose ministerial support was absolutely necessary for the prosecution of Mr Miller's more ambitious projects.[2]

On disclosing his identity to Robert in Edinburgh—as he did, shortly after his gift of the ten guineas, by inviting the poet to take a glass of claret with him at his house in Nicolson Street, Old-town—he had been absorbed in arrangements for printing a pamphlet dealing with his invention for the propulsion of ships by paddle-wheels, or, in his own words, 'triple vessels worked by wheels and cranks,' which would make three or four miles an hour, and to which he suggested 'the *steam engine* could be applied to *work* the wheels so to give them a quicker motion, and consequently to increase that of the ship.'[3] But this attended to, his thoughts kept reverting to the estate on the Nith which, the year before, he had been so rash as to buy without inspection. Dalswinton it was called. He had paid £25,000 for it, rejoicing in prospect at the thought of its many farms, its water, and its great historic interest. The Red Comyn, whom Bruce slew in Dumfries church, had lived there in a tower, the walls of which still stood; and before him, in the eleventh century, the thanes of Galloway had owned it. Its more modern dwelling-house had been built in 1626. The ground was reputed rich, the woods and hills lovely. But Miller, when he went to view this purchase, was 'so much disgusted for eight or ten days' that he felt like going away never to return. The place was in a state of utter exhaustion, the tenants were in poverty, the oats from the best river-side or holm fields would fetch only 25s the acre. But at the end of the eight or ten days his enthusiasm had revived, and he had seen himself as the saviour of Dalswinton and the benefactor of Scotland. He would enclose and drain and plant, and bring sheep from Northumberland to cross with the local breeds. He would convert the marshy loch into a lake deep enough for the trial ships of his donkey-powered paddle-boats. Above all he would find in the outhouses all the space he needed for his constant experiments. Dalswinton house was too small for the ideas of his wife and daughters, but Dalswinton coach-house would serve today for the housing of half a dozen tram-cars. Miller would keep no coach—let his womenfolk complain as they might—but he would have a splendid workshop. To placate the family he would build a new dwelling-house on a new site—well within view of the loch, yet far enough from the stable buildings for perfect privacy in the latter place. He would have it of red freestone, four-square, four-storied and solid, with a wide stone area railed about with iron—rather like a new city bank. If the ladies could not be happy there it was not his fault. His sons were a great anxiety to him, the eldest in particular being very costly and light-minded, and not one of them took the least interest in engines or seeds or cattle or their own country. They sided with their mother and sisters in preferring balls at the Duke of Queensberry's, the Edinburgh and Dumfries assemblies, and frivolous trips to London Mrs Miller's father had been quite a small laird.

It is to be feared that this upright and desperately serious gentleman found more to attract him in the poet than the poet did in him. The poet, however, was grateful, and he discharged his gratitude in the only way open to him—by inserting a flattering reference to the Miller family in the Edinburgh version of *The Vision*:

> Through many a wild romantic grove,
> Near many a hermit-fancied cove,
> (Fit haunts for friendship or for love),
>   In musing mood,
> An aged judge, I saw him rove,
>   Dispensing good.

But Miller had, as usual, conceived an idea. He wanted to have Mr Burns as tenant of one of his farms, for he coveted the credit of such a prodigy on his estate, and he was prepared to play the part of the ideal landlord. Mr Burns must come to see Dalswinton, must take his choice of the farms there—all as yet unimproved—and there would be no difficulty about terms. The banks of the Nith would combine dignity with profit, and would confer honour on poet and patron alike. This business man of nearly sixty was still an optimist. It was the poet of twenty-seven who was pessimistic. He summed up the situation in a letter to Ballantine at Ayr: 'Mr Miller is no Judge of land, and though I dare say he means to favour me, yet he may give me, in his opinion, an advantageous bargain that may ruin me.' Nevertheless he had promised that he would visit Dalswinton and inspect the farms there in May before returning to Mauchline. This was early in January, when he had just planned his Border tour.

He had kept his promise, and found Dalswinton beautiful, but in shocking condition. He would come again, he said, in August, and would then give his decision. From Mossgiel he wrote to Smith:

> I cannot settle to my mind. Farming, the only thing of which I know anything, and, heaven above knows, but little do I understand of that, I cannot, dare not, risk on farms as they are. If I do not fix, I will go for Jamaica. Should I stay in an unsettled state at home, I would only dissipate my little fortune, and ruin what I intend shall compensate my little ones for the stigma I have brought on their names.

At the same time, if farming was to be his lot, he knew that he would 'be happier anywhere than in his own neighbourhood'; and a week after writing to Smith he was admitting to Nicol that his view of Miller's lands and Miller's 'reception of my bardship' had somewhat mended his hopes.

Returning from the Highland tour on 16 September, he waited nearly a fortnight before writing an apology to Miller for his delay in revisiting Dalswinton. The letter prevaricates. He has 'arrived in town but the other day'; he will 'certainly wait on' Miller within the coming month; he is 'determined not to leave Edinburgh' till he has wound up his matters with Creech, which may be a tedious business; if he cannot come, after all, till the late autumn, when Miller will presumably be in town, perhaps Miller's factor will deal with him. With many expressions of gratitude—difficult as coming 'from a little man to a great man'—he encloses two indifferent poems of topical and Ayrshire interest.

The trouble was that he could not think without misgiving of this long-nosed laird who with such 'real though mistaken benevolence' had 'sought him industriously out.' Together with what Creech still owed, there would not be more money out of the Edinburgh venture than such a farm as Miller's would devour in two years or less. So whispered the experience of three generations of Burneses. Was not Jamaica itself to be preferred? By leaving Scotland he could at least endow his dependants with the few hundred pounds his poems had brought. With May Cameron's baby his folly had given him four children to provide for; and his fame had placed a family of adults more or less on his hands. His frequent hints concerning an Excise post—and in the Excise he could fancy a competence not inimical to poetry—had been persistently ignored. Yet to refuse Miller's offer would be to refuse the sole suggestion Edinburgh had made. Also there remained the imperishable glamour of a man's own farm . . . the source of his song . . . the shelter for his muse . . . the nucleus of his human circle. He could not now see a family—father, mother, children—without feeling wild with envy. Might there still not be salvation for him on Scotish soil, if he were married to the right woman?

There was, for instance, Gavin Hamilton's young relative, Peggy Chalmers. She was above him socially, yet not so far above him as to be inapproachable in the circumstances. He was not far gone in love, but could express 'a kind of wayward wish to be with you ten minutes by yourself.' She was not so pretty as her cousin Charlotte Hamilton, who lived with her and her widowed mother; but Robert, though on the best of terms with Charlotte, was more warmly interested in the plainer, elder girl. Peggy was small and dainty, with intelligent hazel eyes that could listen appreciatively, and white teeth, and a store of good sense. She liked reading but not talking about books. She sang Scots songs well and without affectation. Robert had got into the way of consulting her in many small matters. Why not do so in greater? Two days before writing to Miller he had written to Peggy, who was still out of town, telling her that he intended seeing Miller's farms 'on Thursday or Friday.' Now suddenly he was determined to see her first. No matter that Harvieston, her country home, was in the opposite direction from Dumfries. He must have her approval before he gave Miller his decision. Perhaps he would ask for something more than her approval. It happened that attractive invitations had come to him earlier from the Stirling neighbourhood, in which Harvieston lay. Leaving Creech to his levees, he mounted Jenny Geddes and rode out of Edinburgh by the Queensferry way. With him for company went a young doctor called Adair.[4] It was early October.

The trip was in most ways a success, especially for Adair. At Stirling they fell in with Nicol, and made a songful night of it in that same tavern where last time Robert had written the offensive lines on the window. This time, however, he broke the pane. At Harvieston they were storm-stayed for ten days, and Robert asked Peggy to marry him, and Adair fell in love with Charlotte, and Charlotte with Adair. At another place of call, Robert, in amorous mood, made advances to a young lady, still in her teens, named Euphemia, and was chidden but not cast down.[5] At yet another he was 'knighted' by an ancient Jacobite dame with the Bruce's own sword. Outside Dunfermline Abbey he knelt to kiss 'with sacred fervour' the poor flagstones of the Bruce's grave—raging the while with secular fervour against Scotland's neglect of her heroes. Presently, inside the church, he set Adair upon the cutty-stool and, himself mounting the pulpit, held forth at length in Daddy Auld's best manner upon the exceeding sinfulness of fornication. On the way back they visited Queen Mary's prison in Loch Leven. On Saturday, 20 October, after close upon three weeks, they were recrossing the Queen's Ferry into Edinburgh. Robert had collected more songs and airs, had caught a heavy cold, and had been refused by Peggy Chalmers.

This last meant that another of the few remaining paths to happiness was closed. More clearly than ever he could imagine that, with Peggy's clear eyes, linnet voice, wise, plain little visage and country upbringing, his life would have gone well. Happily, however, her refusal had not wounded him. He had been so much more friendly than enamoured that when she confided in him that for some time she had been secretly engaged to a young Edinburgh lawyer, his friendliness was increased by a greater measure of frankness and affection.

Her strong approval of the farm, though she would never be its mistress, weighed with him; and finding in Edinburgh a letter from Miller which had been lying for nearly a week, he answered it at once with apologies. He has been 'a few days' out of town; he is in the doctor's hands with a cold; but he hopes to ride to Dumfries in 'two or three days.' He practically commits himself. Acting on the advice of his friends, he would wish to call Miller landlord sooner than any landed gentleman he knows.

Besides Miller's letter there had been one from home to tell that little Jean, the girl twin, was dead. To Richmond, now on holiday at Mauchline, he wrote:

> I long much to hear from you, how you are, what are your views, and how your little girl comes on . . . by the way, I hear I am a girl out of pocket and by careless murdering mischance too, which has provoked me and vexed me a good deal. . . . I beg you will write me by post immediately on receipt of this, and let me know the news of Armour's family, if the world begin to talk of Jean's appearance any way. . . .

The following week he went to Dalswinton, looked briefly and despairingly at the land again, and returned to town without having lengthened his journey either way by going round by Mauchline. He would have to face Ayrshire and its problems soon enough. After that he would pay one more visit to Dumfries and decide. He would discuss the matter with Gilbert first. 'My brother is an excellent farmer,' he wrote to Peggy, 'and is, besides, an exceedingly prudent, sober man (qualities which are only a younger brother's fortune in our family).' If Miller's farm, of which he now confessed to feeling 'rather hopeless,' should fail, he was even prepared to 'return into partnership' with Gilbert in

Ayrshire, so long as it was not at Mossgiel—that is to say, in spite of the 'something' that had so often whispered in him against all farms, and in particular against a farm in his old neighbourhood, he was prepared to defer to the judgment of others. He invited Peggy to compliment him upon his 'unfathomable, incomprehensible wisdom.'

From the nightmare subject of farms he passed with relief to discuss some of his new material for the *Museum*. Here, anyhow, he knew so perfectly what he wanted that he needed neither advice nor approval. He had set himself to save the folk-song of his country, music as well as words—music, he would say, before words; because he had seen this as the natural order ever since his first love-song in the harvest field at Mount Oliphant. First love, then music, then the poet—then again love, in the shape of a girl to sing the words to the music and kiss the poet and so complete the starry circle. Not all the wise town critics could alter this. Neither could the discouragement of the genteel Edinburgh musicians shake his conviction that an old tune ought to be preserved in its integrity, without modification or modernising. In Johnson he had a 'natural' musician, who was luckily as illiterate and acquiescent as he was enthusiastic about true folk music; while in Clarke, the Episcopalian organist, he had a practical musical editor who was indolent, fond of his glass and all against gentility in music. Clarke easily did for him what he, with his severe musical disabilities, found impossible; yet even here, by virtue of his inner ear and rhythmical memory, he would be master. He had the rare faculty for detecting what he called 'the genius of a tune' under any disguise, and no trouble was too great for him in the matter of discovering dates and sources. If Scotland was ever rich in anything it was in melodies, but everywhere music was disappearing. In all existing printed collections there were not a couple of hundred airs with words attached. Johnson in his first volume had felt compelled to eke out his material with English airs. In the second volume (due to appear in March) Robert declared that every one of the hundred airs would be Scotish, no matter what the words. He had become an inveterate searcher of the old dance and instrumental music books with their peculiar scales and eccentric intervals, which he loved, and a still more inveterate saviour of melodies that lived only on the lips of some country woman or in the catguts of some drunken barn-fiddler. He had clearly in his head several hundred different tunes, many of them with various versions to which he was acutely sensitive, and on hearing them played he could correct the slightest fault in tempo, rhythm, and so forth.[6]

As for the words, it was his humour to be anonymous. The god of rustic song must perform his wonders unhampered by the pedantry of the polite. He had had enough of Edinburgh criticism with the few songs of his that Edinburgh had seen. Asking neither money nor praise for a pursuit that delighted him, he would be free from the cramping comments of the genteel, for whom, after all, his songs were not meant. So, in Vol 11 of the *Museum*, of the forty songs which would have his words, or words transformed by his revision, only one—a political ballad—should bear his name. If they passed for authentic old songs, so much the better; he would even assert their antiquity himself. The title of a dance tune—and it was lucky that all Scotland was dancing mad now—or a scrap of refrain was enough to suggest a plausible reconstruction, but such old words as were found must be piously preserved. If they were too bawdy for the *Museum* they could be kept for *The Merry Muses*. If he went wrong anywhere it was out of charity to the contemporary efforts which were thrust upon him in profusion when the news of his enterprise got about. In his gay and arrogant preface he asked for the collaboration of readers and proclaimed that

> Ignorance and prejudice may perhaps affect to sneer at the simplicity of the poetry or music of some of these pieces; but their having been for ages the favourites of Nature's Judges—the Common People—was to the Editor a sufficient test of their merit.

For such work a harpsichord was much needed, but Robert now had an upper room in St James's Square, New-town, at the home of his and Nicol's friend, Cruik-shank of the High School, and Cruikshank, who was married, had a harpsichord and a musical schoolgirl daughter called Jenny who was glad to pick out tunes for a dark-eyed poet.

But otherwise he was merely hanging about, waiting for Creech. And he was in the old familiar situation—illuminated by success, yet in all his farewells afflicted by a sense of failure and by the doubt whether he would ever be able to settle down either as wage-earner or as poet. Apart from complimentary verses and anonymous songs he had produced nothing these many months. From Stirling came the suggestion (no bad idea as ideas go) that he ought to write Scotish Georgics: from London Murdoch wrote advising that 'this huge overgrown metropolis . . . would afford matter for a large poem.' Several times he had to contradict the rumour that he was going to London. London indeed! Edinburgh was enough, and now the edge was off Edinburgh. As the sessions of the Courts and the University opened late in the year, the smarter folk would not return much before the beginning of December. It was Robert's belief that when they did return they would no longer be interested in him or anything of his. He had had a hint here and there, and though he had expected as much and said so from the first, it was disgusting. There was Ainslie, of course, lodging just across the square and with a supply of the best port stowed under his window-seat. And there was Nicol, always ready to sit up all night,[7] deploring, with some wit but more noise, the iniquities of those in authority (with special reference to the Rector of the High School). And there were many other good fellows, buglike in their fidelity to Auld Reekie in all seasons, who were only too glad to have life supplied to them gratis by one whose gift was life. Still it was time for him to 'return to his shades,' and on 4 November he wrote to Mrs Dunlop that he would be in Ayrshire 'in eight or ten days.' That new trouble was brewing for him at home he had every reason to know. This did not keep him from creating the elements of later trouble in Edinburgh. The May Cameron affair being settled, the girl had gone on her way—doubtless rejoicing that she had obtained the legal admissions of a man in the public eye and with money in his pocket. But naturally May had had a successor. Her name was Jenny Clow.[8] She seems to have been a decent, well-doing girl, but lacking health, vigour and friends.

As usual Robert found it difficult to move. On 1 December

he was still in Edinburgh, hoping to be off 'in three or four days.' On 4 December there was a tea-party given by a spinster friend of Peggy Chalmers, to which for business reasons he must go. On 7 December there would be a later, more convivial gathering, to which he need not, but would go. Other items of business and farewell made him postpone his departure to 13 December.

The tea-party was at Alison's Square, Old-town, between the University and Nicol's house, quite near Mr Patrick Miller's town residence. Robert went from politeness and because Mr Nimmo, his hostess's brother, was a high official of the Excise and a man to keep in touch with. Miss Nimmo herself he did not much care about—though kindly, she was a decided bore. But there was among her guests a fluffy, full-bosomed young married lady, who addressed herself to the poet in so engaging and flattering a manner that he was presently cursing his bad luck in not having met her sooner. Those fair feathery curls, tied back in enchanting disorder—were not 'golden locks a sign of amorousness' in woman? That palpitating presence—and 'the more love in a woman's composition, the more soul she has.'[9] That enthusiasm for poetry, and particularly *his* poetry! That endearing alternation between irrepressible gaiety and something serious, even pathetic! That crying need (for which he had an ear as keen as for folk-song) of 'what every lady does or would do'—everything distinguished her from the usual sprightly but self-contained female that he had been meeting in middle-class Edinburgh society. When, Cinderella-like, she took an early leave—a young family requiring her speedy return to her home across the way behind General's Entry in the Potterrow—she took with her Mr Burns's promise that he would honour her humble abode on Thursday evening (which was the day after tomorrow) at eight o'clock, when she would be alone.

Their conversation had been so marked that, when 'the Ayrshire Ploughman' took his leave, he was rallied by Miss Nimmo upon his success with 'poetess Nancie.' Like so many ageing and good-natured spinsters, Miss Nimmo was something of a sly pander as well as a gossip. She knew enough of her guest's private life to render him a trifle unresponsive to her teasing. But the word poetess was a bait that he could not resist. Who and what was the charming lady? Miss Nimmo's information was deplorably interesting.

He was unable, as it happened, to drink tea on Thursday evening at the Potterrow, and sent his humble apologies. The invitation was at once renewed for the Saturday, to be 'embraced with the greatest pleasure.' In an access of rollicking spirits he wrote to Gavin Hamilton, who had recovered from the gout, enclosing two sets of bawdy verses:

> . . . A hymn of thanksgiving would, in my opinion, be highly becoming from you at present; and in my zeal for your well-being, I earnestly press on you to be diligent in chaunting over the two enclosed pieces of sacred poesy. My best compliments to Mrs Hamilton and Miss Kennedy.

Yours in the Lord,
ROBT BURNS.

Robert was correct in his instinct that Miss Nimmo's guest was no Edinburgh product. He was usually correct in his instincts, though circumstances and the times so often seemed to put him in the wrong even in his own eyes. Little Mistress Agnes McLehose was from the West, and a very little emotion was enough to remove the veneer imposed by five adult years in the metropolitan East. The daughter of a Glasgow surgeon of respectable connexions and good professional standing, she had been born in the same year as Robert and, like Robert's mother, had been left motherless at the age of eight with saintly maternal memorials of the Calvinist persuasion. A further bereavement when she was thirteen, of an only, one-year-married sister (no doubt in childbirth), had imposed a further 'sensibility' upon a disposition naturally light. At fifteen, full of gaiety and good looks and up to her neck in innocent flirtations, 'pretty Miss Nancie Craig' was a Glasgow toast. She had the brightly delicate colouring of the West, with affectionate eyes, a pleasantly retroussé nose, lovely teeth, a chin amenably retreating, childish hands and feet, a soft voice and frank, lively manners. She was imitative and quick-witted, but little care had been given to her education.

At this juncture, however, her father felt moved to send her to an Edinburgh establishment for the daughters of gentlemen. He did so, not so much to improve her mind as to remove her from a too amorous atmosphere, and perhaps in the hope that a boarding-school finish—the latest novelty in Scotland—might enhance his only child's matrimonial prospects and lead her to set a higher value on her charms than if she were led merely by her own amiability. To this end he put her one day into the stage coach at the Black Bull—she being the only passenger—and waved her good-bye with every conviction of parental duty discharged.

He was not aware (as neither was, to do her justice, Miss Nancie) that a young Glasgow writer of the name of McLehose, aged twenty, an admirer who as yet had failed of an introduction, had booked all the other seats in the same coach, which he purposed to enter at a further stage of the journey. An all-day, unobserved, uninterrupted siege, McLehose trusted, would not fail of its effect.[1]

His confidence was well founded. Nancie was nothing if not impressionable, and though when the coach rumbled out of Glasgow she fancied she had left her heart behind, this was a way of wooing she could not resist. She dreamed of it all the six months at school, and on her return, when the young fellow immediately renewed his protestations, promised to marry him forthwith. Her father and others begged her to wait, but she was set upon it, and, as there was nothing superficially against her choice, who was presentable in person and family, she had her way. At seventeen she made a charming bride.

In some circumstances she might also have made a good wife. She was loving, dutiful, cheerful. But she was of the courtesan type, she loved her own way above all things, and James McLehose—for all his bright idea about the coach—was the worst husband she could have had—violently jealous, cruel, a bully and a hypocrite. Their quarrels were soon constant and fierce. Nancie, for all her endearing young charms, had, as she admitted, 'nothing of the spaniel' about her. After three and a half years she got her friends to agree with her that a separation was necessary. He got his to agree with him that she should be regarded as a deserting wife. The first baby had died, two more were alive, another was imminent. Mr McLehose's orders were that the new infant should be sent out to nurse as soon after the confinement as possible, and the other two 'distributed' at once among his relatives. This was done. Sadder, if not much wiser, Nancie went back to live with her father in the Saltmarket.

After two years Dr Craig died, leaving her a tiny annuity; and being wretched in Glasgow, where she was exposed to encounters with her husband and his people, while not permitted to visit her children, she went to live in Edinburgh. McLehose, however, was the kind of man who cannot let a woman be, save in the matter of money. He was for ever suggesting new arrangements, meetings, scenes of reunion. His relatives had begun to grow tired of him and of looking after his children. He announced that he was for Jamaica. But he would go *via* London. Would Nancie let him pay at least a farewell visit—'probably for the last time on this earth'—before he took the coach? Nancie, in spite of her retreating chin, was firm.

Injured, he tried to retaliate by letter. She was to return to Glasgow, there to make her home with 'those endearing pledges of our once happier days,' now definitely rejected by his family. But there was no word of support.

Nancie refused to live in Glasgow. She would, however, go there for the children and assume the full responsibility for bringing them up. In the quality of a delinquent lawyer's wife and a deceased doctor's daughter she obtained £10 a year from the Glasgow Faculty of Procurators and £8 from the Glasgow Faculty of Physicians and Surgeons. With this and her father's annuity she established a frugal home in Edinburgh. One of the children seems to have died about this time, so she had only two to provide for.

Among her Edinburgh kindred were two judges, Lords Craig and Dreghorn, which gave her a measure of social standing. In addition, Lord Craig—seeing how the price of living had gone up since the conclusion of the Colonial war—contributed something to her income from his own pocket, and in doing so acquired a *tendresse* for his interesting, spirited young cousin and certain rights which she permitted without allowing him to overstep them. Lord Dreghorn was different. Something dissolute in his own habits, he emphatically disapproved of women who lived apart from their husbands for any reason whatsoever. Still, the connexion was a useful one. Though it was perhaps easier to see 'Mistress Meiklehose' in her own house than elsewhere—she not being widely or fashionably invited out—she had her own little circle, and there were worse places than her minute, small-windowed, first-floor drawing-room in which to spend an evening. Had Edinburgh been

Paris she would almost certainly have found her niche as the most careful and respectable of *maîtresses femmes*. She had the gifts and the history for such a position, as well as the rigid principle and strength of character to maintain it. As this was Edinburgh she had to be content with platonic friendships. On his way to 'Dawney' Douglas's Lord Craig found it very stimulating to drop in for a quiet chat with the ripe, broody young woman who was a good listener as well as an animated talker, and to watch her pouring out tea into her elegant little cups decorated with birds of paradise. With her irreproachable life, her sweet little children and her tinge of tragedy, she provided a pretty contrast to the Crochallan stories and songs at Anchor Close. The least he could do in return was to gratify her by an occasional introduction to 'literary' people.

For literary people were her aim and admiration, and her secret ideal was a *salon* with herself as centre. Like her Grace of Gordon (for whom she expressed the strongest contempt) she had assiduously mended her own education these few years while undertaking that of her children. She had not only studied the best authors in prose and verse—especially verse—but had 'cultivated the Muses' now and then herself. Ideas for poems 'came into her mind like an inspiration.' As a letter writer she had acquired a style both playful and correct.

At the same time she was religious. Thrown into a panic by the shock of her marriage and the revelation it had brought of her own levity and violence, she had embraced with ardour the strict Calvinism which had been her mother's faith. It provided the guidance necessary to her 'chequered life.' It also provided the even more necessary male 'to shelter me in his bosom' in the shape of the Rev John Kemp of the Tolbooth Kirk. Always ready for a soulful *tête-à-tête* with any of the ewes among his flock, this pastor was what is known among the less favoured as 'a great ladies' man.'[2] Of a type found at all times in the priesthood of all Christian sects, he adhered to the new Evangelicals, of whom Sir Henry Moncrieff was the distinguished leader.

Mr McLehose, after two and a half years of dissipation in London, had gravitated by the usual path to the Fleet Prison. His family advanced funds for his release and outfit, provided he went abroad at once. At last he sailed for Jamaica, whence came high-sounding letters but no money. On these reports of prosperity the learned faculties of Glasgow withdrew their pensions to his wife, and Lord Craig informed the defaulter that he was stopping supplies. Nancie wrote too. Her younger boy, William, was delicate. He had abscesses. She badly needed money. Neither letter elicited any reply. His Lordship went on paying. Gallantly he even made up the £18 difference.

For many months Nancie had cherished only one greater ambition than that she should meet the Ayrshire Ploughman, and this was that the Ayrshire Ploughman should meet her. She had tried again and again, but had failed. Lord Craig was evasive—it would almost seem obstinate. All the forces of religion did not keep her from repeatedly murdering in her heart that brazen, infamous Duchess, who, merely because she was titled, might bid a grateful poet wait upon her in town or country. All Nancie had read by the man, all she had heard of him from the gossips surrounding her, assured her that she alone in Edinburgh was fitted to be his darling friend. Was not her scorn for the great even keener than his? Had she not, like him, been the sport of misfortune and her own impulsive but loveable nature? Did she not, like him, lack coolness and wisdom, and despise design? Gifted, in her humbler way, with a similar 'pathetic elegance of language,' and with 'the delicate refinements of superior minds,' what converse might she not have with him of a sort to which 'the bulk of mankind are strangers?' And he was of the West, as she was. She would not need to go warily with him as with the frigid, critical Edinburgh folk. While she would avoid the least appearance of condescension, how pleasant it would be—on account of the difference in their stations, and because of her 'sweet feminine mind'—to act just for once as the dispenser of favour.

After many disappointments her enthusiasm and importunities had brought about the meeting at Miss Nimmo's house. And all her presentiments had come true! Even Mr Burns's favourite quotations, which he so liked to have 'pat for every occasion,' were those which had been *her* favourites since girlhood. She lived for Thursday night.

But her excitement was to be further fomented by a series

of checks. On Thursday came the message that Mr Burns was unable to drink tea with her. He regretted it much, but something of the utmost urgency had intervened.

She detained the messenger till she had written a note for him to carry back to St James's Square. Would Mr Burns come on Saturday evening instead? She was not offended; she was gay; she was appealing; she would take no denial.

The same day she had what amply consoled her—Mr Burns's acceptance, couched in the most flattering terms, and enclosing a *jeu d'esprit* written specially for her in response to Miss Nimmo's teasing. True, Mr Burns was careful to remind her that fiction was 'the native region of poetry,' and that he was leaving Edinburgh within a week, not to return for two years; but he had 'not often been so disappointed' and he promised her some more 'poetic trifles' if she would like them. On the Saturday night she fluttered over her bird-of-paradise cups awaiting him. There was something bird-like about her—feathery crest, pretty bosom pushed to pigeon height by her stays, snowy fichu folded modestly across (for Mr Burns, true labouring man, disapproved of gratuitous exposures). The few candles were alight, the fire burned brightly, two chairs were placed. What things might not be said and looked and felt within this cosy feminine ark with never a husband near! How 'delightful, when under the check of *reason* and *religion*' to listen to 'the passionate effusions of an elegant mind!' When a knock sounded at the outer door it was with difficulty that the lady allowed her trusted female servant to open it. Next moment the servant entered—with a letter!

In the early hours of that morning, returning from another all-night party—attended by Miss Nimmo, though not by Mrs McLehose—Mr Burns, on stepping from the coach, has fallen and dislocated his knee-cap. Pain has prevented him from sending an earlier message. He will not be able to put his foot to the ground for weeks.

The blow was severe. But the lady was brave; and there was some balm in at least the framing of the news. The crippled poet's warmth—due no doubt to the quantity of port prescribed by Edinburgh's cleverest surgeon[3]—permitted of an even warmer reply. While the messenger waited,

Nancie poured herself forth in the fullness of 'pathetic elegance.' If only she were Mr Burns's sister that she might come to him! Surely they two are temperamentally akin as any brother and sister! Here are some of her own verses for him to condemn! Even if she must flout the censorious by calling upon him (with Miss Nimmo as chaperon) he *shall* not leave Edinburgh without seeing her! Had ever Scotish lady written so to a ploughman before?

Robert waited four days—days of acute physical and mental distress—before he answered this letter. He bore pain stoically, but such an accident at such a moment was a trial indeed. Wood said it might be years and must be months before he recovered full use of the knee-joint. For weeks the leg must be kept stretched on a chair.

In desperation the patient began to read his Bible right through. The first four books of the Old Testament went to his head, and with this and his predicament he was quickly in a state of extreme nervous sensibility. If only Peggy Chalmers had been there with her safe friendliness and her sweet cousin Charlotte, to 'pour oil and wine into his wounded spirit'—thus he wrote to Peggy on the Wednesday. But Peggy was not there, and oil and wine he must have, and were they not being offered in the pretty lady's letter which still lay unanswered? He had never believed in platonic love—for himself; but a tender friendship with a gentlewoman who thought that she did, opened up new possibilities. Glorious as the Bible was, he would soon have read it from cover to cover, and he was sure he was not going to enjoy the New Testament nearly so much as the Old. So that same day, after writing to Peggy, he wrote to the lady of the Potterrow. If he and she had but met in time, he said, things would have been very different; but as it was, he was her friend till he should cease to be, and every day until he saw her she should hear from him.

Next day's news in Edinburgh was the death of Lord President Dundas. Sandy Wood brought it to his patient, and with it the suggestion (strongly backed by another friend and fellow-Crochallan, named Hay) that the Scotish laureate would do well to 'celebrate' the occasion in elegiac verse. The mighty Henry Dundas was the late Lord President's younger brother, and Mr Solicitor Dundas his son. Little matters like the Excise, as well as larger matters, were equally in their hands. The Scotish laureate did not at all like the idea, but reason and prudence overbore his scruples, and instead of sleeping that night he produced twenty couplets with which he was not displeased. He also composed a careful covering letter, which Wood delivered with the poem at the Solicitor-General's house. No acknowledgment was ever received. Robert had not suffered such an affront since the occasion of his dismissal from the Armours' cottage. 'I never see the name of Dundas,' he wrote three years later . . . 'but my heart seems straitened for room in my bosom, and if I am obliged to read aloud a paragraph relating to one of them, I feel my forehead flush and my nether lip quiver.'

The letter to Mrs McLehose met with a happier fate. If she did not reply till Sunday, this was only because she felt the need to collect herself in a ladylike manner and think things over prayerfully. Mr Kemp's sermon helped to this end. In the most refined way she would inform Mr Burns that she was neither a fool nor a wanton, remind him that he was addressing a married woman, and at the same time make sure that he should go on addressing her.

Robert smiled. There are letters that have much power to deflect an early love-flame into the flue of flirtation, and this was one of them. He clearly saw the writer as a 'miss of the would-be gentry' who, unlike at least some 'females of the upper ranks,' could not escape from the bane of boarding-school acquirements. But he also felt the heart of an amorous woman fluttering in his hand, and his own gave decided throbs in response. She had asked him if he could wait for her seven years! Before answering he wrote to Peggy:

> My worst enemy is *Moimême*. I lie so miserably open to the inroads and incursions of a mischievous, light-armed, well-mounted banditti, under the banners of Imagination, Whim, Caprice, and Passion; and the heavy-armed veteran regulars of Wisdom, Prudence, and Forethought move so very, very slow, that I am almost in a state of perpetual warfare, and, alas! frequent defeat.

And he wishes he were either a wild horse, having no desire

that cannot be satisfied, or an oyster possessing neither desire nor fear.

Being, however, neither an oyster nor a wild horse, but a disciple of the Rev Laurence Sterne; and holding that 'whim enters deeply into the composition of human nature; particularly of genius' and that Love is surely no 'present of ribbons that you cannot share among womankind without lessening the quantity each should receive,'[4] he despatched to the Potterrow a letter of the utmost skill.

> Pay my addresses to a married woman! (mark how he twists her phrase) I cannot positively say, Madam, whether my heart might not have gone astray a little; but I can declare upon the honor of a Poet, that the vagrant has wandered unknown to me.

The rest is pure tom-cat flirtation with a she-mouse. But there shall be no deceit about it. So, besides the warning that he is on his honour only as a poet (she having been told earlier that fiction is the realm of poetry), he will have her know that he writes 'because he has nothing else to do.'

But Nancie had humour as well as persistence, and by Christmas Eve she had composed six stanzas for him upon this last hard saying, which she sent instead of a letter. She introduced Apollo, Cupid, Venus, and Minerva, and signed herself 'Clarinda.' While Joseph the porter—who by now knew that he was on a good thing and charged when possible at both ends—waited at St James's Square, Robert indited ten stanzas in reply and signed himself 'Sylvander.' Impossible not to flirt with such a woman. Besides the 'Daft Days' had begun.[5]

Two days after Christmas she sent some lines of a different character:

> Talk not of Love! It gives me pain—
>   For Love has been my foe.

which charmed him so much that he said he would have them—with some additions of his own and a false rhyme mended—for the *Museum*.[6]

The poetess, however, having eaten her 'Yule-tide bread' in solitude was sad and lonely, and was going out of town the following week. She longed for conversation with the man who had created 'so much fun' between two people who had met only once. Could not Mr Burns take a coach and visit her tomorrow or the next day—Friday or Saturday?

Now able to hobble on crutches, he was going on Monday to an ale-house round the corner where some Edinburgh Jacobites were to celebrate the birthday of the Young Chevalier. He had composed one of his worst poems for the occasion:

Tho' something like moisture conglobes in my eye,

and was looking forward to it. But the Potterrow, nearly a mile away in bitterly cold weather, was another matter. To soften his refusal he addressed her as his 'dear Clarinda' and signed himself 'Sylvander.' So no more Sirs and Madams even in prose. 'The idea of Arcadian names in a commerce of this kind' pleased him and seemed to make things safer. In a letter interrupted by portentous callers, so that it was begun one day and finished the next, he begs to know her movements, warns her that he may be gone before her return, promises to make her house his first place of call as soon as he can go so far even in a coach, enlarges on his ideas of a friendship between them upon which separation would have no effect. It is to be a perfectly innocent friendship, but she must know that for him 'there is no holding converse, or carrying on correspondence, with an amiable woman, much less a *gloriously-amiable fine woman*, without some mixture of that delicious passion whose most devoted slave I have, more than once, had the honour of being. But why be hurt or offended on that account?' Why indeed!

Late on Friday night Clarinda wrote that she had changed her plans. She is going out of town on Saturday and returning on Tuesday. In spite of conscious innocence her situation demands that their correspondence should be absolutely secret. He is not to tell a soul. Like himself, however, she is incapable of dissimulation, though only too capable of love.

On the Sunday of her absence Robert wrote to his old Irvine friend, Brown, now married and master of a ship—the *Mary and Jean*—and living at Greenock between voyages to Grenada. He hopes to meet Brown shortly in Glasgow on his way home, when he will have something to tell of 'the other sex.' At this moment he is ready to hang himself for 'a young Edinburgh widow, who has wit and wisdom more murderously fatal than the assassinating stiletto of the Sicilian bandit . . .' so that 'Almighty Love still reigns and revels' in his bosom. Reminding Brown affectionately of their walks in Eglinton Woods, and of his encouragement to a heckler poet, he encloses Nancie's 'Talk not of Love.' Though he could still laugh at her and himself he was clearly impressed with her dear idea. At the very least it was something to take away with him into his shades. There was not in all his world one other young woman to whom he could write as he wrote to her, or from whom he could receive letters such as hers.

Her next letter was cooling. She had returned from the country full of virtue and end-of-the-year resolutions, the chief of which was to bring her Ploughman Poet to Jesus. He had confessed that he had no love for Calvinism. By her decree the Throne of Grace would be their rendezvous, the Father of Mercies their chaperon. While allowing that 'a *little* softness' must be in a friendship 'between people of sentiment and of different sexes,' she lays it down that any 'selfish gratification' (a thing of which man alone seems capable) 'deserves to be styled, not love, but by a name too gross to mention.' But just because, had she been a man she would have been Robert, she must be allowed, goddess-like, to chasten where she loves. Mutual fault-finding is to be the duty and the test of their friendship.

Robert was not so far gone as to swallow this, but he was so gentle in his written exposure of each fallacy that it was easy for her to see nothing but the gentleness—especially as he proposed coming to the Potterrow by chair the very next day—Friday, 4 January. True, it would only be from 5 to 6 P.M. on his way to 'a much-valued old friend' who lived beyond her, and on his way back he would pay a farewell call at Miss Nimmo's. But he was coming. In preparing for this, their first *tête-à-tête*, she got a headache.

Their hour was short, even hurried. It was saddening to learn that Satan was one of Sylvander's 'favourite heroes,' still more so that the much valued old friend to whom he was hastening on was the infamous Nicol, of whom Clarinda had heard nothing good. Yet all the more need to save a wayward poet. He certainly had the gift to turn even such a meeting into 'a paradisaical evening interview, stolen from the restless cares and prying inhabitants of this weary world.' Short as it was, there was time for him to hear much of her history, to speak of his mother to her, to tell her about Jean and his little Bobbie at Mossgiel, to assure her that though Jean had alienated him he could never think of a woman with less affection for her having yielded to him, to promise her a reading of his autobiographical letter (of which he had a tattered copy in Edinburgh) sent to Dr Moore in September, and for much more of tender interest, including her determination that she will make two shirts for little Bobbie with her own hands.

After twice reading the Moore letter which she had next day she sat up a whole night writing to Sylvander. She has found in his autobiography 'not a trace of friendship towards a female.' Jean, she thinks, must be 'either an angel or a dolt.' Her own opinion is that he should not marry till he finds a woman that 'can love as ardently as himself.' As for her, she could forgive even unfaithfulness in a husband if he were kind and self-reproachful. 'Reconciliation, in such a case, would be exquisite beyond almost anything I can conceive! Do you understand me on this subject?'

Only too well Sylvander understood. Since their brief meeting their letters had become more frequent and of a heightened emotion, and Clarinda had made repeated attempts—each provocatively unsuccessful—to be seen by him from his window and to catch a glimpse of him as she walked across the Square. And though he twisted a wry face over her platonic and 'religioso' vein, he was now in love with her half the time. The rest of the time he was cool or frightened. All the time he knew the whole thing to be impossible. He was too experienced not to see how things were heading. This woman would suffer materially if he became her lover. His life was complicated enough without that. When now she wrote asking him to join her in the Leith fly, in which on Saturday the 12th she had to convey her boy who had been ill, it was a relief to him that he could not yet walk so far.

But his excuse reached her just as she was setting out, still hopeful, for the fly; and besides he laid it down that she must not find fault with him unless she wanted occasion to break with him, and said she should not expect a call till *about the middle of next week*. It was too much. She wept with vexation during the tedious journey with sick little William, and that same evening sent a tearful reply. Sylvander is offended with her : he will soon forget her : she wishes she saw him happily married. Which brought Sylvander straightway in a chair. They both had raging headaches. If he was not in love he was as near as makes no matter. She made no question of her condition. Thus, next day :

> I will not deny it, Sylvander, last night was one of the most exquisite I ever experienced. Few such fall to the lot of mortals! Few, extremely few, are formed to relish such refined enjoyment. That it should be so, vindicates the wisdom of Heaven.

Yet, though 'the limits of virtue had been observed,' the lady had doubted during a sleepless night if Heaven, still more if Lord Craig, would have approved. On the Sunday morning, listening to Mr Kemp's discourse, she was in a panic lest she had lost Sylvander's esteem. To remedy this she preached to him evangelically on paper on Sunday evening, at the same time cleverly adopting and echoing as her own, particular sentiments and tastes she knew to be his. He admitted that he liked a woman to be strong on religion. Now they wrote, as often as not, twice in a day, deliciously mingling literature, theology, human misfortune, self-revelation, observation, flirtation, friendliness, gaiety and love-hunger. She became his angel. She noted that another woman praised by him had a thick, bad figure, waddled in her walk and was red in the face. But in spite of all, he suggested no other visit till next Saturday. She preferred Thursday or Friday—'Saturday I am not *sure* of being alone . . .' 'eight will be an hour less liable to intrusion . . .' 'a chair is so uncommon a thing in our neighbourhood, it is apt to raise speculation; but they are all asleep by ten.'

Not only did Robert go on foot from St James's Square to the Potterrow on Friday, but on Saturday he wrote acknowledging his conversion to platonic friendship. Clarinda had refined and exalted his soul, given him a stronger relish for piety, shown him the charm of 'Beauty and Grace in the arms of Truth and Honour.'

These assurances depressed her somewhat, but she was cheered by the belief that he still nourished 'delusive hopes' with regard to her. Was he truly 'the male friend' she had long sought, who could love her 'with tenderness, yet unmixed with selfishness?' She would not hide from him that all other attempts had ended in love-making on the part of the male friend. And 'the man who enjoys more pleasure in the mercenary embraces of a courtezan than in relieving the unfortunate, is a detestable character, whatever his bright talent may be.' She had just been cut by Lord Dreghorn.

Much in the two letters written by her on the Saturday and Sunday after their third meeting would have made Robert in his normal state pull a face. But when they reached him he was far from normal. Shocking news from Mauchline had thrown him into one of his old nervous conditions, and he had been further shattered by a succession of callers—pretentious, critical, verbose—to whom he had been obliged to show courtesy. His conscience tormented him; his father's teaching showed full of truth and wisdom; he was ready to lend an ear to any word of religion.

At Mauchline Jean was again with child past hiding, and was being turned out of her parents' house.[7] Suppose that at this new crisis the Armours took it into their heads to plead the validity of the marriage? It was true that, having mutilated the document, they would stand little chance in a court of law. Still, there was no knowing what tricks they might try. He would not marry the girl now, but he would do what he could for her. As always, his heart went out to the woman in trouble, even when he was the cause, and he could not help dramatising himself as in her place. For Jean's first conception he had written 'O Wha my Babie Clouts will buy?' For her second he wrote 'The Bonie Lad that's far Awa'—and decided that it must go into the *Museum*. And he wrote to arrange for his old friends, the Muirs, of Tarbolton Mill, to take Jean in till he came himself to see to things. Anyhow he was in the way to provide for her. Creech had promised, after an acrimonious correspondence, to settle his accounts on Monday. A week after that his doctor would allow him to leave Edinburgh. Until then he would do all that could be done to be admitted to the Excise, and would give up the thought of Miller's farm. He wrote at once to Lord Glencairn asking for his patronage and announcing that he would call upon him in the following week.

> I know your Lordship will disapprove of my ideas in a request I am going to make to you, but I have weighed my situation, my hopes and turn of mind, and am fully fixed to my scheme, if I can possibly effectuate it. I wish to get into the Excise. I am told that your Lordship's interest will easily procure me the grant from the Commissioners. . . . You have put it in my power to save the little HOME that sheltered an aged mother, two brothers, and three sisters, from destruction. My brother's lease is but a wretched one, though I think he will weather out the remaining seven years of it. After what I have given and will give him as a small farming capital to keep the family together, I guess my remaining all will be about two hundred pounds. Instead of beggaring myself with a small, dear farm, I will lodge my little stock, a sacred deposite, in a banking-house. Extraordinary distress, or helpless old age have often harrowed my soul with fears, and I have one or two claims on me in the name of father. I will stoop to anything that honesty warrants to have it in my power to leave them some better remembrance of me than the odium of illegitimacy.
>
> These, my Lord, are my views: I have resolved from the maturest deliberation; and, now I am fixed, I shall leave no stone unturned to carry my resolve into execution. Your Lordship's Patronage is by far the strength of my hopes; nor have I yet applied to anybody else. . . .

With this letter he enclosed a copy of 'Holy Willie!'

On Sunday night he could only write Clarinda a short paragraph in reply to her two letters, to say how ill he felt, but on Monday morning, brightened by the prospect of Creech's hundred guineas and a favourable reply from Glencairn, he wrote at length. Clarinda wants a male friend. Sylvander will put all else aside and be that friend. But, he asks, after three evenings spent together, 'swift-winged evenings with pinions of down' (he does not count Miss Nimmo's party as one), can she give him a friendship equal to that of which he is capable, a friendship that shall defy 'years of absence and the chances and changes of fortune?' He is not quite sure, but he hopes so. He will call on Wednesday evening. On Wednesday week he will be gone.

Monday morning passed and Monday evening, but no word came from Creech. Robert began to doubt if he could look to any other than God for an equal friendship. In a nervous fury—for the attack was not yet wholly past—he summed up his life. Out of all his triumph what would he take home from Edinburgh? A light friendship with the light-minded Ainslie, difficult friendships with the churlish Nicol and the jealous Richmond, the goodwill of a girl betrothed to another man, the flattering notice of a fascinating but impossible married madam, a very little money, a doubtful reputation, the feeling that he would never write another substantial poem, the fear that he could never earn a livelihood. To Clarinda he could dash off only a few sentences, but to Mrs Dunlop he managed to write a letter that, while disingenuous on points of fact, was emotionally truthful enough to the moment. He hopes to call upon her on his way home next week or soon after his arrival.

> After six weeks' confinement, I am beginning to walk across the room. They have been six horrible weeks; anguish and low spirits have made me unfit to read, write, or think.
>
> I have a hundred times wished that one could resign life as an officer resigns a commission: . . . Lately I was a sixpenny private—and God knows a miserable soldier enough; now I march to the campaign, a starving cadet: a little more conspicuously wretched.
>
> I am ashamed of all this; for though I do want bravery for the warfare of life, I could wish, like some other soldiers, to have as much fortitude or cunning as to dissemble or conceal my cowardice.

Under the pressure of life's dreadful realities and his own weakness he saw to the full the impracticability of anything but friendship between Agnes McLehose and himself. For the moment he even realised to the full the artificiality of the friendship between Clarinda and Sylvander. In violent revulsion he wrote to Peggy Chalmers on the Tuesday. He still figured as a soldier, but in a more desperate martial guise than he had adopted for the older woman. And he had had 'a hairbreadth 'scape, in the imminent breach of love.'

> . . . God have mercy on me! a poor, damned, incautious, duped unfortunate fool! The sport, the miserable victim, of rebellious pride, hypochondriac imagination, agonizing sensibility, and bedlam passions!
>
> *I wish that I were dead, but I'm no like to die!* . . . Come, stubborn pride and unshrinking resolution; accompany me through this, to me, miserable world! . . . Early in life, and all my life, I reckoned on a recruiting drum as my forlorn hope. Seriously though, life at present presents me with but a melancholy path; but—my limb will soon be sound, and I shall struggle on.

Tuesday passed with still no sign from Creech. However, on Wednesday night (23 January)—the fourth meeting at the Potterrow—there were kisses admittedly not of the platonic sort between the Arcadian pair, and Robert's hairbreadth escape was very much a thing of yesterday. They had both been swept into a painful and serious, if also fitful, rapture of love. He is the man who adores her, who loves to madness and feels to torture, who would die a thousand deaths before he would injure her, and who must soon bid her a long farewell. She is his love, and the soul of his enjoyment, and incorporated with his dearest threads of life. 'All else is of the stuff of stocks and stones.' But Robert at first was cheerful; and on the Thursday morning, when the lovers sat in their several places to write to each other—with a next meeting in view on the Saturday—his tone was jocund, affectionate, flattering. He is a lucky devil of a 'poor harum-scarum poet,' she a 'masterpiece of womankind.' Spiteful Fortune, though allowing nothing else, has decreed that he shall give her 'that immortality among mankind, which no woman of any age ever more deserved, and which few rhymsters of this age are better able to confer.' Here surely was a solution almost happy! Dinner time interrupted his missive. After dinner he sat over a bowl of whisky punch with Signor Schetki, talking music and discussing a setting for some farewell verses to Clarinda, till nine o'clock, when he resumed his letter-writing in hilarious mood.

Not so Clarinda. She too began to write before dinner. Upon waking she 'received a summons from Conscience to appear at the Bar of Reason,' not to mention Religion, with dishevelled hair, Reputation darting indignation from her eyes, and other accusers who wanted to know why she had 'no certificate from the Temple of Hymen.' Under the examination she is 'neither well nor happy'—clearly she is very miserable—and she would rather not see Sylvander on Saturday unless she can 'depend on herself acting otherwise.' He must remember that Clarinda's present and eternal happiness depends upon her adherence to Virtue. 'Happy Sylvander! that can be attached to Heaven and Clarinda together. Alas! I feel I cannot serve two masters. God pity me!' When, by the evening, she had not yet heard from him, she continued yet more tearfully—till his letter arrived and sent her happy (after a few more phrases) to bed. He ought not to flatter her so. She is far from perfect—being 'passionate, unsteady and weak.' Still she knows she deserves *some* of his praises, and if he will respect her weakness by the strictest delicacy all may be well. Having slept on it she finished next morning by deciding that 'another interview spent as we ought, will help to procure' repute on earth and peace with Heaven.

On Friday and Saturday morning letters from St James's Square were carried to the Potterrow. Sylvander admits having 'in the moment of fond endearment and tender dalliance' perhaps 'trespassed against the *letter* of Decorum's law,' but denies having 'sinned in the very least degree against the *spirit* of her strictest statute.' He begs Clarinda to trust him and not to 'wound our next meeting with any averted looks or restrained caresses.' (In short, he promises not to seduce her, but she must permit everything short of seduction as he is leaving her so soon.) As Ainslie is anxious to meet her, he is bringing him to the Potterrow for ten minutes on Saturday. A girl friend of Clarinda's, Mary Peacock, is to be there too, but later in the evening there will be only Clarinda and Sylvander.

Lovers they were now confessed. They had kissed and

fondled and wished. They had debated whether anything could be done about Mr McLehose, but it seemed that nothing could. As things were, Robert could certainly have overcome her scruples had he tried. But he saw that for her nothing but unhappiness could come of it; and for himself, he had enough problems without that of a married mistress. He wished her well. All he could do was to use his skill in giving and getting the utmost delight the situation allowed. That night even Clarinda excused him some little *infringement* of the line he himself had marked out.

But there was the next morning, when she always felt bad—and a Sunday morning at that. After church she was impelled to consult Mr Kemp. Mr Kemp listened for an hour and more to her confession. She was in love. Her love was returned. Ought she not to inform Lord Craig? Undone by a late night and Mr Kemp's pulpit appeal, she wept. But the name of Burns was not mentioned. God's minister displayed both delicacy and worldly wisdom. It was all very sad, and he would think about it and would call to see her on Monday evening. Of one thing he was certain. No word should be said to Lord Craig. It could do no good but 'could only make him uneasy.'

While Nancie was comfortably unbosoming herself in the vestry of the Tolbooth Kirk, her lover was undergoing an agony of vulgar humiliation in very different surroundings. Through the officious kindness of Miss Nimmo he had been appointed to wait that morning upon a great and wealthy lady, Mrs Stewart,[8] who had influence in the matter of Government patronage. The great lady did not prove amiable, being an ostentatious, domineering creature, who plied him with impertinent questions about his private affairs, reprimanded him—in spite of her name—for his epigram on the tavern window at Stirling, and generally made it clear that, while she might do what she could for him, he did not deserve it. Robert went back to his attic trembling with resentment, disgust and disappointment. If that was how he was regarded in official circles he might as well give up the Excise idea, and in the first impulse of his rage he began a letter to Nancie to say so and to vent his fury against all who not only flaunt their greatness but 'must also be so very dictatorially wise.' Too agitated to write much he broke off, and in the afternoon sought comfort at Miss Nimmo's, who soothed him with kindly common sense, assured him that her friend was not so bad as he imagined, and sent him away with equanimity restored. Perhaps, after all, he had been over-sensitive to the great lady's lack of tact—and in any case he still had the genuinely sympathetic patronage of Glencairn and Graham of Fintry. That night he continued his letter to Clarinda in a more collected frame of mind, and next morning finished it in perfect serenity.

On Monday night serenity and sleep were equally destroyed by Clarinda's long Sunday letter inspired by her talk with Mr Kemp; and she followed this up by a Monday letter in immediate reply to his, which, to one of his turn of mind, was even more disturbing. If there was one thing Robert hated and feared it was to be henpecked. Long since, of a fault-finding farmer's wife at Mauchline, he had written—'I'd kiss her maids and kick the perverse bitch!' And here was one, than whom 'never woman more entirely possessed his soul,' scolding and preaching to him with all her might. She was 'half-glad' both about his being lectured by Mrs Stewart and about the Excise misgiving, and she spoke of the temptations of Edinburgh to one of his social nature.

But on Tuesday night he called at the Potterrow, to find that they were as happy as ever in each other's company, and she as amenable (outside of letters) as in the circumstances he could wish. He called again on Wednesday. Having dined and drunk late with a baronet, he could not call on Thursday, but on Friday between eight and nine he was once more in the snug little drawing-room. After some violent vacillations it seemed he had accommodated himself to the situation. Indeed he kept himself so nicely and so gaily within the prescribed lines that Clarinda began to be a little glum. He had written 'your person is unapproachable, by the laws of your country.' For him to say this was not quite as she wished, so she tried to arouse his jealousy by hints about Lord Craig, revealing at the same time her own jealousy by her certainty that Mary Peacock had fallen in love with the poet at first sight. Assertively she would 'hold him in her arms' sooner than let him hand about such a poem as 'The Holy Fair,' luxuriously she tells how she could revel in 'innocent' love with him. He had several times asked for her silhouette in wax that he might wear it concealed in a breast-pin next his heart. She will dare to sit for this to Miers, the silhouette artist, without taking a chaperon. After all Mr Miers is said to take only two minutes—barely time for advances to be made or for comment by the gossips.

But the gossips were already busy. Perhaps Mr Kemp dropped a hint to his wife, the lady of title; or the neighbours may have pried. Nancie was not universally popular with her own sex. And of course there was dear, confidential Miss Nimmo, who meant no harm, but still—

In Cruikshank's attic all the while, Robert was writing some of the loveliest country songs in the world—the love song, 'O Whistle, an' I'll Come tae Ye, My Lad!' and the death song:

> Sae rantingly, sae wantonly,
>   Sea dauntingly gaed he;
> He played a spring, and danced it round
>   Below the gallows-tree.

But the Excise business still hung fire; and his knee, though he no longer needed crutches, was still bad; and on Thursday (7 February) he had again postponed his leaving by a week. He was bored. To Richmond, who was out of Edinburgh, he wrote of the city:

> . . . everything going on as usual—houses building, bucks strutting, ladies flaring, blackguards skulking, whores leering, etc. in the old way!

At the same time he was 'crazed with thought and anxiety,' and he wrote asking help from Tennant of Glenconner. Should the Excise fail there was still Miller's farm. He would keep his promise and visit it once more. But this time his father's old friend, the shrewdest farmer in Ayrshire, should go with him. He was prepared to act on Tennant's judgment. Boredom and anxiety together, succeeded by extraordinary gaiety and amorous excitement, made of Friday evening the sweetest of all the evenings yet shared by Clarinda and Sylvander.

A day or two later Clarinda was shocked by receiving a

severe letter from Mr Kemp. Apparently it had come to the
minister's knowledge that his fair parishioner was not exactly
following the advice he had so tenderly and prayerfully
imparted. He may not yet have known the identity of the so
persistent evening caller at the Potterrow, but that there
should still be a persistent caller was enough. Clarinda sent
the letter on immediately to St James's Square, where
Sylvander was about to sit down with a party of male friends
to dinner. Thus Sylvander, while friends and dinner wait:

> I have not patience to read the Puritanic scrawl.
> Damned sophistry . . . the half-inch soul of an unfeel-
> ing, cold-blooded, pitiful Presbyterian bigot cannot
> forgive anything above his dungeon-bosom and foggy
> head.

Sylvander is sure that Heaven looks at things differently, but
he will be to her what she wants and no more. Clarinda is to
name her own terms and he will abide by them. He wants
only her happiness, but he loves and will love her without any
sense of heavenly disapproval. Despising 'the scum of
sentiment and the mist of sophistry,' he will be with her the
following evening.

Clarinda's post-bag was further enriched before then;
for after his dinner-party Sylvander had found strength
to read Mr Kemp's letter, and forthwith had written her
the most splendid declaration she had yet had from him.
Next morning, though 'hunted by fifty devils,' he wrote the
kindliest:

> If I have wronged you, God forgive me! But, Clarinda,
> be comforted; let us raise the tone of our feelings a little
> higher and bolder. A fellow-creature who leaves us,
> who spurns us without just cause, tho' once our bosom
> friend—up with a little honest pride—let them go!

And in the afternoon he wrote a fourth letter (by way of reply
to a lacrimose one from her) proclaiming the very sort of
adoring friendship for which she had constantly asked.[9]

After all this, at their next meeting on Friday night (the
15th), the more hysterical she, the more firm and sustaining, almost platonically affectionate, he. He gave her good
counsel—to hold up her head, to give no information to her
disapproving friends (of whom there were now two, both

male), and to remember that she had done no wrong. She gave him the shirts she had made for Bobbie. On Saturday they had their farewell meeting. Clarinda made Sylvander promise her a rendezvous before the Throne of the Father of Mercies every Sunday evening at 8 sharp. Their good-byes were sweetened by this—and by the fact that, after all, Sylvander was going to be away only three weeks instead of two years. For his efforts and the efforts of his friends had borne fruit. He had received from the Excise Commissioners an order for a six-weeks' course of instruction in revenue work, with an intimation that when that had been completed an appointment would follow at an early date. On Sunday he wrote to Peggy:

> You will condemn me for the next step I have taken. I was not likely to get anything to do . . . it is immediate bread, and though poor in comparison of the last eighteen months of my existence, 'tis luxury in comparison of all my preceding life. . . .'

On Monday, 18 February, Robert rode to Glasgow and went to Durie's Black Bull in Argyle Street. At once he sat down to write to Clarinda, but finished hurriedly upon the entrance of his brother William and Richard Brown. The two old friends had not met since Robert's heckling days. That night at Durie's young William Burns listened to one of the world's best conversations. It was a great evening. Next morning the poet went on to Paisley where there was business to be done and a number of people very anxious to meet him and to show him 'savage' hospitality. The same at Kilmarnock, where he was sad to find his friend Muir very ill. Then two nights of refined kindness equally joined with good advice at Dunlop House.

On Saturday morning, on his way home, he looked in at Willie's Mill near Tarbolton to see Jean.

NOTE. The 'Clarinda' correspondence is difficult material for the biographer. Many of the originals have been lost. Those which survive are legible enough to prove that the printed texts are exceedingly corrupt. The exchanges of letters between Burns and Mrs McLehose were so frequent—sometimes twice a day and even oftener—that they were seldom dated, and the conjectural dates assigned by editors are in some cases palpably wrong. Thus, I have had to make a re-arrangement of the important series of letters that passed during the last week of December 1787 and the first week of January 1788. I take the order of the letters to be as follows, the figures in brackets indicating the order hitherto accepted:

1 (4) Clarinda to Sylvander: I got your lines: they are '*in kind*.'

2 (5) Sylvander to Clarinda: My dear Clarinda—Your last verses have so delighted me. . . .

3 (1) Sylvander to Clarinda: I beg your pardon, my dear Clarinda, for the fragment scrawl. . . .

4 (2) Clarinda to Sylvander: I go to the country early tomorrow morning. . . .

5 (3) Clarinda to Sylvander: Many happy returns of this day to you. . . .

To the variable weather of Scotland and the fact that the
Scotish peasantry lived in two-roomed dwellings, we owe the
many songs in which the lover must shield his mistress with
his plaid. In the cold or rain of the open, or in a draughty
outhouse warmed only by the breath of the sheltering beasts,
he had often quite literally to 'wear' her on his breast to keep
her from perishing. The 'happy fireside clime' of a cottage
was the preserve of 'weans and wife' and often of grand-
parents and poor relations as well. It was no meeting-place
for lovers. This truth, difficult for genteel householders to
grasp, was a commonplace to Robert and Jean and the Muirs
of Willie's Mill at Tarbolton. Intimate matters, whether of
joy or grief, between a young man and woman were not to be
discussed in the kitchen. As soon as the general greetings,
news and thanks had been exchanged, Robert rose and
signalled the girl to follow him. Together they went out into
the dark little stable where he had left his mare.

There is a traditional magic about stables. In the Mill
kitchen Robert had seen Jean as coarse and unlovely,
appealing to pity and justice alone. Inevitably he had
compared her country looks and ways with the looks and
ways of his Edinburgh lady, and had found them wanting.
But in the quiet and intimacy of the stable, remote from
Edinburgh's 'noise and nonsense,' Jean took on a different
aspect. Here she was, 'banished, like a martyr—forlorn,
destitute and friendless' (the Muirs were unable to keep her
longer), and it was all for him and for 'the good old cause.'
Her unshaken fondness and her simple reality dealt hard
blows at the Dresden shepherd and shepherdess of the
Potterrow. The poet had been a skilful Sylvander, but he had
never in that rôle done anything half so skilful as he did now.
He 'reconciled Jean to her fate' while expressly refusing to

marry her. He kissed her to comfort her, but their talk was innocent of fantasy. He would give her a guinea to be going on with. He would support her and see her through. He would take a room for her in Mauchline, put a bed in it and get Dr Mackenzie to attend her. He would call on her parents, make her peace with them, persuade her mother to be friendly—anyhow to the extent of nursing her through her confinement, which was expected within the next month. (After all, Edinburgh fame and Edinburgh gold could do something for a man in Mauchline.) In return she was to promise, 'privately and solemnly' and 'like a good girl,' that 'neither during his life nor after his death' would she attempt any claim on him as a husband, even though any one should persuade her that she had such a claim, which she had not.' And like a good girl she promised. If their parting lacked the platonic element it was at any rate full of peace.

On his way home, calling in at Johny Dove's (which was the Mauchline post-office) he found a packet of letters from Clarinda, which had been lying there since Thursday. Their mood, somewhat *triste* and *religioso*, might make him grimace in the country air, but everything concerning this woman, down to her feather-pated handwriting (the only woman's hand that had ever addressed a love-letter to him) held emotion. And under the absurd flutter of affectation and convention these were passionate love-letters. Though he read that Mr Kemp, while still discharging his ministerial duty toward an erring lamb, had stately withdrawn his friendship, that Mr Wood was coming to lance William's leg and that 'the feeling of Honour is a noble and powerful one,' he also read that Edinburgh was a dreary town without Sylvander, and that Sylvander's unexpected letter from Glasgow had cheered his Clarinda, even as she wrote, like the sunshine that would have been her true god if John Calvin had never existed.

As he urged his mare up the familiar hill from Mauchline to Mossgiel, Robert mused in philosophic vein; and, as usually happened with him, his philosophic musings were the musings of the common man—mingling in equal parts the practical and the pathetic. The chief difference was that they were in a high degree articulate. He arrived cheerfully, and cheerfully he greeted his mother, Gilbert, his sisters, his two children. Bobbie was a fine toddler. Clarinda's dainty town shirts were tried on him amid smiles and sly questions. Black-eyed Bess would hardly look her daddy in the face for strangeness. But there might not be much sitting and talking. On a Saturday in February farm people may not pause before dark. Besides, the newly-returned traveller announced that he must go down again to Mauchline almost at once, as he had important business with the Clerk and others.

Yet climbing the ladder to his bedroom under the thatch, and seated before the little table where all his best poems had been copied out and polished, he managed to answer Clarinda's letter. She too was suffering for his sake. She must be comforted and a libation poured to the polite if no less exigent god of platonic love. Besides, how delicious to be writing to Clarinda from Mossgiel!

> Now for a little news that will please you. I, this morning as I came home, called for a certain woman. I am disgusted with her: I cannot endure her! I, while my heart smote me for the profanity, tried to compare her with my Clarinda: 'twas setting the expiring glimmer of a farthing taper beside the cloudless glory of the meridian sun. Here was tasteless insipidity, vulgarity of soul, and mercenary fawning; there polished good sense, heaven-born genius, and the most generous, the most delicate, the most tender Passion. I have done with her, and she with me. . . .

If he could afford the postage he would write again from Dumfries, where he was going next day to take a last view of Miller's farm; he made no doubt but that the Excise and not the farm would be his fate; he begged Clarinda not to forget her rendezvous at eight on Sunday night.

That afternoon he was very busy in Mauchline. He saw Dr Mackenzie and consulted with Hamilton and found a room in the village for Jean to go into at once—a kitchen room which happened to be unoccupied, in the Backcauseway next door to Dr Mackenzie's house and only a few doors from Smith's former shop on the other side. He bought or borrowed a mahogany bed, to be fetched and put in its place at the earliest opportunity by young Willie Patrick from

Mossgiel. He called on the Armours, and did not leave them till he had Mrs Armour's promise that she would fetch her daughter from the Mill and nurse her when her time came. Having done all these things—at the cost of considerable cash and eloquence, not to mention *finesse*—he returned to sleep at home in the consciousness of a day's work discharged 'with prudence and caution to an astounding degree.'

All things considered, it was as well that he should avoid the ordeal of Mauchline church-going just then. He set off accordingly, as arranged with Tennant, upon his long ride to Dumfries early on Sunday morning.[1] Having settled Miller's business he would make the return journey on the following Sunday. After that, having attended to various matters at home—and it would be easy to spend a third Sunday elsewhere than at Mauchline—he would return to Edinburgh to wind up outstanding affairs with Creech, and, if possible, to persuade the Excise Commissioners to consult his convenience by allowing him to take his course of instruction from the Tarbolton officer. His plans were somewhat grey, but at least they were definite, and no one should accuse him of a lack of seriousness. Before setting out on Sunday he wrote a page of grave philosophising to Brown in case the *Mary and Jean* might sail before he got back from Dumfries.

> . . . almost all that deserves the name of enjoyment, or pleasure is only a charming delusion; . . . When I think of life, I resolve to keep a strict look-out, in the course of Economy, for the sake of worldly convenience and independence of mind; to cultivate intimacy with a few of the companions of youth, that they may be the friends of Age; never to refuse my liquorish humour a handful of the sweetmeats of life, when they come not too dear; and, for Futurity—
>
> > The present moment is our ain,
> > The neist we never saw!

To Dumfries he went 'merely out of compliment to Mr Miller.' He had little doubt but that Tennant—'the most intelligent, sensible farmer in the county'—would counsel him against the enterprise.

At Dalswinton, as Mr Miller was in Edinburgh, his factor,

a pleasant man named Cunningham,[2] did the honours of the estates and offered the Ayrshire visitors the choice of three farms. The weather was favourable. Some, anyhow, of the Dalswinton holm land, lying level with the banks of the Nith, had earth that felt rich between an Ayrshire thumb and finger and gave promise of yielding generously to 'improvement.' The two elder men—in age Cunningham was nearer to Tennant than to Robert—were loud in their praises. Only the younger man stood doubtful and confounded before what all his Burnes blood whispered was a snare for poverty. But he had made up his mind that he would be guided by his father's friend, and here was the shrewd old man unhesitatingly bidding him to enter into an agreement. Himself he could not help being enchanted with the softer beauty of Nithsdale, and as choice must be made he would take those acres by the name of Ellisland that sloped steeply (yes, and stonily as Mount Oliphant itself) up from the river on the opposite bank from Dalswinton house grounds. Here, on a platform site, commanding vistas of wild water up stream and down, a house might very well be built convenient for a poet. Before leaving Dumfries Robert wrote to Mr Miller, promising to call at Nicolson Street in ten days, when, if not before, he would make a definite offer for the farm.

A house would have to be built, as there was none as yet, and for this Miller was prepared to allow £300. Miller's proposal was for a seventy-six years' lease, starting at Whitsuntide, at £50 for the first three years and £70 thereafter. Tennant had pronounced the offer a good one. Robert could only wonder and accept the verdict. On the homeward ride his knee pained him badly, and he was in his solemnest mood. The solemnity of the letter he wrote to Clarinda from Cumnock while his mare was feeding, may have rejoiced that lady. Her image is 'omnipresent' to him: what with absence and memory he is on the way to 'idolatrize it most seriously': he will be with her in spirit that evening 'at the Throne of Grace': he is eager to find a letter from her waiting at Mauchline, having received only one since he left Edinburgh. Yet, of all the letters she had ever had from him, it ought to have alarmed her most. It began with an apology, ended with a farewell and breathed resignation throughout.

Tell me, first of womankind, will my warmest attachment, my sincerest friendship, my correspondence—will they be any compensation for the sacrifices you make for my sake? If they will, they are yours. If I settle on the farm I propose, I am just a day and a half's ride from Edinburgh. We shall meet: don't you say 'perhaps too often!'

Farewell, my fair, my charming Poetess! May all good things ever attend you.

I am ever, my dearest Madam, Yours, SYLVANDER.

Sure enough there was a letter at Mauchline, which had lain there all the week. It was reproachful, even a little nagging, and it was more than a little absurd. 'I wish you had given me a hint, my dear Sylvander, that you were to write me only once in a week. . . .' She has been compelled to solace herself for his neglect by attending a lecture upon 'the Origin of Minerals, Springs, Lakes and the Ocean,' which has 'raised her thoughts to the infinite wisdom and boundless goodness of the Deity.' Robert was annoyed. Something in the tone of her letter caused a violent revulsion. Next day he wrote, not to Clarinda, but to Ainslie, asking him to tell the lady that he had written to her four times and that she was the only person to whom he had written at all. His mood led him to add, for Ainslie's information, an account of that same meeting with Jean which he had formerly described to Clarinda in more seemly but less truthful terms.

I have f——d her till she rejoiced with joy unspeakable and full of glory. . . . I took the opportunity of some dry horse litter, and gave her such a thundering scalade that electrified the very marrow of her bones. O what a peacemaker is a guid weel-willy p——. It is the mediator, the guarantee, the umpire, the bond of union, the solemn league and covenant, the plenipotentiary, the Aaron's rod, the Jacob's staff, the prophet Elisha's pot of oil, the Ahasuerus' sceptre, the sword of mercy, the philosopher's stone, the horn of plenty, and Tree of Life between Man and Woman. . . .

If Ainslie were to give Mrs McLehose some gentle indications of reality, so much the better for all concerned. It appeared that in his friend's absence the young man had become a frequent caller at the Potterrow, perhaps was supplying there the safe male bosom which, since the withdrawal of Mr Kemp's, was sadly needed. Nancie—the more that of late she had suffered 'several little rubs' from the world, including a marked coolness from Miss Nimmo—was anyhow under 'unspeakable obligations' to him.

In whatever form Ainslie delivered the message, Clarinda by 5 March (having then received Robert's welcome detraction of Jean) felt able to write flirtatiously, as well as with continued, though very affectionate reproach. She is glad the Ellisland scheme is prospering, so that the poet may become a 'sober, industrious farmer.' She pities Jean sincerely, and wishes 'a certain affair happily over.' His consideration of postages is unworthy of such a friendship as theirs. 'If I had but a shilling in the world you should have sixpence; nay eightpence, if I could contrive to live on a groat.'

This lively letter reached Robert when he was suffering from the after-effects—always to him dreadful—of a late party the night before. His hosts and all the other guests might go about their business little the worse, but he, though he drank no more than they, must endure a whole day of sickness and headache, together with the pangs of self-disgust and distrust and a sinking sense of his mortality. In this plight he wrote an immediate reply to Clarinda, so humbly apologetic, religious and affectionate that, upon reading it, she saw her Sylvander being all she wished before he left this world. But, that he might not become so all at once, she described to him her strangely melting feelings in bed, reminded him of the many kisses she had given him, longed for next week, and prophesied happiness. Possibly Ainslie had felt it his duty to allude to the well-known charms of village girls, for she added:

> When you meet young Beauties think of Clarinda's affection—of her situation—of how much her happiness depends on you.

Robert, however, on the day following his feebleness, had written her a second letter, wiser and more vigorous, with his customary humour restored. (It is indeed, while affectionately flattering, one of the wisest, most vigorous letters ever written by a man in his twenties to a woman with whom he

was in love.) At the same time he had written to Mrs Dunlop
(who had crows to pick with him), to the dying Muir at
Kilmarnock, and to Brown. A report had reached Mrs
Dunlop that the poet had somewhere raised a laugh at her
expense. He defended himself, and all wits, thus:

> That I am often a sinner with any little wit I have, I do
> confess: but I have taxed my recollection to no purpose,
> to find out when it was employed against you. I hate an
> ungenerous sarcasm, a great deal worse than I do the
> devil; at least as Milton describes him; and though I
> may be rascally enough to be sometimes guilty of it
> myself, I cannot endure it in others. You, my honoured
> friend, who cannot appear in any light but you are sure
> of being respectable—you can afford to pass by an
> occasion to display your wit, because you may depend
> for fame, on your sense; or if you chuse to be silent, you
> know you can rely on the gratitude of many and the
> esteem of all; but God help us who are wits or witlings
> by profession, if we stand not for fame there, we sink
> unsupported.

For the sick man—with whom in many a tavern talk he had
agreed that life was 'no great blessing on the whole'—he set
down his own honest belief with friendly fullness:

> . . . an honest man has nothing to fear. If we lie down in
> the grave, the whole man a piece of broken machinery,
> to moulder with the clods of the valley—be it so; at
> least there is an end of pain, care, woes and wants: if
> that part of us called Mind, does survive the apparent
> destruction of the man—away with the old-wife pre-
> judices and tales! Every age and every nation has had a
> different set of stories; and as the many are always weak,
> of consequence they have often, perhaps always been
> deceived: a man conscious of having acted an honest
> part among his fellow-creatures; even granting that he
> may have been the sport, at times, of passions and
> instincts; he goes to a great unknown Being who could
> have no other end in giving him existence but to make
> him happy; who gave him those passions and instincts,
> and well knows their force . . .[3]

—and after giving the news of his offer for Miller's farm, he quietly added 'if he accepts, I shall sit down a plain farmer, the happiest of lives when a man can live by it.'

To Brown, regarding the above-mentioned passions and instincts, he gave his further belief:

> . . . but I have always found an honest passion, or native instinct, the trustiest auxiliary in the warfare of this world.

Should any one desire to have Robert Burns's philosophy of life in plain prose it is expressed in these four letters, two to women and two to men, all written on the same day; and, be it noted, written on the day following that day of sickness and depression which followed upon a night of over-drinking. It was not for nothing that he differed from the Rev Laurence Sterne. Where that gentleman wrote[4]—'I never drink—I cannot do it on equal terms with others—It costs them only one day—but me three—the first in sinning, the second in suffering, and the third in repenting,' the poet made the marginal comment—'I love drinking now and then. It defecates the standing pool of thought. A man perpetually in the paroxysm and fears of inebriety is like a half-drowned stupid wretch condemned to labour unceasingly in water; but a now-and-then tribute to Bacchus is like the cold bath, bracing and invigorating,' which defence of Lord Buchan's 'Jolly God of Wine' has more of profundity than any condemnation yet penned.

His letter to Brown ended with information concerning 'a certain woman' named Jean Armour, about whom the skipper had made kind inquiries:

> I found Jean with her cargo very well laid in, but unfortunately moor'd almost at the mercy of wind and tide: I have towed her into convenient harbour where she may lie snug till she unload; and have taken the command myself—not ostensibly, but for a time, in secret . . . after all, I may say with Othello:
>
> Excellent wretch!
> Perdition catch my soul, but I do love thee!

On the same day (Friday, 7 March), or certainly within a day or two, he wrote to another man friend, lamenting his weaknesses but declaring his determination to be strong and practical. Whether he chooses the farm or the Excise, 'poesy must be laid aside' for some time, and his mind is 'so vitiated with idleness that it will take a good deal of effort to habituate it to the routine of business.' By Monday evening, after paying several business calls on his way, with the object of collecting small sums owing to him for his Kilmarnock edition, he arrived in Glasgow, there to stay for a couple of nights. He was concerned about his brother William, for whom a place must shortly be found, and he had a parcel of books to fetch for Clarinda. On account of his knee, he left his mare in Glasgow. When at the Trongate he entered the fly (an equipage much associated with Clarinda) it was with the intention of staying not more than one week in Edinburgh.

He stayed, in fact, a fortnight.

Without delay he called on Miller, and the lease of Ellisland was completed. Without delay also he called at the Potterrow, which (as he was this time staying with Nicol) was conveniently near. He had, indeed, to pass Clarinda's entrance every time he went to the centre of the town. He was clear in himself now about her, if he had never been quite clear before. If she could really give him the peculiar sort of devotion she offered, he would take it gladly: and meanwhile he would take with a clear conscience all the sweets that she felt able to grant. Necessarily Jean was much in his thoughts. That Thursday, 13 March, she was once more delivered of twins—this time both daughters—and as Thursday was post day in Mauchline the news reached him from Dr Mackenzie next day. He wrote then to Peggy Chalmers:

> I have discharged all the army of my former pursuits, fancies and pleasures; a motley host! and have literally and strictly retained only the ideas of a few friends, which I have incorporated into a life-guard. . . .
> Firmness both in sufferance and exertion, is a character I would wish to be thought to possess . . .

—and he is sure she will approve of Ellisland, though

> heaven be my help! for it will take a strong effort to bring my mind into the routine of business.

For the next ten days he was so distracted—hearing that both the twins had died, worrying and being worried by Creech (in whose presence he always became helpless), and

obtaining his order from the Excise Board for Ayrshire
tuition—that he became sleepless and was again threatened
with his 'nervous ailment.'

His meetings with Clarinda were as snatched and uncertain as they were sweet; and they were—what meetings
always are when a man and woman both wish to meet, no
matter what their preoccupations—frequent. The two could
scarcely ever make or keep an appointment, but they
arranged a window signal which told him if she was at home
and alone any time he passed. Sometimes they had to meet
warily in the street. Once they went for a walk together—their
only one—she dressed modishly in her high-waisted jacket
and large, feather-trimmed hat. He was so set upon straight-
ening out his life that he even refused tempting invitations
here and there, but each one of his hurried visits and still
more hurried notes to Clarinda breathed tenderness. Even
when rushing off to an important audience with some Great
Man of power in the Excise, he left a gay, tremulous note at
her door:

> I thank you for all the happiness bestowed on me yester-
> day. The walk—delightful; the evening—rapture. Do
> not be uneasy today, Clarinda; forgive me. I am in rather
> better spirits today, though I had but an indifferent night.
> Care, anxiety sat on my spirits . . .

and after being baffled again and yet again by Creech, he
wrote:

> Life, my Clarinda, is a weary, barren path. . . . For me I
> have the dearest partner of my soul: . . . Wherever I am,
> I shall constantly let her know how I go on. . . . Will it
> please you, my Love, to get every week, or at least every
> fortnight, a packet, two or three sheets, full of remarks,
> nonsense, rhymes, and old songs?
>
> Will you open, with satisfaction and delight, a letter
> from a man who loves you, who has loved you, and who
> will love you to death, through death, and for ever?

To make up for what she could not or would not receive from
him, he would give her all the admiration and respectful worship—good measure, pressed down and running over—that
she could take. He would be the platonic lover of her dreams.
On Saturday night (the 22nd) they spent the evening

together, and as parting presents he gave her a pair of little drinking-glasses and a copy of Young's *Night Thoughts*. On Monday—fevered, and 'convulsed with rage' against the monstrous impositions of society—he took the fly to Glasgow. Instead of Creech's one hundred guineas he carried a 'load of care almost too heavy' for his heart.

'Positively crazed' was his own description of his state, and it was so that he rode from Glasgow to Dalswinton to make the final arrangements with Cunningham about Ellisland, and to interview the Dumfries tradesmen with regard to the building of the farm-house. These practical arrangements perplexed and alarmed him, besides being very exacting. He foresaw expenses that would not come within Miller's building allowance. Returning to Mauchline on Sunday, the second last day of March, he wrote asking Creech yet again for the 100 guineas. By the same post he confessed to Cleghorn, the Crochallan and farmer, that he was borne down by anxiety. Next day he began his six-weeks' course, under the Tarbolton Excise officer, in the distasteful 'art of gauging, and practical dry gauging casks and utensils; . . . surveying victuallers, rectifiers, chandlers, tanners, tawers, maltsters, etc.,' with the keeping of books regularly, and the 'drawing of true vouchers and abstracts therefrom'—for all of which benefits he must pay the fees himself. Between whiles he would ride to Ellisland, lodge there in the damp and draughty hovel which was the dwelling of the outgoing tenant, and with his own hands help to build the new house.

'The world sits such a load on my mind,' he wrote to Cleghorn, 'that it has effaced almost every trace of the image of God in me.' The horrid difficulty of earning a livelihood was only aggravated by his prolonged taste of leisure and pleasure. He believed himself seriously enervated. But he was full of fight, or wished to be. He had rung down the curtain upon youth's 'bewitching levity,' and held it quite possible that he had also made his exit as poet. With sublime realism he would let youth and poetry and pleasure go, and would contest to his last fibre for what remained and was worth them all—his 'intrinsic dignity' as a man. To maintain this in the behaviour of life was the fundamental article of his creed, the single matter in which free-will had the advantage over fickle fortune. By this in a world of prose he would stand. For this he would face the most odious realities—even those which were imposed, not by nature, but by the society in which he found himself.

To begin with, he would make public acknowledgment of his marriage with Jean Armour and take her as his wife. Day after day for weeks, walking the plainstones of Edinburgh, crazy for Clarinda, sitting in the Glasgow tavern, riding the turnpike roads to and from Dumfries, half mad with material worries, he had considered of this matter, seeing it as a sacrifice, yet finding no way out of it, as things were, but by the violation of his essential honesty and pride. For long, under the spell of success and his disgust with the Armours, he had felt free from Jean, except as regards financial and paternal responsibilities. But a further turn of the wheel now indicated her establishment as due alike to his manhood and to her nature. She was a woman clearly capable of happiness, and she was the only woman whose happiness was in his power. Was it not also the sole amends he could ever make to the *manes* of Mary Campbell? That he had failed Mary, though only partly by his own fault, had never ceased to torture him, and the lives of Mary and Jean were joined in his, as their names were on the bows of Brown's boat. Then, too, they were working girls. In turning from them to women of another class he would turn from himself. That spring, when Term Day came with its domestic upheavals—only too painfully reminiscent to him of his parting with Mary—it happened that he drank tea with a lady whose drawing-room was rich with a carpet, with silver, glass and china. The talk turned upon servant girls—their stupidities, their rascalities, their occasional, patronisable virtues—till Robert, without saying a word, experienced a final and ferocious dissociation from the 'necessities, the conveniences . . . the caprices, of the important few.' His ferocity was directed more against himself than against his hostess. 'But for the consolation of a few solid guineas,' he had to admit, he must 'almost lament the time that a momentary acquaintance with wealth and splendour' had 'put him so much out of conceit with the sworn companions of his road through life—insignificance and poverty.' If his decision had not already been taken, it would have been taken then.

There was another aspect of the question that was wholly practical. Whatever arguments there had been for his repudiation of Jean, the Ellisland decision now annulled them. He had fought against Ellisland. As poet, as instinctive creature, and as child of the old, careless Scotland, he had shrunk from the fate of husbandry. But all the men and women he had trusted had declared in its favour. Clarinda and Peggy had urged it. He had no great reason to trust his own judgment. Necessity drove. And if Ellisland, then Jean. Town-bred or even county ladies might see nothing impossible in the idea of a bachelor farmer with two illegitimate children setting up in a new neighbourhood. But a ploughman knew better. Whether Clarinda guessed it or not, there could be no Ellisland without a wife sooner or later, preferably sooner, and a working wife at that. If so, who but Jean? Were Mr James McLehose to oblige them by dying at once, who could see his relict, in her befeathered hats and gauzes and ribbons and fichus, serving the gaudsmen with their 'twal' 'oor' brose on Nithside?

Robert admitted that there was 'little romance' in the contemplated marriage; yet the more he thought of it (especially once he had made up his mind), the more he liked it. And the more he expatiated on its good points to those closest in his confidence, the further good points appeared. When he gave it out one day, as if by accident, in Gavin Hamilton's house (before a mixed company which included Aiken of the bursting waistcoat), by referring casually to Jean as 'Mistress Burns,' his own self-approval and her joy brought him a sense of peace and a new consciousness of strength. When Hamilton wrote[5] asking him to stand security for Gilbert for the Mossgiel rent, he was able to give the proper refusal with an assurance which otherwise would have been hard to seek. Already, he pointed out, he had handed Gilbert some £200, partly as a gift, partly as a long loan without interest. Later he hoped to give more. But to shoulder the responsibility of an additional lease, with a wife and children on his hands and a farm to stock, would be madness.

On the whole Robert thought it best that Clarinda's first hearing of the event should be through Ainslie or other friends. Then she could write to him, and he would know from her manner of taking it how he must reply. He had a clear conscience, but there was sorrow and a certain awkwardness. He could only hope for the best from a 'sweet feminine mind' which had so often urged that his and her passions were glorious only when 'under the control of reason and religion.' At the worst he would take his accustomed stand upon the letter of the law. In giving to another what she could not legally accept and had steadfastly refused in Nature's way, he was doing her no wrong. If they could not now go on as before, it would be of her choosing.

When it came to his knowledge that the lady was furious—that she was accusatory and opprobrious to the extent of forbidding any retort or explanation by him, he could only shrug.[6] This, after all her preaching and platonics! He was hurt, of course, deeply hurt, and deeply disappointed. He could not think of her without emotion; and he had allowed himself to be almost persuaded that a real lady could keep up a thing like this with a man; that it would be practicable to continue by letter and visit a delightful sentimental friendship that might even have impassioned interludes. Why not? Now that she had shattered the illusion he was also disgusted; and his disgust shed a favourable light upon Jean. Thank Heaven he was getting a wife who was at least honest under every trial in her 'sacred enthusiasm of attachment' to him, a wife who had 'not a wish but to gratify his every idea of her deportment,' a wife, above all, who was free from 'the multiform curse of boarding-school affectation.' All the better that she was unable to write a letter. Had she not as fine a figure as Mistress McLehose, and a far finer singing voice? Robert had never cared to dwell upon Clarinda's vocal efforts, which were emphatically of the drawing-room *via* the boarding-school.

In fine, though he saw in wedlock 'the circumstance that buckled him hardest to Care,' the farther removed he was from the 'noise and nonsense' of Edinburgh, the more he was satisfied with the girl who, after all, had once been deified by him as his country Muse with bare legs and holly-clad brows.

She had never ceased to love him, and she had never ceased to attract him. So, instead of living at Mossgiel, he came to share the kitchen in the Backcauseway and the mahogany bed—for both of which he had paid out of his poems—and he was more and more pleased with her and himself. He wrote to Kirkoswald for three or four stone of sea-bird down for a feather mattress. One day, when brother William was visiting them, he was made to take Jean pillion to Glasgow that she might have her miniature done there and set into the very breast-pin which had contained Clarinda's more flamboyant profile. In being dislodged poor Clarinda's face was broken, and the pieces were put away in a cardboard box. Under Jean's picture was inscribed by Robert's order:

To err is human, to forgive divine!

PART FIVE

Dumfries

In the same year that Robert Burns strove to make his peace with his world and his conscience—affairs often at variance but rarely independent of each other—one Wolfgang von Goethe was taking similar steps with a similar purpose. He discharged his mistress, the Countess von Stein,[1] made an honest woman of Christine Vulpius, and heaved, one imagines, a sigh of manly virtue over the transaction.

But the German's problems were those of a gentleman and a highly established official, greatly alleviated by the fact of poetic fame. The Scotsman's, on the contrary, were the far more excruciating problems of the common man, which, in his circumstances were aggravated by the element of poetry. His fame itself was both peculiar and dubious. In many quarters he was denounced as subversive, even atheistical;[2] and there was foundation for his belief that in Edinburgh—the place that counted—he had merely been taken up as a fashion and was now laid aside. Mr Samuel Rogers, aged twenty-six, was able to visit the Scotish capital in 1789 and to meet there everybody of literary note, without hearing anything about a ploughman poet of sufficient interest to enter in his journal. Young Mr Walter Scott, though he was later to boast of his two chance Edinburgh glimpses of a certain 'high-souled plebeian,' significantly failed to pay his respects throughout the next eight years of constant private and professional visits to the Dalswinton vicinity. As regards Dumfriesshire, whither both fame and notoriety had preceded the newcomer, the figure of a poetical farmer was rather an object of suspicious curiosity than of neighbourliness.

Moreover, the Weimar lover and lyricist was in his fortieth year while the Mauchline one was only in his thirtieth. Twenty-nine is an early age for any artist to conform himself to what the men of his time and place happen to have declared to be life. It was certainly too early for a truly Scotish singer to conform to a world ordered by the anglified and mostly third-rate lairds, lords, lawyers, lecturers, and ladies of late eighteenth-century Edinburgh. Fresh from indigenous country comedy and country tragedy, he had mingled in their world and his heart condemned it. It was a world which for such as them provided perhaps the easiest, most leisured, most complacent existence known to social history; while for such as him it furnished one of the hardest and most humiliating. Yet, of course, though it had left a bad taste of humanity in his mouth, it had impressed him deeply. With a head handicapped by self-education—which is always half-education—a mind overawed by Scotish, double-extra-Burnes traditions of learning, and a soul tortured by gratitude for the favours accorded by various kind and cultured persons, he could see no other way for himself but the one indicated. Neither, apparently, could anybody else. The mountains of Jamaica, which for so long had offered at least an imaginary covert for the hunted fox of a man's freedom, were now barred as completely as were these other escapes, the ways of Jolly Beggary or drum and fife. In Edinburgh he had heard enough of the Indies to know that to a man of his kidney Scotland overseas was yet more oppressive than Scotland north of the Tweed, and when James Smith went there, as he shortly did, Robert had a clear idea of the conditions in which his gay friend would meet with an early death.[3]

Also he was increasingly subject to weariness of life. Repeated nocturnal intimations of mortality, and the 'day-after' malaises which now followed on an evening of the mildest dissipation, kept him well within sight of the hour when he should have no choice but to conform to the dust; and as he rode that summer up and down through Galloway he came more and more to regard life through the upgathering, informing frame of death. For long it had been his midnight terror, then a grief never far away. Death—the mangled grouse at Mount Oliphant; young John at Lochlie wilting like a cut, unwatered flower; the father slowly consumed like an elm bough that will not burn, and Luath stiff across the threshold; Mary in the new grave at Greenock with her baby and his; three children of his and Jean's in the Mauchline kirkyard; friend Muir coughing his life out at Kilmarnock. But now he lost the fear of it for himself. He even had occasional longings for it. Was it not the one way of escape for poor men? One June night, half a mile from where his farm was building, in the smoky, draughty room of which he had the temporary use, he got out his long-neglected Edinburgh Commonplace Book and wrote:

> I am such a coward in Life, so tired of the Service, that I would almost at any time, with Milton's *Adam*—
>> Gladly lay me in my mother's lap,
>> And be at peace.

At the same time he was a proud man, and he wished ardently to be a resolute one. He hated 'the language of complaint.' He blamed himself primarily for misfortunes and difficulties and for the ill-doing of others whom he had foolishly judged as finer than they were. Disbelieving in a future Hell and sceptical about a Heaven,[4] he held that human behaviour was yet of eternal importance. That no honest man lives in vain, was his creed; 'never, never to despair,' his motto; to 'build resolve . . . on reason,' his touching endeavour. A being such as his, subject all its days to the combined torments of Tantalus and Sisyphus, may lend strong support to the theory that this world itself is Hell. But that it may be so tormented, it must also be quick in every part to the delicious miracle of existence. So it is crucified. In a life-long crucifixion Burns summed up what the common poor man feels in widely severed moments of exaltation, insight, and desperation. In the recognition and acceptance of this he may have found some solace. It was certainly the grand factor (if crucifixion may so be named) in his peculiar attitude toward criticism and his unshakable estimate of himself as a people's poet. If he could choose nothing else he could choose to stand by the common poor man and by the common poor man's magnificent, unspoken philosophy, without which, when all is said and done and sung and written, the world would be intolerable. That human decency and human worth have for the most part their dwelling among the poor he had a perception more constant, more pressing and more experienced than any other man of his epoch. It was strengthened by his Edinburgh adventure to such an extent that personal ambition, hitherto a driving force in his life, almost ceased to operate. To Cunningham—now his 'first and dearest friend'—he wrote at this time:

> There is not a doubt but that health, talents, character, decent competency, respectable friends, are real, substantial blessings, and yet do we not daily see those who enjoy many or all of these good things, contrive, notwithstanding, to be as unhappy as others to whose lot few of them have fallen? I believe one great source of this mistake or misconduct is owing to a certain stimulus, with us called ambition, which goads us up the hill of life, not as we ascend other eminences, for the laudable curiosity of viewing an extended landscape, but rather for the dishonest pride of looking down on others of our fellow-creatures, seemingly diminutive in humbler stations.

And he had proved by his actions that these were not mere words.

But there is no going back in life. For all his loyalty and his conviction that he was the poor man's poet, Robert could not look chiefly to the men and women of his own class for intelligent understanding or companionship or literary stimulus. He must accept, though on unequal grounds and weighed down by gratitude, whatever of friendly intercourse was offered by cultured persons because of his talents and his season of fame. And he must have news of the world from which, by his marriage, he was further dissociating himself. This need is hardly disguised by the gay good-humour of the language in which he addressed a Crochallan brother that April. His overpowering fear of solitude led him to what now seems the exaggerated statement that he had only one other Edinburgh correspondent left.

> The world of wits, and *gens comme il faut* which I lately left, and with whom I never again will intimately mix— from that port, Sir, I expect your gazette: what *les beaux esprits* are saying, what they are doing, and what they are singing.

Crucifixion was the poet's own word for his fate. He was no evangelical. He particularly detested what he called the 'sugared up Jesus' of the Rev Mr Kemp's Sabbath discourses and of Clarinda at her writing-table on the morning after a too-amorous *tête-à-tête*. The Gospel story had never appealed to him. But the sign of the cross was in all he was and did. To use phrases of his own, he was continually beset with 'a damning conjuncture of circumstance,' 'a choice only of different species of error and misconduct,' or 'an irreconcileable war between my duty and my nearest wishes,' which, when one comes to think of it, is precisely the fate of the common poor man who feels strongly yet is not an anarchist. At the best he is confronted by two conflicting evils, between which he must choose; at the worst by two conflicting truths from neither of which he can escape. Such were the warp and woof of Robert's life, like the criss-cross of his plaid. Crossing his belief in honesty was the knowledge that his world was impossible for an honest man who was also poor and a poet; crossing his intelligent progressiveness in politics was his loathing of unfairness toward any individual, even if the individual were a king; crossing his low opinion of humanity were his worship of individual worth, his craving for friendship and his dependence on the social occasion; crossing his tragic premonition regarding his own fate were his delight in life's good things, his happy domesticity, his wish to be respectable and rich, his love of bawdry and his determination to make the very best of a bad job; crossing his sacrificial championship of the poor was his hunger for educated and even elegant companionship.

One day in April Mr Robert Burns and Miss Jean Armour had together crossed the Backcauseway to Morton's tavern, where they had an appointment with a local laird who was also a justice of the peace. Here in the ball-room, which served other purposes besides penny reels, the pair restored and put on record their old unlucky contract of marriage. Gavin Hamilton, who had drawn the new document in form *secundum artem*, was in professional attendance. The gift of the bride's father was a punch-bowl of dark marble, hewn and hollowed in his own building yard. The gift of the bridegroom to his mother was his father's silver watch. Now that he was to be head of a new household he must buy himself a new watch and a new family Bible.

Later in the month, though it was still private outside of Mauchline, Robert had sent Smith the jovial intimation that 'a certain clean-limbed, handsome, bewitching young hussy' had been given a matrimonial title to his corpus, that he reckoned on 'twelve times a brace of children' against his twelfth wedding day, that it was plain as a pikestaff why a twenty-four gun battery was a metaphor he could readily employ, that he wanted as his first present to Mrs Burns one of the Paisley shawls he had admired in the Linlithgow shop, and that Smith was to look on this letter as a 'beginning of sorrows.'[5] On 25 May he wrote to Johnson of the *Museum*: 'I am so enamoured of a certain girl's prolific, twin-bearing merit that I have given her a legal title to the best blood in my body, and so farewell rakery!'—this being accompanied by a humour so mounting and spreading that some tight-lipped survivor has seen fit to tear away the flower of the peroration. Next day—the date from which the Ellisland lease began—he wrote more guardedly to tell Ainslie that the matter was now public, and that though the step had added to anxieties for the future, it had also given a stability to his mind and his resolutions unknown before. The letter, containing some carefully phrased encomiums of Jean, was manifestly meant for the information of Clarinda. It was written on the same afternoon—the Term Day—that he had drunk a cup of tea, still in the character of a bachelor, with the lady who was so gravely exercised about the servant question.

The lady's attitude toward women of Robert's own class, besides hardening his heart against Clarinda, might well make him doubt if Mrs Dunlop would 'entirely enter into the motives' of his marriage; so he addressed his announcement of it next day not to the widow but to her son, with whom she was then staying at some distance from her home. When, however, she replied herself, with a dozen shrewd, kindly questions and good wishes and the offer of a fiddle as a wedding present[6]—though at the same time she indicated that as a bachelor he would have kept a larger circle of friends—he answered confidentially and at length.

From this interchange arose a fuller, livelier correspondence than before. The poetical Clarinda was now definitely
out of the picture. The Ayrshire widow provided a prose, not
to say prosy substitute that befitted reformation. She liked
his letters—those 'of a Poet breathed from the heart of a
Christian'—even better than his poems: and she was a
woman. Approaching sixty, slightly deaf and blind, not very
robust, and with none of the vanity of pretended youth, Mrs
Dunlop would have been shocked had anybody suggested
the presence of any but the most placid elements in the
interest she so openly displayed. 'I have been told,' she had
written, 'Voltaire read all his manuscripts to an old woman
and printed nothing but what she approved. I wish you would
name me to her office'—whereupon she had appointed
herself without more ado. But that there was none the less a
powerful jealousy in her friendship Robert quite understood.
When in winter he had sent her from Edinburgh some verses
beginning:

> Clarinda, Mistress of my soul,
> The measured Time is run!

she had begged to know 'who our song "Clarinda" was
addresst to?' She had already reproached him with reading
her letters carelessly; she hated the contacts brought about
by his satirical and humorous verses—which she would have
destroyed; she particularly hated his friendship with Nicol.
Now that he was marrying his village 'fault,' partly at least
from a sense of duty, she felt more than ever secure from
possible Edinburgh sirens in her position as his soul's
mistress. In April she had given him books—Dryden and
translations of Virgil[7] and Tasso—which, read for the first
time, filled him with 'a thousand fancies of emulation' and
despair. As a wedding gift she gave a tent-bed, and her son
presented a nice little heifer toward the Ellisland stock. If her
protégé could not help cracking an occasional joke over her
solemn gentility and smiling over the mis-spellings in her
interminable letters, he was deeply grateful and affectionate
toward 'la plus aimable de son sexe,' particularly when so
many others seemed disposed to ignore him.[8]

Everything went on very tardily. The period of Excise
instructions at Tarbolton had been prolonged by necessary

visits to Dumfriesshire, and during a severe spring Robert had caught two bad colds in the course of his exposed comings and goings on horseback over the forty-six miles that lay between Mauchline and Ellisland. At no time could he stand a wetting with impunity, and the room lent to him in the hovel of the outgoing tenants at Ellisland was 'pervious to every blast that blows and every shower that falls.' He had endeared himself there, however, in the face of strong initial hostility to the old woman of the house. By the middle of June he was dividing his time equally between the two places, spending eight to ten days in each. Though alarmed at times by unwarrantable exhaustion, and by a growing suspicion that Ellisland was 'no such pennyworth' as he had been taught to expect, it was not in him to enter upon any new thing without zest. He threw himself into making a home. Creech's hundred guineas had come on 30 May.

Adam Armour was helping to raise the farm-house and to dig the spring below into a well and to clear and enclose the fields. The existing barn and byre stood parallel with gable ends pointing north and south, the river being to the east. The new dwelling-house was to join the southern gables. It was to be fifty feet long, with the living-room looking out on the river, a parlour looking westward, and between these a small kitchen bedroom. Upstairs there were to be attics for servants and children. An ambitious house. Robert was master of works, digger of foundations, carter of lime, collector of sand and stones. He was not so good a builder as his father and he was a lax overseer. The local workmen hired by him took their time and more; and the Dumfries merchants, who believed he had made vast sums out of his poems, overcharged him when possible, which, no doubt, was usually. But though he resented being cheated he had the pride and the wit to attribute most of his losses to his own lack of business acumen.

More trying was the critical attitude of neighbour farmers toward one with such peculiar credentials. Except for a jolly good fellow away at Brownhill, from whom Robert had early asked advice and friendship, most felt it to be no recommendation that in the streets of Dumfries the incomer was liable to be hailed by persons of quality, members of the Dumfries

Caledonian Hunt. Also he was known to be importing—as if there were none good enough in the neighbourhood—two overpaid farm lads and a woman from Ayrshire, and his furniture, if you please, was being made for him by the Mauchline wrights. The neighbourly suspicion with which William Burnes had been watched piling up his clay walls by the Doon was mild beside that with which his first-begotten was observed raising his stone walls by the Nith. The native heads were shaken with dismal delight. Failure was prophesied. The builder was the more sensitive for his own suspicion that the prophecy was correct.

Some of the gentry accorded more flattering notice, especially the laird of Friars' Carse, a once monastic property, of which the grounds nearly adjoined Ellisland and were the loveliest in all the lowlands. Captain Robert Riddel, or, as he was usually called, Riddel of Glenriddel, having heard of Burns from various friends and Masons, had immediately decided to show hospitality to the poet and had intimated the same to his lady. They were young people but childless, the children born to them having a way of dying soon. From the first time Robert entered their house—a square, whitewashed, slate-roofed mansion, that enclosed some ancient rooms within its modern walls and stood welcomingly at the end of the level carse from which it took its name—he found it 'more pleasant than at all the houses of fashionable people in this countryside put together.' His host was a magistrate, a Fellow of the Antiquarian Societies of London and Edinburgh, a member of the Literary and Philosophical Society of Manchester, an amateur composer and a hearty drinker. He had further an immense fist and a stentorian voice. If anything piqued the visitor it was the somewhat marked decorum of his hostess. Though pleasant to look upon, and so young, she preserved a detachment which seemed to proclaim with needless clarity that no poet would find in her a prey. But her social courtesy left nothing to be desired. Robert was given a key of the grounds that he might wander there at will and was introduced to an ancient little laburnum-hung summer-house, within which there was a fireplace and a table and a stone seat once the tombstone of a long dead Scotish knight. Where should a poet compose if not here?

Robert did compose—lines serious and contemplative to order, and more spontaneously a song. This renewal of intimacy with the gentry had the effect of increasing his tenderness for Jean, and it was while strolling in Glenriddel's woods that he made the love-song to her, 'O' a' the airts the wind can blaw.'

Word from Edinburgh furnished additional argument for seriousness, perhaps for marital tenderness. Jenny Clow was expecting a baby in November, and this time Robert made no question of his paternity. He would offer to adopt the child: but more than ever was a godly, righteous and sober life indicated for the bard.

Having acknowledged his marriage socially and civilly, he now approached the Church with his confession that two springs earlier he and Jean had contracted an irregular union before two witnesses. The Session could only demand the attestation of the witnesses and order the couple to endure ecclesiastical reproof.[9]

These things were complied with, and on 5 August at Mauchline

> 'compeared Robert Burns with Jean Armour, his alledged Spouse' to be 'solemnly engaged to adhere to one another as husband and wife all the days of their life.'

Whereupon Robert gave a guinea note for the Poor: whereupon the Session 'absolved the said parties from any scandal': whereupon the record was signed by Robert and Jean, who thus purged their ecclesiastical offence, and by Daddy Auld, who thus triumphed: whereupon, after their long excommunication, the pair were given their lead 'tokens' admitting them to the next Holy Fair to be celebrated at Mauchline, which happened to be the following Sabbath: whereupon Robert got moderately drunk.

August 5 was a common Fair Day. After the business with the Session, Robert wrote to Glasgow to merchant McIndoe—the same from whom he had had the silk for his mother and sisters—ordering 15 yards of black lutestring at 5s 9d the yard, the very best that could be got, for Jean to make herself fine for church. And in spite of his tribute to Bacchus he managed to write several other letters later in the same day. Robert was never too drunk to write a letter.

Soon after he and Jean had partaken of their first communion[10] as a recognised couple he was riding south again alone. He had been bidden to dine for the first time at Dalswinton House on 16 August.

Though the 'noxious swamp' had already been transformed by Miller into a loch deep enough to float his experiments with paddles, the house of new red stone with its red stone areas and its white marble mantelpieces and its high, almost nineteenth-century windows looking north that the loch might be seen from them, was not yet completed, and it was to the little seventeenth-century house in its hollow that the tenant of Ellisland made his way that afternoon. He wore his Sunday waistcoat fastened with six onyx buttons set in silver, his gold breast-pin containing a wax profile of Glencairn with the inscription outside, *Mon Dieu et Toi*, and his face was respectfully composed, as befitted a 'little man' when a guest of the Great. He was graciously received by the lady of the house who, while she would never dream of inviting Jean, conveyed her high approval of his marriage. The landlord had a world of agricultural theory to lay down and the approaching trial of Deacon Brodie in Edinburgh to discourse upon. As for the tenant, he narrated how he was trying, with the sympathy of Captain Riddel and the assistance of Peter Hill (now gone from Creech to a business of his own) to start a book club in the neighbouring parish of Monkland. The idea was that farmers and farm labourers and village people should have a subscription library and the chance of buying at stated intervals any book they might wish to possess. Hill would secure second-hand copies as cheaply as possible and Robert would undertake the whole management. Nothing of the kind had been tried before in a country parish.

But Mr Miller was too full of his own plans to afford much interest or practical help. He was going to make trial on Dalswinton Loch of his very latest paddle-propelled boat, and dreamed that she might register five miles an hour. If this private trial was a success he would make a more costly experiment next year with a larger boat on the Forth and Clyde Canal. Meanwhile that autumn, armed with an introduction from Mr Dundas to Mr Pitt, he was going to

London to offer the King a new small kind of war vessel with a new small kind of gun (all his own invention) which was now lying temporarily rigged at Leith. He had already spent over £3000 on her, and his loyal wish was to make a present of her on the surely not unreasonable condition that her rigging and equipment (running to a trifle of £1000) should be completed at the Government's expense. With such things on hand it was no wonder if the banker-laird could not unbend his mind for so obscure a matter as the Monkland Friendly Society, though doubtless he quite approved of it.

Before leaving the dining-room Mrs Miller had made it evident that she too was a kind of poet. Couplets had a way of occurring to her as to Clarinda, *impromptu*. Without much pressing she gave vent to several of these in the drawing-room 'to the admiration of all present,' including Scotia's bard, who could see nothing for it but to beg forgiveness of his 'household gods, Independence and Integrity' and to go 'agonising over the belly of his conscience' not for the first time. Later in the evening it almost looked as if some tribute might be paid to his own talents. One of the ladies present, seating herself at the harpsichord (when in London Mr Miller meant to purchase one of the much talked-of 'Piano Fortes'), treated the company to an anonymous song from the *Museum*. When she had ended amid applause, great admiration was expressed for the air, and Mrs Miller wondered if Mr Burns knew by whom were the words, which began 'Raving winds about her blowing.' Mr Burns replied that they were his own 'very best.' Because it associated two things he loved—wild winds and young womanhood—he had a weakness for this song, quite irrespectively of its artistic merits. But his hostess did not share the author's feeling for his verses. They were in truth somewhat grandiose though eminently songful, and she admired them as little as he did her post-prandial efforts. But herein lay the difference. Where *he* had ground his teeth and lied, *she* signified her opinion without a word, a smile or a frown, by merely turning her head away from her informant. The fact that a woman might so act with impunity only because she was rich, indicated his position more brutally than any calculated insolence could have done.

After all that has been said on the other side of the question, man is by no means a happy creature. I do not talk of the selected few, favoured by partial heaven, whose souls are tuned to gladness amid riches and honours, and prudence and wisdom. I speak of the neglected many, whose nerves, whose sinews, whose days, are sold to the minions of fortune.

So he wrote next day, describing his visit to Mrs Dunlop with a frankness which he always allowed himself in letters to his middle-aged Muse. He had restrained himself with difficulty from quoting the text about pearls and swine to Mrs Miller. Instead he had reminded himself that after all his songs were not intended for her or her like. Not in drawing-rooms must one look for 'the precious importance' or 'the divine efficacy' of human life, but rather 'among the obscure recesses of disappointment, affliction, poverty and distress.' And he smiled to recall how much better Jean or his mother sang than all these ladies.

On his first return to Mauchline after the Dalswinton dinner he found some difficult and expensive matters waiting for his attention. One concerned William. In spite of several half-promises in Edinburgh and Glasgow the lad had not yet found a place. Robert believed his brother was clever and wished to see him 'a first rate hand if possible.' So now he offered to bind him a year or two, on 'almost any terms,' if he might be got into a good saddler's.

The other matter was more complicated as Clarinda was involved. The friendship with Nicol had never been to Mrs McLehose's taste, and more than once she had relieved herself by telling the poet damaging stories about the schoolmaster. Only half believing it, and inclined to attribute even that half to the malevolence of Nicol's headmaster, Adam, Robert had repeated one of the stories to Cruikshank, referring to his informant vaguely as 'a lady.' Cruikshank in turn had repeated it to Nicol. As Cruikshank liked Adam no better than Nicol did, the matter might have ended there, had not a violent new quarrel involving litigation sprung up between Nicol and Adam, causing Nicol to demand from Robert the name of his tale-bearing lady friend. This Robert had refused to do. He was now informed by Nicol that if he persisted in his refusal he would be served with a summons to appear in court there to divulge the name. It was a pretty kettle of fish for the intending farmer! Robert wrote firmly but mollifyingly to Nicol, acquainted Clarinda of the situation and begged Ainslie first to confer with her and then to call on Nicol with or without the disclosure of her name as she should decide. His letter to Clarinda was short and formal, requiring no acknowledgment. As he heard no more of the affair, Ainslie would seem to have handled it adroitly or Nicol to have given way.

On the top of these things it was harvest, with himself binding behind an inadequate team of borrowed reapers and putting in two stacks a day. There was daily annoyance and the loss of two hours caused by working without the centre of a farm-house. Each evening he was dog-tired, sometimes despairing over a parcel of land that looked to him like the very 'riddlings of creation.' He wrote to Peggy Chalmers to tell her for the first time of his marriage and to boast a little of having 'laid aside *éclat.*' And he wrote to Graham of Fintry making a definite, unapologetic request for a gauger's division in the Ellisland vicinity by the following summer. The salary of a simple gauger had recently risen to £50 per annum, to which prize money and perquisites should add another £20. Though he still tried to be hopeful about the farm, it was 'in the last stage of worn-out poverty' and would 'take some time before it pay the rent.'

If goodness dwells among the poor, poverty is yet a bad thing—'less or more fatal,' as Robert knew, to the native worth and purity of even the noblest souls. But there is a worse thing than poverty, and that is the fear of it. In Robert the fear had been early implanted and steadily nurtured by the events of hunger, bankruptcy and 'roup.' For a time he had escaped from it. But now that he was married and committed to a farm, with his money melting and Ellisland grinning stonily at him, it had more power than ever before to gnaw at his vitals when he was at all cast down.

The harvest weather turned so bad that the reapers had to take cover from the desolating rain, and their master, smitten with the 'fashionable influenza,' retired to a bed where, as he said, he could at least be preserved from being chilled to death by suffocating with smoke. In the intervals of work and illness he wrote affectionate, practical letters to Jean, calling her 'Dear Love,' bewailing 'these cruel separations' and subscribing himself 'ever, my dearest Madam, your faithful husband and humble servant.' He sent new songs to Johnson and wedding anniversary verses—in the approved English manner—to Riddel. A kindly and practical reply from Fintry cheered him. In February he would visit Edinburgh to clinch the Excise business and to get from Creech the £50 that was still owing. Three days before the end of September, though still weak from his illness, he was up at three in the morning and riding to Mauchline, rhyming as he rode. Jean always came some miles to meet him, and mounted pillion for her return journey.

BURNS, *the Ayrshire Bard*, is now enjoying the sweets of retirement at his farm. Burns, in thus retiring, has acted wisely. Stephen Duck, the *Poetical Thresher*, by his ill-advised patrons, was made a parson. The poor man, hurried out of his proper element, found himself quite unhappy; became insane, and with his own hands, it is said, ended his life. Burns with propriety, has resumed the *flail*—but we hope he has not thrown away the *quill*.

Thus—in comfortable congratulation that Mr Burns had been saved by his country's efforts and advice from the sad fate of Mr Duck—the *Edinburgh Advertiser* of 28 November.

The statement ranks high among other items of newspaper comfort in taking no account of facts. It was to be the spring of the following year before Robert and Jean were nearly settled in Ellisland, let alone enjoying such sweets as it offered. The pious hope regarding Robert's quill, however, was quickly fulfilled to an embarrassing degree. Already that month he had made a first journalistic effort, intended for what he described as that 'most blasphemous party London newspaper,' the *Star*,[1] and directed against Mr Kirkpatrick, his parish minister, for the manner in which that Evangelical, when celebrating the centenary of the landing of William of Orange, had seen fit to heap pulpit obloquy upon the Stuarts. The poet's point of view was that as the Stuarts had suffered in their lives the full penalty for their faults, it was unbecoming in a Christian or a gentleman to pursue them with invective after their deaths! He was in fact not so much proclaiming Jacobite leanings in himself as accusing his minister of a lapse of manners. His minister would have found Jacobitism easier to forgive.

Partly because he was confident of presently adding the exciseman's rod to the flail (in which implement as a mainstay against despair he had not the *Advertiser*'s trust) the tenant of Ellisland was in fighting trim that winter. Having prepared a provocative preface for Johnson's third volume he frothed into further gay defiance of the genteel world with the song:

> I hae a wife o' my ain,
>   I'll partake wi' naebody;
> I'll tak cuckold frae nane,
>   I'll gie cuckold to naebody.

which, for all its unimpeachable morality, was not calculated to placate his drawing-room critics.[2] As he rode his new horse, Pegasus, to attend the New Year Fair at Ayr, he composed a scathing elegy upon a dead old lady of title and wealth (amassed in Jamaica) whose funeral pomp happened to impose acute discomfort upon him and Pegasus, as had her living state upon the poor in her Ayrshire acres. This too would go to the *Star* with a couple of letters, one appropriately signed 'Tim Nettle.' A kindlier elegy on the Old Year for a provincial newspaper opened:

> For Lords or Kings I dinna mourn,
>   E'en let them die—for that they're born!

For private circulation he had braced himself to a poem in classic English couplets, which he called 'The Poet's Progress.' It vituperated the critics for their 'cureless venom,' denounced the 'vampire booksellers' and gave a lively, unmistakable description of Creech in that rôle. In contrast with the portion of these 'truly blest' ones he pictured the lot of the heartbroken son of the Muses who, like a poor dead horse by the hedge:

> Lies, senseless of each tugging bitch's son.

Thus Mr Burns's quill, under what he drily called 'the favors of the Nithsdale Muses'—in addition to forty new-old songs for Johnson, one of them called 'Auld Lang Syne,' which it was his humour to allege was more old than new though the reverse was the case.

But Mr Burns did not find his flail—as Dr Moore assured him Virgil had done—agreeable with literary pursuits. On the contrary, by December he was envying his cocks and drakes because they had no thoughts beyond the dunghill, and the Dumfriesshire rooks and magpies because they could fly away.

In the last week of November he had convoyed two cartloads of gear from Mauchline—live stock and implements and furniture (including beds, as there were no 'concealed' beds in Dumfriesshire), his books, his heavy putting-stone (of which he was proud because few besides himself could swing it), the marble punch-bowl, and a cask of the younger Tennant's distilling, with more plenishings and wedding-presents. The clock and some other new things were delayed at Mauchline in the making. Not that this mattered; for in the first week of December (which happened to be the week of Peggy Chalmers's wedding) the farm-house was not yet ready for habitation, though Jean arrived then with a servant girl whose father had made Robert promise that he would supervise her behaviour and exercise her regularly in the Shorter Catechism. It was as well that the baby Robert was not to be brought from Mossgiel till May, for when at last at the end of January[3] his father limped[4] across the threshold with his wife on his arm preceded by the servant girl bearing bread and salt upon the new Bible, it was into a damp, unplastered building, to sleep at one end while the walls at the other were barely completed.

Before many weeks were out, however, the place was full of human beings. Early in the year old Uncle Robert died in poverty, and Ellisland was at once offered as a permanent home to one of the orphaned girls,[5] and summer work there was promised to one of the boys. Another boy had already been employed on the farm and was being apprenticed in the spring to Mr Armour in Mauchline. In return a sister of Jean's would come to Ellisland and Robert's sister Agnes would shortly join the company. William too was with them for the first ten days of February. All efforts to place him in Scotland had failed. Now, fitted up by Robert with a new greatcoat, velvet vest, and shirts coarse and fine, he was going to Cumberland, and by stages from there to London, as had one of his grand-uncles from Kincardine so long before.

Ellisland at least enabled the poet to make the large gesture that he loved. In cheerful letters he described himself as

playing the patriarch's part, surrounding himself with
man-servants and maid-servants and flocks and herds, and
begetting sons and daughters two at a time. Was not his
face turned Zionwards? At family worship he gave out the
Psalm:

Lo, children are God's heritage,
The womb's fruit His reward,

and he rejoiced to hear Jean's voice piping up 'with the
pathos of Handel's *Messiah.*' For Jean was again proving
fruitful without delay, and by the end of the summer there
would be another mouth to feed, if not two!

The neighbours, invited to the house-warming, left reassured as to the failure of Ellisland. Nine or ten cows, four
horses, some young cattle and several pet sheep! Sliced
potatoes given to an ailing beast! Mr Burns and his family
feeding in a carpeted parlour apart from the four servants!
Yet the servants eating almost as well as the family—good old
beef, a Nith salmon, fresh or smoked, a glass of fine punch
on the shortest notice—such punch as there was none in
this neighbourhood, for young Tennant's whisky bore five
waters for strong toddy or six for ordinary! Then the rows
of books! The volumes of stage plays! The dishes of pierced
ware from Leeds ranged along a mahogany sideboard! Not
so were things done by tenant farmers in Dumfriesshire!
Above the parlour fireplace hung a plaque profile of the Earl
of Glencairn flanked by two smaller ones of Edinburgh
gentlemen.[6] Mrs Burns wore black silk stockings to church,
and a lace collar and kid gloves and a brooch of pebbles set in
gold; and Mr Burns passed his evenings with the magistrate
at Friars' Carse or with the Duke's factor at Drumlanrig
House, or sitting in his own fine, but untidy spence over
letters, poems and what not, so that he was never to be seen
about his fields till after nine o'clock, which was his breakfast
hour! He need not have had the inscription, 'Robert Burns,
Poet' put on his collie's collar. Any man could see for himself
that here was no farmer! In the warmth of the moment the
host at Ellisland had permitted himself to talk freely of himself to guests who had 'as much an idea of a rhinoceros as of a
poet,' a mistake quickly brought home to him. Replying to a
letter in which William asked for advice he gave his brother

but one item of counsel: 'Learn taciturnity; let that be your motto.' This with another shirt and a hat for the emigrant.

In the last week of February he set out on Pegasus to spend not more than a day or two in Edinburgh. Clarinda had heard from Ainslie that he was coming, and he found a letter from her awaiting him. He was a villain; he was a traitor; he was to reply only if he pleaded guilty to villainy and treachery. By word of mouth Ainslie gave him a further message. So long as he remained in town the lady would avoid her window sooner than catch a glimpse of him as he passed.

Strung by this to a useful if unhappy tension, Robert discharged his business with remarkable celerity. He saw Fintry, got Creech to stand and deliver the outstanding £50, and was back at Ellisland by the end of the month.*

On his return he was exasperated by the unfinished state of the farm-house. The workmen had merely marked time. Not till nine days later did he reply to Clarinda's Edinburgh letter. He begged her to pardon him if he could not carry complaisance 'so far as humbly to acquiesce in the name of Villain merely out of compliment' to her opinion, much as he esteemed her judgment and warmly as he regarded her worth. In a fury at her failure, Clarinda retorted that she would have him know she had regarded his letter with a smile of contempt, nay, that she was thinking of showing all his letters to the world! He did not reply.

During March and early April, while the landlord of Ellisland still hung vainly about the ante-rooms of St James's and Downing Street, neither giving nor getting satisfaction because of the King's illness, and the evasive politeness of Mr Pitt, his tenant was successful in establishing a local friendly society. This too in the teeth of ministerial opposition. For Kirkpatrick, the local pastor—'in himself one vast Constellation of dullness'—was naturally against the scheme. But with the moral support of Riddel, and his own ardour as secretary, treasurer, donor and committee, Robert had carried it through. Soon he heard that similar societies on a larger scale were being started elsewhere in the country. He derived a more personal benefit in that he could buy books

---

* See note at end of chapter (p.308).

more cheaply for himself while catering for the library. He was determined to study English literature, of which till now he had the scrappiest knowledge, and he was full of plans for severe poetic discipline.

Alone one May morning by the river with his seed sheet knotted round his neck, he saw a doe hare shot, but not killed, by a lad from a neighbouring farm. His rage at seeing the creature drag herself away across the dewy grass to die was great. He swore frightfully and nearly threw the sportsman into the Nith. 'There is something,' he wrote to Cunningham, 'in all that multiform business of destroying, for our sport, individuals in the animal creation that do not injure us materially, that I could never reconcile to my ideas of native Virtue and eternal Right.' But here too was surely matter for an English poem something in the style of Cowper? He wrote one in five stanzas and sent it to Dr Gregory. Dr Gregory was not enthusiastic. Possibly, he thought, if the metre were altered to something more correct and polished, the word 'fellow' changed to 'person,' 'shot' to 'wounded with a fowling piece,' 'blood-stained' to 'bleeding,' and 'form' (the shape left by an animal crouching in the grass) to 'some place of wonted rest,' the poem might be fit to send to a lady. 'Dr Gregory,' wrote the poet, 'is a good man, but he crucifies me.' Such a letter as Gregory's demanded a polite and categorical reply. 'Of all boring matters in this boring world,' groaned Robert, 'criticising my own works is the greatest bore.'

But hardly less trying were the unblushing demands made upon him for his criticism of other people's works—items from the 'inundation of nonsense under the name of Scotish poetry' constantly submitted to him with a view to publication by subscription. Here was indeed a 'horrid task' and one full of 'dreadful articles.' With his house unfinished, and spring staring at his exhausted fields, he must pronounce delicately upon a prospective book of verse by Davie Sillar,[7] upon another by Lapraik, the Ayrshire neighbour who had won his admiration at Mossgiel with a poem to which his claim of authorship had been proved fraudulent; and upon the poetic remains of a Lothian husbandman, 'highly respectable for every accomplishment and virtue which adorns the character of a man and a Christian'—which remains included 'two complete and regular tragedies,' a three-act farce and a complimentary address to Mr Burns in forty-one stanzas. To do Mr Burns justice it was two months before he brought himself to dispose of these, and he then did so firmly, refusing to read the tragedies, declaring that the poem to himself was too long 'by a damning degree,' and stating that his own 'perhaps as much accidental as merited' success had 'encouraged such a shoal of ill-spawned monsters to crawl into public notice, under the name of Scotish Poets, that the very term Scots poetry borders on the burlesque.' This, however, did not keep the worthy man's book from appearing, nor Robert from becoming one of his subscribers! It was shortly followed by another address—this time from a young lady in London—accompanied by a poem on the Slave Trade in 400 verses for his advice and encouragement, and this in turn by an address from a poetical milkmaid employed by the Dunlop family. Not one who sent complimentary verses failed to ask confidently for praise and favours. Clearly this was to rank among the sweets of retirement. Dr Moore, without even sending complimentary verses, remitted a copy of *Zeluco* with the request for a detailed critical appreciation.

Robert's disgust over the native efforts made him for a time the more amenable to counsels from Dr Moore and others, that he should 'abandon Scotish stanza and dialect and adopt the measure and language of modern English poetry.' Dramatic subjects particularly seethed in his mind. In Dumfries there was a small theatre that took from £18 to £25 a night in the season and turned away so much money that a larger house was soon to take its place by subscription. If there had been any tradition of Scotish dramatic writing there can be no doubt that there was a people's dramatist in Robert Burns. But Calvinism had seen to it that there was no such tradition. So he was hopelessly at sea and alone, and was confused though never deceived by the supremacy of English fashions. As things were, he met and immensely liked the men and women of the stock company, asked them out to the farm on Sundays, wrote excellent prologues for them, and planned to write plays.

As a journalist and lampoon writer for the newspapers note had been taken of him. Peter Stuart of the *Star* asked him to become a regular contributor at a salary as large as that which he expected from the Excise. But he refused without the least hesitation.[8] He would rejoice, he said, to be an occasional contributor. In return Stuart might supply him with free copies of the *Star*. Nothing else would suit his view of himself as a writer. The true bard is an aristocrat. It amused him to write political rhymes and slashing prose letters under the signatures: 'Agricola,' 'John Barleycorn,' 'Peter Nettle,' 'Duncan McLeerie,' 'Nithsdale,' but the amusement would cease if he were to accept money for them. As it was, his newspaper activities gave a new handle to his enemies, and he was presently obliged to disclaim some facetious and tasteless verses that ridiculed the Duchess of Gordon in the *Star*. He had not written them—the Duchess herself believed that Dundas was at the back of the trick—but his denial came late, and mischief was done.

The incident, upsetting as it was, did not make him more cautious. Once more that summer a breath from the outside dissipated his weariness and timidity as though they had never been. The clarion call came from France. There was to be Liberty, Equality, and Fraternity in the world. The Bastille fell in July. Instead of the mountains of Jamaica Robert's eyes beheld the rosy dawn of human freedom. It was enough. He joined gaily in a heresy hunt—on the side of the heretic—with the rousing doggerel 'The Kirk's Alarm,' and though the heretic recanted and was forgiven, and the satirist discovered how 'much more venial is it in devout men's eyes to be guilty of heresy than of satire,' he did not care. On the occasion of national thanksgiving for His Majesty's recovery, he denounced the whole affair in lightly blasphemous psalmody as 'a solemn farce.' At the same time he redoubled his efforts for Johnson who, contrary to all expectations, was calling for a fourth volume, and he resumed with vehemence several correspondences that had lapsed, especially with Crochallan comrades. On Sundays, taking his family to his parish church (when he was not playing truant in a dissenting congregation), he sat staring at the hostile preacher from beneath his challenging arched eyebrows. '. . . from such ideas of my Creator,' he wrote to Mrs Dunlop, 'good Lord deliver me!'

In August Jean was delivered of a black-eyed boy who was named after Mrs Dunlop—Francis Wallace—and through her after the illustrious Scotish patriot she claimed as her ancestor. Robert's mother came to welcome her first grandchild to be born in circumstantial wedlock, and waited till the late autumn. The lavish summer, and the large party at the farm before it was in working order, had made inroads on capital. Robert grimaced a little as he enclosed two pounds more on loan in a letter to William. William had fallen in love and had asked his brother what he ought to do about it. Robert replied:

> I am, you know, a veteran in these campaigns, so let me advise you always to pay your particular assiduities and try for intimacy as soon as you feel the first symptoms of passion; this is not only best, as making the most of the little entertainment which the sportabilities of distant addresses always give, but is the best preservative for one's peace.

His capital was melting, but he was still hopeful. He had not let Fintry forget him; and in the nick of time, as it seemed, his name was entered that August in the Excise list for active employment, with the official note: 'Never tryed; a Poet.' By the middle of September, furnished with an oilskin 'dreadnought' for all weathers, he undertook the duties of a gauger over ten parishes. This entailed, among other things, riding 200 miles a week.

Much has been said in commiseration of a poet-Exciseman, and some of this has been based on the apologies and lamentation of the man concerned. But Robert's early apologies and lamentations have only to be read with care to show how conventional they are and how largely a sop to the conventionality of others. There was much that was uncongenial, much even that was humiliating in the work of a gauger. None knew this better than he. But he knew also better than most men how much of the uncongenial and humiliating there is about most work that is done for a livelihood. The Exciseman was not one whom most people delighted to honour. But most people were fools. The Exciseman's post depended upon a combination of harshness and obedience, an attention to detail and a perfection of book-keeping which were difficult to reconcile with a poet's temper. But what of the position of the tenant farmer who must think all day and every day of small gains and smaller chicanes? And what of the journalist in the pay of a party newspaper? Some social stigma there might be attached to Excise activities; but Robert had studied his duties carefully beforehand and he could see no shamefulness in them. They demanded firmness, quickness and many other good qualities. They took a man about the country and to the fairs—to wool fairs and feeing fairs and onion fairs in some of the most ancient villages of Scotland—enabled him to study his fellows, allowed him alternately to meditate and to be in diverting company. By means of them, if he persevered, a man could provide for his wife and children throughout his life and after his death. If a man could neither be a laird on his own acres nor a beggar without a care beyond his wallet, the Excise-man's job was as good as any other for one of nature's bards. This bard had worked hard to get it, and there is not the least doubt that having got it he was delighted with it. The fact that he was on friendly terms with the local magistrates was a point in his favour and argued early promotion.

With energy and high spirits he threw himself into the stamping of hides and gauging of malt-vats. Smugglers who thought they were going to have a soft mark in a poet were disappointed. Here was a strict, well-informed, conscientious officer, who had not for nothing lived at Kirkoswald and had a smuggler for his grandfather. If it amused Mr Burns to discriminate—to turn a blind eye upon the poor peccadilloes of old wives on a Fair Day, or to refrain from exacting fines that would come to less than the cost of prosecution—it soon became known that the new gauger had eyes like gimlets for silk and home-made candles, a very fine nose for tobacco and tea and brandy, and no mercy for the dishonest trader on any scale worth mention. Of the same opinion was the District Supervisor. For after three months' trial his note opposite to the 'Never tryed; a Poet,' was 'Turns out well.'

It was a lively autumn, and Robert, released from the

farm, enjoyed himself. Ellisland was now his picturesque and cosy home, where he did no more work than to sow and plough on occasion and supervise his family. His idea was to keep it as a dairy farm, chiefly for butter and cheese, the making of which could be left to the women. In a very short time his reputation as a wit and improviser had spread through his ten parishes. They were lovely in the autumn weather and were well furnished with inns and with cottages containing singing women, serviceable to him as any Edinburgh harpsichord. The news from France was more than ever stimulating, and at home in September there was a political contest.

Dumfries was an entertaining place for talkers and for observers of mankind, and its 5,800 inhabitants were richly provided with taverns in which to exchange their views. Robert's own favourite centre was the Globe in the High Street where Jock and Meg Hyslop, the proprietors, were always glad to see him and to give him a bed upstairs if the weather was bad or if he or his horse were disinclined for the six miles home. But if he liked he could step along to the King's Arms; where he would be among the gentry. There was an increasing number of landowners and even of ladies who were glad to engage him in conversation.

The fight for the Dumfries Burghs was still a very personal affair. It took no account that year of French politics. For the last six years the seat had been held for the Tories by Sir James Johnstone, a middle-aged soldier and local landowner, who was a good quiet man. But the Duke of Queensberry, who had always supported Johnstone, was anxious this year to wreak a personal revenge upon Pitt. Having ratted badly over the Regency Bill his Grace had been deprived of his office of Lord of the Bedchamber. His Grace would therefore do his best to have a Whig returned, and to this end he had selected a puppet—'a youth by no means above mediocrity in his abilities'—namely young 'Peter' Miller, Dalswinton's eldest son, who was not yet come of age.

It might have been thought, and was doubtless at first taken for granted, that Miller's new tenant, himself 'a little tinctured with Buff and Blue,' and having few powerful friends who were not Whigs, would have put his talents as a ready rhymer at the service of his landlord's family. But besides being a ready rhymer Miller's tenant was that incalculable thing a poet: and while to himself his politics, like his theology, were crystal clear, to others they had a way of appearing 'abundantly motley.' In this particular election he saw no principle at stake worth 'three skips of a cur dog.' He would keep clear of party, enjoy the spectacle of 'Dukes, Earls and Knights' paying their court for once to 'Weavers, Tailors and Cobblers' and take his stand as a Tory-Jacobin Whig-Jacobite—a stand in which he was not unlikely to be suspect on both sides.

As the pied piper of the election he could at least indulge to the full his bent for personalities. His chief detestation was the Duke of Queensberry.

Had Robert himself been born to the peerage instead of to the plough it is highly probable that he would have regarded 'Old Q' with amused tolerance. As the Man of Feeling said, the Duke at least 'had none of the hypocrisy of pretending to virtue or disinterestedness,' and if he was selfish, grudging no price for any enjoyment, he was also gracious, witty and a begetter of splendour. But not having been born a peer, Robert inclined rather to Emma Hamilton's verdict that the great landowner (who had abused her behind her back) was 'a nasty old son of sin' and 'an avaritious beast of human nature.' To Robert his gambling on the turf and in politics, his brazen debaucheries, his cynical neglect of Nithside, and his uniform meanness to the poor of Nithsdale, made him the very embodiment of the rich and wicked oppressor now so gloriously being overthrown in France. Beside him Judas Iscariot appeared a sympathetic character. 'Judas Iscariot,' said Robert comparing the two, 'was a sad dog to be sure,' but 'Iscariot, poor wretch, was a man of nothing at all per annum, and by consequence, thirty pieces of silver was a very serious temptation to *him*.'

Throughout September Robert turned out spirited election ballads for the Tory candidate, championed the cause of liberty in France, and revelled in that 'exhibition of human nature' which was local politics. For the first time in his life he felt financially secure. The Excise appointment and the French Revolution between them had restored much of the old gay mastery of life. Meeting with Nicol at one of his houses of call, and being joined by another jovial soul on holiday—Allan Masterton, a musical friend of Nicol's—his gaiety spurted high in one of the world's best Bacchanalian poems.

More formally he celebrated a drinking match at Friars' Carse between Captain Riddel and two other magistrates, to determine which gentleman should last be capable of blowing a little ebony whistle, a Scandinavian trophy which had many times changed hands on these terms. The three justices competed in strong claret and Patrick Miller lent his long nose sedately to the contest as umpire. The gallant host was the first to disappear under the table after his sixth bottle. He was followed by Laurie, the Parliamentary representative of Dumfries County, who drained his seventh without drawing breath, an effort he owed to the memory of his grandfather who, after three days and three nights, had seen a hardy Norseman sink before him. The winner was Fergusson of Craigdarroch, who in Edinburgh, as Right Worshipful Master of the Canongate Kilwinning Lodge, had once had Burns 'assumed a brother of the Lodge.' He it was that now blew the whistle and passed out after his eighth bottle in triumphant oblivion. Though Brother Burns was not actually present at Friars' Carse, his poem on the occasion has all the spirit of immediacy.

NOTE. see p.300. It appears probable that on this visit Burns saw or communicated with Jenny Clow, who had borne him a son, that he wished to adopt the boy, and that she refused. See the letter to Mrs McLehose quoted on page 326 *post*.

Though in town for so short a time, he relieved his feelings by at least two letters to women—one to Jean, his 'Dearest Friend,' describing Creech's settlement as less than fair; the other to Mrs Dunlop to say that never before had he found himself so unhappy in Edinburgh.

But with all his readiness, his heavy, vigorous frame and his flaming vitality, Burns had a flawed constitution; and with the oncoming of winter he knew that his treble undertaking was going to outpace his strength. In one day he might have to pay twenty-four visits before seven in the evening. He had given of his best to the Excise, shirking nothing. He had written many thousands of words in verse and in prose (often enough groaning over his accomplishment as an elegant correspondent, which, however, did not save him from spending laborious hours in rewriting and correcting and transcribing afresh those difficult epistles which he held as due to his patrons). Now the farmer's hard autumn brought him sharply against the limitations of his energy.

All at once his high spirits flagged. One October night, having worked late at some harvest task against cold and exhaustion, he was overwhelmed as dark came on and the stars came out, by the remembrance of Mary, dead just about this time three years before. In a transport of grief he addressed a song to her 'in Heaven.' During November he was tired—too tired even to want to write letters—and in December he went down so completely under one of his nervous attacks with persistent headache and weakness of the limbs[1] that for over a fortnight he could not ride, could not even attend to his Excise books, and had to lie down much of his time. Death again filled his mind—Muir's and Mary's. He no longer feared it for himself, but now that he had undertaken such frightful responsibilities in the world it held a new threat. Neither could he endure the thought of Muir's or Mary's or his own complete extinction. Yet could an honest and a thinking man hope for immortality?

Jesus Christ, thou amiablest of characters! I trust thou art no imposter and that Thy revelation of blissful

309

scenes of existence beyond death and the grave is not one of the many impositions which time after time have been palmed on credulous mankind.

Depressed as he was, he could not avoid a flash of sceptical wit. The same is evident in a belated epitaph he now made for Muir—the human uttering its challenge to the Divine—

> If such Thou refusest admission above,
> Then whom wilt Thou favour, Good God?

During these obscure attacks, which affected not only the nervous but the muscular system, attacks of which the duration increased as he grew older, his mood fluctuated. At times, even during the onslaught, he could pull himself together, make efforts, be witty and even wise; but for the most part he lost his grip on life and was crushed by fear, particularly by the fear of poverty. It was, however, precisely when he was in this reduced and tremulous state that he saw most clearly the falseness of his position. Bound by his marriage to compete in respectability with equals who were not poets, stuck ankle-deep in farm clay, pledged to subserviency as a petty official, like a man in a nightmare, helpless but exquisitely sentient, he watched the Muses waving their mocking farewell from a far distance. Summoning all his will and reason he would condemn this clairvoyance as part of his malady. It was man's part to fight despair. Besides he knew that he had only to walk by the Nith after heavy rains (when the current would be red and roaring as he loved it, because it recalled the red waters of the Ayr) to commune with the Muses again. He had only to take a sheet of paper from Dugald Stewart's little portable desk to start inditing verses upon that eternal theme which provided equally 'the turtle-feast of the Sons of Satan and the delicious secret sugar-plum of the Babes of Grace,' so vigorously that coming upon some of them long afterwards, a more gentlemanly poet found his scanty white hair rising up on his head in horrified disapprobation.[2] He had only to play awhile with his baby boys and to find to his pleasure that they were stout and fiery with a proud carriage of their young heads and an unsubdued glance in their black eyes, to ask himself how he could despair. He had begotten sons ill fitted for a slavish life, and he would breed them up to be honest, hard men. No creeping into lower branches of the 'learned professions' for them. But they must be fitted for the fight, and for this one must make some money. Who would not accept the necessary insults offered by the world to his own freedom when acceptance was the only means of preserving the freedom of two princely infant sons? It was the old panacea, noble but unavailing, of the proud man who has given himself into the hands of the shearers.

But duty, resolve, sacrificial emotion, even with the aid of profanity, will not suffice the free soul which lets itself be bound. Sooner or later it must have truancies as well, if only for the sake of human nerves under the pressure of bondage. All January and February Robert's nerves were 'in a damnable state.' He knew that so far as he was concerned Ellisland was accursed. 'A ruinous affair on all hands,' he wrote to Gilbert. It had undone what he needed more than anything else, his 'enjoyment of himself.' 'But let it go to hell!' he added, 'I'll fight it out and be off with it.' Gilbert could repay nothing. The farm must go.

Its expensive failure did not improve his never very warm feelings toward Miller. Though he had dined more than once at the new Dalswinton house, had admired the marble mantelpieces and the 'Piano Forte,' had learned how Miller, in the process of purchasing the 'Piano Forte,' had been the means of doubling the inadequate allowance of a worthy bastard of the late King, had championed Miller's eldest daughter (later Countess of Mar) against an uncomplimentary, drunken Lord of Session, and had politely copied out another man's verses for Mrs Miller, yet he had begun to resent his landlord's rather frigid atmosphere and his taking of a poet's deference as his due. What did not grate upon him bored him. He resented Miller's well-meant suggestions for improving Ellisland. He hated the present of £5 which Mrs Dunlop sent him for his thirty-first birthday. Somewhere, somehow, a man and a poet must break out or die of bitterness and *ennui*. In Jean, dear woman and best of farmer's wives, there was no understanding of bitterness, nor was there medicine for *ennui*.

Mrs Dunlop was not the only one to write him a birthday letter. Clarinda, having heard from Ainslie that he had not been well, seized her chance and sent him friendly greetings without a reproach. He replied, friendly too, but frank:

> . . . Though I were conscious that I had acted wrong—
> and I am conscious that I have acted wrong—yet would
> I not be bullied into repentance. . . .

At last she had his admission for what it was worth to her! And she had more. For in the same letter, trusting that as it had pleased him, so it might her, was the address 'To Mary in Heaven.' Clarinda replied by threatening the publication of all his letters to her.

Sylvander did not much care. The love of women was necessary to him, but equally necessary his absolute domination as the male. He would give immediate passion and lasting tenderness, but to no woman would he subjugate himself. If Clarinda could not give the free, unreproachful, delicious love which was the solace and 'blood-royal of life' to poor men and poets, there were others who could and did. During the final weeks of the election, when, amid unprecedented excitement, young Miller had been returned, Robert had slept many more nights than usual in the upstairs bedroom of the Globe. Owing to the extra pressure of business the Hyslops had imported a niece—a buxom, merry golden-haired girl from the East country—to help in the house. Anna Park, though young, made no particular claims to chastity. She had warmth and to spare for a poet—perhaps for any man who knew how to ask for it.

Throughout the spring that followed Robert's delight in Anna gave savour to his life, and her softness towards him intensified his championship of all frail women as compared with mercenary ones. To William (who was soon going to London and had written asking for more good advice and an introduction to Murdoch) he wrote warningly in capitals of 'Bad Women' and of the dangers and expensiveness of 'Whoring.' But he was furiously on the side of a pretty 'night-nymph' who, by the rulings of Creech, Lord Dreghorn and other lawgivers in Edinburgh, had been 'banished furth of the city and liberties for ever.' 'It is written,' he dashed off to Peter Hill:

> 'Thou shalt not take the name of the Lord thy God
> in vain': so I neither say 'God curse them!' nor 'God

blast them!' nor 'God damn them!' but, may Woman
curse them! may Woman blast them! may Woman damn
them! . . . And when many years and much port and
great business have delivered them over to vulture gouts
and aspen palsies, then may they be tantalised with the
impotent desires, which like ghosts haunt their bosoms,
when all their powers to give or receive enjoyment are
for ever asleep in the sepulchre of their fathers!!!

With equal fury he rejoiced when he learned that upon a
second appeal this immoral English namesake of his (Miss
Margaret Burns was her professional, not her real name) had
got the judgment reversed. And he greeted with delight the
trick played on Creech by a waggish London editor. Threatened with a libel action unless he would withdraw the
statement that 'Bailie Creech, of literary celebrity in Edinburgh, was about to lead the beautiful and accomplished
Miss Burns to the hymeneal altar,' this editor had published
the counter-statement thus:

We have now the authority of that gentleman to say that
the proposed marriage is not to take place, matters
having been otherwise arranged to the mutual satisfaction of both parties and their respective friends.

Not that sweet Anna Park of the Globe was any Miss
Burns. She was neither vicious nor venal. She was merely a
hearty, gay and lavish Scotish barmaid, self-forgetting and
inducing self-forgetfulness. With his arm round her waist the
Exciseman felt once more debonair and blessed and reckless
and a truant. That summer poesy throve.

Yestreen I had a pint o' wine,
    A place where body saw na;
Yestreen lay on this breast o' mine
    The gowden locks of Anna.

He believed it was his best love-song, though in its unexpur-
gated edition 'not quite a ladies' song.'

The Kirk an' State may join an' tell
    To do sic things I manna;
The Kirk an' State may gae to hell
    An' I'll gae to my Anna.

Ainslie, who made one of the harvest-home party in the
autumn, found his friend cheerful, though a blow had lately

fallen on the family. Poor William, who had reached London in March, and had written home eagerly for shirts trimmed at the breast such as were the only wear there, had died of typhus after two days' illness in July. Murdoch, however, had not sent the news till seven weeks later, after which in due time it reached the farm accompanied by much moralising and the bill for the funeral. Ainslie, on his part, had to tell of another young William's death. In August Mrs McLehose had lost her delicate boy.

None the less, and though Robert was himself just recovering from a severe quinsy with prolonged low fever, they were merry at Ellisland with dancing and kissing games.

It was the first time Ainslie had seen Robert in the homespun family circle, and he was astonished. Could this exuberant man in the corduroy breeches, drab tail-coat and clumsy gaiters, whose sallies made the women shriek with high-pitched laughter, be the same that had gravely enchanted drawing-rooms in town? The Edinburgh law clerk, who had always had compressed lips and was becoming prematurely middle aged, observed his friend critically, heard him boast of being 'a mighty tax-gatherer before the Lord,' and watched his uproarious mirth which communicated itself to cousins and sisters, babies, neighbours and farm hands. He might, as he said, still go 'pretty frequently among the great,' but to Ainslie's way of thinking he was as much Exciseman now as poet, and the picture of him thus should go far to cure Mistress Nancie of any lingering *tendresse*. Nancie should be duly informed of it all, and of how satisfied the poet seemed with his countrified wife, once more an expectant mother, who declared laughing that 'oor Rob could hae done wi' twa wives.' There was no denying that she was treated by her husband with conspicuous affection, for all that she was careless of her personal appearance and as broad in the beam as in her racy tongue—so much so that Syme of Barcailzie,[3] breakfasting for the first time at Ellisland on 1 September, declared that in celebrating 'bonny Jean' Robert had exhibited his 'poetical genius'!

In the talk that passed between the friends the poet made out a cheerful case for himself. In spite of a bumper crop—'the finest the land had carried this twenty years'—he would have to give up the farm. But he hoped also to 'quit this corner of Scotland.' Owing to his influence with Fintry and others, he had the expectation of immediate promotion in the Excise, and once placed on the 'Register of Persons Recommended for Examiner and Supervisor,' as he was assured he would be shortly, he looked forward to a speedy Supervisorship in some more congenial district. Then all his cares would be at an end. Rail as he might against the 'execrable office of whipper-in to the bloodhounds of justice,' he had not found in it any of 'these mortifying circumstances he was led to expect.' He told Ainslie of a new and successful departure made by him when appearing recently before the magistrates along with the other officers for the rendering up of defaulters. He had begged off all those on his list who were, in his estimation, too poor to pay their fines, and had got the bench (two out of the three magistrates had been competitors for the whistle at Friars' Carse) to double the penalties of sinners who could well afford to pay. One result of this was that his own share of the spoils (for each gauger was entitled to a commission on the fines recovered) would work out proportionately larger than that of any other Exciseman present! He was counting on £50 or £60 prize money. And well he could do with it! He had paid the bill for poor William's illness and funeral without delay. His capital was melting at Ellisland even more quickly than he had foreseen; and this though they all worked, as he put it, as hard as 'an Edinburgh bawd on a Sunday morning.'[4] But he still believed that over a period of years the place could be made to pay, and he was going to ask Mr Miller's consent to sub-let. One of the family—Gilbert or a cousin—might step usefully in, and so the work and money might yet be recovered.

Ainslie carried back to Edinburgh the image of a man filled with plans and sure of himself. He and Nicol,[5] envying a little their friend's great expectations, picturing him as one who would presently be giving himself airs as the worldly superior of all law clerks and schoolmasters.

But the chief reason of Robert's confidence that autumn was that he had written a long poem—his 'first essay in the way of telling a tale,'—which he knew was as good and better than any belonging to his Ayrshire days. A funny fat friend of Captain Riddel's, an Anglo-Swiss antiquary and literary adventurer named Grose, who was a perfect Falstaff of learning himself and a skilled picker of the brains of other men for the compilation of vast guide-books, having exhausted England and Wales in four mighty volumes, had come to seek fresh blood in Scotland. Riddel, Robert and Syme (who, like Grose, could draw) all had given him free copy, Robert's contribution being a prose account of Alloway Kirk, with some of the supernatural doings there that he had heard as a child when his father was rebuilding the ruined walls. The only return he asked was a little drawing by Mr Grose of the place where his father now lay and where, he said, he desired his own bones to lie when his time should come. But one day, idling from dawn to dark by the full-foaming Nith, a proceeding poor Jean found as reprehensible as it was incomprehensible (such is it for a poet to wed his muse!), he had found the whole story turning from prose to poetry on his hands. Hour after hour he gave himself over to it, taut with the need to cope in a single unbroken effort with the heavenly coincidence of a sudden vision and verbal material ready to hand. Once at Kirkoswald, taken with a local tale that involved Alloway, he had attempted a rhymed narrative. Now these abandoned stanzas served him. Jean, coming to scold and get him home for food, found him perched upon the turf-dyke with tears running down his face. His power had not left him! The Muses had not deserted! Renewed by the streaming autumn current and by the embraces of golden-haired Anna, he was his old bardic self and more. His narrative ran to two hundred and twenty-four lines, and not all Doctor Moore's pedantic strictures when the poem was sent to him, not all Ainslie's judicialness when it was recited to him, would bring the author to believe that 'Tam o' Shanter' was not the peak of his achievement.

> Care, mad to see a man sae happy,
> E'en drowned himself amang the nappy!
> As bees flee hame wi' lades o' treasure,
> The minutes wing'd their way wi' pleasure:
> Kings may be blest, but Tam was glorious,
> O'er a' the ills o' life victorious!

He had succeeded too, as never before, in grafting his native tongue upon a stem of English undefiled:

> But pleasures are like poppies spread,
> You seize the flower, its bloom is shed!
> Or like the snowfall in the river,
> A moment white—then melts for ever;
> Or like the borealis race,
> That flit ere you can point their place;
> Or like the rainbow's lovely form,
> Evanishing amid the storm.

It was a unique achievement, and he knew it.

He was studying hard. He had displayed to Ainslie his new complete Shakespeare, his Jonson, his Wycherley, Congreve, Vanbrugh, Cibber, Macklin, Garrick, Foote, Otway, Sheridan, and his proud little shelf of French dramatic authors in the original—Molière and Racine, Corneille and Voltaire—all of whom he was reading with a view to writing humorous and historical plays for production in the Dumfries theatre. He had been asked to contribute to a new periodical called *The Bee*. The end of the year saw him joining recklessly in another heresy hunt against the orthodox and backing a bill for £20 at three months for a man who had helped in the building of Ellisland and happened to be pressed for money. All the while he was visiting his lovely Anna, and coming away from the Globe 'o'er a' the ills o' life victorious,' without the help of ale more than a reasonable glass.

But the year 1791 opened badly and went on worse. Throughout January Robert knew financial pressure. He owed money to Hill for books—£8 and more; Ellisland was still all outlay and no profit; Jean was going to have another baby in April; Anna Park was due to have one even sooner. Robert felt not so much guilty as furious. He was ready to admit himself guilty of extravagance and folly, but was overwhelmed by the gross and fatuous unfairness of society. If he had not happened to be poor who would blame him for the sterility of Ellisland or the fertility of Anna? Who shook their heads at Miller for his costly experiments in field and workshop? Who refrained from greeting the Duke of Queensberry though he robbed half-starving folk to pay for his heartless amours ? For the man of family and fortune :

> *His* early extravagances and follies are fire and spirit ; *his*
> consequent wants are the embarrassments of an honest
> fellow ; and when, to remedy the matters, he sets out
> with a legal commission to plunder distant provinces
> and massacre peaceful nations, he returns laden with the
> spoils of rapine and murder ; lives wicked and respected,
> and dies a Villain and a Lord.

Unfortunately for Robert a lord who was not a villain died
at the end of January. Glencairn, having been for some time in
poor health, had gone to Lisbon. But the sunshine did him no
good and the longing came over him to see Ayrshire once more.
He died on board ship as they were drawing into Falmouth.

Robert mourned sincerely and wrote a dignified and beautiful Lament. Hoping to be an inconspicuous follower at his
patron's funeral, which it was thought would be in Scotland, he
went to the expense of a dark grey tail-coat and bought a pair of
black gloves. But the interment took place at Falmouth, and to
the service held at the same time in Ayrshire the poet was not
invited. Nor did his Lament, which he sent to the Earl's sisters,
evoke response. One sister asked the other to deal with it, and
that other allowed months to pass without acknowledgment.
Seven months later Robert wrote asking if he might publish it
in *The Bee*, but the matter was not thought worth replying to.
The poet felt his loss the more for this neglect, and though
by February his name duly figured in the Examiners and
Supervisors' list, he saw his chances of promotion deferred.

Ever careless, and a somewhat clumsy rider, he came down
with his horse in February and broke his right arm. Arriving
so at home he was met by an unexpected visitor. The poetical
milkmaid, patronised by Mrs Dunlop, had chosen that
moment to come from Ayrshire seeking words of comfort
and advice from a fellow poet. Cursing with pain and galled
by the remembrance of how bad the girl's poems were, the
master of Ellisland excused himself. She returned to Ayrshire in maidenly disappointment. Mrs Dunlop was vexed.

Before he was able to write again with any ease, two
poetical proposals were made to him. Dr Moore suggested
a collection of fugitive pieces 'reconsidered and polished
to the utmost of your power' to be published once more by

subscription. He was against Robert's practice of sending copies of any new piece round to friends. He was in fact prudent and businesslike. The other proposal came from a Scotish minister through a London publisher. It was thought to issue a new edition of Michael Bruce's works, of which the proceeds should all go to the dead shepherd-poet's mother who was old and poor. Would Mr Burns, out of his sympathy with the poor, edit, arrange and subscribe for the volume, and contribute a few lines of his own?

To the first proposal, Robert's reply was perfectly imprudent, unbusinesslike, characteristic and aristocratic. In truth the thought of his Edinburgh edition always made him feel a little sick. He would not repeat the experiment. He believed, moreover, that a new book of poems under his name would not meet with a very favourable reception. This he did not care to risk, not now so much because he was timid, as because he was in a new way sure of himself and of how he wished to stand as a poet. Above all he would refuse to regard poetry as a commercial proposition. He rhymed best when he rhymed 'for fun,' and for posterity (of whose support he felt quite confident). It pleased and it suited him to hand his pieces about as he wrote them, to post them to friends and acquaintances and even enemies, to copy them carefully out into the interleaved copies, a few of which he had insisted upon having from Creech of the Edinburgh edition, or into manuscript books for special friends like the Riddels or Mrs Stewart of Stair. For the Riddels he had begun to copy out a selection of poems into one manuscript book and letters into another, and had written a little preface so that the whole should have a unique and personal value. It was his only way of doing a royal favour. He would never relinquish it for methods more impersonal and calculating.

To the second proposition he replied with equal peremptoriness. Michael Bruce's publishers might have any or all of Mr Burns's own unpublished pieces, including 'Tam o' Shanter,' and Mr Burns would gladly edit the work.

So he truly wished it—to give with a friendly gesture all his best to help the memorial to a dead poet who had been poor and to feed a poet's mother who was alive and still poor. But though the prospectus was announced in due course, it was not carried out. Doctors Blair and Moore would not have it. Not the poet but the poet's patrons, it seemed, must decide what he should do with his own. Besides there was a difficulty. The works of Michael Bruce, said Doctors Blair and Moore, were moral in their tendency. Any juxtaposition of pieces by Robert Burns, especially the juxtaposition of such a piece as 'Tam o' Shanter,' would be a 'gross violation of propriety.' Robert Burns, accordingly, was permitted only to edit, to arrange and to subscribe for the new book.

There were others who could find a use for his reckless offers. Soon afterwards he had a 'fine fair letter' from Creech, speaking of a new two-volume edition which could not possibly be expected to pay, asking for it every new thing written since the last edition, and offering in remuneration a few free copies when the book should appear! It is one thing to make a lordly gesture and another to be taken for a fool. Robert was infuriated but helpless.

Since he had booked for Jamaica he had never needed cash so urgently. In March the builder whom he had backed for £20 was unable to meet the bill. On the last day of the month Anna Park, away now at Leith, had a baby girl. By some accident the child was given the same name as Robert's first illegitimate daughter—Elizabeth. Jean's new baby, born on April 9, was another boy. They had him christened William Nicol.[6] There is no sign that Jean was unduly upset about the little new Elizabeth. Jean was generous and humble-minded and simple, and being herself warm-blooded, was rich in understanding of the flesh, especially her husband's flesh. She knew he had that spark of restless fury in him which no one woman could satisfy. As for her, she was satisfied with being his wife. When Anna Park's baby could be carried to Mossgiel she would suckle it with her own. After all she was used to nursing twins. She would give it out that she was fostering a dead neighbour's bairn.

Far worse to her was the absolute decision that the farm must be given up for a narrow first-floor house in Dumfries and that Miller would not allow them to sub-let Ellisland. The fact that Ellisland was looped off by the river from the rest of the Dalswinton property had made Miller wonder more than once if it would not be best to part with it. His expenses with the new house had been great, and it was proposed that he should purchase a troop in the Dragoons for his soldier son William, at the cost of £3,600. Just then a neighbouring proprietor, named Morin, who had capital and could wait for tired acres to recover, offered him £1,900 for Ellisland.[7] Though a landlord's refusal under these circumstances to an unsuccessful tenant could hardly be regarded as sharp practice, Robert was angered by the conjunction of the heavy loss to himself with the credit for kindly patronage retained by Miller. Miller would always be able to represent himself as one who had made a good offer to a poet who, by his own shortcomings, had not been able to avail himself of it. Yet in hard fact the gain was all on Miller's side, and the poet was losing his work, his money and his farming reputation.[8]

In the early summer Robert met with another accident. He was the kind of man who is always knocking up against things, falling, cutting or bruising his fingers, losing his possessions or forgetting them, so that Jean would scold at him for that very impetuosity of movement which had arrested her eye and caught her fancy when she first saw him in Morton's tavern ten years earlier. This time, before his arm was quite healed, he fell and injured his leg.[9] In June he had to hobble to Gilbert's wedding, for which he obtained three days' leave from his Excise duties. Gilbert was marrying a Kilmarnock girl—another Jean.

Shortly after the wedding came a careful letter from Clarinda enclosing a poem by herself. Robert replied with verses. They began:

> Sweet Sensibility, how charming,
>> Thou, my Friend, canst truly tell;

and ended ambiguously:

> Dearly bought the hidden treasure
>> Finer Feelings can bestow.

To which Clarinda:

> Yes, Sensibility is charming
>> Tho' it may wound the tender mind, . . .
> Sensibility! sweet treasure,
>> Still I'll sing in praise of thee!
> All that mortals know of pleasure
>> Flows from Sensibility.

She also begged to know if Mr Burns had read this or that?

During the course of this politely tender interchange Jean was at Mauchline with the children, and Robert did unexpectedly well with his August sale of crops. The Dumfriesshire buyers had crowded to the farm in the hope of a bargain and the assurance that according to custom they would be permitted to help themselves to drinks. But the Ellisland brew was so profuse and so potent that the partakers were soon bidding against each other to the tune of a guinea an acre above the average. Robert, who remained sober enough to appreciate the epic scene, described it realistically afterwards, though not to Clarinda. At the end there was a hand-to-hand fight out of doors between about thirty people, while indoors men lay about on the floor so overcome that their lapping dogs were soon too drunk to stand. Even in that intemperate county 'such a scene of drunkenness,' wrote Robert, 'was hardly ever seen.'

During the past eighteen months public as well as private affairs had stiffened the rebel in Robert and forced him to define his own political position. Since the split between Fox and Burke over the French Revolution in February 1790, and the growing Tory hostility toward the revolutionaries, he had taken his firm stand as a Foxite. The discourtesy of the Glencairns in the matter of his poem, and Miller's refusal to let him sub-let the farm, were events that emphasised his Jacobin leanings. In the middle of June the Earl of Buchan had written asking him to assist in pretentious celebrations, alleged to be in honour of the poet Thomson, but really designed to display his lordship as a patron of letters. Robert kept him waiting for an answer as long as the Glencairn family had kept him. He then sent a mock-modest letter of a technique peculiar to himself. Its phrases, while giving no offence to the complacent recipient, could arouse shouts of ribald laughter when he repeated them aloud. He also addressed some verses to Thomson, later to be published in a revolutionary sheet:

> Dost thou not rise, indignant shade,
>   And smile with spurning scorn,
> When they wha wad hae starved thy life
>   Thy senseless turf adorn?

Such was his mood in November when he had to sell his stock and implements before removing from the farm. On this occasion there was neither jolly drunkenness nor unexpected profit. It resembled far too much the enforced sales at Mount Oliphant and Lochlie. His failure and loss were made evident to the world, and there had been friction beforehand over the renunciation of the lease signed in the presence of Miller and Morin. Morin had found fault with the unfinished condition of the fences and offices, and had insisted that it was Burns's part to leave them in perfect repair. Burns maintained that he had already done his full and losing share in reclaiming what was practically waste ground when it came into his hands. A further cause of dispute was the value of the manure which now lay on the farm and was Burns's property though he could not profitably remove it. On every count Burns had to yield.

If there was one thing he endured hardly it was this position of unjust helplessness. He wanted to smash the society which forced so unnatural a thing upon him.[10] Anyhow he must smash something. On the day of the 'flitting,' which followed hard upon the sale, Adam Armour was there to help. The journey to Dumfries with the loaded carts was made with feelings roused to boiling point. Trotting at the tail of the last cart was the only beast they were taking with them—the nice little heifer that was Colonel Dunlop's wedding present and that Jean had refused to part with. Robert had parted with his pet sheep, his putting stone, his £300 of good money. On arriving at Dumfries he remembered yet another matter, left inadvertently behind, but still in his power. With his diamond he had inscribed verses on many of the Ellisland window panes. These, at least, neither Miller nor Morin should have. Young Adam was sent trudging back in the November evening. Being young he carried out his orders with a right good will. That night after dark there was the sound of splintering glass by the banks of the Nith.

A man's failure is doubled when he fails under the eyes of his wife. Jean was not backward in blaming her husband for the Ellisland fiasco. A fiasco it was, though not for the reasons she supposed. He, knowing the true reasons, was more conscious of his failure than she, and so he found himself for the moment, at least, incapable of his father's masterful ruling: 'Let there be no gloomy looks in this house!' Jean was not a shrew; but for a time there was wifely scolding in the new home, which consisted of four upstair rooms in the Wee Vennel, and after all no place to be found for her nice little cow. For Robert's writing-table and bookshelves, instead of the pleasant parlour commanding the Nith, there was a mere closet wedged between the two front living-rooms. Happily he was undisturbed by the noise of children. He still composed mostly out of doors and could revise his songs or write his letters peacefully among his babies. But the accusing face of his spouse as she cooked in the small back kitchen was destructive of a poet's peace. He must get away, if only for a few days. He would spend a week in Edinburgh and say a last farewell to Clarinda.

Clarinda was going to Jamaica! She was sailing in February in the *Roselle*—the very ship in which he had meant to embark if he had failed of his Edinburgh edition. Her astonishing decision had been made known to him before he left Ellisland, not by herself—it was long since she had written—but by Ainslie. Mr James McLehose, twelve months after learning of his son William's death, had suddenly become an assertive father and husband. He was earning £1,000 a year and had a good home to offer. He regretted his past behaviour and piously purposed reform. He desired that his only remaining son should be put to the best boarding-school in Edinburgh where French and fencing were taught. He requested his wife to join him. All this was accompanied by a bill for £50 and a characteristic threat. Should his dear Nancie refuse to carry out his wishes, her boy would be permanently removed from her.

After much agitated heart-searching and repeated colloquies with female and clerical friends, Nancie had decided upon the Christian course. It was indeed difficult for her to do anything else. She would trust that time and Jamaica had improved her husband out of knowledge, and she would undertake the rôle of the forgiving wife. Upon hearing of it Robert was sure it was all wrong, but what could he do? Nothing, but seize the chance to say good-bye to her at a moment opportune for himself.

If Sylvander was depressed, Clarinda was uplifted by the general approval of her circle and thrilled by the picture of her self-sacrificing self being greeted by a penitent and wealthy husband on Kingston pier. She was in fact in an uppish mood, when the chance, unexpected as it had been long sought, presented itself for the castigation of her poet. She seized it without scruple. After her lengthy silence this was the letter that Robert received from her one gloomy November day shortly after his move:

> SIR,—I take the liberty of addressing a few lines in behalf of your old acquaintance, Jenny Clow, who, to all appearance, is at this moment dying. Obliged, from all the symptoms of a rapid decay to quit her service, she is gone to a room almost without common necessaries, untended and unmourned. In circumstances so distressing, to whom can she so naturally look for aid as to the father of her child, the man for whose sake she suffered many a bad and anxious night, shut from the world, with no other companions than *guilt* and solitude? You have now an opportunity to evince you indeed possess these fine feelings you have delineated, so as to claim the just admiration of your country. I am convinced I need add nothing further to persuade you to act as every consideration of humanity, as well as gratitude, must dictate. I am, Sir, your sincere well-wisher.   A.M.

Not a word of her departure nor of her feelings. Just this. But if this did not rouse Sylvander nothing would!

She was right: though as usual her rightness had not the expected results. Sylvander was ready to admit his faults to himself, to his wife, to God and to all the world. He was ready even to exaggerate them. But he would never submit to the useless humiliation—cursed to him that gives and him that takes—of platonic fault-finding. He was depressed and self-accusing enough when her letter reached him, but such a challenge could not be refused. All he needed was a drink or two (not over much) to nerve him to an effort of irony which His Grace of Queensberry himself could not have bettered:

> It is extremely difficult, my dear Madam, for me to deny a lady anything; but to a lady whom I regard with all the endearing epithets of a respectable esteem and old friendship, how shall I find the language of refusal? I have, indeed, a shade of a lady, which I keep, and shall ever keep, in the *sanctum sanctorum* of my most anxious care.[1]. . . . By the way, I have this moment a letter from her with a paragraph or two conceived in so stately a style that I would not pardon it in any created being except herself; but as the subject interests me much, I shall answer it to you, as I do not know her present address. I am sure she must have told you of a girl, Jenny Clow, who had the misfortune to make me a father (with contrition I own it) contrary to the laws of our most excellent constitution, in our holy Presbyterian hierarchy.
>
> Mrs M— tells me a tale of the poor girl's distress that makes my very heart well blood. I will trust that your goodness will apologise to your delicacy for me, when I beg of you, for Heaven's sake, to send a porter to the poor woman—Mrs M, it seems, knows where she is to be found—with five shillings in my name; and, as I shall be in Edinburgh on Tuesday first, for certain, make the poor wench leave a line for me, before Tuesday, at Mr Mackay's, White Hart Inn, Grassmarket, where I shall put up; and, before I am two hours in town, I shall see the girl and try what is to be done for her relief. I would have taken my boy from her long ago, but she would never consent.

> I shall do myself the very great pleasure to call for
> you when I come to town and repay you the sum your
> goodness shall have advanced . . . and most obedient,
>
> ROBERT BURNS.

Sylvander was in Edinburgh only one week. His parting
with Clarinda on 6 December was heart-rending. But he
returned sure of himself, refreshed, bubbling with song, and
having a lock of his platonic, evangelical, impeccable,
incorrigible mistress's hair in his pocket-book.[2] Once more
the distant mountains of Jamaica had wrought a miracle
in Scotland. Clarinda loved him: Clarinda forgave him:
Clarinda, in kissing him and being kissed, had ceased to be
exercised about Jenny Clow. As for Sylvander, he had done
what could be done for Jenny,[3] had bidden Anna Park
God-speed, and had arranged for his child by her to go to
Mossgiel.[4] By 15 December he had written six affectionate
letters from Dumfries, most of them containing songs, to his
'dearest Nancie,' his 'ever-dearest of women,' his 'ever-
beloved' and 'ever-sacred Clarinda,' 'the most accomplished
of all womankind' and 'the first of all God's works.' Toward
the end of the month, a seventh, very hurried letter conveyed
three songs, one of which was 'Ae fond kiss and then we
sever.'

Mrs McLehose's farewell did not come till the end of the
month. It was as full of religious adjurations as of loving
protestations. She commanded him not to write to her in
Jamaica, wished him happiness, and bade him meet her in a
glorious eternity.

Poor Nancie! It was her fate always to be taken at her
word. As she made her comfortless departure from Leith—
rendered yet more comfortless by an unfriendly letter that
reached her from her husband at the last moment—the man
she could have 'lived or died with' was drinking tea with a
delightful female out of blue and gold-rimmed Chelsea cups
(specially made in London with the family crest engraved
on each one), almost as cosily as he had drunk out of her
bird-of-paradise ones in the Potterrow. And he was exchanging anew old vows of friendship. Clarinda's exit had in fact
been forestalled by the entrance into Robert's life of another
lady, far younger and more cultured, and considerably
cleverer.

The circumstances of this entrance had been such as to forward intimacy without delay. One morning before dawn, a highly original picnic party had set out from Friars' Carse. Captain Riddel's younger brother Walter and his wife Maria[5] had newly arrived from Antigua *via* Mayfair. Maria, aged nineteen, and not long emerged from her first experience of child-birth, was in wild spirits. She wanted to explore the lead mines at Wanlockhead, some thirty-five miles away, and she insisted that the poetical ploughman, of whom she had heard so much, should go with them. So it was arranged. They would ride twenty miles to Sanquhar, breakfast there hungry as hawks, and then go on in a postchaise and descend the mines. Maria was all for adventure. She had been in a ship that pirates had chased, and it had struck on a rock, and she had as nearly as anything been wrecked. Down in the mines she cut her gloves to ribbons and tired everybody else out (especially the poetical ploughman who felt quite faint underground); but she would not desist till she had seen more and done more than the only other woman who had ever preceded her. Mrs Robert Riddel waited above ground. Relations between the two branches of the Riddel family were not going to be easy. Walter, who had seen exciting foreign military service while in his teens, was very handsome, but neither very honest nor very clever. He was in fact a gentlemanly rake, and an entirely frivolous person who quickly made himself obnoxious to his sister-in-law. Maria— talkative, opinionative, witty, intelligent, easily bored, capricious, and careless of the conventions (when it suited her)—might not be actually obnoxious, but she appeared too alarming for country comfort.

It was easy to see that she was a spoiled little girl. Daughter of the Governor of St Kitts and the Leeward Islands, she had been used since childhood to queening it over Englishmen and natives, and she was by nature unusually vivacious. At fifteen she had exchanged satirical and amorous effusions with the London wits. At sixteen she had written a book (still in manuscript but ambitious of appearing in print) on her travels. Now, at nineteen, she was a wife and mother, an amateur naturalist, a professed republican—to her Dundas was the 'arch-fiend'— and a passionate reader and playgoer.

She disliked realism and Miss Burney, and sought relief from 'the dull realities of life' in Mrs Radcliffe. She was chestnut-haired and slender, though with a good bosom amply displayed. Her keen, piquant face comprised a pointed chin, a large mouth, an inquiring tip-tilted nose, and alert hazel eyes. Like so many women who habitually enhance their charms by art—Maria made up her face and added to her not too profuse locks—she was delightfully free from self-consciousness, and she knew too much of the usages of society to have undue reverence for them. Though she had made a mistake about her husband, and probably knew it, she had a true instinct for men of genuine character or gifts, and she was more popular with men than with her own sex. She had only to hear the life story of Mr Burns to be crazy for a meeting, had only to shake his hand and look into his eyes to determine upon winning him for her friend. Her husband had just bought (though he had not yet paid for) an attractive little estate four miles out of Dumfries. There Mr Burns must come as often as he would, perhaps oftener. He must see her natural-history museum, and use her interesting English and foreign library. He must bring his poems and criticise hers. He must introduce her to Mr Smellie in Edinburgh, so that her book might be printed. She even called (a thing no other lady either in Ayrshire or Dumfries had done) on Mr Burns in his own house, and there surveyed the situation in the time that it took Jean to dust a chair. Her conclusion was that the poet, though a kind and affectionate husband, was not in love with his wife.

More than any other woman of fashion, with the possible exception of the Duchess of Gordon; with whom she had traits in common, Maria appreciated Robert Burns's quality. And because she was younger and fresher than the Duchess of Gordon and less, as yet, the prey of her own caprice, she was more receptive and capable of genuine reverence. An Englishwoman—even, it might be said, a foreigner—she was not in any great degree able to estimate his poetic achievement. To his poems in dialect she was largely deaf, while his English verses, except in so far as some of them were written in compliment to her, struck her as chiefly remarkable for being the work of a ploughman. But simply as a man, by his aspect, his force, his talk, his immense variety of moods, in all of which he radiated life, he impressed her deeply. She had met and was to meet many distinguished men and several men of genius; but she found none possessed of 'sorcery' in the same degree as Mr Burns.

Robert lost neither his head nor his heart. For that in a woman he needed an element of pathos, something wistful, if it were only in her situation. Maria, well placed and conscious, could never move him as Clarinda, with all her absurd, muddle-headed flamboyance, had moved him. He positively disliked her capriciousness, her coolness, her sureness, her chatter. But it was impossible for him not to take pleasure in the friendliness and freedom and youthful admiration of her company. The evenings spent at Woodley Park may not have been pleasanter than those at Friars' Carse, but they were more stimulating. Without losing his heart it was good to have his heart-beats quickened now and again by a young and practised hand.[6] Besides, Maria professed to be as ardent as himself over the way things were going in France, and as enthusiastic for reform and the rights of the people at home. That February, when he despatched to Paris four carronades, which he had been instrumental in seizing from a smuggling brig in the Solway, he could count on Maria's approval, whatever other heads might be shaken. He had bought the guns himself for £3, bidding for them at the sale of the confiscated cargo, and they had gone at his expense—a present from a people's poet for the French legislative assembly to use against its enemies and the enemies of the labouring man!

Robert had been embarrassed by Maria's demand for an introduction to the blunt 'old sinful Smellie.' But she would have it, so he wrote a diplomatic, apologetic letter informing Smellie of her desire. He might have spared himself the pains this letter evidently cost him. Before February was out, Maria had returned from a brief visit to Edinburgh, with her manuscript accepted and the Crochallan in her pocket. When later he came to Dumfries he danced attendance upon her at a Caledonian Hunt Assembly, and gallantly reproached her for having married a soldier when there were printers and naturalists like him alive. With funny fat Grose, on the other hand, she had quarrelled so violently and with so strong invective (Robert being present on the occasion) that the antiquarian declared it impossible that he should ever come under her roof again. Her tantrums could be shocking. But as the months went on her friendship became a more important and amusing element in Robert's life. 'Were I to lose you,' he wrote, 'it would leave a Vacuum in my enjoyments that nothing could fill up.' Dumfries, a gossipy, censorious little place, believed the worst of the friendship, but Walter Riddel—'my friend and your husband,' as Robert called him—did not make this mistake. He cared no more than Maria for what the Dumfriesians said, and rightly held the intimacy to be without injury to himself. It was, however, an understood thing that when he was away from home, as he often was, Robert should discontinue his visits. Also, neither Christian names nor Arcadian were used. Limits of decorum must be observed, even by Antiguans.

Robert was still only a gauger. Instead of the hoped-for Supervisorship in a new place, he had been given a Footwalk in the Dumfries Third Division. But he did not grumble. He was saved the expense of a horse and the farm was off his hands. The worst of the work was that, even without the farm, it ate his leisure. Yet he saw no other way to his desire—'literary leisure with a decent competency'—but by Excise promotion. So he persevered, sometimes cheerfully, at other times in terrible despondency.

That spring he was cheerful. Opposite his 'character' for the year in the official record was written 'The Poet; does pretty well.' In February he had been promoted to the First or Port Division at £70, with a £15 or £20 bonus. At a dinner he had made a tremendous hit by singing 'The deil's awa wi' th' Exciseman'; and on the occasion of his making that song—the day he had waded sword in hand through the waters of the Solway to subdue a crew of smugglers more numerous and better armed than the men at his own back—he had proved himself to be a brave as well as a diligent officer. Less spectacularly he was helpful to juniors and indulgent to ageing officers, and his own temperamental shortcomings were balanced by a talent for administration which prompted him to suggest several highly practical improvements. His immediate superiors in Dumfries, Mr Findlater, who had become Supervisor only the year before, and Mr Mitchell, the Collector, were able to appreciate the value of these suggestions, and were both his particular friends and well-wishers.

Another encouragement in the spring was a diploma including him among the Royal Archers of Scotland. Though slow in acknowledging this honour—even then a considerable one—he was pleased. He composed his quarrels with Miller and with Creech, and having some ready money from the sale of Ellisland stock, he paid all his debts, including that for the stone on Fergusson's grave. He wrote to Creech giving his consent to the scheme for a third edition in two volumes, offered 50 pages of new poems, including 'Tam o' Shanter,' and asked in return 20 copies to present to patrons and personal friends. He would be at peace with all men.

Dissipation of the expected poetic leisure at Dumfries was not caused by the Excise alone. When it became known that Mr Burns would bestir himself to help any man whom he judged had been unfairly treated, and that all the influence at his disposal was also at the disposal of each honest acquaintance, he was much sought after. New friends and old enemies applied to him for introductions to 'the Great.' Wilson, the Tarbolton quack and schoolmaster, whom he had pilloried as Dr Hornbook, had long since begged unblushingly for favours. Now a local dominie in trouble had his case taken up and money lent to him by the poet. Maria had protégés to whom Robert could be useful. Besides which, all the good fellows in Dumfries, who knew not how to wile away their own leisure, had discovered a man whose company was incomparable. The Hyslops at the Globe were as friendly as if Anna Park had never been and gone. More friendly perhaps because of her. After all Mr Burns had shouldered his share of the business, and warm men like him were the best for the trade. Quickly he had become a figure in the town, and his acquaintance embraced all ranks. Haugh, the blacksmith, who lived on the floor above, and Syme, who was commencing Collector of Stamp duties in an office on the ground floor, were his cronies. Syme had bought the 23-acre croft of

Ryedale near Dumfries and built a bachelor cottage there, and Captain Hamilton of Arbigland, Robert's landlord, whose town lodging was just opposite, were alike pressing with invitations to dine at their country homes. For the local farmers he wrote letters of love or dispute, and for a brother Exciseman, Gillespie, he undertook to woo by letter and by song the blonde young daughter of a smuggler in his district. There was never an evening after his six o'clock tea that he could not pick up in a stroll along the High Street two or three friends in whose company to receive the news brought by the 8 o'clock post. Sometimes he went with them to the Globe; sometimes to the less reputable Coach and Horses. Again, he would take chosen ones home to sit round the marble punch-bowl, while Jean, wearing the first gingham gown to be seen in Dumfries, waited upon them, untidy but happy. However merry or long at the Globe he might be, she never once heard his step unsteady on the steep stair at night, or knew him miss having a look at the sleeping children.

The problem he never learned how to solve was to drink level with the lairds, as they insisted he should, yet not to lose control as it almost seemed they wished him to do. Often because of it he refused their invitations. Hamilton of Arbigland tried vainly for twelve months to get him out to dinner. At other times he went, and was able to keep his head and reach the drawing-room with a steadier hand and eye than his host.[7] Once, to prove how steady he was, he threaded the embroidery needle with which one of the ladies was working. But there were times when he drank as much as any gentleman, and to some gentlemen's malicious joy, put away constraint and led the company as entertainer and lawgiver, without respect of persons. Then 'Robin's confounding wit,' as Syme called it, ran riot.

Throughout Scotland during the earlier months of 1792 there was a sense of prosperity and easy money. At the end of February, Pitt had declared that 'there was never a time in the history of the country when from the situation of Europe we might more reasonably expect fifteen years of peace than at the present moment.' It was only cautious old croakers like Patrick Miller[8] who talked gloomily of inflation and of a bubble that would soon burst, even as his precious Spanish ram had blown itself out that March and died, having taken from it in the autopsy 'about half a mutchkin of water.'

And if money just then seemed freer than usual, so were topics of conversation more profuse and exciting. Tom Paine's *Common Sense* was replacing *The Fourfold State* not only on the weaver's bookshelf but in the libraries of Dalswinton and Friars' Carse. A wave of emotion had swept through the land uniting generous-minded men without regard to their stations. All the topics were in reality only one topic—the French Revolution.

Foreign agitations in the name of liberty had always been popular north of the Tweed. The Scotish breast by its history and the Scotish brain by its training were both responsive to cries for freedom. At this particular time the warlike compatriots of Wallace and of the Covenanters were also the intellectually adventurous contemporaries of David Hume and Adam Smith. A Boswell, for all his Toryism, was eager to reflect in his proper person the glory of the 'brave distrest Corsicans'[1]: the compressed lips of a Patrick Miller and the mobile mouth of a Robert Burns had denounced with equal indignation the 'execrable' slave trade in America. All classes and parties had been solid for Abolition. In May there was widespread anger over the rejection of the Bill at Westminster.

Unhappily any Scotish miner or salter, or indeed any Carron iron-smelter, might legitimately have envied the lot of the Carolina negro,[2] and any Scotish child-labourer in one of the new cotton mills would certainly have been happier and healthier as a distrest little Corsican. More unhappily still, neither a Miller (though he had been a colliery owner and a shareholder in the Carron foundry) nor a Burns (though he had descended the lead mines and had turned shuddering from the 'hell' of the Falkirk furnaces) noticed this discrepancy.

With the French Revolution it seemed at first as if foreign sentiments and home realities could still be kept unrelated; as if yet again a distant battle cry might provide no more than a stimulant (pleasantly diluted with self-congratulation) for the Caledonian heart, and fresh matter for discussion (comfortably abstract) for the Caledonian mind. Dugald Stewart had been in Paris and had returned as innocently enthusiastic as his pupil Lord Daer: the Earl of Lauderdale had addressed the French mob as a sympathiser: Dalrymple and the Erskines were ardent for the liberties of 'the people.' When our poet despatched his four carronades to the Legislative Assembly, he was merely expressing in concrete poet's fashion what thousands of his countrymen felt, irrespective of station, and at first perhaps irrespective of party.[3]

But even today guns travel less quickly than news, and in 1792, while the gauger-poet's parcel of iron was still on its way from Dumfries to Dover, the whole face of things changed. France had declared war against Great Britain's ally, the Emperor of Germany. Even before this declaration, Mr Pitt and his colleagues had begun to suspect Robert's addressee in spite of that body's alleged friendliness; and Talleyrand, after sounding the British Ministry (in careful phrases learned from Dominie Murdoch) as to their feelings about the possible attack by the French on the Emperor's Flemish domains, had been slighted at a levee and cut by the Queen at a drawing-room. The gauger's gift was stopped at Dover, and a note of his name and effusive dedication was sent to the proper quarter. Soon afterwards another gauger— author of *The Rights of Man*—was mobbed at the very place where the unlucky guns lay. In August, Louis XVI was deposed and the British Ambassador recalled. In September the National Convention was summoned.

Nowhere was the war-cloud darker than over Scotland. And in the shadow of the cloud the cold home-truth emerged. Scotsmen possessed no single free institution. The Church, the town councils, the criminal courts were unchecked. Places and the press were in the pockets of the Tories. And the Scotish Tories were not simply corrupt: they were without the compensating qualities of political tradition or of patriotism. Their hearts were where their treasure was—in London.

The Whigs, though they had intellectual standing, were politically negligible. As a domestic factor public opinion hardly existed. There was, as we have seen, small implication either of Whig influence or of public opinion in young Patrick Miller's representation of the Dumfries Burghs. In Dumfries, as elsewhere in Scotland, the county member was elected by the freeholders, a small body practically controlled by Government; and the burgh member, who sat for a group comprising four or five burghs, was awarded his majority by a judiciously 'refreshed' municipal conspiracy.[4] Miller's return having been merely Queensberry's little revenge on Pitt, His Grace turned high Tory again with perfect political cynicism.[5]

Made at last alive, by their interest in France, to the evils at home, the genuine Scotish Whigs quickly declared themselves for domestic reform. In England societies of the 'Friends of the People,' calling for 'a full, free and equal representation' had come into being. Now, with a central body in Edinburgh of which Harry Erskine was the leading spirit, they were established all over Scotland. They disclaimed extreme measures and stood by the ancient institutions of the country, but they demanded a shortening of the duration of Parliament, an end of political corruption and 'a redress of real grievances.'

At first their case appeared hopeful. There were no cruel despots in Scotland, only corrupt institutions. The Scots were not apt to be extreme or excitable like the French. Surely then they had only to be shown the crying need for perfectly constitutional changes for such to be brought about without pain or delay? So Professor Stewart, beaming rhetorically upon his students in Edinburgh, and the Dean of the Faculty of Advocates eloquently pacing Parliament Square in company with his Whig friends; so Miller and Riddel, rationalising over their claret at Dalswinton or Friars' Carse; and so, in his more personal, impassioned way, Robert Burns at the Globe or seated with Maria and her harp in the Woodley Park drawing-room.

But those who declared for reform had also to maintain their declaration against the war, an attitude that was every day more provocative to the ruling section. Soon the mildest advocacy of change at home came under the head of disaffection. Then was the honest Scotish Whig faced by a fresh discovery. Speech, the one thing in Scotland which had been free, was free no longer.

There were few, if any, real Jacobins in Scotland; but from midsummer the word was hurled at any man who expressed his sympathy with the French or his disapproval of going to war with them, and by the turn of the year it included any critic of home affairs. Even the man of property who advocated reform was now 'a cause and shield of popular delusion.' The landless critic was something worse. The execution of the

French king in January, with its aura of infidelity and its train of atrocities, divided the Whigs and added enormously to the ranks of the self-styled Tories—'saviours and maintainers of their country,' whose chief claim to either designation was that they possessed no public principle but devotion to Henry Dundas. The British declaration of war in February completed their supremacy.

The strange thing is that the Scotish Tories were timid even to panic. Dundas 'had the means of rewarding submission and of suppressing opposition beyond what were ever exercised in modern times by one person in any portion of the empire.' His supporters 'engrossed almost the whole wealth, and rank, and public office, of the country, and at least three-fourths of the population.' Yet the meeting together of three or four 'disaffected persons' became conspiracy, not more than a dozen guests (whose names were taken down by the Sheriff's officer) could assemble for Fox's birthday dinner, and written Tory tests were instituted for new men at the Bar, which if they did not subscribe, forbade their entrance. When it took all Miller's dourness and Erskine's prestige and Stewart's popularity for these men to stand firm and remain vocal: when a harmless old gentlewoman, because she spoke feelingly of freedom, was suspected of hiding a bijou guillotine and of practising upon it with chickens and mice 'against the time when French principles should come to Scotland';[6] we can infer the situation of lesser like-minded persons. Pitt, scenting sedition among Scotish 'labourous folk,' had issued a proclamation forbidding the sale of Paine's works. Since an effigy of Dundas had been burned in some of the country places 'the whole lower orders' were credited with 'a thirst for bloodshed and anarchy.' Dundas's system of espionage, which was already widespread, was thereafter supplemented everywhere by amateur endeavour. The frequently inadequate reports of informers 'working with ferocious bitterness and systematic zeal' lacked neither direct sanction nor substantial rewards from headquarters.[7] A man's livelihood might easily depend on his subservience. In the case of a small official, that subservience would extend beyond his official capacity to cover his behaviour as man and as citizen.

It has been truly said that the French Revolution found Scotland out.[8] It did more. It revealed individual Scotsmen to themselves, to each other, and to the world at large. A mere handful emerged from the trial bearing with them the full lustre of their courage. Of these Harry Erskine was one. In his staider way Patrick Miller was another. Men more obscure than these had far larger sacrifices demanded of them and did not shrink. Was Robert Burns of their company?

There has never been any doubt about his convictions. He was for France, for Freedom, for Reform, for the People—all in capital letters. Neither rationalism nor the decapitation of crowned heads (as such) shocked him.[9] Though physically courageous and temperamentally warlike—as witness him sword in hand subduing the Solway smugglers—he was in principle an ardent pacifist. 'War,' he cried, 'I deprecate: misery and ruin to thousands are in the blast that announces the destructive demon.' Sometimes thus fierily, again with humour—'I am better pleased to make one more than be the death of twenty'—he repeatedly expressed his detestation of organised warfare. He appreciated its futility in general and its disastrous results to labouring men in particular. He would advocate arms in one case only—the case of invasion. Nothing but the catch-cry of that 'just and necessary war for all that is dear to us' could deceive him. And of all wars he was most opposed to a war undertaken against the French. So much for his convictions.

Equally there has never been any doubt about his indiscretions. It was not in him, when occasion offered, to refrain from the revealing gesture, the effective witticism or the impetuous outburst. Of the first sort of indiscretion the carronades incident was positively typical. So, negatively, was his action on a gala night that 30th of October in the Dumfries theatre. It was at the close of the last long and successful day of blood-sports (loathsome as war to Robert) by the gentlemen of the Caledonian and the Dumfries and Galloway Hunt, which 'had drawn together almost all the genteel families in the three southern counties,' so that 'there never was on any occasion such an assemblage of people distinguished for their rank, fortune and elegance of manners, seen in this place, or perhaps in any provincial town in

Scotland.'[10] During the morning hours Mrs Burns at her marketing and Mr Burns on his official business had been jostled in the streets by 'pimps and chairmen . . . hairdressers, milliners' apprentices, grooms and valets, carriages driving and bustling backwards and forwards.'[11] And now at night Lord Hopetoun's box (His Lordship was in Robert's view an obnoxious person) 'exhibited an assemblage of nobility rarely to be seen in one box in the theatres of the metropolis.'[12] There was only one little flaw in the proceedings. When, to conclude the happy season and the successful performance of *As You Like It*, 'God Save the King' was called for by this fashionable gathering, a shout came from the pit for 'Ça ira.' It was quickly and easily drowned, and the incident, accompanied by some counter shouting and a brief scuffle among the groundlings, was not so serious as to need reporting in the local newspaper. Still it did not go unnoticed. Nor did it escape remark that Mr Burns, who was himself in the pit, remained seated throughout the singing of the triumphant, loyal strains with his black felt wideawake pressed firmly on his head.[13]

His calls for embarrassing toasts in mixed company belong also to the second sort of indiscretion in which he frequently indulged. Already warned by several loyal or innocuous toasts the gauger would rise glass in hand to propose 'the last verse of the last chapter of the last book of Kings!' Or, following the drinking of Pitt's health in a large party which included men holding His Majesty's commission, he would ask for 'the health of a better man, George Washington.' Or, worse still, when it was his turn to utter a post-prandial 'sentiment,' he would say 'may our success in the present war be equal to the justice of our cause,' or maybe 'may we never see the French, nor the French see us!'

For the third sort of indiscretion his pen was more apt than his tongue.

'Go on, Sir!'—he wrote to Captain Johnston, the promoter of *The Gazetteer*, upon receiving a prospectus of this daring new paper which was to be independent, reforming and anti-war. 'Lay bare with undaunted heart and steady hand that horrid mass of corruption called politics and statecraft.' This, a fortnight before the annexation of Savoy by France,[14] was one of the many indiscretions in prose and rhyme which led 'Moderate' Whig friends, such as Mrs Dunlop, to fear that the poet was a misguided 'Wild.' *The Gazetteer* was notorious for its advanced views, and Robert did not merely subscribe for it, he contributed to it and caused others to do so. He prevailed upon Riddel of Carse, who was a delegate for County Reform, to send a tendencious article signed 'Cato'; and for himself, besides verses which had no special political significance, he sent others of which the meaning could not be missed.[15] So much for Robert's indiscretions.

Unmistakable convictions with constant indiscretions do not invariably imply courage. How did the poet behave when he learned, as he did for the first time at the end of 1792, that there was to be an inquiry by the Excise into his political conduct?

There is only one reply. He flew into a humiliating panic. He abased himself in disingenuous disclaimers and needless apologies. In the same breath he was innocent of all disaffection, begged to be forgiven, and promised that it should not occur again. His letters on the subject, with their Micawberish protestations of 'manly' independence and domestic sentiment, make pitiful reading. It was by the wickedness of 'some scoundrel enemy' that he had been maligned. He was a husband. He was a father. Near half a score of innocent beings and 'the prospect of many more' were dependent upon him. What would become of them, if his Excise promotion were denied or delayed? What, still more, if he were discharged?

A few weeks later, Erskine of Marr, a rich Edinburgh Whig who had heard of the discharge as a fact, wrote to Robert Riddel inviting his contribution to a subscription headed by himself. The Erskines and others would see to it that a poet suffering for his convictions should be kept from want. Here then was the reply to Robert's theoretical question. But Robert had not waited to put the question in practice. During the interval he had eaten his words and was committed to a diet of humble pie more upsetting to his stomach than many festive nights. In an appeal to Fintry he had washed his hands of *The Gazetteer* thus:

> Of Johnston I know nothing. One evening, in company with four or five friends we met with his prospectus, which we thought manly and independent; and I wrote

> to him, ordering his paper for us. If you think that I act
> improperly in allowing his paper to come addressed to
> me, I shall immediately countermand it.

His utmost affirmation, even to a Whig patron, was that in his opinion 'an alarming system of corruption has pervaded the connection between the executive power and the House of Commons.' Of the King he remarked, 'His private worth it is altogether impossible such a man as I can appreciate.' Possibly he expected Fintry to relish the subtlety of this characteristic ambiguity. It is hard to believe that on this occasion he really enjoyed it himself.

Erskine's kindly and practical offer had been the outcome of considerable alarm in Edinburgh, an alarm fostered by the poet's own alarmist letters to his friends. Nicol, under the veil of banter, had sent serious temporising advice. His 'dear Christless Bobby' should consider St Paul's precept, that 'we ought not to resist the Higher Powers' and should take the Vicar of Bray as his exemplar. . . . 'What concerns it thee,' wrote the Latin master, 'whether the lousy Dumfriesian fiddlers play "Ça ira" or "God Save the King?" Suppose you *had* an aversion to the King, you could not as a gentleman use him worse than He has done. The infliction of idiocy is no sign of Friendship or Love. . . .' To which Robert returned a suitably facetious reply couched in oriental vein, admitting the wisdom of the counsel, and calling himself 'A puddle-headed, rattle-headed, wrong-headed, round-headed slave.' But he knew well enough, and he knew that Nicol knew, how disingenuous under the circumstances was the analogy with the famous Vicar. By his oft-spoken convictions, by his lifelong championship of individual integrity, and by his unequalled gift for bold, witty, fiery, popular improvisation, he was born to be the declared troubadour of the hard-pressed body of his fellow-countrymen who were now holding out against ever-mounting odds in the name of liberty. If ever, in the words of Clarinda, Mr Burns had 'an opportunity to evince he indeed possessed these fine feelings he had delineated so as to claim the just admiration of his country,' it was now. Yet that December, when 160 delegates from 80 societies of 'The Friends of the People' assembled from all over Scotland to form their first convention in

Edinburgh; when his most powerful patrons joined with men worse placed than himself (and equally endowed with wives and children) to pass some moderate resolutions of Parliamentary reform, and to close the proceedings with the oath 'to live free or die,' Mr Burns was not among them. He was afraid—afraid for his family, his livelihood, his promotion. By his own admissions there is no other conclusion. Just as his strong and heavy frame was somewhere flawed, so his magnificently vital and vocal spirit was somewhere infirm. He was content to write:

> In Politics if thou would'st mix,
>   And mean thy fortunes be;
> Bear this in mind, be deaf and blind,
>   Let great folks hear and see.

—or to ease his bitterness by an abstract diatribe in the form of a catechism:

QUERE. What is Politics?

ANSWER. Politics is a science wherewith by means of nefarious cunning and hypocritical pretence we govern civil politics for the emolument of ourselves and adherents.

Q. What is a Minister?

A. A Minister is an unprincipled fellow who, by the influence of heredity or acquired wealth—by superior abilities or by a lucky conjuncture of circumstances,[16] obtains a principal place in the administration of the affairs of government.

Q. What is a Patriot?

A. A Patriot is an individual of the same description as a minister, only out of place.

—or to bemoan his unique bad luck in politics as in love. *He* has only to set his heart on a particular woman for her to be unattainable. If *his* 'resentment is awaked' it is sure to be where it 'dare not squeak.' And he pictures his soul as 'flouncing and fluttering round her tenement, like a wild finch caught amid the horrors of winter and newly thrust into a cage.'

> O fie on silly coward man!

—he might well write the line just then. Before the end of the year he had learned the results of the official inquiry. It had resolved into an 'admonishment' and a reminder that it was his business 'to act and not think.' The Surveying General Examiner was a friend of Mrs Dunlop. In the background was the well-disposed Fintry. Allowance would be made for a poet who would promise future 'silence and obedience.' The poet did so promise. The matter was closed. His description of himself to some of his friends as only 'partly forgiven' and with his hope of promotion 'blasted,' derived perhaps as much from anger as from fear.[17]

Though all the seas round Britain were calm, the March of 1793 came in at Dumfries with two days of tempest without rain, such as nobody could remember before. The wind raked the Drumlanrig woods—soon to be worse treated by His Grace himself on behalf of a daughter whose illegitimate paternity he was not the only one to claim—plucking up the ducal ashes and firs by the roots and breaking and twisting firmer trees 'as if on purpose.' At Dalswinton two of the stoutest beeches were down and the orchard was wrecked. The proprietor, surveying the damage from the doors of his now little-used workshop, found in the gale a symbol of the political tornado and rejoiced grimly in his own sagacity. When buying this estate on the Nith he had also purchased 22,000 acres on other river banks which 'from climate and soil' were destined in his opinion to become a 'centre of power and consequence,' namely the banks of 'the Ohio and the Missysippie.' His equally sagacious friend, Mr Pulteney, had chosen lands in the back parts of New York State and on the Tennessee. Now that the declaration of war in February had brought Scotish trade to a standstill and was like to ruin many Scotish lairds, Patrick Miller's thoughts were in Kentucky, where he would fain lay out another four or five thousand pounds. Scotland was no longer a place for the planting of capital. It was well that poor Burns had failed with Ellisland and Morin bought it for cash. With the best credit this was not a time for borrowing. Almost he thought of selling Dalswinton. But he had grown unexpectedly to love the place, which helped his belief that it would justify his outlays and reward his patriotism, given time and economy.[18] The need for this last must be brought home to Peter, who was taking life and his Parliamentary duties with equal lightness in London. Peter should be reminded that had he depended for a livelihood on his own efforts, he would now be fit for nothing more distinguished than to cart dung on a farm. As for William, if it might be done without dishonour, he must sell out of the Dragoons. The repercussions in Scotland of the French Revolution had convinced Miller that commissions in a smart regiment were contemptible snobbery. Besides, it could not be right 'to run the risk of one's life voluntarily in a war of which we disapprove.' But this too would cost money. As an example of thrift he would give up his carriage and horses, would keep only a farm pony for his practical needs—let his wife and daughters complain as they liked—and he would neither visit nor entertain. A bottle of wine would more than serve him for a month, and he reckoned that the coat he was wearing, which nine months ago had cost him half a guinea, would still be decent in another nine months. General Goldie, though he was a man of fortune and on the Staff, had paid sixpence less for his and made it last as long.

These prudent resolves were greatly reinforced by the failure of the Glasgow Arms Bank at the end of the month and an unheard-of spate of Scotish bankruptcies. The Miller stables were emptied, and that summer Peter was requested to buy and send to Dalswinton a book entitled *An Enquiry concerning Political Justice and its Influence on General Virtue and Happiness*, by a writer named William Godwin[19]—'in 2 vols quarto, price £1 16s boards.' Peter was also reminded that it might be as well to make inquiries among the Whig journalists in London as to the possibility of employment for Mr Burns, should he lose his Excise position on political grounds. In April, Miller had been reminded of the poet's existence by a presentation of Creech's new edition[20] with a covering letter in which he was described as 'a gentleman to whose goodness I have been much indebted,' 'a patriot who was in a venal, sliding age, stands forth the champion of the liberties of my country' and 'a man whose benevolence of heart does honour to human nature.' And at the end of the summer this was followed up by a modest note which took the liberty of addressing a not very good little song to the prettiest of the Dalswinton daughters. The one-sided quarrel was made up.

Mr Burns was endeavouring to be prudent and practical.
Having bowed his neck to the spiritual humiliation imposed
by the war, he had now to deal with its financial problems.
Where a Depute Chairman of the Bank of Scotland moved
his spare capital abroad and wore an old coat, a gauger-poet
without a penny of capital[1] was forfeiting something like a
third of his annual income owing to the cessation of imports.
His family was both growing up and increasing. For some
time past the Wee Vennel house had been too small, and at
Whitsun they were moving to a larger one at the top of the
steep Mill Vennel beyond the lower end of the High Street.[2]
In November Anna Park's Elizabeth had come to them from
Mossgiel, and in the same month a legitimate baby girl—an
arrival for some reason dreaded by Robert[3]—had made the
sixth young one at home and the eighth in existence. She,
too, had been christened Elizabeth (after Mrs Robert
Riddel) and, as often happens with an 'unwanted' child, had
become her father's particular darling and delight. He was
always dandling her in the doorway, crooning a 'random
clink' to her and studying her fragile little face with fearful
devotion. Of his many 'tender ties' it was this delicate new
one that most 'unnerved courage and withered resolution'
while at the same time it demanded a renewed endurance and
inspired fresh lyricism. For a time crucial political questions
gave way to the primitive vision of life he shared with his
forefathers—'this short, stormy winter-day of our fleeting
existence'—which so healingly turned itself into song:

> Ye banks and braes o' bonny Doon,
>> How can ye bloom sae fresh and fair;
> How can ye chant, ye little birds,
>> And I sae weary, fu' o' care!

and which led a man also to make the best of a bad job.

As the eldest boy—a docile creature unlike that 'ramplor devil,' the second—was now of school age, his father had begun to feel concerned about education. He wrote to the Town Council reminding them that he was an honorary burgess and begging that in the matter of school fees he might be granted the full privileges of an ordinary freeman. This was granted. At the same time the committee of the new Public Library, to which on its foundation six months earlier he had presented a copy of his poems, resolved by a large majority to make Mr Burns a free member, thus sparing him the initial fee of half a guinea and the quarterly subscription of half a crown. Like the reduction of school fees to a freeman, this was a compliment as well as a considerable financial relief. Mr Burns was making the best of his dear-bought subservience.

But it was telling upon him. His mortification and his anxiety between them were stretching him once more upon the plain man's rood, and he lacked the plain man's crassness of endurance. The flaw in his physical constitution corresponded only too well with the flaw in his spirit. Early in the year, suggesting himself for temporary work that would involve harder wear and tear, he had still been able to allege his strong physique. But within three months of that he was reduced by mental suffering, and by the only nepenthe he could find for that suffering, to the mercy of the 'terrible trinity—Rheumatism, Cold and Fever.' In April he had an attack of rheumatic fever that aged him. After it he was borne down by the furies of extreme *ennui*. Constantly he used the word 'boredom.' He was so bored with Creech's forthcoming edition that he could not bear to correct the proofs himself. 'I am not interested in any of those; blot them at your pleasure,' he wrote, sending them to Mr Tytler in Edinburgh. And though Tytler's pleasure, like his 'most correct taste,' was of a peculiarly exasperating quality, the author made no remonstrance. He was too sick and too sad. He was fully alive only when he was writing a song, or when he had enough drink in him to perpetrate an indiscretion. Then, for the moment, he was his careless, proud self. But on each day after, when—as it did—the indiscretion came home to roost, he was abject in apology, and once more he died the death.

'May the last king be hanged in the entrails of the last priest!'
Resoundingly he uttered this at night; and next day—chal-
lenged by some young blood in uniform—he alleged in
humble exaggeration his own 'drunkenness' as an excuse,
and protested his loyalty to his 'idiot King.' Having impro-
vised scathing lines on General Dumouriez's desertion from
the Republican Army, he rushed upstairs to conceal his
copies of Paine's books with Haugh the blacksmith. Having
presented one evening De Lolme's *Constitution of England* to
the Public Library with the inscription 'Mr Burns presents
this book . . . and begs they will take it as a Creed of British
Liberty—until they find a better,' he went before breakfast
the next morning to efface the inscription with trembling
hands.

It was enough to undermine the health of a far sounder
man. During a long-deferred trip through Galloway upon
which he rode at the end of July with Syme, he was touchy
to the point of hysteria. He could hardly abide to see a
nobleman's mansion even from the distance,[4] became frantic
with rage over an accident to a new pair of white-topped
Wellington boots for which he had paid extravagantly (the
more frantic that they were spoiled by an impulsive kindness
on his part to an old clergyman who was afraid to wet his
feet—whereupon somebody had twitted him with being
'priest-ridden'!) and reached the climax of impotent fury
when a lady asked him to write an epitaph on her pet dog.
This, to the singer of freedom and the bard of human dignity,
when in Edinburgh men who thought as he did were awaiting
their trial for 'sedition'! For the Government, having resolved
on a policy of ruthless coercion, had chosen Scotland as the
most favourable ground for their initial operations. They
could count on the subservience of Scotish judges and the
pusillanimity of Scotish juries.

In August, because he had advocated reform, and had
bought and distributed copies of Paine's *Rights of Man*,
Thomas Muir, son of a Glasgow merchant, was brought
before a packed jury and sentenced to fourteen years at
Botany Bay. Three other leaders—men no better placed
than Burns—received the same savage verdict. A Methodist
parson was transported for having taken part in an address

against the war. Successive editors of *The Gazetteer* had been imprisoned. It was under such pressure that 'Scots wha hae' was written, by a man who dared not put his name to it in any Scotish publication, and at a time when all hope of Scotish freedom, even in the matter of mild reform, was indefinitely postponed. The poet's disgust 'gagged by his office' bit the more deeply into the very tissues of his frame. Yet at the same time that he wrote one of the world's most famous songs of liberty, he acceded to the fine lady's request. He wrote the epitaph on the lap-dog!

From this time onward, every contemporary account shows the poet under a cloud. And the Dumfries cloud does not resemble that dark but enlivening shadow, under which at Mossgiel his awakening genius showed clearer, as buds on a flowering tree show clearer against a thunder-cloud than against sunshine. Under the Dumfries cloud there is a sinister vagueness of outline, a subtle treachery of disintegration, which has been variously ascribed to drink, to dissipation and to social ostracism. 'His wit,' says one, 'became more gloomy and sarcastic,' and his conversation assumed 'a misanthropical tone' unknown to it before. 'Mysterious insinuations' against his character were whispered about and reached Edinburgh. Dome-headed Dugald Stewart, in colloquy with bewigged Mackenzie, was grieved to report 'that Burns's conduct and manners had become so degraded that decent persons could hardly take any notice of him.' And though the Man of Feeling hoped that Professor Stewart had been deceived by exaggerated rumours, he did not fail to pass them on, and to recall his own dictum that Burns's great admiration for the poet Fergusson had betrayed a 'propensity to coarse dissipation.' Reports of his drinking and worse were circulated by friends as well as by enemies and by Whigs as well as by Tories. Young Archibald Lawrie of Loudoun, spending an evening with his father's famous protégé when passing through Dumfries, found him uncertain of mood and over-indulgent in his potations. Professor Walker found him hospitable, but 'too opinionative and broad,' 'violent in praise and censure' and 'not brooking contradiction.' We get the unwitting picture of a suffering man and of a rich vitality that has 'dwindled down to mere existence.'

The potations, of course, the attempted dissipation, the coolings of certain hospitalities, were the symptoms not the cause of the disease; and though they in their turn were to become contributory factors helping to form a deadly circle, they were in themselves of no degree worth notice. Neither posterity nor contemporary observers have seen fit to label as inebriates men like Walter Riddel or Walter Scott or even that mighty drinker, James Hogg; yet at no time did Robert Burns's regular allowance of stimulant come near to that of the two first-named gentlemen, and on his most excessive occasions he never got half so drunk as did the Ettrick Shepherd on 'no occasion' at all. It was a common enough thing for a gauger to be admonished for intemperance, yet Robert's heaviest indulgence never interfered with his efficiency in a task beset with detail, or brought upon him so much as a 'complaint.' He never drank in the morning or in secret, or alone, except when the task of a difficult letter called for a bottle beside the ink-horn. When he dined with the gentry he had that embarrassing way of withdrawing with the ladies to drink tea with them upstairs while his host pushed the bottle about. None the less every observer, and himself most of all, knew that he was drinking dangerously more than his constitution would stand, and that where one pint will amply serve good-fellowship for a night, two will barely drown misery for an hour. Crucifixion none the less if it be needless, is thirsty work. Never had his 'standing pool of thought' so often and so urgently called for defecation.

For female society of a confidential and stimulating kind Robert had come to depend largely on Maria Riddel. Her conversation contrasted refreshingly with Mrs Dunlop's long, ill-spelt, hardly decipherable dissertations, which continued to arrive by post. These, the recipient had got into the habit of laying aside for a later perusal which did not always take place. But Maria and he could scold each other without pain or boredom, and could have tender passages without suffering from heart ache, all of which was pleasant. She had given him a topaz for the engraving of a new seal upon which he had set his heart, and had helped him to work out his device of 'armorial bearing' in proper style.[5] And he had searched all the haberdashers in Dumfries till he found a pair of French gloves without which he had heard her exclaim she 'could not exist'—a pretty compliment to her hands and her political views.

But that summer—the summer of the Terror in France, the burning of Tom Paine's effigy in Dumfries and the savage sedition trials in Edinburgh—Maria was in London with her husband enjoying the season. The pretty lint-locked Lorimer girl too—the smuggling farmer's daughter for whom Robert had conceived a tenderness while wooing her unsuccessfully for his friend Gillespie—was gone. In spite of the attentions of two other gaugers, she had eloped to Gretna Green in the spring with a young English squire named Whelpdale. Mrs Robert Riddel, though hospitable, provided no intimacy. A further depressing interchange of letters with Clarinda, after a too long, too unaccountable silence, had gone far towards rendering that divinity a 'ci-devant goddess.'

Mrs McLehose had been back in Edinburgh since the previous August, but had purposely kept the poet in ignorance of her return. She was ill, disillusioned and badly shaken. True, she had once more failed to play the spaniel to her husband, but she was only too glad now to be a sheep that would never more stray an inch beyond the Rev Mr Kemp's safe fold.

Arrived at Kingston pier in April she had been the one woman on board the *Roselle* to find no welcome awaiting her, but this was the least of her troubles. No attempt was made in her new home to discontinue or even to conceal the presence of an ebony mistress and a thriving family of little mulattos which represented James McLehose's mode of passing the time while his Nancie was self-denyingly platonising with Robert Burns. Further it was Mr McLehose's pleasure to display for his Scotish wife's edification the way he had with the natives—a way involving frequent corporal punishment, at which he required her attendance. We cannot wonder that the Northern Woman of Feeling felt her evangelical resolves melt in the climate of Jamaica. With a doctor's certificate that she should not be expected to survive the summer there, she sailed back within two months of her arrival and reached Leith with £21 in her pocket.

Observing her ban on letters to Kingston, Robert had

written twice during the autumn to her friend Mary Peacock asking for news; but Mary, instructed by Clarinda, had not replied. A third appeal—urgently dated 6 December, the first anniversary of their farewell—begged for the Kingston address so that the fourth volume of the *Museum* might find its way there safely. This Nancie dared not risk. She was bent upon a legal separation and alimony. Who could tell what rash inscription the poet might not write on his fly-leaf for Mr McLehose's bilious eye to light upon? So Mary answered with cautious news of the return. Her letter arrived during Robert's visit to Mrs Dunlop at Christmas, and by a suspicious piece of carelessness on the part of Jean it slipped behind a chest of drawers and was not found till some weeks later. Robert's reply, a fortnight afterwards, coincided with his undertaking of 'silence and obedience' that closed the Excise inquiry. Its violent assertiveness was a relief 'like the opening of a vein' to one who had just failed in a vital assertion. He longs for a letter from Clarinda. 'But first,' he dictates, 'hear me.'

> No cold language—no prudential documents: I despise advice and scorn control. If you are not to write such language, such sentiments as you know I shall wish, shall delight to receive, I conjure you, by wounded pride! by ruined peace! by frantic disappointed passion!... be silent for ever!... Mind my request—If you should send me a page baptised in the fount of sanctimonious prudence, by heaven, earth and hell I will tear it to atoms! Adieu; may all good things attend you!
>
> R.B.

Satisfied with this effort, which was achieved 'without a scroll,' he made a copy for insertion in Robert Riddel's album of his prose MS. It was not the first letter to Clarinda that Sylvander had felt obliged to compose with the aid of a bottle and glass. When it came to the actual insertion he did not feel quite so sure of it. Still, it expressed something he felt strongly and continuously; so he compromised with this note for Riddel's benefit—'Letter to a Lady. I need hardly remark that the foregoing was the fustian rant of enthusiastic youth.'

The attachment was broken, perished at the core by

Clarinda's own doing. To the end Sylvander would carry about with him some of the tendrils, and at times could make believe that they lived. No past emotion ever lost all its power to move him. But these tendrils were faded and rootless. When at length Mrs McLehose answered his letter begging him to write 'in friendship,' he replied sadly and—by his own statement—sottishly, complaining of lost fame and lost friends (Ainslie among the rest) and protesting that when a fair one's toast is called for he still gives 'Mrs Mac.' But he never went to see her in Edinburgh, nor did she come to Dumfries. No more letters passed between them. The Arcadian affair was finished.[6]

One thing alone was a living source of satisfaction in the gauger's depleted life. Soon after the publication of the fourth volume of the *Museum* in the previous autumn, an Edinburgh civil servant named George Thomson[7] had been minded to make another collection 'of the most favourite of our national melodies' on a scale much 'more elegant and superb.' Symphonies and accompaniments were to be provided 'by the first musicians on the Continent,' special use being made of 'the delicate harmony of Pleyel,' that 'most agreeable composer living,' and each native air should have an instrumental prelude and conclusion, the better to fit it for 'concerts both public and private.' As the scheme was to have the patronage of other wealthy amateurs of Scotish song, such as the Hon Andrew Erskine, pecuniary profit was to be 'quite a secondary consideration' and the promoters were 'resolved to spare neither pains nor expense.'

Thomson's sins, which were flagrant and many, may almost be forgiven him because of the timely vehicle he thus provided for the poet's crippled Muse. With all its superb elegance his collection cannot compare, as a collection, with the *Museum*. Thomson had neither taste nor reverence nor pecuniary decency, though he claimed all three. What Robert called 'simple,' he pronounced to be 'silly.' And Pleyel, who did not scruple to alter Beethoven's MSS, never had the slightest suspicion that a ploughman, who could not sing a tune, might know more about folk-song than he himself could have learned in a lifetime. Robert's words were altered; his directions about rhythms, melodies and accents were disregarded; all his sure, delicate, passionately practised knowledge was ignored. Yet Robert did not much care. He was under the compulsion of making and mending songs at a time when no other kind of poetry was possible for him. He worked with the hautboy-player Fraser, with the country fiddler Gow, whom he had met at Blair Castle, and with the organist Clarke,[8] who was teaching the McMurdo girls at Drumlanrig. He worked even with the 'narrow, conceited' and dishonest musician Urbani, because Urbani sang beautifully. While still providing for Johnson's fifth volume he became the very soul of Thomson's first. He had begun with the promise to contribute a score or so of new ballads, but soon he took over the provision of airs as well, and embroidered both words and airs with his sound, sensitive notes. Now on his own bookshelves he possessed in various collections 'all the music of the country.' However they might be set at nought he would register his musical opinions. Song-making, after all, not political reform, was his 'trade.' At the same time it was the best anodyne for life's paralysing problems. What did Robespierre matter so long as a man could write:

> O my Love's like the red, red rose,
>   That's newly sprung in June:
> My Love's like the melodie
>   That's sweetly play'd in tune.[9]

And what did it matter if Thomson thought it a poor, foolish song? It was a song for his own folk. Once more he was the Bard, whose products were 'either *above* or *below* price'; for he had refused to consider payment as being 'downright sodomy of soul.'[10] He had Thomson's promise that his contributions should be anonymous. Thus he could see in print some at least of the battle hymns and songs of liberty which owed their impulse to the Revolution. Thomson's first volume was out in July. With much fuss he persuaded the poet to accept a five-pound note for his part in it! When Nicol and Masterton came for a week's vacation in the late autumn they found their friend in good spirits. Maria, though not her husband, was home from London. She had met Mr James Boswell and was happily exhausted with her conquests in the metropolis. She even invited her

poet—oftener than he could come—to visit her in her solitude;
and her poet substituted her name for Mary's in one of his
songs to Mary Campbell and invited her to contribute verses
of her own composition to Thomson's English items. Also,
having added new original numbers to his *Merry Muses*, he
handed it about. Whatever he abjured he would never abjure
bawdry.[11] Thomson, indeed, had felt impelled to warn Mr
Burns that 'however gay and sportive the muse may be' she
must 'always be decent,' that some of our native writers had
'confounded simplicity with coarseness and vulgarity,' and
that he must make it his business never to wound 'that charming delicacy which forms the most precious dowry of our
daughters.' By way of reply, Mr Burns indited a spring song,
that was not at all for the boarding-school miss, and has
indeed, so far, proved too broad for any biographer.

But the year ended badly. The delicate Elizabeth was ill—it
seemed seriously—and Dumfries was full of irritating young
officers—'epauletted puppies,' as Robert called them—who
thronged the taverns and the theatre, stared insolently through
him and drove home constantly the sense of his ignominious
position. He could neither avoid nor abide them. As often as
not, in spite of her republican views, Maria Riddel had a
'lobster-coated' escort. When he reproached her with encouraging them she laughed. As Walter was still away the
poet was not invited to *tête-à-têtes*, and he had to content himself with meetings in company, or occasional encounters at the
play or in the street. A 'lobster-coated' escort never seemed far
away. Maria had no objection to making her gauger fume.

At New Year a hideous thing happened, which to this day
is attributed in Dumfries to a 'rag' on the part of gentlemen
wearing the King's uniform and bent upon amusement at
the expense of a too haughty poet whose 'hands were not
altogether clean of the coom of Jacobinical democracy.'
Robert had been invited to a festivity at Friars' Carse. His
host and fellow guests had seen to it that he drank level with
them, and by the time they were mellow he was wrought up
to recklessness. The ladies having retired from the table,
some gentleman suggested that their own emergence into the
drawing-room should partake of the nature of an amorous
raid. To each stalwart Roman a Sabine was allotted. The

only poet among them should take his hostess. A man was a man for a' that!

Robert was ready primed. It would not be the first kissing frolic in which he had taken the lead. Such fun might have cropped up as easily at an Ellisland Hallowe'en, a Tarbolton penny bridal or an Irvine Hogmanay. In this toilsome world these were among the few carefree holiday moments permitted to lads and lassies of the people. But alas! here were neither farm hands nor hecklers. This was a frolic of the gentry—a frolic moreover which had another object than general laughter and happiness and the sweet abstract effluence of love. So when Robert had carried out his part with hearty despatch and all the latitude the occasion called for, he was stupefied to find himself alone. The lady—she who had always been so kind and so prim—was genuinely outraged. The gentlemen—who had failed to play their own parts—were less ingenuously shocked. Yet not three months earlier most of them had taken part in the Saturnalia of the Caledonian Hunt.[12] The whole thing was a trick, and what it now came to was a question of class. A gauger in liquor had affronted Mrs Riddel of Glenriddel. *This* was unprecedented and unforgivable.

Some of the ladies saw through the affair. Two—one a married woman, the other unmarried—tried to beg off the too-ready guest. But Mrs Riddel would not listen, and her husband, the Captain, caught among his fellow officers, allowed things to take their course. Class, after all, is class. Robert left the house disgraced.

After some furious hours at home he wrote to ask Mrs Riddel's pardon with an abasement so exaggerated that it is impossible to believe wholly in it. It was a catastrophe and he was contrite. But writing 'from the regions of Hell, amid the horrors of the damned,' a large part of his tongue was in his cheek.

Perhaps Mrs Riddel suspected as much, or she resented the plain statement that her husband had been as blameable as her guest. Anyhow she did not answer the letter. Robert felt the rebuff, which came as a surprise, as severely as the deprivation which followed it. Apologetic verses to his host remained without acknowledgment. Still unreconciled, he learned in April that Captain Riddel had died. He was stricken with real grief, and the same morning of the death wrote an affectionate sonnet 'to the memory of the man I loved,' which appeared under the obituary announcement in the local newspaper. But Mrs Riddel was still unforgiving, a behaviour which removed all sense of obligation toward her for past kindnesses. When next Robert walked in the woods of Friars' Carse it was to survey every stick there bitterly and secretly with a commercial eye for one of his Highland acquaintances[13] whom he desired to buy the property. Sooner than let it fall into the hands of her brother-in-law, whom she now 'most cordially hated,' the widow was insisting that it should be put up for sale.[14]

On the first day of April the Woodley Park estate had also been advertised for sale. Walter had failed to pay up the purchase money—£1,600. Though he had spent £2,000 on improvements, the place now fetched only £1,600. Already in February Maria and the children (her husband being again away) had been packed off to Tinwald House on the Duke of Queensberry's lands. But Woodley Park or Tinwald House, Maria's doors had alike been closed to Robert as firmly as the doors of Friars' Carse since the unfortunate party. She had not been at the party herself, but, like many others, she had heard her sister-in-law's version of what had happened, and for all her vaunted republicanism she had stood in with her own class. The next time she met her poet he was stared at severely and passed by with a look that 'froze the very life-blood' of his heart. He must be given a lesson. His letters of entreaty and explanation were ignored. Robert felt this more than all the rest, and his heart was hardened against Maria and against all ladies. Ladies were simply not genuine women. Even Mrs Dunlop could not bear nature or truth, must be flattered, had to dictate manners and morals to a man for no other reason than that he was her social inferior.

'What is there in riches that they narrow and encallous the heart so? I think that were I as rich as the sun I would be as generous as day; but as I have no reason to imagine my soul a nobler one than any other man's, I must conclude that wealth imparts a bird-lime quality to the possessor at which the man in native poverty would have revolted.' When he wrote these words to Cunningham, now his chief confidant by post, it was not merely of financial meanness that he spoke.

There was the petty misery of returning and demanding the return of books and manuscripts which had been pledges of special friendship. Very angry, and with nerves badly jangled, Robert eased himself by launching lampoons at Maria and her husband. In epitaph Walter was a despicable fool and Maria a silly, rouged, venomous gabbler without wisdom or heart.

> We'll search through the garden for each silly flower,
> We'll roam through the forest for each idle weed,
> But chiefly the nettle, so typical, shower,
> For none e'er approached her but ru'd the rash deed.

When, after some trouble, he recovered his MSS book from Mrs Robert Riddel he transcribed some of these attacks into it; and as he handed and posted various copies about,[15] rumours of them at least must have come to Maria's notice. She had only too many friends who were anxious to foment the quarrel.

In the winter, throughout several weeks of extreme nervous depression bordering upon illness and accompanied by the usual rheumatic pains, he had been able to write none but spiteful things and not many of these. He complained to Cunningham of his 'deep incurable taint of hypochondria,' which had 'from the first' poisoned his existence, and of his three demons 'Indolence, Business and Ennui.' It took him all his fluctuating strength to carry out his Excise duties, but he did carry them out more than conscientiously, thinking out reforms and economies which, being adopted at head-quarters under strict injunctions of anonymity, reduced the work by a whole division.

In a particularly sunny March—which induced Patrick Miller to send to London for some melon and celery seeds and two female swans ('as I am satisfied that all the swans here are males')—life brightened considerably for Robert, though the rheumatic pains still haunted him. In losing the Riddels he had lost his never very strong social confidence, and he shirked the invitations that still came from the sort of people he called 'Honourables and Right Honourables.' But two individuals, a man and a girl, had come upon the scene to heal his pride and restore his flagging spirits. These made all the difference to him throughout that summer, and it was under their soothing influence that he got off a packet of forty-one songs to Johnson and wrote the lovely lines:

> The winds were laid, the air was still,
> The stars they shot along the sky;
> The fox was howling on the hill,
> And the distant echoing glens reply.

The new male acquaintance, though born in the Stewartry, had been educated in France, where he had begun to practise as a doctor, and he was a sympathiser with the revolutionaries—so much so that as one of the National Guard he had been present at the King's execution. Dr Maxwell probably came as near as any man in Scotland to being a true Jacobin.[16] He at once became the leader of the more extreme Whigs in Dumfries, and with Robert Burns (whose physician and most intimate friend he became), Syme of Ryedale and one or two others, formed a little coterie to talk politics. Their meetings, sometimes behind locked doors, enraged the 'Loyal Natives,' a much larger club of the other persuasion, which existed ostensibly 'For preserving Peace, Liberty and Property, and for Supporting the Laws and Constitution of the Country,' but really to bully and spy and swill, and call traitors all who differed politically. The 'Savages,' as Robert called them, thought the worst of Maxwell's friends. Were certain rhymes to come to their notice, Syme feared they might cut Robin's pipe.

The new female 'divinity,' who had lightning in her eye, witchery in her smile, and an 'adorability' of charms which involved the weary gauger once more in 'the guileless simplicity of Platonic Love,' was the smuggling farmer Lorimer's daughter who, at eighteen, had returned to her father's house from a short, disastrous marriage. Her squire Whelpdale had proved to be vicious, weak, dishonest, and a maniacal spendthrift. And here she was, as sweet as ever and far more attractive—'one of the finest women in Scotland'—needing to be visited and comforted and championed. She was not clever like Maria, but she was poor and pretty and unlucky, and she had flaxen ringlets and 'eyebrows of a darker hue,' and she was song-inspiring. Before she went away, Robert, on Gillespie's behalf, had written the admirable song, 'Poortith Cauld,' for her. Now that she was 'the lovely goddess of his inspiration' and his 'Bonnie lassie, artless lassie,' whose 'smiling sae wiling, wad make a wretch forget his woe,' he wrote at least ten songs to her from himself, some of them as good as any he had yet written.

> Beyond thee, dearie, beyond thee, dearie,
>   And oh! to be lying beyond thee;
> Oh, sweetly, soundly, weel may he sleep
>   That's laid in the bed beyond thee!

—of which Thomson in his genteel-facetious manner wrote:

> In the name of decency, I must beg a new chorus-verse from you. 'O to be lying beyond thee, dearie,' is perhaps a consummation to be wished, but will not do for singing in the company of ladies.

'Do you think,' Robert asked Thomson in this connexion:

> that the sober gin-horse routine of existence could inspire a man with life, love and joy—could fire him with enthusiasm, or melt him with pathos equal to the genius of your Book? No, no!!! Whenever I want to be more than ordinary *in song*; to be in some degree equal to your diviner airs, do you imagine I fast and pray for the celestial emanation? *Tout au contraire!*

Again:

> Conjugal love is a passion which I deeply feel, and highly venerate; but somehow it does not make such a figure in poesy as that other species of the passion—
>   'When Love is Liberty; and Nature Law.'

And again:

> Musically speaking, the first is an instrument of which the gamut is scanty and confined, but the tones inexpressibly sweet, while the last has powers equal to all the intellectual Modulation of the Human Soul.

He might have alleged the presence of Chloris[17] as much as the responsibility of Jean when that summer he refused an opening by which he could have thrown off at least official thraldom at a stroke. In May, Mr Perry, editor of the London *Morning Chronicle*, made him a remarkable offer through Patrick Miller, junior. Through Patrick Miller, senior, the word had gone out that Mr Burns's talents were being lost to the world. So far as he and others could see, not one poem of note had been produced since the bard left Ellisland. Except for the obituary sonnet on Glenriddel the past year had seemed a blank. The 'cargoes' of songs that kept sailing from Dumfries to Edinburgh did not seem to these observers to count as poetic output. So they had laid their well-meant plans and this was the result. If Mr Burns would consent to reside in London he could count on five guineas a week as 'occasional correspondent' of the *Chronicle*, and would be paid extra for reporting and general contributions in prose and verse. Here was a chance for the anonymous laureate of the Whigs and the man of independent soul. Lately Robert had felt the wish to write 'little Prose essays'; now he was offered the vehicle for prose and verse alike, from the fondest love lyric to the most scurrilous political squib. In London he would not lack friends, familiar or powerful. There was Murdoch for one, and Dr Moore for another. Nor would Jean and the children want for company among the thriving colony of Ayrshire folk who had made their home near the Strand.[18] In theory, at least, he should have leisure. Even allowing for Excise perquisites his income would be almost thrice what he was earning and would earn yet for some years in Dumfries.

But it involved what he had always instinctively hated— the idea of living by his pen. And it meant making a break and taking a risk. He must leave Chloris for Grub Street, Lincluden and Sweetheart Abbey for Westminster and St Paul's, the 'trotting' Scotish streams for the majestic Thames. The beloved known must be exchanged for the dreaded unknown, the country town for the city, the sure prospect of Excise promotion for the gamble of journalism and the different thraldom of party. He had always been timid. It is doubtful if at any time he would have done it. At thirty-five he knew his courage, and perhaps his physical strength, unequal to such a demand.

> You will know my political sentiments [he wrote to Miller], and were I an insular individual, unconnected with a wife and a family of children, with the most fervid enthusiasm I would have volunteered my services: I then could and would have despised all consequences that might have ensued.

With the letter he sent a copy of 'Scots wha hae' to be published anonymously, and some verses, including the spiteful ones on the Riddels. Of these the *Chronicle* printed only 'Scots wha hae.' In return for free copies of the newspaper, Robert offered Mr Perry occasional unpaid contributions.

It is on the whole a relief that we are not asked to contemplate the Ayrshire bard as a newspaper correspondent, though it would have been interesting to have read his report in the *Chronicle* of the Duke of Queensberry's splendid arrival in Dumfries that 18th of June. We do read that to meet his Grace 'the Magistrates and Trades with colours flying and drums beating, many gentlemen and a great concourse of people went out of town,' and that 'the populace unharnessed the horses and dragged him in his carriage through the streets.' But this is not the poet's description. It occurs in one of old Patrick Miller's letters, and ends drily—'When he got to the King's Arms I paid my respects to him.'

That evening at sunset, a friendly young man[19] saw the poet strolling in marked solitude on the shady side of the street while on the other side all the fashionable flocked unnoticing to an Assembly. The young man reined in his horse. 'Are you not joining us?' he asked. Robert shook his head. 'That's all over now,' he said, and he quoted:

> Oh, were we young, as we ance hae been,
> We sud hae been galloping down on yon green,
> And linking it ower the lily-white lea—
> *And werena my heart light I wad dee.*

After which his young friend accompanied him to the Mill Vennel for a glass of punch and a heartily amusing hour before going on to his more genteel appointment. It is an incident often exaggerated. If the gentry were chary of noticing the poet, the poet had a poor opinion of the local gentry as having too much 'dissipation without fashionable gaiety.' That autumn saw buckish rowdyism at the Assemblies and in the theatre, and the only nobleman at the Races—Maule of Panmure—to celebrate the wooing of 'a very beautiful and valuable young girl,'[20] daubed a harmless inferior's hair with mustard and stuck toothpicks all over it. In Syme's congenial company Robert raged at such things. Syme, though a mighty Nimrod, was sensitive to beauty in trees and temperaments. In his 'Robin,' whom he loved 'more and more,' he found the chief solace for life in Dumfries.

The French decree, promulgated in the early summer of
1794, that no quarter was to be given to the British and no
prisoners taken, did more than many apologies to secure
Robert's position on the Excise. Quickly following upon this
decree came what destroyed with equal efficacy the hope of
home reform and the fear of Scotish Jacobinism, namely,
the scare of invasion. Civil nervousness had already been
dissipated by the downfall of Robespierre and the end of
the Terror. And 'as soon as it was understood among the
commonality that the French were determined to subdue and
make a conquest of Britain . . . there was a prodigious stir and
motion in all the hearts and pulses of Scotland.'[1]

The call to defensive arms was one that no Scot could
withstand. The Whigs especially were eager to show their
loyalty, and the staunchest opponent of the war abroad was
prepared to eat alive the first Frenchman who landed on
British soil. Though Patrick Miller now brought his son out
of the Dragoons he 'would think meanly of any man that
would hesitate a moment to take arms in defence of his
country.' The invasion scare was, of course, only one scare
the more; but it was an effective scare, uniting in a single idea
such men as Miller and Queensberry, and bringing into the
common fold such notorious stragglers as Dr Maxwell,
Robert Burns and poor little Moir, the scapegrace printer of
the *Gazetteer*, whose bank-manager turned suddenly into
a benefactor when his customer appeared clad as a volunteer
for home service!

By the turn things had taken, the long-despised Whigs
found themselves in possession of unexpected political
power, and soon they were flattering themselves that the
King with his Tory advisers might be superseded by the
Prince Regent with a Whig Ministry. Dr Maxwell and his

friends at first shared this hope. In a by-election for the Stewartry of Kirkcudbright, the Whig candidate, Heron of Kerroughtree, who happened to be a popular man, actually looked like carrying the seat, and Robert threw himself into versifying on his behalf, with the more ardour that the opposing candidate had the support of the hated Earl of Galloway. Heron, reading one of his ballads and appreciating at once how important an ally the poet was, showed the utmost friendliness. He consulted Syme as to the best way of helping him, and Syme obtained from Robert himself a statement of the whole Excise position. Robert shrank from the new social intercourse involved. He was more than ever 'ill at ease with the Honourables and Right Honourables,' and would entreat Syme or another to accompany him to Kerroughtree. But he needed all the influence he could get, and he was delighted to be approached as a bard and a patriot. He could now style himself openly the laureate of the Whigs, and a certain proportion of the Dumfries Whigs were 'Honourables.' Though he definitely preferred the society at the Globe or at Lorimer's farm to that of the quality any-where, he consented that summer, after a year of refusals, to dine with that heavy drinker, Hamilton of Arbigland.

The quarrel with Mrs Robert Riddel was not to be made up and Robert regarded her as a definitely malevolent person who deserved 'no kindness at his hands.' But the case with Maria Riddel was different. In the general warmth Maria felt that her offending friend had been enough punished. Whatever rumours had reached her she knew nothing of the most offensive 'Monody.'² She was, besides, heartily bored and uncomfortable in her temporary home—a 'crazy, rambling, worm-eaten, cobweb-hunting chateau'—which was moreover turning out less temporary than her again absent lord had led her to expect. Her children kept having infantile ailments (she had produced a second daughter within a few days of the birth of Robert's legitimate Elizabeth) and she was weary of being left 'as usual . . . *tête-à-tête* with myself.' A dose of the poet's infallible 'sorcery' would do her good. She could easily convey a hint to him slight enough for withdrawal should he fail to take it. We are not told of such a hint, but lacking it Robert would hardly have seized, as he did, the chance of her birthday in November to address to her some sentimental lines reproaching her with faithlessness—'Canst thou leave me thus, my Katy?'—to which she at once responded with similar lines protesting her continued affection. It was at least a reconciliation in rhyme. Robert seems to have left it at that. But in January Maria took the further initiative by sending a book on loan to the Mill Vennel with a letter and one of her poems for criticism. To this Robert replied amiably, though with a certain coolness and in the third person, 'Mr Burns's compliments to Mrs Riddel . . . is much obliged to her for her polite attention in sending him the book . . . has not that time to spare which is necessary for any belles-lettres pursuit,' but would take kindly the loan of another new book of hers—the translation of *Anacharsis's Travels*—before she presents it to the Public Library. Maria sent the book, and their friendly correspondence was renewed. Though she does not appear to have invited him to Tinwald House, the poet was able once more to scold his fair friend with affectionate candour by letter for her caprice and her levity.[3]

Like many other well-placed Whigs, Maria had allowed her liberalism to pale somewhat before the cry for 'loyalty,' and she had not approved of Robert's reported indiscretions. But now she was safe to befriend him again. With Maxwell and Syme he had joined the Royal Dumfries Volunteers. Twice a week at least he might be seen wearing the uniform—a short blue jacket, half lapelled, with red cape and cuffs and gilt engraved buttons, a white kerseymere vest and buckled breeches and half gaiters, white stockings, a black velvet stock, shoes tied with black ribbon, and a round stiff hat, turned up on one side with a gilt button and surmounted by a cockade and black feathers. For this loyal splendour he owed his tailor £7 4s. Though he was awkward in handling fire-arms, he was an enthusiastic recruit. His martial verses ran like wild-fire round the country and he was punctual on parade. Politically, officially, and socially his prospects had brightened.

But as usual there was a flaw. He was not well. In January he had undertaken the temporary duties of a district supervisor on account of another man's illness, and riding through many weeks of iron frost followed by unaccustomed deep snow, he realised with a sinking heart that after labouring at least two or three years more, a supervisor's lot—'so hard and full of drudgery that it would put nearly a complete bar to every species of literary pursuit'—would be the sum of his attainment, while even so his salary would be only £120 rising to £200. Could he hope to attain the coveted standing of a collector, with a salary rising from £200 and that 'literary leisure' which was 'the summit of his wishes,' before premature old age deprived him of the strength to enjoy it? Already he was conscious of a threatening stiffness in his frame and a waning of his energy, once so abundant that he had spent it like a wastrel. Assiduous volunteering and the coining of election songs under the spur of stimulants were further drains on his strength throughout the spring. Though he had the great satisfaction of seeing his man win the seat, his nerves were in a bad way. Small mishaps produced a wholly misproportionate anxiety. In April he explained with needless passion a trifling lapse of memory about some wine barrels. In May, he who had always had strong, beautiful teeth, suffered from violent toothache. And all the while he worried over his debts.

There was reason enough for this, though the emotion aroused, in his case as in his father's, was symptomatic and amounted to unreasoning panic. Commercial depression had not passed with the fear of revolution. The price of meal had risen to almost double. His bare salary of £70 was all he dared count upon while the war lasted, and his temper was not frugal. To pay the rent of his new house he had been obliged to borrow a few guineas from Hamilton of Arbigland. His pride had forced him to protest when Thomson the year before sent him £5 for all his work; but he made a very wry face that May when Thomson's 'regardlessness' of expense consisted of a picture for the poet and a shawl for the poet's wife! At the same time he was obliged to beg Creech for three more copies of his third edition, to be sent at his own charge![4] It was truly 'in unison with his present feelings' that he enclosed seventeen epigrams, 'mostly ill-natured,' to the Edinburgh publisher. He was incapable of saying to any one of these people what he thought of them. What he did think is clear to us now between the lines of his letters; but it was concealed in such far-fetched irony of polite compliment that at the time his correspondents received it complacently as the unskilfulness of a self-educated man.

In June there were some unfortunate local military doings, upon which the poet was cautiously silent in public, though they must certainly have been the topic of his warm comment behind locked doors with Syme and Maxwell. The press-gangs were busy in Scotland. A family of Irish tinkers—father and two sons—called O'Neil, had for the second time resisted the attempt to press them. In the fight a sergeant and two privates had been hurt, and one of the privates, after having a leg amputated, died. The O'Neils' house near Dumfries, where they had been monstrously assailed, was burned to the ground, and the old man, with one of his sons, was imprisoned, while the other—'aged about 22 . . . a stout well-made man with dark hair hanging loose . . . small round hat and tied shoes'—got clear disguised as a woman. He was outlawed and the others were condemned to be hanged. But the O'Neils were Catholics and there was a fair sprinkling of Papists among the Dumfries gentry. These despatched Maria Riddel as a Protestant go-between (she being known to have a wheedling way with the men) to Edinburgh to plead for the resisters. Delighted with her mission, Maria persuaded Harry Erskine to act without a fee; and when, in spite of his eloquence, a hanging verdict was brought in, she appealed to Mr Fox in London and obtained a commutation of the sentence. So Maria covered herself with glory and mercy.

The other incident, which happened two days after the O'Neil affair, ended more tragically. A Volunteer regiment, the Breadalbane Fencibles, had for some six months been billeted at Dumfries, and during that time had become on very friendly terms with the inhabitants. The morale of the regiment, however, was bad owing to the injudicious conduct of some of the officers, and one day upon the arrest of a defaulter, several of his comrades tried to release him from the guard-room. The affair—unsuccessful and bloodless as it was—ended in four of the ringleaders being sentenced to be shot and a fifth to 500 lashes, a part of the general punishment being that the condemned men made a six-hour journey out of town in a mourning coach with their coffins following behind, and later drew lots that would spare one of their number.

At the end of a hopeful rather than a happy summer, a summer in which the main poetical output was political—and local politics at that—Robert was forced by a sudden sorrow to recognise the waning of his life force. In the hope that the more bracing air of Mauchline might restore her, little Elizabeth had been carried to Mossgiel; but in September came the news that she was dead, and as it happened to be a very busy time on the Excise, her father could not so much as go to her funeral, which was in Mauchline churchyard. He grew ill with grief. For two months he could hardly write. He did, however, by a mighty effort of will and a forcing of his nervous system, carry on his over-exacting Excise work. Constantly he had to stimulate himself to the point of efficiency. When at length he had thrown off the more outward signs of sorrow, it was noticed that he had acquired a habit of rubbing his shoulders, and he often complained of shooting pains. Dr Maxwell gave these the name of 'flying gout,' with the facetious hint that they were the result of a too indulgent youth. If he had put them down to a too strenuous boyhood there might today be more respect for the well-meaning man's diagnosis. At the time, what was probably no more than a professional jocosity was taken almost as literally by the sufferer as it has been since by too many biographers. It does not seem to have occurred to anybody to recall that the irreproachable William Burnes had been equally in his way a victim of premature senile decay.

In November Robert took to his bed with a second attack of rheumatic fever. This time, for some days at the crisis, his recovery was uncertain. Towards Christmas he was better, but still too ill to accept a tempting dinner invitation from Syme for the 17th, though he managed to compose a rhymed refusal. At New Year, sick of confinement, he managed to crawl along to the Globe for some Hogmanay cheer and company. Unhappily, while crawling back home alone in the snowy small hours—pausing, it is said, to rest his damaged heart—he fell into a drowse. So he caught a new chill, and

Jean had to put him to bed again. The next time he emerged from the house was three days before the end of the month, when he insisted upon attending a Mason meeting close by his own door.

During the opening weeks of the year, public and private misfortune had combined to harass him. An unusually bad harvest, and worse management, made it difficult for working folk to buy meal at any price whatever. Some days there was not a grain in the Mill Vennel house. Occasional riots took place in the street outside.

At the same time there was a temporary renewal of political persecution. The passing of the Sedition Bill had damped Whig hopes and put fresh restrictions on liberty of speech and assembly. On 12 January, the date of the annual re-election of the Dean of the Faculty of Advocates in Edinburgh, Harry Erskine, who had long held the post unchallenged, was opposed and overwhelmingly defeated by Henry Dundas. In December, gaily refusing to be gagged by his office, he had presided at a meeting of protest against the Sedition Bill and the war. In London, his brother Thomas, after a successful advocacy of the prosecuted 'democrats' at the State trials, had been carried home shoulder high. But in Edinburgh not all Harry's popularity could prevent his being made an example of. On hearing of the election result[5] his fury was so great that he took a coal axe and hewed from his door the brass plate bearing his lost title. Robert, in and out of his sick bed, wrote a pithy ballad.

But, in his reduced state, poetical composition, like other efforts, was becoming spasmodic, and the deep-set terrors which had enslaved his early youth—poverty, debt, and failure—resumed their domination. At the very time when powerful friends like Heron and Fintry were at last scheming in a practical manner to help him, he could see nothing in the future but friendlessness and ruin. Mrs Dunlop was offended with him poetically, personally and politically.[6] She considered that he had behaved badly about her poetical milkmaid, and she could forgive neither his 'utter contempt' to her hints, his failure to answer categorically the many points in her letters, nor his damning, persistent friendship with Nicol. Exaggerated stories had reached her of his

'temeraire conduct' and his intemperance. He had not
received a line from her during twelve months past. Ainslie
wrote seldom and with dryness. When in February Robert
begged Clarke the schoolmaster, who now had a good
position in Forfar entirely owing to Robert's efforts, to let
him have back some of the money lent three or four years
before, Clarke was 'furnishing a large house' and could only
send one guinea and promise another soon. The admirers
among his equals who had so eagerly sought the bard's
interest and company seemed suddenly to be few and far.
They had been drawn by his rich spontaneity. Now they were
repelled by the sight of effort and impending weakness. For
himself they had never felt any deep concern. They had only
wished to bask in his vitality while it lasted. Imaginatively
he had always known life's cruelty. Now, between the consciousness of his own failure and the full revelation that
self-interest directed the 'ingrateful tribe' of his friends, his
heart was crushed as between two millstones.

Yet he was still subject to moods of hopeful self-deception.
Considering that Mrs Dunlop was what she was, that she had
four sons and a grandson in the army, and that two of her
daughters had married French Royalist refugees, it is strange
that Robert did not realise what she must have thought of
his last letter with its drastic comment upon the execution
of Louis and Marie Antoinette. He was, however, simply
puzzled and hurt by the withdrawal of her friendship and the
non-appearance of those long, warm, scolding, dull, unreadable letters which had been used to reach him with three
times the frequency of his replies. Even if he *had* offended,
surely if she learned that he had been ill and bereaved . . . ?
On the last day of January he wrote a heart-to-heart appeal,
telling of Elizabeth's death, of the meal famine, of his own
grave illness and present weakness, and begging above all to
know in what he had transgressed. For Mrs Dunlop he had
always piled on the gloom with a liberal hand. Now it might
be that his honest but calculated realism would fail of its
effect on the good lady. As a vindication and a peace-offering
he enclosed his volunteering verses—'Does haughty Gaul
invasion threat?' She was in Ayrshire, so he might expect her
answer in a couple of days. She did not reply.

The same month he had planned to write a journal for Cunningham of prose and poetry; but this fell through. His heart was outrun by the daily demands, often in arrears through indisposition, and the plans of stimulated hours drifted into the limbo of fatigue. Under exertion his voice faltered and his hand shook. Sometimes he needed help in rising from his chair. Pains in his joints, particularly in his hands and feet, made him sleepless. But his will held, and he kept up work and—less equally—appearances. The good Syme saw nothing amiss on Sunday, 21 February, when Robert dined alone with him at Ryedale and they soberly consumed only one bottle of port between them. Folk in Dumfries often ailed with cold and rheumatism and quinsies.

His own belief that a large part of his ailment was due to 'hypochondria,' due in its turn to worry, and conquerable by a 'commanding' of the 'mind and spirits,' was furthered by the opinions of his friends and doctors who were reassured by the sufferer's capacity to pull himself together on occasion. One fine spring day, for example, he was leaning listlessly against the outside of his house, when he recognised coming along the footway the daughter of his old friend Aiken of the bursting buttons. She, for her part, saw only 'a tall, gaunt, rather slovenly-looking person of sickly aspect,' whom she would never have connected with the vivid, vigorous young man she had often met twelve years before in her father's house at Ayr. But the moment he spoke her name she knew him; and when, after some persuasion, he had gone in to shave and smarten himself to be carried off by her to the house of a mutual friend where she knew he would be well received, he led the party in cheerful, resolute talk till midnight.

For all such feats, however, whether it was attending a Lodge meeting in April or replying in rhyme to his friendly old Colonel's[7] inquiries after his health, he paid in pain and melancholy next day or sooner, and, feats apart, the slightest difficulty or mistake toppled him over into an abyss of fear and depression.

Jean and the doctors had hoped that with the coming of summer they would see a real increase of strength. They were disappointed. At the end of a lovely May[8] he was weaker than ever and often in bed half the day. Yet how generally his illness was under-estimated is shown by a card handed in by Maria Riddel at the beginning of June. She hoped he was better. She wanted him to copy out and send her a recent love song of his, which she had heard was good; and she invited him to accompany her in uniform to the King's Birthday Assembly. Thus he could display his loyalty, and their reconciliation would be public and complete. It would be their first meeting since their quarrel. The moment was well chosen. Once more the Whigs were hopeful. Parliament had been dissolved in May, and Heron had retained his seat— this time in preference to a younger son of the hated Earl of Galloway; and to celebrate that victory, Robert had written one of the best of all his political ballads. The gallant Volunteer would be led back to genteel favour under the wing of the fascinating philanthropist.

It was not an occasion for which Robert felt the need to 'command his spirits.' He gave Maria a black picture of his health; and though he sent her some pastoral stanzas to prove that the Muses had not wholly deserted him, he would not copy out the love song. 'No,' he declared, 'if I must write, let it be Sedition, or Blasphemy, or something else that begins with a B, so that I may grin with the grin of iniquity and rejoice with the rejoicing of an apostate angel.' And he pertinently added—'Man delights not me, nor woman either!' By this time, in constant colloquy with Maxwell, he saw through the political manipulation which was all that the invasion scare amounted to.

Jean, who had been pregnant again since November, was anxious and unhappy. This it was to have married a poet! The brightest thing in her life was a girl of eighteen, sister to the Exciseman who had taken a minor part in the capture of the smuggling brig on the Solway.[9] Young Jessy Lewars had got into the way of dropping in to help the overwrought wife and mother, who was herself still under thirty. In so doing she had become the most 'platonic' and perhaps also the sweetest of all the sick laureate's divinities.[10] He called her by no Arcadian name. She was just Jessy. But when all else had proved to be illusion—patriotism, friendship, fame, even in some degree 'the fireside clime of weans and wife'—Jessy, by her mere presence, convinced him that young love was no fraud. Jessy stood to the poet for Nelly Kilpatrick and Peggy Thomson and Mary Campbell, and for Jean before she had become part of a scheme to defeat him. His eyes followed her healthy figure as she moved about the kitchen in her sleeveless print jacket and homespun skirt, tending his children good-naturedly and preparing the gruel which was almost the only food he could swallow. He scribbled loving notes to her, wrote tender lines with his diamond on the empty tumbler before handing it back to her; and because he was himself amorous to the last gasp, he lay in wait for that 'bewitching, sweet, stow'n glance o' kindness' which he had found so much the best thing in life.

It was already some time since he had written for her one of the best of all his songs. Jessy could sing. Being a really superior girl, she could even play the harpsichord, and had a keyboard instrument of some kind in her home. One day, visiting her father, Robert had got her to play for him upon it, and he promised her words to her favourite tune if she would let him hear it. At once the wise Jessy had played an old Scotish nursery-rhyme, an odd difficult air, which she sang to the now forgotten jingle:

> The robin cam to the wren's nest,
> An' keekit in, and keekit in

—which alone was enough to make the bard fall in love with her. Within half an hour he had mastered the melody and meted to it a poem which must have proved to him that at least the lyric muse had not yet flown:

> Oh, wert thou in the cauld blast.

That Jean, the wife, could look on indulgent and unreproach-ful, is her high title to fame, and of this her husband was passionately appreciative. They had never been on more affectionate terms. It was a marriage in which from first to last each party had been honest.

These two ignorant women, Jean and Jessy, were the only people in Dumfries to know the full gravity of Robert's 'protracting, slow, consuming illness.' By midsummer, however, it became clear to Maxwell and others that the thing had gone too far and that the patient must be got out of Dumfries without delay. Built on what was practically a low island, surrounded by bogs and undermined by hidden streams and springs of water, the 'third town for importance and elegance in Scotland' was the worst in the world for a depressed, nerve worn, rheumatic, heart subject. Maxwell, apparently after consultation, said that if the patient wished to recover he must go for the remainder of the summer to country quarters, and there indulge in sea-bathing, horse exercise, glasses of port wine, and iron water. He was already being heavily dosed with mercury.

How any physician, even of that age, seeing the wrecked and emaciated body, 'reduced nearly to the last stage' by 'an excruciating rheumatism,' the hollowed, scarcely recognisable face, and the spirits that had 'fled, fled,' could recommend riding and immersion in Scotish seas is hard to explain.[11] Perhaps it was the Parisian fashion of the day in therapy. The patient, however, was not concerned with questions of therapy. 'What way in the name of thrift,' he demanded frantically with a glance at Jean's figure, 'shall I maintain myself, and keep a horse in country quarters, with a wife and five children at home on £35?' If only Maxwell or another could have brought him the information that, by an order of the Excise Board, he was to receive little less than his full pay, and that a young probationer had been put in to do his duties gratis, the effect would have been more sedative than an ocean of salt water and more truly stimulating than much port wine and iron. But for some careless reason the information was withheld, so the invalid was left thinking that £35 a year—the usual half-pay of a gauger absent through illness—was all he could count upon, and that his debts—£30 in Dumfries and some trifles in Edinburgh—would force upon him the necessity to make Gilbert bankrupt.[12]

Yet by some means he managed to leave Dumfries on 16 June, and, though scarcely able to stand, went by himself to lodge at a place on the Solway about eleven miles from Dumfries.

Because it had a spring of mild chalybeate-water, which was contained in a red stone tank the size of a kitchen table, the place was dignified by the name of a spa. It was the Brow Well, no less. But provision for a sick man there was none. It was a mean, dilapidated, dismal little clachan, consisting of a dozen cottages and an inn that was no more than a cottage itself. For the spa some rickety benches in a broken shed did duty, and a twenty-yard 'esplanade' of tufted sea-grass. There were wonderful expanses of sea and sky; but throughout this cold, grey July it was unutterably cheerless, especially to one whom the sea had always saddened. Here were no 'trotting' brooks. Here were only spread waters, as shallow as they were dangerous. By the sea—especially by this sea—even love seemed an illusion:

Love swells like the Solway but ebbs like its tide.

At last the solitude that he had dreaded, that he had even sometimes perjured himself to avoid, was complete. He was alone. And he was broken. He knew, if no one else did, that he was dying. At the inn, where he stayed, he found a Bible, over which he pondered much, with an occasional grin to think how Syme and Maxwell would tease if they saw him at it.

Yet he tried hard to be hopeful without hope, and to carry out the doctors' crazy orders. Each day he waded shakily—he had to wade a long way to get the required depth—into the chill Atlantic water that he might stand obediently up to his armpits till it was time to drag his aching joints out again and slowly dry himself and sip his allowance of port. Riding was beyond him, even if he could have hired a horse, and he had no money. When the small supply of port gave out at the inn, he managed to walk a mile with the empty bottle to the next village; but here he had to offer his engraved pebble seal as security for payment, an offer indignantly refused by the innkeeper's wife, who knew who he was and felt honoured in serving him. Except for one letter, begging Clarke to send another overdue guinea by return of post if he could, and bidding his protégé farewell—'Adieu, dear Clarke! That I shall ever see you again is, I am afraid, highly improbable'— he seems to have had no heart for writing throughout the first fortnight.

The first break in his solitude was on the nineteenth day. Maria Riddel, who had herself been ill (by her own account, seriously), was convalescent not many miles away, and, hearing of his presence at the Brow, she sent a sympathetic invitation and her carriage to bring him to dine. He went;

and as soon as he entered the room she saw death in his looks. On the mere prospect, however, of this so singular meeting he had recovered wonderfully some of that 'stubborn something' which he had at least once had occasion to remind her was a key to his character. 'Well, madam,' he greeted her, 'and have you any commands for the next world?'

Maria, shocked as she was by his cadaverous aspect, did not lack a retort. It seemed a doubtful question, she assured him, as to which of them would first reach the next world. She for her part was counting upon him to write her epitaph.

Considering that he had already done so, and in the cruellest manner, it was a shrewd stroke. The poet, however, did not give himself away. Noticing that she really showed traces of illness, he expressed the tenderest concern for her, and the two sat them down to a *tête-à-tête* meal at which the topic was death. That it was his death and not hers was tacitly admitted between them. Maria was overwhelmed with love and admiration and shame. To her dying day she could never be got to admit that Robert Burns's poetry was so enthralling as his talk. This time he spoke seriously, simply, firmly and—as she expressed it, 'without any of the ostentation of philosophy'—of his end as likely to come soon. He lamented bitterly that he must leave his family poor and Jean in so dreadful a plight. But he was vivacious on the subject of his eldest boy's talent, and he assured Maria that he had never felt any real enmity to the people whom he had lampooned in his verses. One thing distracted him. With his illness had come a nervous concern both about his vagrant poems and the results of his general poetic carelessness. Spurious ballads bearing his name had been sung and offered for sale in the Dumfries streets. Critics and enemies in plenty 'watched for his halting.' To save himself from being 'blamed for trash I never saw' and 'defrauded by other claimants of what is justly my own,' he had proposed that Thomson should print 'on a cheap plan' a collection 'of all the songs of which I wish to be called the author.' Pending this, he had written a certificate for Thomson's second half-volume (not to be published till 1798) declaring that the songs by him there were published by his authority, and empowering Thomson to prosecute any one who issued reprints without permission. One of his dearest wishes now was that he might have time to select and edit his works. But of this, he told Maria, he saw small chance. So he sat talking of the things nearest his heart, and face to face till evening the strangely assorted pair made their peace with each other and with themselves. They met again for tea-drinking the next day, after which they said good-bye.[13]

The day before his dinner with Maria he had started wildly writing letters again. To a request from Thomson for more songs he replied, 'Alas! is this a time for me to woo the Muses?' Yet he enclosed some new lines, and some older MSS with marginal comments, and promised more songs. He wrote also to Cunningham entreating him to do what he could in Edinburgh to persuade the Excise to allow him full pay, declaring that the new baby, if a boy, should be named after him, admitting that his spirits were fled and his bodily suffering great.

A few days later he wrote to Gilbert, delicately indicating the financial position,[14] commending Jean and the children to his care, and drily stating his belief that he was dying—

> Dear Brother,—It will be no very pleasing news to you to be told that I am dangerously ill and not likely to get better. . . .'

There, by the treacherous Solway tide, not only his dreaded solitude but his humiliation was complete. He had become a beggar, and a beggar to those before whom he had most loved to vaunt his pride. On the same day that he wrote to Gilbert he wrote to his father-in-law imploring him to send Mrs Armour to Dumfries within the next fortnight—the utmost he thought Jean could reckon on before her confinement; and signed himself 'your most affectionate Son,'—than which we have no more gushing superscription of his on record. In Gilbert's letter he had merely said 'remember me to my mother.' It was the only farewell Agnes got from her eldest son.[15]

Two days later—when he was feeling somewhat better and believed himself to be benefiting by the treatment—the post brought a communication which came down like a hammer-blow to his labouring heart. The tailor from whom he had bought his Volunteer uniform early in the preceding year was

dissolving a partnership, and an attorney named Penn had
been instructed in the usual way to collect outstanding debts.
The letter was Penn's formal demand for £7 4s!

To any man hard pressed for money, such a common form
request would have been annoying. To Robert, in his morbid
and critical condition and with his lifelong horror of debt, it
was murderous. From the moment of its arrival it was never
out of his thoughts. £7 4s!—a third of his annual salary as a
sick man! And if he failed to pay, a debtor's prison! Thus he
conceived it—'the horrors of a jail.'

The same day he wrote three letters. In two of them, which
were requests for money, he represented himself as a man
whose health would be coming about finely but for his
anxiety. The first was to Thomson asking for £5 by return of
post, 'not gratuitously,' but as an earnest of songs to come.
Had he not that very morning written lines on his old
favourite theme of running water?[16] The second, which
also held out hope—as a borrower must—was to his cousin
at Montrose beseeching the speedy loan of £10, bewailing
Gilbert's affairs and fearing there was no choice but to 'cut
him up.'

The third letter contained no word of his poverty. It was
an announcement of his approaching death, a farewell and
a desperate appeal for one word of kindness to his 'poor
palpitating heart'—addressed to Mrs Dunlop. Though the
writing of it is broken and blotted so as to be hardly
recognisable, there lurks in it some trace of that 'confounding
wit' which, addressed to a portentous correspondent, we
are so much too apt to attribute to portentousness in the
writer. Why, he asks the widow, are her letters, 'at once
highly entertaining and instructive, still denied to a dying
man?'

In the contradictoriness of these three letters written in one
day, we may find some clue to the scepticism of the poet's
doctors, who were not used to prescribing for poets, and the
optimism of his friends, who trusted in his vitality. Here was
a man who was at the same time, for reasons suited to his
various correspondents, both dying and recovering!

Jessy Lewars had been sending him the home news; but
only now, having given the salt-water treatment a fair trial,

did he write her a letter that was for Jean. 'My dearest love,' he wrote:

> . . . It would be injustice to deny that it has eased my pains, and I think has strengthened me ; but my appetite is still extremely bad. No flesh nor fish can I swallow ; porridge and milk are the only things I can taste . . . I will see you on Sunday.—Your affectionate husband,   R.B.

Sunday, however, found him still at the Brow, and the following Sunday also. For all that Dr Maxwell might say, riding eleven miles was out of the question, and there was some difficulty in getting free conveyance. The weather was 'very rainy, coarse and boisterous' and he dared not risk a wetting. A Dumfries baker's van had failed him. At length he was promised a gig—the first seen in Scotland—by a local farmer, Clark of Lockerwoods.

During the week Syme rode out bringing Cunningham's reply which had been sent with privately anxious inquiries through Ryedale. Cunningham was doing his best with the Excise but could guarantee nothing. Syme was scared by Robin's looks. But he could still hope that 'the vigor of his former stamina will conquer his present illness.'

On the day following the letter to Jean the amazing invalid had walked inland by field paths and beside flowering hedges—a quarter of a mile each way—to drink tea with two more ladies, the wife and daughter of the minister of Ruthwell. It was actually fine, and the sun at setting poured in to the Manse windows. The younger woman, horrified by the visitor's sunlit face, which showed him like a corpse but for the glowing, still dangerous eyes, went to pull down the blind. But Robert stayed her hand with one of his warm smiles that charmed her as it had charmed so many other women. 'Thank you, my dear, for your kind attention,' he said, 'but oh! let him shine! He will not shine long for me!'

The fatigue of this visit brought on a fresh attack of fever next day, and he could not start for home till 3 o'clock on the afternoon of Monday, the 18th. When, that evening, he climbed down from the spring-cart at the bottom of the Mill Vennel which was too steep for the horse, he could not stand upright. But Jessy was there. Crouching and tottering, with a parched tongue, a rigor in all his being, and looks that were 'hollow and ghastly,' he managed with her help to reach his own door. Jean was 'quite speechless' with terror. They could not get him up to the smaller of the two upstairs rooms, where the yellow boxwood bed had been prepared for him, so he was put into the kitchen bed. At once he sank into an intermittent stupor.

But an urgent word would bring him out of it for half an hour together and he kept begging Jean to 'touch him and remind him when he was going wrong.' When Findlater or Lewars called he gave them his dying orders lightly and rationally. 'Don't let the Awkward Squad fire over me!' he begged one of his fellow Volunteers; and at night he managed to write at least one letter—a second summons to Mrs Armour to come at once.[17] He was able also to read the letter—kindly enough, but guarded and disapproving—which came at last from Mrs Dunlop.

Then for a time his follies, sins and failures came all at once to mind, and seeing how he was leaving Jean and the children he took the full blame on himself in an agony of penitence and self-accusation terrible to see. He must not die. Maxwell had pronounced him to be better. Repeatedly in delirium he called for Cunningham and for Syme, and when, first thing on Tuesday morning, Syme came in and took his hand he 'made a wonderful exertion.' 'I am much better today,' he said, raising his voice strongly, 'I shall soon be well again, for I command my spirits and my mind. But yesterday I resigned myself to death.' Seeing his face and Jean's, Syme went without hope. But 'never, never to despair' was still Robin's motto. Having left him for a few minutes alone Jean came back into the room to find the bed empty and himself sitting in a corner with the bed-clothes about him. He was 'building Resolve'—though not, alas, 'on Reason.' It took the two women to coax him back to bed. Knowing as they did that his strength was gone, they whispered together that he must have had some kind of a fit. The next day, Wednesday, they heard him shout very loudly and peremptorily for 'Gilbert! Gilbert!' but Gilbert was not there.

On Wednesday night he lapsed into a condition in which the doctors were compelled to see that his heart could not hold out much longer, and his brain refused to take in the good news which now, too late for his consolation, kept arriving at the house by letter or word of mouth—that James Burness gladly sent £10; that Thomson, by return, sent £5 and a practical suggestion for a subscribed edition of songs; that Fintry assured him of so slight a diminution of salary that the enclosed donation of £5 would cover it.[18]

Jessy was his only consolation. She had put the four little boys to sleep at her house and had come herself to sleep with Jean. All that night Dr Maxwell sat by Robert's bed and in the very early morning two neighbours took his place. Jessy, seeing for herself that the end was near, ran for the children who, in the true Scotish fashion, must assemble to see their father draw his last breath. The four, headed by ten-year-old Robert, stood round the bed. But here were to be no pious injunctions. The poet roused himself: he looked passionately at his boys: and with passion he cursed by name the attorney, Mr Penn, who had sent in the bill for his Volunteer uniform. It is even said that in that extreme moment he made one last desperate effort, and that his nerves served him so far that he rose to his feet in the bed and stepped eagerly forward. Though 'much the child of disaster' and with all his errors on his forehead, the son of William Burnes would have no one say he had not played the man. But from that he relapsed into unconsciousness, and by five o'clock in the morning, into death.

Jessy took the children out for a walk along the river banks, and they brought back bunches of wild flowers and grasses and sprigs of birch and hazel and hawthorn to strew over the dead poet. Jessy knew the growing things he liked best. He had shown her one of the last fragmentary poems now thrust among the disordered papers in his desk:

> In gowany glens the burnie strays,
> Where bonie lasses bleach their claes;
> Or trots by hazelly shaws and braes
>   Wi' hawthorns gray,
> Where blackbirds join the shepherd's lays
>   At close o' day.

And though it was too late in the year for some of his favourite plants to be in blossom, she and the boys found daisies and foxgloves and harebells and some late dog-roses. Her brother, the gauger, came in and sat laboriously writing letters for Jean. Jean, sitting by her hard-won husband's body, could do little more than wonder when her pains would come upon her.

But she had many helpers now from near and far. As soon as the news got about in Dumfries, the house was busy with callers. Men and women quite suddenly realised that here lay one who was the Poet of his Country—perhaps of mankind— as none had been before, because none before had combined so many human weaknesses with so great an ardour of living and so generous a warmth of admission. Certainly none had ever possessed a racier gift of expression for his own people. The more for having sinned on all points wherein the common man is tempted to sin, both to glory and repentance; the more for having walked the valley of the shadow of compromise while yet retaining in his breast the proud, soft, defiant heart of a man. Burns was perceived by many to be the jewel of Scotland, death sometimes has a way of giving these sudden insights.

Now that poor Robin was dead, all the birds of the air fell a-sighing and a-sobbing to some purpose. The hat was handed round for the widow and children[19] and, in true Scotish fashion, the Dumfriesians grudged neither trouble nor expense for a burial. Between the Thursday when Burns died and the following Tuesday when he was 'interred with military honours and every suitable respect' in St Michael's churchyard,[20] enough money must have changed hands to have paid his debts many times over. Both the Angus-shire Fencible Infantry and the Cinque Ports Cavalry were stationed in the town. Such an occasion was a godsend to these and to the Gentlemen Volunteers—good drinkers every man. In addition all the 'important people of Dumfries and its neighbourhood' expressed a wish to join in the procession—as, for example, the Hon Charles Jenkinson,[21] of the Cinque Ports Cavalry, and Maule of Panmure, who, though the one had lately made the loyal declaration that he would never shake Mr Burns by the hand, and the other had not long since spurred Robert into scarifying verse, now both desired prominent parts in 'the obsequies of the Scotish

bard.' Besides, on the same night as the obsequies there was
to be a ball.

Early on Monday morning the coffin was privately taken to
the Town Hall, where 'a vast concourse of persons,' some
from long distances, gathered by one o'clock. The dead
Volunteer's sword and unpaid-for hat were laid on the coffin
lid, and amid showers of rain with occasional sunshine the
procession formed. Fencibles, infantry, and cavalry lined the
streets for the half mile that lay between the Town Hall and
the grave. The drums were muffled, the bells tolled. So
Robin went to his last lair.

The Dead March in *Saul* (a piece of the sort which the poet
had always found repugnant to his musical taste) was played.
Three volleys by the 'awkward squad' were fired over the
grave, which was 'in an outside corner of the overstocked
churchyard,' and 'a desirable situation,' consisting of 'a space
of 9 feet by 7 free and unincumbered.' 'The spectacle,' we are
assured, 'was in a high degree grand and solemn.' Syme was
able to forget his grief for a while in the perception of how
well he had organised the ceremony, as indeed he had. At
home Jean, who all the morning had endured the pains of
labour, gave birth to a ninth child, a boy.

The *Edinburgh Advertiser* of the same date announced the
poet's death, appealed for funds for his widow, and felt sure
that 'the public, to whose amusement he has so largely
contributed,' would 'learn with regret that his extraordinary
endowments were accompanied with frailties which rendered
them useless to himself and his family.'

Five evenings later, when dusk had fallen and the churchyard with its crowd of tombs standing as high and square as
houses, was locked, a young man and woman might have
been seen approaching the south wall. While the young man
waited outside, the lady, young, slim and athletic, climbed
the wall, made for the new grave, and kneeling, planted in
the freshly turned earth some laurel plants and 'emblematic
flowers.' It was Maria Riddel—her squire the son of 'old
sinful Smellie,' the Crochallan.

Notes

Part One. Prelude
CHAPTER I

1 Galt's Laird of Kittlestoneheugh not only stakes 'more than the whole value of his estate,' but the person of his only son to be devoured in the promised land of gold by hunger and mosquitoes. *The Entail*, ch.i.

2 They were entrusted with poor relief besides acting in a small way as bankers to the well-to-do.

3 At no period have the *women* of Scotland been open to the charge of sloth.

CHAPTER II

1 £5 sterling.

2 The poorest kind of barley.

3 As a journeyman James would be earning 6d a day, about one-third of an English carpenter's wage at that same time.

4 When all was over they were able to obtain certificates from the parish minister stating that they had 'no hand in the late wicked rebellion.'

5 It was in keeping with Robert Burnes's fate that the 'Forty-five, which ruined him, might as easily have helped him. For it enabled Parliament to make a clean sweep of the clan system and all the mediaeval jurisdictions that for centuries had stood in the way of good government in Scotland.

CHAPTER III

1 The bean-woman allowed each customer to suck a piece of bacon for flavouring, but not to bite the piece or take it away, as it must serve for all who came.

2 Allan Ramsay had tried to set up a theatre, but it had been suppressed by the Kirk.

3 Alexander 'Jupiter' Carlyle, minister of Inveresk.

Part Two. Father and Son
CHAPTER VI

1 Then close upon a shilling a day.

2 Dr James Beattie, professor of moral philosophy at Marischal College and a leading opponent of Hume.

3 Some time before 1780 Murdoch made a tour in France. Possibly it was before his return to Ayr.

4　This class-consciousness was no new thing. Burns has recorded as one of his earliest memories his fury one Sunday in church, when he saw a pretty young servant girl having to rise and come out of a pew to make way for the loutish son of a laird, her master.

CHAPTER X

1　See Burns's letter to Niven, Nov 3, 1780.

2　From Lochlie Burns attended a singing school for two months. None but sacred music was allowed.

3　The dating of 'Mary Morison' has been the subject of controversy. The weight of evidence is in favour of the period to which I have assigned it, yet the style indicates the period of Burns's maturity. The probable explanation is that the song as we now have it is not the original version, but a recension made some years later.

4　This did not prevent her from boasting later on that she had inspired them.

5　In November 1781 the Guild paid Burnes £160 for it.

6　The young man was married and doing well as an attorney.

CHAPTER XI

1　The circumstances of Burns's life at Irvine are admittedly obscure, but they are not so perplexing as his biographers have been apt to suppose. The perplexity has arisen from the assumption that Peacock and the thievish partner whose drunken wife caused the conflagration were one and the same. It is certain, however, that they were not. Peacock's shop was never burned down, for it still stands in the Glasgow Vennel. The shop that was burned down was in the High Street. Therefore the 'partner' whom Burns speaks of but does not name, must have been somebody he took up with after his quarrel with Peacock.

CHAPTER XII

1　It is always stated that Burnes died of premature senile decay.

2　The circumstances of the transference from Lochlie to Mossgiel, as here set down, have been deduced from Alexander Tait's poem 'Burnes in Lochlie.'

3　The late Sir Edward Tennant, 2nd baronet, on being raised to the peerage commemorated the origins of his family by taking the title of Baron Glenconner. Of John Tennant's descendants living today the best known is, of course, his great-granddaughter, the Countess of Oxford and Asquith.

Part Three. Mossgiel

CHAPTER XIII

1　Before his father's death Burns had commonly used this convenient phonetic spelling. Now Gilbert and he used it increasingly, though the family did not adopt it till some time later. When not Burns he always wrote his name Burness, never Burnes.

2   Later she married happily and was respected by all. Today the wealthiest of all the blood of Burns, and the only one to reach the peerage of the United Kingdom, is descended from the child she bore to the poet.

3   Well-meaning biographers have said that Robert endured a prolonged period of depression during the summer after his father's death. Meanwhile the most reliable chronology has quietly removed the grounds for this assertion. The biographers, however, have not as yet seen fit to withdraw it.

4   The races were actually run on the road which, just below Mossgiel, is level.

5   See 'A Mauchline Wedding.' This delicious fragment is not well known as, owing to the exuberance of the poet's amorous fancy, it is seldom included in popular editions of his works. The only text we have is from a copy which Burns afterwards sent to Mrs Dunlop of Dunlop and from which he deliberately omitted the last line of one stanza. Not much conjecture is needed to restore it. In a note, however, he gravely explains the lacuna as due to defect of memory inasmuch as the poem had been composed some time before, but was now being committed to paper for the first time! Burns was an apt pupil of Sterne.

6   In spite of the distance he was regular in his attendance at Tarbolton Lodge, and as Depute Master often occupied the high chair, which he did, it is said, with conspicuous dignity.

7   We have Burns's own word for this, but no actual record. Possibly he had a rough musical short-hand of his own devising, which he used and destroyed his notes when they had served their purpose.

CHAPTER XIV

1   The plebeian sinner paid a guinea.

2   His inward agitation induced an attack of 'slow fever' (see letter to James Tennant, 13 Sept 1784).

3   A loose, short-sleeved print jacket.

4   Burns went on with his music. He and James Tennant got up a large singing-class at Ochiltree, which he attended ardently for three months.

CHAPTER XV

1   To this day 'Death and Doctor Hornbook' is a sore subject with the Tarbolton schoolmaster's descendants. In placing the poem I have followed the Chambers-Wallace chronology instead of the Scott Douglas, which seems to refer to a later, completed edition of the earlier draft so plainly dated by Gilbert.

2   Now known as *The Jolly Beggars*.

3 The powerful faction, even in Ayrshire where the Old Light continued to burn more strongly than elsewhere.

4 Stair House, of which the widow, Mrs Stewart, was mistress, and in the kitchen of which Davie Sillar, ably seconded by Burns, had gone courting.

5 The only 'decree' that has been preserved is the so-called 'Court of Equity.'

6 As it turned out Lapraik had only adapted the poem from one he had seen two years before in *Ruddiman's Weekly Magazine*.

7 Biographers have often ascribed the idea of publishing to the fact that Burns was unable to find the money for his passage. An examination of dates and letters (as well as Burns's own express statement) negatives this.

8 He had acted for Hamilton in the ecclesiastical courts, where, in the ardour of his rhetoric, he had used injurious expressions about Mr Auld for which he afterwards had to apologise.

9 It is noteworthy that Burns, who was a good judge of his own work, could never be induced to make another effort of the kind. 'The Cotter's Saturday Night' succeeded as he had intended it should succeed, as an exhibition piece.

CHAPTER XVI

1 Unknown to all save Jean and himself, one of the back windows of Dove's tavern commanded a side attic window of the Armours' cottage.

2 Burns too was a snuff-taker.

3 This was David Sillar's opinion of the Tarbolton folk.

4 Unable to decide the delicate question whether he should include Aiken, he wrote that same night to Hamilton asking his advice and signing himself 'the unfortunate Robt Burns.' Hamilton smoothed over the difficulty, and Aiken was enabled to give free rein to his benevolence.

5 Burns's beautiful and characteristic handwriting was formed at this time.

6 Mary Campbell's Ayrshire places cannot be named with certainty.

7 Auld, of course, would do so in ignorance that an irregular marriage had taken place.

8 Though Burns's Bible has been preserved, Mary Campbell's has not. The facts point to its later destruction by Burns.

9 Aiken having asked for these verses Burns hastened to oblige— showing that their quarrel was quite made up.

10 In other words—*if through bad luck you have been found out.*

CHAPTER XVII

1 My reconstruction of that part of the narrative to which this fragmentary undated letter is the clue, is admittedly in some degree conjectural. Conceivably, though not probably, Burns

wrote to Smith without solicitation about the time of Jean's return. In any case the emotional essentials must have been as narrated, and Lockhart must have dated the fragment too early, thus misleading all subsequent biographers, who have accepted his date without question, and by so doing have greatly wronged the poet with respect to Jean.

2 It was a cautious selection, excluding all the satires except 'The Holy Fair' (out of deference to his family and those many friends who disapproved strongly of such pieces), and consisting of some twenty subject poems, seven epistles, a few odd verses, epigrams and epitaphs (including the most serious one on himself) and only three songs. Even so, Wilson the printer shook his head—'Ah, Rab,' he said, 'it winna do unless ye begin your buik wi' mair sprinklins o' serious bits.' In make-up, under Burns's own direction, it was the comeliest volume Wilson had ever produced.

3 The 'Reply to a Tailor,' perhaps the most profoundly Scottish poem ever penned. It links Burns with the courtier Dunbar across three centuries by a bond deeper than any discipleship. As yet he had not read a line of Dunbar.

4 Even in company Burns had the capacity for stillness.

5 When, five months later, he wrote a flowery letter to Miss Wilhelmina, enclosing the song and asking her permission to print it, his letter remained 'delicately' unanswered. When he and his eyes were safely under earth a summer-house was built on the spot where he had stood, and facsimiles of both song and letter hung within. The lady retained the original of the song and boasted of its author's attentions till she died at the age of eighty-eight, a virgin. It was published after her death in a collection selected 'by a society of gentlemen,' with the following note—'Composed by Robert Burns from the emotions of gratitude and esteem which he felt for the worthy family now living there for the kindness and attention they had shown him.'

6 The evidence points unmistakably to a renewal of love relations, anyhow of a fitful sort, between Burns and Jean Armour at this time.

7 One at least of these times he had to appear on the cutty stool with Jean beside him.

8 Near Irvine. Mrs Allan, mother to their gaudsman, was Mrs Burnes's half-sister, and had shown Burns kindness in his heckling days.

9 The exact date of his visit to Peggy is not known. It may have been a week or two later, when he gave her one of his own three copies of the poems inscribed with indifferently poetic but truly heartfelt lines: And when you read the simple artless

rhymes,/One friendly sigh for him,—he asks no more,— / Who, distant, burns in flaming torrid climes,/Or haply lies beneath th' Atlantic's roar./

10   The full text of this important letter will be found printed for the first time in Professor De Lancey Ferguson's edition of Burns's letters, now in the press.

11   Burns was living at home again, for though the Armours' warrant was still in force his success had gained him county influence, and he knew they would not dare proceed (see letter to Richmond, 1 Sept 1786, in De Lancey Ferguson's book).

12   Of which Aiken alone accounted for 145.

13   The incorrect assertion that the poems were published *in order* to pay for his passage has been so constantly repeated that the correct statement can bear underlining.

14   The *Nancy* did not in fact sail till 4 or 5 September.

15   Without, however, marrying Jean.

16   Provided this could be brought about by a mutual friend, as his own acquaintance was not sufficient to permit of such a liberty.

17   Without giving up all idea of Jamaica, Burns now began to make inquiries about the Excise (see letter to Aiken, 8 October 1786).

18   On the face of Wilson's account, which has been preserved, Burns should have been in pocket some £54; but as the printer's honesty was never questioned, we can only reconcile Burns's express statement by supposing that there were other expenses besides those entered.

19   Lord Cockburn.

20   He died two years before Burns. His younger brother, who succeeded as fifth Earl of Selkirk, settled the Red River with Highland emigrants and thus founded Manitoba.

21   No doubt all was done with Burns's consent, if not by his suggestion.

22   Typhus.

23   In the Bible Burns gave to Mary there are signs of some one having tried, with a wetted thumb, to obliterate his name.

Part Four. Edinburgh
CHAPTER XVIII

1   This in contrast to the regular brothels of Edinburgh, which were conducted in so seemly a manner that it is related that once, at Assembly time, an old minister from the country was entertained in one with food and conversation without any suspicion on his part as to the character of the establishment.

2   It was supposed to make the journey to Edinburgh in sixty hours, but its first trip actually took seventy-four.

3   It was lent to Burns by a son-in-law of Tennant of Glenconner.

4 As Burns wrote, 'we can easily distinguish our laughter-loving, night-rejoicing neighbours—when they are eating, when they are drinking, when they are singing, when they are,' etc.

5 Richmond later married Jenny.

6 If he had to sail, Burns was going to risk the Savanna route.

7 Though the fact is not recorded, it is highly improbable that Burns did not join in the 'daylight procession' from the New Kirk (Old-town) to St Andrew's Church (New-town), especially seeing that an Ayrshire New Light Minister was conducting the service. The Rev James Wright was an enthusiastic Mason, and it is on record that his sermon on this occasion on 'the Union of Love to God and love to Man' met with great acceptance. The collection was for 'indigent brethren.'

8 When later this poor man learned what he had missed he was frantic with chagrin. He undertook to print the work of the very next stray versifier that came along—and lost his money.

9 Considerably less since 1780 when the duty began on Scotch claret.

10 Carlyle of Inveresk.

11 Carlyle of Inveresk.

12 Letters to Temple.

13 Preface to *Blair's Sermons*.

14 During the revolutionary period Mackenzie was to become very useful to Dundas and to Pitt in London as a pamphleteer. In 1799 he was made Comptroller of Taxes for Scotland.

15 Burns's own phrase. Creech later became Lord Provost of Edinburgh.

16 Lord Erskine, LC.

17 Cockburn's *Memorials*.

18 It is for this reason I quote so fully a letter which—even allowing for the jargon of the time—is distressing to read.

19 Dugald Stewart had handed his copy of the poems to Mackenzie with this explicit idea.

20 By this costume—the livery of Fox—besides smartening himself up for town visits Burns proclaimed himself a Whig.

21 An attempt has been made to prove that Burns was made welcome to a meeting of the popular Kilwinning Lodge as early as 7 December, but the claim remains to be substantiated.

22 But Creech was to take the odd shilling of all non-subscribers' copies.

CHAPTER XIX

1 His French, however, was a failure, so that when he addressed a French lady in that language she could make nothing of it. And he found only too true the Ayr schoolmaster's warning as to the importance of the classics among persons of culture. So

much so that he later took some lessons in both French and Latin.

2 Blair's junior colleague, a gifted man who later disappeared under a cloud. He fled the country in such circumstances that pious editors of Burns's letters felt it their duty to mutilate and disguise all references to him. They even went so far, in the case of letters addressed to Dr Greenfield, as to substitute the names of blameless correspondents, such as Mrs Dunlop.

3 Cromek's *Reliques*.

4 Burns to the end of his days kept up a correspondence with Smellie. The latter carefully preserved the poet's letters, but one of his grandsons, who inherited his grandfather's papers, though not his disposition, destroyed them all because he disapproved of their tone—a literary crime so atrocious that it hardly bears thinking about. Other destroyers 'on broad moral grounds' were Greenshields of Kerse and Dr Currie. Thomson shamelessly falsified the letters in his possession for his own ends, and even Clarinda was not blameless. No great figure in literature has suffered more than Burns from posthumous vandalism.

5 It was Burns's instinctive theory that old dance or 'Bacchanalian or warlike tunes, taken slow and soft, can be used for amorous or pathetic words.' In fact many an existing tune to 'a droll song' was an ancient Romish chant burlesqued, so that its re-union to serious words was an act (however unconscious) of poetic justice, triumphantly carried out in practice. The tune to that bawdy song, 'The Grey Goose and the Gled,' was of such a kind. Burns's later air to the above, 'The Banks o' Doon,' was a reminiscence from Playford's old opera, *Apollo's Banquet*, which had been modified by nearly a century of ignorant singers till it was become a folk tune.

6 Two years passed before the order was executed, two more before Burns could pay for it. The stonemason then wished to charge interest on the sum, £5 10s. Burns refused. 'Considering,' he remarked, 'that the money was due by one Poet for putting a tombstone over another, he may, with grateful surprise, thank Heaven that he ever saw a farthing of it.'

7 By Shenstone. The well-meant comparison is Mrs Barbauld's.

8 These expressions, written in irony some twenty years later by Francis Jeffrey, express the sentiment current in 1786.

9 A poem now lost.

10 Father of the hero of Corunna.

11 'A person whose immense vanity, bordering upon insanity, obscured, or rather eclipsed, very considerable talents . . . He

had a desire to be a great man and a Maecenas *à bon marché.*'—
Sir Walter Scott's *Journal*, 20 April 1829.

12 Dr Blair replied the same day at great length commending his wisdom and giving much advice upon the importance of humility. This letter from the reverend doctor (who had subscribed for a single copy of the poems) reached Burns as he was mounting his horse to leave Edinburgh. It had such an infuriating effect that with imprecations he thrust it half read into his pocket.

CHAPTER XX

1 A Glasgow bookseller asked for fifty copies for subscribers.
2 He had wished to do it for Muir of Kilmarnock.
3 Burns had found that the great body of Scotish folk melody was Highland.

CHAPTER XXI

1 In 1788 he became Lord President of the Court of Session, a position he held till his death soon afterwards.
2 Here, as elsewhere, my account of my great-great-grandfather has been compiled from family tradition and papers, as well as from the well-known sources mentioned in the *Dictionary of National Biography*. Among other Dalswinton documents I have in my possession a curious anonymous pamphlet of which I have been unable to trace any other copy, though possibly one may be hidden somewhere in the National Library. It bears the date 1813 and the imprint of Robert Jackson, Dumfries, and is entitled 'Letter/from ——/to his Friend in London,/on the present State/of Public Affairs,/recommended to the serious consideration/of Every Man of Property/in Great Britain and Ireland.' It professes to be a digest of conversations held by the writer with 'our old friend Mr Miller, whom we left, seven and twenty years since, busily employed in making experiments for the improvement of cannon and muskets, and also with a view to the improvement of naval architecture'; but this is a transparent fiction, for the contents of the pamphlet—a most engaging medley of acuteness, ingenuity, simplicity, egoism and anecdotage—make it clear that the author is Miller himself, who was then over eighty years of age. The pamphlet is very full on two subjects (1) Miller's invention of the carronade, and (2) fiorin grass. As to the former, Miller's claim is treated by the writer in the *Dictionary of National Biography* as a mere tradition unsupported by evidence or probability, but Miller's own account of the origins of the gun (which is given in the pamphlet in the first person) is so circumstantial that it can only be rejected on proof of the document being a forgery. As to fiorin, Miller in 1813 was 'confident that this grass will have the effect to furnish much additional food for

man and beast, as many fields now lying waste will be covered with it.' The latter part of the prediction proved only too true, for fiorin grass took so kindly to Scotish soil that it soon became a pestilent weed. The supposed virtues of fiorin were first preached by an Irish clergyman, Dr Richardson, of Clonfeckle, to whom Miller in his enthusiasm erected a monument at Dalswinton which is known to this day as 'Miller's Maggot.'

I may add that, although the 'Letter' contains a good deal of personal reminiscence, the name of Burns is not mentioned. Perhaps the silence is eloquent.

3 *Quarterly Review*, vol xix p.532. Miller was undoubtedly the first to suggest the application of steam to navigation.

4 Adair, introduced by Lawrie of Loudoun, was the son of an Ayr doctor and related to Mrs Dunlop.

5 Later the lady 'manifested a disinclination to speak on the subject of her meeting with Burns.'

6 Although Burns himself speaks of 'taking down' tunes from the singing of country girls, it does not follow that he was capable of doing so in the ordinary way. The holographs containing musical extracts are among the rarest of Burns MSS, and the extracts bear all the marks of having been laboriously copied from a score by one who had none of the command of musical notation that is necessary for the taking down of a tune. It is most probable that Burns evolved some kind of musical shorthand of his own, which, aided by his remarkable musical memory, enabled him to convey a tune to Clarke or another, and that he destroyed his rough notes once they had served their purpose.

7 One morning Nicol's class, on arriving at school, found their master very much before them. He and a stranger in blue and buff were stretched out on the forms sound asleep.

8 It has been suggested, without proof, that May Cameron and Jenny Clow were the same person. It seems unlikely that a girl of this class would change her name, and both names are on record.

9 These opinions of the poet, as also that quoted on p.270, appear as marginal notes in his hand in his copy of Sterne's *Koran*. Another note to Sterne's remark in the same work—'St James says "Count it all joy when you fall into divers temptations"'—is a single eloquent 'Ah!'

CHAPTER XXII

1 The coach left at 8 A.M. and arrived at 6 P.M.

2 Three times married—twice to ladies of title—Mr Kemp died just in time, though at a fairly advanced age, to escape citation as co-defender in divorce proceedings.

3 Dr Sandy Wood—tall, black-eyed, woman-loving—who had

an inspired touch for a bruise and equal good gifts in diagnosis and song, but was 'in all other respects perfectly illiterate'— according to Carlyle of Inveresk.

4 These are further marginal notes made by Burns in his copy of Sterne's *Koran*.

5 The old Scotish saturnalia, which lasted from Christmas Eve to the first Monday of January.

6 Mrs McLehose's rhyme to 'joys' was 'those.' Burns substituted 'prize.'

7 Burns must have been kept constantly in touch with affairs at Mauchline, and his most frequent and intimate correspondent, one thinks, must have been his brother Gilbert, a fluent letter-writer. We know that over the whole Edinburgh period Burns was helping Gilbert financially (Nicol always maintained that by Burns's own account £300 went to Mossgiel in cash). But no letters passing between the brothers during this time have been preserved. It is highly significant. In many respects Gilbert is the unknown quantity in his brother's life, and he continued to be so after his death. Contemporary biographers got astonishingly little material out of Gilbert.

8 The identity of the lady is obscure. She was certainly not Mrs Stewart of Stair or Mrs Dugald Stewart, but more than this cannot be said.

9 Burns was now the better fitted to play a platonic part at the Potterrow in that, being out and about again, he was able to visit Jenny Clow upon occasion.

CHAPTER XXIII

1 Wallace has assumed, in spite of the poet's express statement in a letter written on the Saturday, that he did not leave for Dumfries till the Monday. Considering that there is nothing to contradict the express statement, my conclusions as to church-going seem inevitable. As 1788 was a leap year, Burns's return journey must have been on a Sunday—2 March.

2 Father of Allan Cunningham.

3 Cf last stanza of the 'Address to the Unco Guid.'

4 Again in the *Koran*.

5 Hamilton's request bears no date. It was probably made before the parish knew of Burns's decision with regard to Jean, but certainly not before the decision had been reached.

6 If any letters were exchanged on the subject, they have been destroyed.

Part Five. Dumfries
CHAPTER XXIV

1 Though Goethe did not actually marry Christine Vulpius till later, his intention was implied by this public acknowledgment.

2 This year—1788—J. Maxwell, 'Poet in Paisley,' published his *Animadversions on some Poets and Poetasters of the Present Age, especially R—t B—s, etc.*, which faithfully reflected the opinion of many orthodox people, calling Burns 'infidel poet' and 'champion for Satan.'

3 'There is no encouragement for a man of learning & genius here,' wrote a friend in Jamaica to whom Burns had sent a copy of his poems.

4 'That we are to live for ever seems *too good news to be true*. That we are to enter into a new scene of existence, where exempt from want and pain, we shall enjoy ourselves and our friends without satiety or separation—how much should I be indebted to anyone who could fully assure me that this was certain!'—Letter to Cunningham, 16 Feb 1790.

5 The same month, writing to a Glasgow friend, he says, 'my Rib begs her compliments to you.'

6 It does not appear that the fiddle was given. Perhaps Burns, having successively tried to play the guitar and the French horn, had despaired of himself as an executant.

7 Burns liked the *Georgics* the best of Virgil, whom in other respects he found a '*servile* copier' of Homer. After the *Odyssey*, which he had read in Pope's translation, he thought the *Aeneid* poor. Dryden he judged to be Pope's master 'in genius and fluency of language.'

8 That autumn Burns conveyed his request (with poems enclosed) for the honour of an introduction to Mr James Boswell, who, busily engaged upon his *Life of Johnson*, seems to have been on a short visit to Auchinleck. All that came of it, so far as we know, was that Boswell docketed the letter the same day as from 'Robt Burns the Poet expressing very high sentiments of me.'

9 See letter to Smith, 26 June 1788.

10 In the Kirk-session minute appears: 'NB—Notwithstanding the great noise, there are only twenty fornicators in this parish since last Sacrament.'

CHAPTER XXV

1 Peter Stuart, editor of the *Star*, had been a devoted friend of Robert Fergusson.

2 Rebuked by Mrs Dunlop, he admitted that there might perhaps be among his works 'a stanza or two not quite fit for a clergyman's reading to a company of ladies.'

3 For some mid-winter weeks the Burns couple were lent rooms by a Dumfries gentleman in his vacated summer-house near Ellisland.

4 He had damaged his knee again that winter.

5 She was called Fanny and later married Adam Armour.

6 Dr Blacklock and Ainslie.

7 Burns allowed Sillar to include his own 'Epistle' and subscribed for eleven copies.

8 He also refused that summer to consider Mrs Dunlop's
suggestion that he should be the first occupant of a chair of
Agriculture at Edinburgh.

CHAPTER XXVI

1 At such times Burns seems to have dosed himself with Glauber
salts, perhaps prescribed by Mundell, his Dumfries doctor.

2 William Wordsworth, who upon being shown some of our
poet's letters with their enclosures, exclaimed upon their
'profanity and impropriety of all sorts' and found therein
'everything which is most shocking.' (From 'A Day with
Wordsworth,' *Blackwood's Magazine*, June 1927, containing
three letters written by James Patrick Muirhead, the first dated
September 1841.)

   Byron also read some of 'Burns's unpublished and never-to-
be-published letters' with comments which are well known.

3 Syme, who was from Edinburgh, was introduced by Alexander
Cunningham.

4 As already noted (see p.181) Edinburgh brothels were conducted with the strictest propriety, and the Sabbath was
punctiliously observed. As Saturday nights were apt to be busy
the mistress of the establishment was hard pressed to get her
young ladies dressed and packed off to church in good time.

5 Nicol may also have been at the harvest home. He had recently
bought a cottage and lands not far away.

6 Thus Burns characteristically offended Mrs Dunlop (Nicol
being her *bête noire*) more than he had pleased her by his
naming of the other boy.

7 Fourteen years later Morin was able to resell Ellisland for
£4,430.

8 Burns admitted that Miller allowed him 'some little consideration' for his lease.

9 Sillar chose this time to ask for a loan. Burns replied that he was
not master of ten shillings. After this the friendship seems to
have cooled.

10 His mood was possibly not improved by the 'duty call' paid by
him with Jean at the hostile manse before their removal.

CHAPTER XXVII

1 The wax silhouette of Clarinda was in fact, as we have seen
earlier, put away in pieces.

2 This time he had it set in a ring.

3 She is never again heard of. Burns appears to have satisfied Mrs
McLehose that, allowing for his fault, he had done his utmost
for the girl.

4 Anna Park is said to have married a soldier and to have died later in child-birth.

5 Maria was Walter Riddel's second wife. His first had died at child-birth, leaving him a vast sugar estate in Antigua.

6 Mrs Walter Riddel performed also upon the harp and the piano.

7 According to one Dumfries hostess, Burns, when at her house, always left the table with the ladies.

8 Miller had now been for nearly two years Deputy Chairman of the Bank of Scotland.

CHAPTER XXVIII

1 Boswell collected by private subscription in Scotland, and despatched to Paoli £700 worth of 'cannon and warlike stores.'

2 Till 1775 Scotish colliers and salters (thousands of men, women and children) were slaves in every sense of the term. From that date they were no longer legally bought and sold, but they continued in virtually the same condition till June 1799.

3 The preceding year a Glasgow gentleman had sent to Lafayette a device for artillery carried by horses, which device was successfully used at the battle of Maubeuge in June 1792. And early in 1792 a subscription by Glasgow people 'to aid the French in carrying on the war against the emigrant princes or any foreign power by whom they may be attacked' reached £1200.

4 The procedure was this. Each of the self-elected burgh councils elected a delegate; and these delegates elected the member. One or more of the delegates received a bribe, and one or more of the town councils was 'refreshed' so that a majority might be assured.

5 In the autumn of 1791 Burns had been introduced to the Duke of Queensberry and had spent the evening with him so pleasantly, that he afterwards wrote enclosing his drinking-song, 'The Whistle.' '. . . he treated me,' Burns admitted, 'with the most distinguished politeness, and marked attention. Though I am afraid his Grace's character as a Man of Worth is very equivocal, yet he certainly is a Nobleman of the first taste, and a Gentleman of the first manners.'

6 Mrs Fletcher of Saltoun—see her *Autobiography*.

7 This account of the effects of the French Revolution in Scotland with the phrases quoted is taken from Cockburn's *Memorials of His Time*, 1779-1830. 'Everything,' he says, 'not this or that thing but literally everything, was soaked in this one event.'

8 By G. Malcolm Thomson in his *Short History of Scotland*.

9 'What is there in the delivering over a perjured Blockhead & an unprincipled Prostitute to the hands of the hangman, that it

should arrest . . . attention . . . ?' (letter to Mrs Dunlop, 12 Jan 1795).

10 From the *Dumfries Weekly Journal* of 30 October. It was probably in connection with these gaieties that Burns was introduced at Friars' Carse to Farington. The diarist, who had been astonished in Glasgow by the vogue of Burns's poems and by the fact that the print-shops displayed pictures of the Alloway cottage, thought the bard looked like 'a mechanic or tradesman.'

11 From R. Heron's *Observations made on a Journey through the Western Counties of Scotland*, 1792 (vol ii).

12 *Dumfries Weekly Journal.*

13 In any case Burns was always enraged by 'the roar of Folly and Dissipation' of the Caledonian Hunt festivities—in his view 'Profligacy and outrage . . . without those bright talents which might throw a kind of veil over mischievous Folly and un-principled Wickedness.'

14 November 1792.

15 Burns's most political contribution was a compliment to the Whigs, praising Fox, the Earl of Lauderdale (one of the founders of 'The Friends of the People'), Lord Shelburne (the supporter of Parliamentary reform), Thomas Erskine and General Norman Macleod of Skye, who was a keen reformer.

16 The parenthesis is clearly introduced to fit the case of Dundas, who was, in most senses of the phrase, a self-made man.

17 'Complaints' of trifling errors, bearing with them a possible 'admonishment,' were locally recorded in the Excise eight times a year. Burns, who was known to be 'exemplary in his duties' and 'jealous of the least imputation on his vigilance,' had endured no more than his fair share of such complaints, and in the preceding May had been for the first time 'admonished' for the slip of entering 160 instead of 16 lbs of green tea in his books. He must therefore have known that an 'admonishment' was not a head office affair as was, for example, a 'censure' or 'reprimand,' and that it had not even a cumulative effect upon a man's record. On the other hand, considering the political situation, he may with reason have feared that the merest remembered 'complaint' of alleged disaffection would militate more than recorded sins against promotion.

18 His belief was justified. In 1785 he had bought Dalswinton (including Ellisland) for £25,000. In 1822—seven years after his death, aged 83—his executors sold it (without Ellisland) for £120,000.

19 The interesting fact that Mrs Godwin (Mary Wollstonecraft) became 'a particular correspondent' of Burns's, is now for the

first time revealed in Syme's unpublished letters. Born the same year as Burns, she died the year after him.

20 In February Burns had to remind Creech of the belated payment for his third edition—presentation copies for distribution 'among a few Great Folk whom I respect and a few Little Folk whom I love.' Miller the new Earl of Glencairn, Robert Riddel, Graham of Fintry, and McMurdo were among the 'Great'; Mrs McLehose and 'dear-bought Bess', his daughter by Lizzie Paton (now aged 12), among the 'Little.'

CHAPTER XXIX

1 Gilbert was unable to repay any of the £300 which his brother had by then lent to him in all. Nicol's estimate of this sum had been questioned. It is now verified by Syme.

2 It was a detached, two-story house, with a kitchen, a parlour, two bedrooms and some closet and attic rooms. The rent was £10 or £12 as compared with the £6 or £7 of the Wee Vennel rent.

3 'I am not equal to the task of rearing a girl,' he wrote two months before her birth, 'besides I am too poor. A girl should always have a fortune.'

4 In spite of this he enjoyed an evening with the Earl of Selkirk, and owed it to the Earl that his boots were ultimately repaired!

5 Burns had lost his old seal, which was appropriately engraved with a heart transfixed by cross darts. This new one was to have a holly bush, a shepherd's stock and horn and a wood lark perched on a sprig of bay; with two mottoes—*Wood-notes wild*, at the top, and *Better a wee bush than nae bield*, at the bottom. It was later made for him in Edinburgh. He was much upset by the loss of the early seal, given probably by James Smith or by Muir of Kilmarnock—anyhow by a friend since dead. It is characteristic that Burns searched long for the true Scotish 'stock and horn,' a rude musical instrument made from the thigh-bone of a sheep and pierced much like a recorder, having a loose oaten reed thrust into it and being fixed at one end into a cow's horn with the end cut off.

6 It served the lady well, however. After Burns's death, with his letters and legend as her stock-in-trade she realised her ambition and became the centre of an innocuous salon in Edinburgh. It included Ainslie (who had become the author of various religious works for the young), Thomas Campbell, James Gray (author of *The Sabbath in the Mountains*), and Mr Graham (author of *The Sabbath*). Lord Craig stood by her financially and she obtained judgment from the Court for £100 a year from her husband. She lived to be 82, and though her memory became hazy on most subjects, she could 'still summon up appropriate quotations and allude aptly to the

Scriptures and quote the Paraphrases,' and bridle at any mention of the 'electric' ploughman.

7   A grand-daughter of Thomson's was Catherine Hogarth, wife of Charles Dickens.

8   Clarke was so 'shamefully careless' that he lost irretrievably some of the airs Burns had collected.

9   The original which here inspired the poet was one of the earliest songs he had ever seen in print. There still exists a stall-sheet dated 1770 and containing among its 'Six excellent new songs' the love-song 'O fare-thee-well my own true love,' which bears in boyish handwriting—'Robine Burns aught this buik and no other.'

10 '*No*,' he exclaimed to a friend, 'if a friend desires me, and if I'm in the mood for it, I'll write a poem, but I'll be damned if ever I write for money.'

11 That year Burns's humour was particularly broad. He admitted and gloried in it, as did the many friends who found bawdy verses enclosed in their letters. He must have added considerably to his private collection, which was lent by special request to the Hon Andrew Erskine who suffered from low spirits. One item, at least, was by 'a Revd Doctor of the Church of Scotland,' to which Burns's comment was, 'Would to Heaven a few more of them would turn their fiery zeal *that way*!'

12 'When universal Scotland all was drunk.'

13 McLeod of Raasay.

14 It would appear that under Robert Riddel's will Friars' Carse was made the subject of a trust for sale, the proceeds to be divided between the widow and Walter; but the trustees were given a discretion to offer the estate to Walter charged with an annuity for the widow. The latter course would have been more profitable to Mrs Riddel, but she was prepared to pay for the pleasure of spiting her brother-in-law.

15 In his last letter to Mrs McLehose he enclosed his 'Monody on a lady famed for her Caprice,' supposed to be pinned to Maria Riddel's carriage: If you rattle along like your mistress's tongue,/Your speed will outrival the dart;/But, a fly for your load, you'll break down on the road/If your stuff be as rotten 's her heart!

16 Dr Maxwell has been identified with the unnamed agent denounced by Burke in the notorious 'dagger' speech of 28 December 1792.

17 The fact that Mrs Whelpdale had the same Christian name as Mrs Burns was unfortunate, especially as, since the affair with Clarinda, Burns had lost his taste for amorous sobriquets. But in spite of his feeling that an Arcadian name attached to a

simple country girl was 'a high incongruity,' he could see
nothing for it but to address Jean Whelpdale as his 'Chloris.'

18   Jean had a brother, Robert, in London doing well as a weaver-
merchant. The Kilmarnock folk were particularly strong there.

19   David McCulloch of Ardwell, a new-made brother Mason.

20   Patricia Gordon of Halleaths.

CHAPTER XXX

1   Galt, in *The Provost* (chap xxviii), where he writes ironically of
the volunteering 'joukerie-poukerie' of the time.

2   She did not see it till after Burns's death, when she did not
recognise herself as its subject. (See her letter to Currie from
Tunbridge Wells, July 1800, in the Currie Correspondence.)

3   But he no longer trusted her. He altered the first line of some
verses once written for her—'Thine am I, my faithful Fair' to
'Thine am I, my Chloris Fair,' and though she had been the
confidante of his other affairs, she never learned from him who
Chloris was.

4   The whole question of Burns's refusal to accept payment for his
work is liable to misunderstanding now as it was in his lifetime.
Had Creech, Thomson and others known how to deal with
the situation, there can be no doubt that Burns would have
accepted his just earnings. If a man like Henry Mackenzie had
undertaken to act for him throughout, as he did at first, in a
business capacity, much friction and folly would have been
eliminated. As it was, the position was a false one, and for the
sake of his pride Burns felt compelled to make the gesture he
did.

5   The votes were 128 for Dundas to 38 for Erskine. Walter Scott
and Jeffrey were two of the 128, Jeffrey unwillingly so.

6   For 'Tam o' Shanter,' which Burns had sent her, Mrs Dunlop
had not a good word to say. Her request for the removal of a
'blot' from 'The Twa Dogs' for Creech's new edition, namely
the lines: Till tir'd at last wi' mony a farce,/They set them
down upon their arse,/had gone disregarded. 'Friendly advice,'
she had written, 'when wholly overlooked makes one feel themselves mean, officious, and in the present case indelicate.'

7   Colonel de Peyster, Commandant of Burns's Volunteer company, was a French Canadian—a charming old man, jovial and
cultured, with whom Burns had become on very good terms.

8   The weather is recorded as unusually fine, but there was a 'light
east wind' which may well have spoiled the sunshine for one in
Burns's condition.

9   Mr Lewars had also been one of the wooers of Jean Lorimer.

10   'Chloris' was either estranged or gone away. She became, in
succession, a governess, a prostitute and a vagrant, and died
aged fifty-six at a lodging near the Potterrow.

11 'The illness is the whole system debilitated and gone.' This, from Syme, is the nearest we have to a contemporary diagnosis. Though mercury was given there is no suggestion of syphilis. Sir James Crichton-Browne on the evidence diagnoses endo-carditis following rheumatic fever, a condition for which the modern treatment is prolonged rest.

12 During his illness some one offered him £50 for his *Merry Muses*. He refused with rage. Syme puts his Dumfries debts at £50.

13 Mrs Riddel must have driven back with him to the Brow on the second day, if indeed the tea-drinking did not take place there, as she later wrote to Currie mentioning 'that miserable cottage I saw him in for the last time by the seaside.' (Same letter as note on p.365.)

14 As in Burns's Edinburgh days, it is strange that the corre-spondence between the brothers, which must have been considerable, has not been preserved. We are almost forced to the conclusion that Gilbert regarded it as not too creditable to himself and so destroyed it. There seems a certain aridity in the wording of this farewell.

15 Agnes passed the remainder of her life with her favourite, Gilbert. She lived to be 87.

16 'Crystal Devon, winding Devon'—addressed to Margaret Chalmers, to whom his thoughts now turned.

17 Mrs Armour was away in Fife.

18 Unknown to Burns, Fintry had a scheme to get him transferred shortly into the Excise office at Leith, where he would have easy duties and a salary rising to £200.

19 The Rev Dr Hugh Blair was among those who refused to subscribe.

20 Burns had told Grose that he wished to be buried in Alloway, yet we are told that he himself gave the order that he should lie in the churchyard of St Michael's, a temple in which the family pew had oftener been occupied by Jean than by him, as he was a frequent deserter to the dissenting body of the Anti-burghers where he paid for a single seat. On his death-bed he must have felt obliged to give up the Alloway idea because of expense. The funeral with its procession was arranged by Syme.

21 As Earl of Liverpool, this celebrated nonentity—'my friend Jenkinson,' as Pitt called him—was destined to hold the office of Premier for one of the longest periods on record.

I have not been able to see all the extant MSS of 'The Court of Equity.' The following text has been collated from the three MS versions in the British Museum, viz. a full version, apparently of Mauchline date (EI), and a fragmentary copy of the same with a few variations (E2)—both in the Egerton Collection—and a revised version (H) in the Hastie Collection, which appears to have been made later for the benefit of Johnson. I have based the text on EI, noting the principal variations and enclosing in brackets the passages that are not common to all three versions. The title, 'The Court of Equity,' by which the verses are generally known, is not Burns's. The Egerton versions have no title. The Hastie version bears in Burns's hand the title 'Libel (*i.e.* indictment) Summons.'

In TRUTH and HONOR's name AMEN
Know all men by these presents plain.

This twalt o'May[1] at MAUCHLINE given
This year 'tween eighty five and seven
WE, FORNICATORS by profession,
As per extractum from each session;
And by our BRETHREN constituted
A COURT OF EQUITY deputed:
With special authoris'd direction,
To take beneath our strict protection,
The stays-unlacing[2] quondam maiden,
With GROWING life and anguish laden,
Who by the Scoundrel[3] is deny'd
Who led her thoughtless steps aside;
[He who disowns the ruin'd Fair-one
And for her wants & woes does care none;][4]

[The Wretch who can refuse assistance
To those whom he has given existence;][5]
[The knave who takes a private stroke
Beneath his sanctimonious cloke;][6]
[He who when at a lass's by-job
Defrauds her wi' a fr-g or dry-b-b][7]
[The Coof who stan's on clishmaclavers
When lasses hafflins offer favours;][8]
All, who in any way or manner
Distain the FORNICATOR'S honor,
We take cognisance thereanent
The proper JUDGES COMPETENT.

First, POET BURNS, he takes the CHAIR
Allowed by all his title's fair;
And past nem. con. without dissension,
He has a DUPLICATE pretension.
The second, SMITH,[9] our worthy FISCAL,
To cowe each pertinacious rascal,
In this, as every other state,
His merit is conspicuous great.
RICHMOND the third, our trusty CLERK
Our minutes regular to mark;
And sit dispenser of the law
In absence of the former twa.
The fourth, our MESSENGER AT ARMS,
When failing all the milder terms;
HUNTER, a hearty willing BROTHER
Weel-skilled in dead and living leather.
Without preamble less or more said,
WE BODY POLITIC aforesaid
With legal, due WHEREAS and WHEREFORE
We are appointed here to care for
The interests of our CONSTITUENTS
And punish contravening truants;
To keep[10] a proper regulation
Within the lists of FORNICATION.

WHEREAS, our Fiscal by petition
Informs us there is strong suspicion,
You, COACHMAN DOW and CLOCKIE BROWN,

Baith residenters in this town,
In other words, YOU JOCK and SANDIE
Hae been at wark at HOUGHMAGANDIE;
And now when it is come to light
The matter ye deny outright.[11]
YOU CLOCKIE BROWN,[12] there's witness borne,
And affidavit made and sworn,
That YE hae raised a hurlie-burlie
In Jeany[13] MITCHEL's tirlie-whurlie;
[And bloostered at her regulator
Till a' her wheels gang clitter-clatter.][14]
An' farther still, ye cruel Vandal,
A tale might ev'n in Hell be scandal,
Ye've made repeated wicked tryals
With druggs an' draps in doctor's phials,
Mix'd, as ye thought, wi' fell infusion,
Your ain begotten wean to poosion.
An' yet ye are so scant o'grace
Ye daur set up your brazen face
An' offer for to tak your aith
Ye never lifted Jeany's claith.—
But though by Heaven an' Hell ye swear[15]
Laird Wilson's sclates can witness bear,
Ae e'enin of a Mauchline fair,
That Maggie's masts, they saw them bare,
For ye had furl'd up her sails
An' was at play at heads an' tails.

YOU COACHMAN DOW[16] are here indicted
To have, as publicly ye 're wyted,
Been clandestinely upward-whirlan
The petticoats o' Maggie Borlan;
An' gied her canister a rattle,
That months to come it winna settle.
An' yet ye offer your protest,
Ye never herry't Maggie's nest;
Tho it's weel-kenned that, at her gyvle,
Ye hae gien mony a kytch an' kyvle.

THEN BROWN & DOW above-design'd
For clags and clauses there subjoin'd,

WE COURT AFORESAID CITE & SUMMON
That on the fourth o' June-in-comin
The hour o' Cause, in our Court ha'
AT WHITEFORD ARMS, YE ANSWER LAW.

[BUT, as reluctantly we PUNISH,
An' rather mildly would admonish;
Since better PUNISHMENT prevented
Than OBSTINACY sair repented.—

THEN, for that ANCIENT SECRET'S SAKE
You have the honor to partake
An' for that NOBLE BADGE you wear
YOU, SANDIE DOW, our BROTHER dear,
We give you as a MAN & MASON
This private, sober, friendly lesson.—

YOUR CRIME, a manly deed we view it,
AS MAN ALONE can only do it;
But in denial persevering,
Is to a SOUNDREL's name adhering.
The BEST O' MEN hae been surpris'd
The BEST O' WOMEN been advised;
NAY, CLEVEREST LADS hae been a TRICK O'T
AN' BONNIEST LASSES TAEN a LICK O'T.
Then Brother DOW, if you're asham'd
In such a QUORUM to be nam'd
Your conduct much is to be blam'd.
See, ev'n HIMSEL—there's GODLY BRYAN,
The auld WHATRECK he has been tryin;
When such as he put to their han'
What man on CHARACTER need stan'?
Then, Brother dear, lift up your brow
And, like yourself the TRUTH avow;
Erect a dauntless face upon it
An' say, 'I am the man has done it;
I SANDIE DOW get MEG wi' wean
And's fit to do as much again.'
Ne'er mind their solemn, rev'rend faces,
Had they—in proper times & places
But SEEN and FUN'—I mukle dread it,

They just would done as you and WE did.
To tell the TRUTH's a manly lesson
An' doubly proper in a MASON.

YOU MONSIEUR BROWN, as it is proven,
Meg Mitchel's wame by you was hoven;
Without you by a quick repentance
Acknowledge Meg's and your acquaintaince, }
Depend on 't, this shall be your sentence. }
Our beadles to the Cross shall take you,
And there shall mither naked make you;
The raep they round the pump shall tak
An' tye your han's behint your back;
Wi' just an ell o' string allow'd
To jink an' hide you frae the crowd.
There ye shall stan', a legal seizure
Induring Maggie Mitchel's pleasure;
So be her pleasure dinna pass
Seven turnings of a half-hour glass:
Nor shall it in her pleasure be
To louse you out in less than three.
THIS, our futurum esse DECREET,
We mean it not to keep a secret
But in OUR SUMMONS here insert it,
And whoso dares, may controvert it.][17]

THIS, mark'd before the date and place is
SUBSIGNUM[18] EST per BURNS the Preses.
                    [L.S.]   BURNS.

This summons & the signet mark
Extractum est per Richmond, Clerk.
                              RICHMOND.
At Mauchline twenty fifth of May
About the twalth hour o' the day
You two in propria personae
Before design'd Sandie & Johnie,
This SUMMONS legally have got,
As vide Witness underwrote;
Within the house of John Dow, vinter
NUNC FACIO HOC—Gullelmus Hunter.[19]

NOTES

1. This fourth o' June. H.
2. stays out burstin. H.
3. Rascal. H.
4. H.
5. E2 and H. The latter has 'subsistence' instead of 'assistance.'
6. E1 and E2, not H.
7. H.
8. E2 and H.
9. Next MERCHANT SMITH. H.
10. And Keep. E2. Keeping. H.
11. And now the matter's come to light
    Your part in 't ye deny outright.'
    —E2.
    And now when facts are come to light
    The matter ye deny outright.'—H.
    E2 breaks off here.
12. First you, JOHN BROWN. H.
13. Here and 12 lines farther on 'Jeany' has been corrected from 'Maggy,' but the correction has not been made throughout.
14. H.
15. 'But tho' ye should yoursel manswear.'—H.
16. 'Next SANDY DOW, you're here indicted.'—H.
17. The whole of this bracketed passage is omitted from H.
18. SIGILLUM. H.
19. At Mauchline, idem date of June/Tween six & seven, the afternoon,/You twa, in propria personae./Within design'd, Sandy and Johny,/This SUMMONS legally have got,/ As vide witness underwrote :/Within the house of JOHN DOW, vinter,/ NUNC FACIO HOC, GULIELMUS HUNTER.

Index

CANONGATE CLASSICS